Democratic Capitalism

The Way to a World of Peace and Plenty

Ray Carey

First published by AuthorHouse 04/27/04

ISBN: 1-4107-9028-2 (e-book)
ISBN: 1-4184-2810-8 (Paperback)
ISBN: 1-4184-2809-4 (Dust Jacket)

Printed in the United States of America
Bloomington, Indiana

This book is printed on acid-free paper.

To Dennice, my wife and best friend

ACKNOWLEDGEMENTS

Four people have been deeply involved in this work on democratic capitalism for over five years: Warren Lewis edited, Michael Hartoonian tested material in classrooms and with civic groups, Barbara Brengel provided administrative assistance, and Jef Gully helped in developing computer skills and setting up the website. I am indebted to them all for their considerable talents and unfailing good humor.

Many have provided support and advice over this long process. They include Reuben Anderson, Les Brualdi, Marge Cordes, Diane Dunlap, Msgr. John Graham, Regi Herzlinger, Ed Liddy, Dan Loritz, George Maloney, Linda and Shaw McKean, Bob Mickelson, T. Ballard Morton, Mike Osheowitz, Joe Pichler, Al Reposi, Selma Rossen, Ian Ross, Sr. Margaret Ryan, Richard van Scotter, Bill Wheeler, and John Whitehead.

My family have been supportive during the long effort and managed never to run out of democratic capitalism jokes including on the T-shirts. This wonderful family includes my wife of 53 years, Dennice; our children, Sheila Bryan, Dr. Lisa Carey, Michael Carey, and their spouses Dr. Matthew Ewend and Kristen Carey. The preface describes how our six grandchildren added motivation for this effort.

The picture on the cover of our grandson, Kelly Carey-Ewend, was taken in 1999 by his other grandfather, Kurt Ewend of Saginaw, Michigan, a good man who died too young.

TABLE OF CONTENTS

PREFACE

The young boy on the cover pondering beauty is my grandson, Kelly. This book is dedicated to Kelly and my other grandchildren, Jenner, Nash, Abigail, Patrick, and Adam. I want them to grow up in a world where they can reach their full potential and contribute to a harmonious whole.

My grandchildren will learn from family, team sports, school bands, medical research teams, and other group efforts that their individual development depends on hard work and cooperation. They will learn that when each contributes strength to the group, and each benefits from the strengths of others, performance is improved and life is more fun. I hope that their schools address this dual development of individual attainment and social cooperation.

In this book about democracy and capitalism, I examine the economic-political system in which all gain as each gains through participation, cooperation, trust, and sharing. With these motivations, and the private property and competition of capitalism, material scarcity can be eliminated and the quality of lives improved. I propose democratic capitalism as the rational alternative to the folly and violence that fills human history, in which the only animal capable of reason has killed more of its own species than any other creature has done. Animosities and violence will gradually end when educated citizens and trained leaders structure human affairs through the economic common purpose that improves all lives.

It is satisfying to realize that Jenner, Nash, Kelly, Abigail, Patrick, and Adam will be the first generation to live in an interconnected world based on freedoms. Convergence of people and commerce in the Information Age will transcend the flaws of traditional institutions. Wars and material scarcity will disappear in a freedom-based, unified world where the simple idea of individual development in a harmonious whole prevails. Citizens of this interdependent world will demand the education and good health necessary to make human freedoms universal. Information Age technology is making education of the whole world possible. With the non-freedoms eliminated, my grandchildren's children and their grandchildren will live in a steadily improving world.

This book identifies the significant parts, their connections, and the actions necessary for society to benefit. My proposed rational order is based on my experience combined with the wisdom of thinkers from many disciplines. My own practice of democratic capitalism provided me a confident view of the latent power of people that could be released when they were free to develop and contribute. My studies found the wisdom of many specifying how to organize human affairs to give all people their best chance.

READER'S GUIDE

Chapter 10, which can be read as a summary of this volume, contains ten hypotheses that, if validated, will lead to the ideal of a world of peace and plenty, the means to attain the ideal, and the process to confirm the ideal and specify the means.

Chapter 1: Citizens' Choice

Reformers made a bad choice in the nineteenth century when they selected Karl Marx's flawed solution to the distribution-of-wealth problem instead of John Stuart Mill's evolutionary refinement. This choice set the stage for the bloodiest century in human history, the 20th.

In the late 20th century, the United States government made a bad choice to support short-term and greedy ultra-capitalism instead of democratic capitalism. The record concentration of wealth that resulted limited the spread of economic freedom and provoked global social tensions and violence.

The various political processes have never found the rational organization for human affairs. Power-adoring and untrained leaders have persistently led to folly and violence. The needed citizens' choice for the 21st century requires a higher quality truth-searching process to educate citizens and train leaders to support the superior economic system, democratic capitalism.

Chapter 2: The Personal Development of a Democratic Capitalist

Because the proposals in this book are an integration of my experience and study, I describe my own discovery of democratic capitalism and the extraordinary potential of people when they become involved, cooperate, produce, innovate, and share. In my experiences over many years and in many countries, I discovered and tested the principles that I later confirmed through studying the wisdom of many.

Included is a description of *Care and Share*, a profit-sharing and ownership plan that I designed and implemented as CEO of ADT, Inc. Such programs are part of the solution to the maldistribution of wealth that has persistently corrupted capitalism.

At the end of my business career, I was puzzled as to why the principles of democratic capitalism are not applied to all aspects of human organization. After studying this question for years, I became even more puzzled that the simple principles of democratic capitalism have yet to become the template for a comfortable and peaceful society.

Chapter 3: The Social Development of Democratic Capitalism

In 1776, Adam Smith defined a new industrial system that could eliminate material scarcity, but he warned of the threat from speculators. Smith's vision of economic freedom was complemented by the political freedoms in the new American republic.

Robert Owen provided early experimental verification that investment in human capital produces results superior to the mercantilist practices of his time.

Karl Marx and John Stuart Mill enlarged the definition of democratic capitalism by examining worker ownership as a way to distribute wealth broadly. The manifestos of both Marx and Mill contain the radical proposal that improvement in industrial performance and the worker's quality of life are synergistic. Marx's vision was contradicted by the totalitarian governments erected to implement his distribution of wealth plan.

Review of the historical growth of democratic capitalism also includes Condorcet's summary of the work of the Enlightenment; the examination of the American democratic experiment by Tocqueville; and the march toward freedom described by the German Idealists Kant, Hegel, and Marx. Kant also proposed the imperative of law, not violence, in the relations among nations in order for economic freedom to function.

Marx's axiom that social progress depends on movement to a superior economic system is contrasted to the flawed cultural tradition in which reformers are conditioned by a contempt for commerce and a love of state.

Chapter 4: How Democratic Capitalism Works

Although democratic capitalism is not taught in Business Schools as a coherent commercial philosophy and practice, most of the companies designated by *Fortune* magazine as the "100 Best" practice its principles. These companies have found democratic capitalism, as I myself did, through trial and error. The common features include a fundamental morality broadly understood, customer loyalty, high levels of productivity, job security, meritocracy, minimum structure, action orientation, and a compensation system that is both fair and perceived to be fair.

Only in the democratic capitalist environment will the cognitive power of involved, contributing, sharing people be fully released. Consequently, democratic capitalism has become a competitive necessity in the Information Age.

For democratic capitalism to reach its full potential, it needs a financial capitalism that is subordinate, not an ultra-capitalism that is dominant.

Chapter 5: Worker Ownership: The Democratization of Capitalism

In the coupling of democracy and capitalism, wealth distribution determines whether the coupling is one of tension or of synergy. Broad wealth distribution motivates wage earners to produce and innovate to their full potential. Broad wealth distribution recycles surplus back into the economy to maximize growth, adds spendable income to make free trade work, and provides a sense of unified purpose. Concentrated wealth inverts each of these requirements for economic growth and social cohesion.

Forms of worker ownership, such as ESOPs, stock options, and profit-sharing stock-purchase plans have grown in the United States based on their economic logic. Worker ownership is growing in other parts of the world wherever people are pursuing economic freedom by privatizing industry.

Chapter 6: The Economic Logic of Democratic Capitalism

The positive effect on both supply and demand by democratic capitalism is described along with productivity increases that support broader wealth distribution in a non-inflationary way.

Macro- and microeconomic policies of the U.S. government are examined and criticized as an inversion of economic logic: Monetary matters needing control are freed, while operating matters that should be left free are controlled. The result is a capitalism that neither provides the nonvolatile and patient capital specified by Adam Smith nor protects the world's economies from the speculators about whom Smith warned.

The priority for large dividends to maximize long-term shareholder value is stressed in order to balance income, appreciation, and security.

Chapter 7: The Rise of Ultra-Capitalism

A historical review of the conflict in commerce between those providing goods and services and those making money on money shows that the traditional flaw of concentrated wealth was multiplied many times over the last quarter of the 20th century. The result, ultra-capitalism, was caused by several forces: the excessive volatility caused by floating the dollar in 1971, excessive liquidity caused when ERISA's new pension funding went mainly to the stock market, easy credit for speculation, and deregulation coupled with the suspension of market disciplines.

Ultra-capitalism caused another boom/bust cycle, slowed the world's economic growth, and threatened world peace. Many nations had their economic momentum reversed by ultra-capitalism, but the most egregious example presented is Indonesia, the fourth-largest nation in population and the largest Muslim nation.

Although wage earners are now the major source of new investment capital, the intolerable contradiction is that wealth has nevertheless become even more concentrated.

Chapter 8: Conflicts in Capitalism: An American Tragedy

This play depicts how the building and selling of products and services has been dominated by the short-term and greedy demands of ultra-capitalism. The play also shows why many CEOs are victims, not promoters, of ultra-capitalism.

Chapter 9: Enron: Poster Boy for Ultra-Capitalism

The bankruptcy of Enron in 2001 is analyzed as a case study of the corrupting elements of ultra-capitalism that threaten the world's economy. Emphasis must be placed, however, not only on greedy and immoral executives but also on the structural imperfections in government that allow Enrons to happen. The government that is supposed to control currency and credit for the general welfare, instead, provides easy credit for speculation. This traditional impediment escalated in the last quarter of the 20th century into a dominant force because the lobby power of Wall Street is not constrained by the democratic power of reformers. The reformers have a different agenda and lack understanding of the necessary macro-reform of fiscal, monetary, and regulatory policies.

Specific tough reforms are proposed that would prevent Enrons from happening. They are contrasted to the superficial and even hypocritical "reforms" coming out of the political process.

Chapter 10: The Way to a World of Peace and Plenty

This concluding chapter presents hypotheses in a logical structure, that is, the first hypothesis must be validated before the second one can be addressed, and so on with the succeeding hypotheses.

Hypothesis #1: Affirmation of Marx's axiom that social progress depends on movement to a superior economic system. The persistent failure of reformers to act on this axiom has resulted in the failure to place culture and political structure in support of economic freedom, in turn resulting in continued folly and violence.

Hypothesis #2: Definition of democratic capitalism as the superior economic system.

Hypothesis #3: Affirmation of economic freedom as a potentially universal system because it has demonstrated its capacity to improve lives under both democratic and authoritarian governments.

Hypothesis #4: Indictment of the domination by ultra-capitalism that causes the world's economy to function at a fraction of its potential.

Hypothesis #5: Indictment of government privileges that have resulted in a banking system that favors the few and does not control currency and credit for the general welfare.

Hypothesis #6: Indictment of the political gridlock in the United States between those who support ultra-capitalism and those who do not use their democratic power to reform fiscal, monetary, and regulatory policies but waste it, instead, on micro-intrusions into free markets.

Hypothesis #7: Indictment of the faulty truth-seeking process that has caused the gridlock. Presentation of the process of Aristotle and Francis Bacon that could unify scholarly disciplines, bridge the managers and thinkers, and find common ground for the secular and religious.

Hypothesis #8: Identification of an agent of change: universities with their responsibility to educate citizens and train leaders and rediscover their obligation to unify and elevate.

Hypothesis #9: Identification of an agent of change: institutional investors with the democratic power and fiduciary obligation to replace ultra-capitalism with democratic capitalism.

Hypothesis #10: Presentation of the ideal: plenty, based on a rising standard of living and a sense of economic common purpose, provides the opportunity for peace when the United Nations, with the United States of America in a cooperative role, displaces violence among nations through the rule of law.

Hypotheses #1-5, and #10 about democratic capitalism and ultra-capitalism are examined in book I. Hypotheses #6-9 are examined more fully in book II. See the Carey Center for Democratic Capitalism website: *www.democratic-capitalism.com.*

CHAPTER 1

Citizens' Choice

The pace and complexity of the forces for change are enormous and daunting, yet it may still be possible for intelligent men and women to lead their societies through the complex task of preparing for the twenty-first century. If these challenges are not met, however, humankind will have only itself to blame for the trouble and the disasters that could be lying ahead.

Paul Kennedy, 1994[1]

In this book on democratic capitalism, I argue that the universal, timeless, human urge for freedom, peace, and plenty can be satisfied by a superior form of commerce, the synergistic coupling of democracy and capitalism.

During the 20th century, hundreds of millions of people were able to live with more freedom and greater comfort than ever before in human history through democracy and capitalism. During the same century, over one hundred and sixty million people, most of them non-combatants were killed by governments.[2] On November 1, 1911, an Italian pilot dropped the first bomb from a plane on Arab civilians near Tripoli.[3] Both noble attainment and obscene failure have carried their momentum into the 21st century. On September 11, 2001, Arab fanatics used planes as bombs to kill thousands of civilians in New York City.

History demonstrates how difficult it is for humans to stop the folly and violence. The human future, however, should be better than the past has been because the demonstrated capacity of economic

---

[1] Paul M. Kennedy, *Preparing for the Twenty-first Century* (New York: Random House, 1994), p. 349.

[2] R. J. Rummel, *Death by Government* (New Brunswick, New Jersey: Transaction Publishing, 1994), p. 13.

[3] Sven Lindquist, *A History of Bombing* (New York: The New Press, 2001), p. 1.

freedom to improve lives and unify people has been enhanced by the Information Age revolution.

The worldwide opportunity to attain peace, plenty, and unity is promising, but we need an understanding of the reasons for persistent failure. Only when the impediments to social progress are recognized can they be neutralized. Identifying the end and the means for social progress is more complex in an open society because the process itself must be free. This places a special responsibility on the universities to organize multi-disciplinary education for students of every age.

Citizen education about social progress must include an understanding of Adam Smith's (1723-1790) definition of the free market system that could eliminate material scarcity. This was a breakthrough concept, for society had until then been dominated by predatory forces battling over finite resources. Smith saw that the means to this new ideal was the wealth production possible from the combination of involved, well-paid workers; private property; competition; and the increased productivity of the Industrial Revolution. Free markets based on these components needed only a government that would support universal education, good health, and a monetary system designed for the general welfare.[4]

Realization of Smith's vision depended on those elements of society sensitive to the human condition: universities, the media, the religions, and the arts, to analyze, refine, and promulgate this new opportunity premised on economic freedom. Their consensus would have resulted in a restructure of governments in support of democratic capitalism.

By the middle of the 19th century, although the extraordinary improvement in the lives of millions, particularly in America, had validated Smith's vision as attainable, a far different pattern had become clear. As Karl Marx (1818-1883) decried in his economic writings, workers in most cases were herded together in wage-slave conditions, and the monetary system was still designed for the benefit of the wealthy and privileged.

---

[4] Adam Smith, *An Inquiry into the Nature and Causes of the Wealth of Nations* (New York: Modern Library, 1937; first published in London, 1776).

In 1848, both John Stuart Mill[5] (1806-1873) and Karl Marx[6] identified the way to create more wealth by involving workers in a cooperative environment and then distributing wealth broadly through ownership participation by the workers. Mill offered practical evolutionary means to this end; Marx offered a flawed, revolutionary approach to restructure commerce and society.

A century-and-a-half after Marx and Mill agreed on the end but proposed different means, the following statements seem clear to me, but they need analysis and testing and then either acceptance or rejection by those responsible for guiding social progress:

- Economic freedom continues to demonstrate the capacity to improve the lives of all people.

- Marx's collectivism was tried in several forms but failed in almost all cases to improve lives.

- In the United States, the political right, with help from the political left, supports finance capitalists who continue to obtain government privileges and concentrate wealth.

- The political left concentrates political power and tries to redistribute wealth through collectivist intervention.

- Because political gridlock protects special privileges, the government does not properly support economic freedom.

- Universities, the media, the religions, and the intellectual community have yet to discover democratic capitalism as the best way to improve lives and eliminate the violence.

---

[5] John Stuart Mill, *Principles of Political Economy with Some of Their Applications to Social Philosophy* (Fairfield, New Jersey: Augustus M. Kelley, Publishers, 1987; first published in London, 1848).

[6] Karl Marx, *Capital* (New York: Penguin Books, 1990; first published in London, 1867); Karl Marx and Friedrich Engels, *The Communist Manifesto* (New York: Penguin Classics, 1985; first published in London, 1848).

- The Information Age revolution has the potential to transform and unify the world through democratic capitalism.

Democracy as a social philosophy means equal rights, equal responsibilities, and equal privileges for all; capitalism as an economic system means private ownership of production and distribution motivated and disciplined by competition. Democracy and capitalism become synergistic in democratic capitalism because they support and enhance each other. From democracy comes the involvement and participation of all; from capitalism comes the energy and resources to excel.

In democratic capitalism, capital and labor are not in conflict because the source of capital and the people doing the work are the same people. All become owners in general ways through pension and savings plans and in more direct ways through ESOPs (Employee Stock Option Plans), stock purchased in payroll savings plans, and profit-sharing distributed in stock. Ownership is the motivation that maximizes surplus; broad wealth distribution builds demand and sustains economic growth. On the global level, incremental spendable income from these plans makes free trade a universal benefit. Because rising compensation is productivity based, it cannot be a cause for inflation.

Governments need to give priority to economic freedom by providing civic order, fiscal and monetary policies that distribute wealth broadly, and capital for growth that is stable and patient. Governments can also design realistic programs for better education, good health, protection of the environment, and assistance for people to learn how to help themselves.

Democratic capitalism is built up from individual development in a harmonious whole. Because of the power of cooperation, the whole is greater than the sum of the parts. The benefits deriving from this simple foundation have been confirmed by the wisdom of many thinkers over many years. Economic freedom that can improve lives and stop the violence is a potentially common ideology because it has demonstrated this capacity under both democratic and authoritarian governments.

Many believe that society cannot sustain or improve itself without a common ideology defined as a body of doctrine, including ways through which to put the ideal into operation, that is, the end and the means. Economic freedom is acceptable to all cultures because it addresses the needs of all people for food, clothing, shelter, education, health, and hope; further, it can unify people through a growing sense of interdependence in pursuing these goals.

Beginning with this common ideology, the progression from economic freedom to political freedom becomes possible. Ethnic and religious animosities recede before growing worldwide affluence and education, while problems of over-population are resolved by the same forces. The world's environment will be protected by cooperative action, funded by optimum economic growth from capitalism built on sensitivity to the human condition and planning for the very long term. Each generation assumes responsibility for the next generation to make the world a better place. The culture refines and promulgates the commercial means to make the ideal become the real.

An ideal world of peace and plenty is the common goal of innate human yearning, the secular goal of both divine providence and of humanistic perfectibility. This is the natural or rational order in human affairs that was sought by the 18th-century Enlightenment philosophers. The question is not the universality of the goal but why the only species capable of reason has persistently failed in attaining it.

Despite the demonstrated capacity of economic freedom to be the common ideology that improves lives and unifies people, the world continues to be dominated by folly and violence. Consider the following mistakes that happened a century apart, caused by poorly educated intellectual and political leaders, that led to disastrous social consequences. If these human errors had been avoided by a more rigorous truth-seeking process, the course of history would have been changed for the better:

- Late-1880s: The world was moving towards economic freedom. The process was imperfect, but more and more people were improving their lives through the coupling of democracy and capitalism. Reform-minded intellectuals were excited by Marx's legitimate criticism of the excesses of capitalism, but they did not subject his radical theories to rigorous examination, including a synthesis with the refinement of free markets as presented by Mill. Reformers working within a narrow spectrum of knowledge made a tragic error in choosing Marx over Mill and missed the opportunity to move the world towards peace and plenty. The bloodiest century in history was the result of their error.

- Late-1990s: Mexico, Indonesia, Malaysia, and many other countries were—despite various imperfections—making impressive progress in improving lives by moving towards economic freedom. Their economic growth depended on stable, patient capital. Instead, lethal ultra-capitalism struck with short-term, volatile, speculative capital. Economic momentum was reversed, social upset was caused within the countries, and tensions increased among nations. Indonesia, the world's fourth-largest country in population and the largest Muslim nation, had through economic freedom reduced the percentage of their people under the poverty line from 40% to 10% in only a few decades. This nation was suddenly thrown into economic reverse and more than 50% of Indonesians were forced back to living in poverty (see chapter 7). A downward social spiral was precipitated by bad economics that ended the Indonesian sense of economic common purpose and would cause religious, political, and ethnic chaos for years to come. The media failed to examine the economic causes, converted the unnecessary economic tragedy into a political event, and thereby failed to inform the public.

- Late-1990s: Under Mikhail Gorbachev, Russia had gone through an extraordinary, bloodless revolution and was prepared to move towards economic freedom. After Boris Yeltsin replaced Gorbachev, he depended heavily on the advice of American government officials, academic economists, and finance capitalists to apply "shock therapy" to effect a quick transition to "free market" capitalism. None of the foreign advisors and none of the Russians involved demonstrated comprehension of the complexities of the management of change or of the disciplines required for economic freedom to function well. The result of their collective errors and the inevitable corruption proved to be the worst peacetime economic disaster of the twentieth century and the worst asset stripping in history when hundreds of billions of dollars of economic value crucial to Russian economic growth was bled out of the country into foreign bank accounts.[7]

In the late-19th century, following Marx, the world took a wrong turn toward communism, socialism, and collectivism that resulted in the bloodiest century in human history. In the late-20th century, following the implosion of communism, the world failed to make the correct turn toward economic freedom. Instead of uniting in economic common purpose, the world turned again to violence, epitomized by the attack on America, September 11, 2001.

The common denominator of these failures was lack of an understanding of exactly what economic freedom means and what support it needs from government and the rest of the culture, if it is to succeed. The world had naturally looked to the United States for leadership, the country that had demonstrated how to couple democracy and capitalism in order to improve lives, but the United States failed spectacularly. Instead of leading the world towards economic freedom, it led to ultra-capitalism, a hardening of mercantilism and finance capitalism that treats the worker as an expendable cost commodity, and takes making money on money quickly as its dominant mission. The best opportunity in human history to improve all lives, unite the world in economic common purpose, and stop the violence, was lost. Many emerging economies suffered the reversal of their strong economic momentum; many others went into decline—including the American economy; and, the world's economic growth slowed by half.

---

[7] Stephen F. Cohen, *Failed Crusade: America and the Tragedy of Post-Communist Russia* (New York: W. W. Norton & Company, 2000), p. 28.

Also lost was the opportunity to use a rising standard of living to lift relations among nations from traditional force of arms and geopolitics to the rule of law and global collaboration. Instead of strengthening the U.N. and world cooperation, the United States weakened it by unilateral actions. America, the "light on the hill," became known around the world instead for "the American model" of short-term and greedy capitalism, and a cop-of-the-world attitude.

The reason for the failure of American leadership was abandonment of essential purpose by the United States government, which is mandated by its own founding document, the U.S. Constitution, to "promote the general welfare." Instead, the government's fiscal, monetary, and regulatory policies were increasingly providing lobbied privileges to the few to make money on money. A failure of the democratic process was to blame because the citizens had failed to benefit from the clear advice of Adam Smith about economic freedom as the means, what is required, and what to avoid. In the 19th century, America ignored further benefit of Marx and Mill's advice about how to maximize and distribute wealth. American education did not present citizens with the opportunity to earn the functional knowledge of these vital matters, and consequently they were unable to express the will and wisdom upon which democracy depends. The lobby power of finance capitalism and, finally, ultra-capitalism filled the vacuum.

The citizens' choice between a world of peace and plenty or more folly and violence was further illuminated during the 1990s in two books. In 1992, Francis Fukuyama proposed in *The End of History* that, the economic and social logic of economic freedom having become clear and in the absence of any competing ideology, the world was moving towards democracy and capitalism.[8] A few years later, Samuel Huntington wrote in *The Clash of Civilizations* that the bipolar world aligned with either Russia or the United States was being replaced by fault lines among a half-dozen cultures along which the sad history of human violence would continue to run.[9]

---

[8] Francis Fukuyama, *The End of History and the Last Man* (New York: The Free Press, 1992).

[9] Samuel P. Huntington, *The Clash of Civilizations and the Remaking of World Order* (New York: Simon & Schuster Touchstone, 1996).

Many regarded the 9-11 attack on America as confirmation of Huntington's bleak view.

I take the opposite view. The goal of peace and plenty in the 21st century is uniquely attainable, and the means—democratic capitalism—is identifiable through multi-disciplinary truth-seeking protocols. Theses supportive of this conclusion are organized in the following four categories and are offered to serve as stimulants to a process of analysis and synthesis. One result of this synthesis should be a curriculum for citizen education, at all ages, and in all parts of the world. Another result should be a political agenda for promoting the general welfare nationally and globally.

- *Reaffirm Idealism*: People unify by believing in an ideal and working towards it. The elimination of material scarcity and violence through economic freedom is the means for humans in all cultures to reach their full potential.

- *Refine Capitalism*: To reach full potential, capitalism needs broader wealth distribution and ample, low-cost, non-volatile, patient capital. Thus sustained and democratized, global capitalism can eliminate material scarcity, improve the quality of lives, and unify people. Conversely, the capitalism now dominated by abandonment of market disciplines, speculation, instabilities in the monetary system, treatment of workers as cost commodities, and a feeding frenzy in executive compensation, is provoking a populist revolt against global capitalism that can ruin this best-ever opportunity for social progress.

- *Restructure Government*: Citizens need a functional understanding of fiscal, monetary, and regulatory matters so that they may pressure their representatives to democratize capitalism and eliminate privileges lobbied by ultra-capitalists. By combining the principles of participatory democracy with Information Age technology, the government can fulfill its missions at dramatically

9

lower cost, and it can eliminate wasteful micromanagement.

- *Reposition Foreign Policy*: The global mission of the United States should be to promulgate economic freedom while recognizing that moral economic leadership and warrior-state geopolitics are mutually exclusive. Only a growing sense of worldwide economic common purpose can phase out reciprocal atrocities. All countries have the responsibility to use economic freedom to improve the lives of their people in ways consistent with their cultures and at their own chosen pace. By accepting this reality, the United States can become a strong team-player while purging its own imperfections.

21ˢᵗ Century Citizens' Choice:
Peace and Plenty or More Folly and Violence?

The human species is poised at the beginning of the 21st century either to use its reason to build a world of peace and plenty or to fail again and repeat its history of folly and violence. America, the world's most powerful nation, will be pivotal in the direction taken, which makes American citizens ultimately responsible.

Democratic capitalism that has demonstrated the capacity to eliminate material scarcity, elevate spirits, and unify people, was rational when Adam Smith first defined it, but because of the impediments, it was only partly attainable. Now it is both rational and attainable because the Information Age has further raised productivity and can function only with educated, involved, and motivated people. For the first time, democratic capitalism has become not merely an ideal but also a competitive necessity.

American citizens are still confused, however, by the lack of a comprehensive and integrated agenda to implement democratic capitalism fully. Many citizens are disenchanted with their government because it is dominated by the special interests of both the collectivists and the finance capitalists. The vision of the American Founders of a better life for all has been confirmed as attainable, but early fears of overgrown government and wealth concentration by the financial oligarchy have also proved to be well founded.

The Founders of the American republic successfully separated church and state, but they failed to separate finance capitalism and state. This violation of democratic principle inevitably results in the concentration of wealth and the lobbied domination of political power by the few. The threat to both democracy and capitalism from this violation is increasing.

The fate of the world will be heavily influenced by the choices made by American citizens. If, however, the government does not reflect the people's will and wisdom, where do the citizens go for help in the exercise of their ultimate responsibility? Fortunately, opportunities for education and political action are numerous:

- Universities: An epiphany in the universities, perhaps led by young philosophers, would enlighten their overdue responsibility to perform the multi-disciplinary examination of the optimum organization for human affairs. For those who have abandoned idealism, this is a difficult task because too many remember the "single solutions" that have failed because they were political and top-down. An examination of the history and philosophy of democratic capitalism, however, reveals the economic solution that is built up from individual development in a harmonious whole.

- New Political Leaders: During times of urgent political reformation, open societies tend to produce great leaders. A platform based on the end and the means of a system with the demonstrated capacity of democratic capitalism, will be enormously attractive to the majority because it is basically a restatement of the promise of "life, liberty, and the pursuit of happiness" for all. The potential idealism that can unite and energize will result from an understanding of the power for good inherent in the proper coupling of democracy and capitalism. America needs leadership in this direction.

- Institutional Investors: The peoples' capital managed by institutional investors is now the largest source of investment capital. Institutional investors ought, therefore, to identify and promote the agenda most likely to lead to the kind of economic growth that gives comfort and security to wage earners. This requires a change by the institutional investors who during the 1990s functioned paradoxically as the shock troops of ultra-capitalism. To meet their fiduciary responsibility to wage earners, institutional investors must recognize that surplus is maximized only by the involvement of all, and motivation is sustained only by broad wealth distribution. Institutional investors are the change agents best positioned to identify the agenda and organize the lobbying forces to countervail ultra-capitalism in a short time.

- Business Schools, Law Schools, and Schools of Public Administration: If democratic capitalism does, in fact, maximize surplus and govern best, then it should be presented especially in the schools that train leaders for industry and government.

- Unions: If democratic capitalism maximizes surplus by the greatest development of each and then spreads wealth broadly, then its promotion should be the mission of unions, including their powerful pension funds.

- Civic Groups: Thousands of civic groups and NGOs (non-governmental organizations) represent the best of democracy in their dedication to make the country better; however, they lack a comprehensive, integrated agenda. By using Information Age technology, these groups could begin to develop the people's agenda for reform with a goal to identify those matters of common agreement. Taking this approach, most civic groups and NGOs would find much to agree on and be better prepared to instruct their political representatives.

- The Popular Media: Television, radio, and the print media must recognize that their special responsibility in a free society can be met only if their analysts, writers, and speakers are trained in the many disciplines that reflect human affairs. Most in the popular media are economically illiterate though sensitive to the human condition—a bad combination that regularly leads to misinformation and misdirection.

- The Internet: The truth-searching process that can lead to greater ideological synthesis among all cultures needs to be facilitated by the most democratic of media, the Internet. The analysis, debate, challenge, and experimental verification process must be made available on the Internet for universal access and critique. As the various hypotheses supporting democratic capitalism become available and survive debate, they will gradually become the building blocks for the best organization of human affairs.

- Religions: Religions can recognize that economic freedom is built on the worth of each individual and represents a common secular goal of harmony. When religious people come to understand that economic freedom can eliminate material scarcity, elevate spirits, and unify people, then they will affirm this secular ideal as the way to achieve the goal of a just society.

The 18th-century Enlightenment first challenged humanity to apply scientific truth-searching protocols to the management of human affairs. The intellectual community was, however, culturally conditioned to reject an economic solution to the problems of society; consequently, society was not consistent in its application of reason. Although rigorous truth-searching in the natural sciences became improved, expanded, tested, and codified, equivalent protocols have not been developed for the human sciences. This default has been the cause of continuing folly and violence in the world.

The Information Age is the technological basis of a truth-searching revolution that simultaneously educates, inspires, and unifies. Use of the Internet also forces recognition that cognitive power is released best in an environment of democratic capitalism. The Internet can become the catalyst for a worldwide truth-searching revolution that I call "Enlightenment II."

The world's most successful societies combine economic freedom with certain minimum disciplines, such as the rule of law. In emerging economies, an architecture of law must be put in place, one block at a time, to provide the foundation for economic freedom to function. An intellectual architecture of theorems applicable to the best organization for human affairs can similarly be constructed when many people all around the world participate in the building process and see it grow. In an open society, this responsibility rests with the universities, stimulated and held accountable by civic groups, democratic capitalists, institutional investors, NGOs, religions, unions, and the media. Peace and plenty in the 21st century is uniquely attainable, but it will depend on the quality of truth-searching by this second Enlightenment.

CHAPTER 2

The Personal Development of a Democratic Capitalist

I am a self-taught democratic capitalist. Starting at age 28, I had the opportunity to change a company environment from mercantilist to democratic capitalist, that is, from hierarchical and fearful to participatory and cooperative. I was plant manager for five years, and then president for seven years, of the Electro Dynamic Division of General Dynamics. Later, for eighteen years, I was CEO of ADT, Inc., the world's largest electronic protection company.

My personal development in democratic capitalism was a trial-and-error process, but I was fortunate in these companies to have opportunities to make mistakes, and time sufficient to correct them; twelve years in one company and eighteen in the other, enough time for my thorough empirical education. To benefit from the experience, however, required that I bring the right instincts and an open mind.

When I retired in 1989 and became a student of the philosophy and history of democratic capitalism, I was confident that I understood a highly productive arrangement for the industrial environment. I did not realize then how thoroughly this ideology could be extrapolated to society in general. It was exciting to find that this arrangement, for which I had been searching during forty years of trial and error, had already been defined, tested, and refined by Adam Smith, Robert Owen, John Stuart Mill, Karl Marx, and others. Along with the excitement came a sad recognition that the educational establishment had failed society by not presenting this best coupling of democracy and capitalism for student inspection.

A generation after Adam Smith, Robert Owen proved in his spinning mill near Glasgow that an investment in human values produces profits and sales growth superior to the results of the mercantilists who depended on cost containment and, frequently, exploitation. I developed this conviction on my own, for it was not part of the curriculum at Harvard Business School, where I took my MBA. Once learned, however, these principles became clear, and my view confident. I have learned through my experience what Robert

Owen learned through his, namely, that investing in human capital produces results superior to those competitors who suppress initiative and oppress the human spirit.

Gardner, Massachusetts

Gardner was a perfect place to grow up. A city of 20,000, Gardner offered good education, good people, and a pervasive work ethic—pervasive in the sense that even while playing three varsity sports, I always had part-time jobs. Pervasive in the sense that the early morning, around 6:45, was punctuated by whistles, audible throughout the city, identifying the several companies as they summoned their workers to the 7 a.m. shift. The whistles blew again at noon when many workers walked considerable distances home for lunch, while the rest opened their lunch boxes at their work. Eating out for any meal was a rare event in celebration of something special.

The legacy from my mother, dad, and sister completes the list of family values. Included was a sense of being part of a whole; being the same as, not different from. Being a part of a whole brought with it a feeling of personal responsibility to contribute to the benefit of the whole. Life in Gardner was New England egalitarian, with its emphasis on equal opportunity, not equal condition.

Football was a large part of my young life. I could not have articulated this conclusion while I was a high school co-captain, but I was already aware that good performance comes best by developing individual talent and harmonizing individual effort with teamwork. As president of my junior and senior classes, I also had some early leadership experience. Leadership to me always meant contributing to the environment to encourage everyone to do their best.

Another legacy from my dad, a life-long enemy of untruth and hypocrisy, was his rigorous truth-searching, enhanced for each of us by the benefits of education at a Jesuit college, Holy Cross. My dad was devoted to sports, but he was also the salutatorian of the class of 1920. Whether in sports, studies, or matters of public interest, my dad disciplined me to move past the superficialities and perceptions to search for the truth. He did this in the time-honored way of constant, probing questions.

Gardner is home to a mixture of ethnic groups. Many of my football buddies spoke English with a French accent. French was the language they spoke at home and at the "French School." Besides the French Canadians, Yankees, and Irish, the other ethnic groups were mainly Baltics: Finns, Poles, Swedes, and Lithuanians. Catholics worshiped at the French, Polish, or Irish churches; the French and Polish churches conducted services in their native tongues. Despite ethnic differences and ethnic pride, most had a feeling of being part of a whole, a feeling that each of us was pretty much the same as everyone else. The only ones whose cultural conditioning proved to them that they were different from everyone else were the Yankees who lived "uptown." Typical of New England, they were the ruling class; their companies wore family names, and they were run on nepotism. Only Yankees belonged to the Gardner Boat Club, which gained its superiority by exclusion: No Jews, no Catholics, and no boats.

The worth of each individual, personal responsibility, and being part of a whole, were deeply embedded values from my childhood. Years later, I recognized them not only as first principles of democratic capitalism but also as the core values of a free society. Global capitalism will not reach its full potential if economic leaders, such as the United States, lose this common ideology, the best coupling of democracy and capitalism. We shall decline as a result of undisciplined individualism on the one hand and excessive concentration on ethnicity and religion on the other. I certainly did not realize any of this in Gardner in the early 1940s, but I was conditioned to the social duality of individual effort in a harmonized whole.

Like most young people in Gardner, I worked. From age 10, I mowed lawns, delivered the *Saturday Evening Post* and *Colliers*, and delivered groceries. My first factory job, at age 15, was at Andersen Wood Turning Company. As the youngest and newest worker, my jobs varied from unloading the wood from the freight cars to going for coffee and jelly doughnuts for the whole work crew.

Andersen made bowling pins, and the demand must have been strong, for we were working nine hours a day, six days a week, that summer. I was so proud of my new work status that I was the only worker who did not shake off the heavy layers of sawdust before leaving the plant: I wore it like a badge of honor walking home. By the end of my first summer of work, I was running the simplest machine, a drum sander—a useful device for getting rid of fingerprints.

In August, another part of my perfect childhood kicked in when my family moved to a rented cottage on Cape Cod. August on Cape Cod became a cherished part of every year, provided by my extraordinarily hard-working father who commuted on the weekends until he could join us for his two-week vacation. One of my greatest regrets now is that my dad did not have the opportunity for the fun and satisfaction that I have enjoyed throughout my whole business career.

My dad and my wonderful mother fulfilled the eternal contract among the generations by providing their son and daughter with opportunities greater than those they had known. The first in his family to have earned a college education, my dad then spent a stressful existence as an Irish-Catholic middle manager in a WASP environment. "Irish need not apply" signs were still seen in Boston when my dad was job-hunting. My mother's father had been a factory worker with eight kids. Somehow, my grandparents had saved enough to educate my mother, who became a piano teacher and church organist.

On Saturdays and vacations during my junior and senior years in high school, I worked with several football friends moving stoves around in a warehouse. To us, it was a choice job, for we were being paid to do a job that doubled for us as weight training. Class distinction in this environment was performance based, depending on whether one could pull a heavy stove onto the hand truck from the high-torque long end of the stove or from the easier middle. Like weightlifting, loading from the long end required a combination of strength and technique, and this exercise diversion also made the time go faster.

My education as a democratic capitalist continued when, at age 16, I drove a two-ton dump truck for the Gardner Parks Department. This work also was good physical conditioning; we mowed parks with big gang-mowers, and we dug graves. Most of the workers were middle-aged men, including my Uncle Ed, but I was pleased with the additional responsibility as driver, and I assumed that it justified my wages of 45 cents an hour.

Every morning we shaped up at the back of one of the cemeteries. As we drove out, the work gang, riding and chatting in the back of the truck, would remind me to stop at the front gate where they would recover their lunches in brown paper bags stashed behind the big stones marking the entrance. I assumed that the bags contained lunches, but why leave them there? Only after a while did I make the connection between my having been designated as driver and the contents of those brown paper bags.

Holy Cross, 1944-48

In July of 1944, a few weeks after graduation from high school, at age 17, my Navy career began in the V-12 Naval Officer Training program at Holy Cross College in Worcester, Mass. In the fall of that first year, I played in Fenway Park on the Holy Cross football team against Boston College. Other less clear memories of the next five semesters were of tough Engineering courses, military discipline, and running up and down hills at 6:00 a.m.

In early 1946, I was on a ship in San Diego harbor and the war was over. As I had no interest in a career as a peacetime Naval officer, I had left officer training to go into regular Navy service. In June of that year, I was transported across the country in one of those "cattle car" trains and, having accrued enough points, was discharged in Boston.

Back at Holy Cross in the fall, I majored in Business Administration and received my degree two years later. Most of the courses were in Philosophy, Ontology, Epistemology, Cosmology and other ambitious subjects that Jesuits love to teach. All of the hard questions were examined, and since it was a Catholic school, all the answers were also given. Morning mass was compulsory, and although half of the students were asleep, the Jesuits promised us "sanctification by osmosis." In a sports environment, I quarterbacked the team that won the fiercely competitive intramural football league two years in a row; my teammates and I are still proud of that record. In my senior year, I was elected to Alpha Sigma Nu, the scholastic honor society—I was good at cramming. My classroom work did stimulate any number of bull sessions over a few beers that provoked some genuine truth-seeking. They were a tough group, and syllogistic imperfections were loudly criticized, though not so loudly as any evidence of hypocrisy. Time spent at Holy Cross reinforced the conditioning of my youth by my dad: Both experiences contributed to that elusive capacity to "think straight."

Very little of what I learned at Holy Cross as a Business major, however, had anything to do with real-world business, as I would soon find out, and none of it had anything to do with democratic capitalism. Holy Cross, at that time, was sorting itself out after the war, so I am not inclined to be critical of the curriculum or the quality of the teaching during a period when students and professors alike were returning from military service. Since then, nevertheless, Holy Cross has been a disappointment to me. They, like every other Liberal Arts college that I know about, are failing in their stated mission of preparing students for citizenship and leadership, if we agree that an understanding of political-economic fundamentals is needed for intelligent citizenship and effectual leadership in America and the world today.

Carey Scholars

I now provide modest financial assistance to my "Carey Scholars," a group now of over four dozen students who help me understand what they are—and are not—learning at college. Most of them are Black and Hispanic graduates of Cardinal Hayes High School and Aquinas High School in the Bronx, New York. Two have gone to Holy Cross; the others elsewhere. Iram graduated from Holy Cross and Fordham Law School; Marleny is at the 'Cross in the class of 2006. Julissa, a practicing attorney, was one of the 1993 class of Carey Scholars who now has a degree from Harvard, a graduate degree from Cambridge, and a Law degree from Columbia. Tony, also of the class of 1993, graduated from Skidmore, worked for a few years for a bank, and in 2003 was working on his MBA at the Tuck School at Dartmouth.

Cape Cod

During college summer vacations, I worked on Cape Cod, usually drawing on my Irish heritage as a good digger. I claim the record for digging a seven-foot-deep, seven-foot-wide new cesspool in the shortest time, but after getting through the tree roots, it was easy digging. I enjoyed the physical labor because among the good jobs is one that totally engages the body with no mental effort.

My democratic capitalist education took on new dimensions the summer of 1948 when I decided to become an entrepreneur and a conglomerate. I borrowed $400 from my dad and bought a 1936 pick-up truck in order to start a landscaping business, a landscaper then being someone who mow lawns but has a truck. As a new entrepreneur, I recall the cash-flow terrors that first week as I sat by the side of a back road worrying about how I was going to get my first job with all of this debt hanging over me. The jobs came, however, and I soon learned how to be a capitalist, "extracting maximum surplus value" from my workers by paying them $1 an hour while I was charging the customers $1.25.

My business plan was typical of conglomerates: One business had nothing to do with the other business, and was just another effort to make money. The only synergy was use of the truck for transportation to my evening efforts to sell Wearever cooking utensils. I would drive by my friend's house at about 6:30 and call out, "Where to, tonight, Abigail?" Abigail would point me in the right direction, and shortly I'd be working my flip charts for a half-dozen bored, mid-week work widows, whose husbands were away in either Boston or somewhere else at work. After lecturing the women about the evils of cooking with water and then pouring the nourishing vitamins down the drain with the hot water, the real excitement came when I baked a cake on top of the stove to prove the extraordinary thermal capabilities of these aluminum pans.

Many years later, when I was honored to be invited to join the Board of the Kroger Company, I kidded everyone that it was due to my former business relationship with Mrs. Pettingill, the daughter of the founder, Barney Kroger. Mrs. Pettingill had been not only my landscaping client on Cape Cod but also my first sale as a peddler of pots and pans. I did not reveal to my Kroger friends that I had almost blown the sale. I was trained to sell "the whole package," and when Mrs. Pettingill kept asking for prices on two individual pieces, I attempted to direct her attention back to the $125 package. Finally, in exasperation, she exclaimed: "Of course I want the whole package, but I also want extras of these!" Mrs. Pettingill made me relatively wealthy at a young age; I earned a $45 commission that first night.

As the summer wore on, I learned about the fourth element in the template of democratic capitalism, *competence*. Without realizing it, I was adopting the template that I talk about in this book. The first three elements were already in place: Thanks to family, church, and school, I was firmly locked in on *integrity*; my operation already had *maximum freedom* and *minimum structure*, for I could have carried my whole administration in my hat-band, if I had had a hat. My freedom was total, for I was completely on my own, but I quickly found out that the flip side of freedom is discipline, learning never to party so late as to miss the 8:00 a.m. start next morning.

My competence gap opened up before me one evening in August, when I proved to be better at lawn work than at baking cakes, and my conglomerate began to come unglued. The evening started badly: One woman was so bored that she was attending her second Wearever session of that summer, and she kept interrupting me to ask why the price of four pans was now less than the price for the three that she had bought earlier in the summer.

Later, I might have pointed out that free markets are inherently deflationary and that, while the effects of this phenomenon worried both Adam Smith and Karl Marx, it constantly drove prices down and benefited the consumer. On the other hand, I might have commented that if Alan Greenspan, future head of the Federal Reserve Board, would take a few years to understand this, why shouldn't she? I mumbled something about needing to check on that question, and I fled to the kitchen to bake my cake, where competence failed me and disaster struck.

Instead of the beautiful one-piece cake I usually baked, this cake came out of the pan in several hundred small pieces. I went back into the living room, almost inclined to fold my flip-charts and steal off into the night, when I heard the hostess's daughter shrieking in the kitchen. The disaster she had discovered was not the cake in pieces but that it had been consumed by their Great Dane. I left that night with a substantial sympathy sale but with little soul-satisfaction.

The incident provoked a conglomerate strategic review. Had I been spending so much time rooting around in the dirt tending lawns under the hot sun that I had lost the delicate touch needed to bake on top of the stove? Did I need an even deeper analysis? Was lawn-care the core business or were the pots and pans? I tried to apply the value test of the long-term-shareholder (me), but I was distracted by the social-benefit question: What is best for the worker? (also me).

Clearly it was not a short-term earnings question, for I usually made about $20/hour selling pots and pans, compared to $1.25/hour on lawn care. Nevertheless, I decided to concentrate on what I enjoyed, the lawn business, so I modified my mission statement to say something about doing more of what I was good at while avoiding non-strategic acquisitions.

Harvard Business School, 1948-50

The hardest thing about HBS was getting in. In 1948, thousands of veterans, all of us on the GI bill, were trying to get into HBS. Luck was with me during the all-important interview. The gentleman conducting the interview asked the profound question: "Why do you want to go to Harvard Business School," and then he just sat there saying nothing. After I had run out of brilliant explanations, I looked to him for help; receiving nothing but silence, I poured forth an even less coherent torrent of information. Perhaps the interviewer found this technique made a boring day shorter, maybe it helped determine the candidate's capacity to arrange thoughts under stress. By accident during this torture, I discovered the truth of what the books tell you is the key to selling: Find the self-interest of the customer, no matter what it may be. I was muttering something about starting a garbage collection business on Cape Cod that summer when "Steely Eye" became quite animated and proceeded to pour out his woes about getting his garbage collected on Cape Cod. By the end of the interview, we were practically slapping each other's backs. Later, I exchanged the garbage career for landscaping, but by then I had already been admitted to HBS.

The shining light at Harvard Business School in those days was General Georges Doriot. During class time, the General probed deeply, and he also arranged for students to do a protracted study of a selected company on site. Doriot was an excellent professor, but his near canonization was helped by the lack of stimulation in many of the other courses. In the General's spare time, he organized American Research and Development, an early venture capital firm that helped launch companies such as Data General. Several years after I graduated, we chanced to be on the same airplane, and he told me that he had seen Frank Pace, CEO of General Dynamics (see below, my work at General Dynamics). The General had asked Frank how his brilliant Manufacturing student, Ray Carey, was doing at GD. I found his memory amazing because I had had been one in a class of 50 students and had neither become individually acquainted with the General nor conceived of myself as particularly "brilliant" in his class.

One of the deans joked that our group was trying to go through HBS on athletic scholarships. We did spend a lot of time in intramural sports. I quarterbacked the team that lost in the playoff finals to a team quarterbacked by "Spook" Matthews, a football star from Georgia Tech. Other than General Doriot, I don't remember the names of many professors, but I can still recall the names of players on my team—and even key plays—in that unimportant game over 50 years ago. Some might regard this as evidence of a personality defect, but I believe that playing football taught me more about individual development in a harmonious whole than did most of my course work. Most of the educational process was then—and, I believe, continues to be—tilted toward individual development.

Aristotle taught that "excellence" is attained in all matters, including association among people, in the same way one learns to play the flute: practice, practice, practice. Football was my flute lessons. Over 12 years of high-school, college, and grad-school football, usually as team captain, I practiced fostering an environment of harmony—the giving and borrowing of strengths, the teaching and learning from the team process—in which each player could achieve his best. Football taught me that 2 + 2 in a team environment adds up to much more than 4. More important than what I learned in my course work, "Football Philosophy 101" taught me how dramatically performance is improved when each has the opportunity for self-development enhanced by an environment of trust and cooperation.

In the various classes, I assimilated knowledge about the protocols of business from control systems to balance sheets and P&L statements. Beyond that, I remember little of what my professors may have been trying to teach me. In those days, relating the study of Business to the needs of American society and the world for peace and plenty, was rarely a part of the curriculum. Through the years, I have been disappointed in the slowness of the Business School to respond to the challenges of capitalism that I detail in this book.

During the spring of 1950, the recruiting effort at Harvard Business School was heavy. I knew that I wanted to work with people, preferably in manufacturing, but I was selected to fly to New York, my first plane trip, to be interviewed by an advertising agency. At a long lunch, the candidates were graded on their capacity to smoke cigars and tell dirty stories. I flunked on both counts.

About the time I retired from my active business career, I wrote my first letter to Harvard Business School in a campaign to get my alma mater to examine democratic capitalism. In that letter to the dean, I described HBS as "a soulless institution with opportunities lost," and on that score, I have not yet changed my mind. After the turn of the millennium, the reputation of capitalism is sinking, the reputation of Business Schools in general is sinking, the standing of proud HBS is declining in the all-important ratings of top Business Schools, and the performance of some HBS graduates in corporate scandals such as Enron is an embarrassment.

In response to all these circumstances, Dean Kim Clark conducted a study that, according to a letter to all graduates, will "delve deeply, understand root causes, and identify actionable long-term solutions." If my premises about democratic capitalism are correct, this deep delving will eventually lead to the conflict between the bankers and the builders, and to the dominance by ultra-capitalism. Success of Dean Clark's program will require great courage and extraordinary statesmanship because HBS is an institution where most of the buildings are named for bankers and most of the money in the recently announced $500 million capital campaign will come from finance capitalists and ultra-capitalists.

Democratic Capitalism

Dean Clark states in the letter that all first-year students take a course in Business Ethics. With due respect to the Dean, this is tactics without a strategy. When the moral philosophy of the capitalism in practice is Social Darwinism; the form of capitalism being taught celebrates "the American model" of ultra-capitalism and its "creative destruction," "downsizing," and "wage arbitrage"; and as long as the prime goal of most new graduates is to make a million dollars by age thirty, then a first-year course on Business Ethics is tokenism.

I will continue to promote the presentation of democratic capitalism in both Business Schools and Liberal Arts courses because democratic capitalism maximizes the profits, presumably the mission of the Business Schools, and democratic capitalism improves the human condition, presumably the mission of a Liberal Arts education.

Dewey-Almy

After graduation from Harvard Business School in June of 1950, I got a relatively high-paying job, $325/month, as an assistant to the sales manager at Dewey-Almy Chemical Company in Cambridge, Massachusetts. My first job was to promote a new product called Cryorap, a shrink-fit plastic to wrap chicken and other meats. A few months after starting this job, I was asked to go to the new factory operation in Lockport, New York, to help with the recruitment and hiring of factory workers.

When I arrived in Lockport, the factory manager, Jim Giles, greeted me by saying: "Congratulations! You're the foreman of the Press Department." After explaining to Giles that I was there to help with the hiring of new people, Giles repeated, "No, you're the foreman of the Press Department." Convinced, I asked, "What's a Press Department?"

For the rest of the year, I was a swing-shift foreman, that is, I worked from 4 p.m. to 12 midnight one week, from12 midnight to 8 a.m. the next week, and 8 a.m. to 4 p.m. the next, except that the actual hours on every shift were usually three hours longer.

The presses were four-color printing presses to print the producer's name and insignia on the roll of plastic material as it flew by on the printing press. I still cringe at the thought of mixing up the greens and yellows on one run I approved at 3 a.m. Things get to be confusing on the graveyard shift.

Lockport was a UAW union town, so I had my first experience with a strong union. The people, including the union officials, however, were familiar to me: They were the same kind of people I had grown up with in Gardner, Mass.

Lockport memories include having dinner at the union chief-steward's house. The invitation pleased me for several reasons, including my first chance to view a home television. It was a very small and very snowy screen. Another time, I learned that in an environment of trust, people become involved and accountable, and they welcome an opportunity to compete. Without fanfare, I began to put up the production numbers for each shift. My friend, the union steward, asked what I thought "this BS" would accomplish. Most of the workers, however, would sneak a glance, and productivity in total began to inch up. I had taken an early lesson in people's desire to get involved and make a contribution.

Electric Boat

In the spring of 1951, I walked into Electric Boat Co., in Groton, Connecticut, and got a new job. My fiancée, Dennice, was teaching at Connecticut College, a few miles up river, and we were planning to be married later in the summer.

Electric Boat was not sure what to do with someone with an MBA. They had been building submarines almost from the first, and most managers had been promoted from the trades or were engineers. By request, I spent the first six months working in various trades "in the yard." Subsequently, I was placed in a dead-end job.

Lacking any opportunity for self-development, I went to the head of personnel and said that if I could not learn and grow, I would have to leave. The manager said that he had nothing for me but that I could interview for the position of "assistant to the nuclear projects coordinator," even though I met few of the profile qualifications such as a degree in Nuclear Engineering. Despite this, I convinced Bill Jones, the recently appointed coordinator, that I could help him in his new position.

This was the very beginning of the atomic sub program, and Jones had been recently appointed to this position with its grand title. The sub-heading to the title should have been: "Keep Admiral Rickover happy, and you're doing a good job." Hyman Rickover later came to be known as the father of the nuclear navy.

During the next few years, I coordinated the weekly "Critical Items Report" with information gathered from the engineers to be sent to Rickover's department. I recruited, organized, and managed a department of a half-dozen manufacturing engineers who supervised the delivery of critical components. I worked in Arco, Idaho, where the first prototype of the nuclear reactor and the steam turbine for the *Nautilus* was built and tested. I also represented Electric Boat at the weekly progress meeting, at Westinghouse Atomic Power Division, located outside of Pittsburgh.

At these meetings, the genius of Rickover became clear to me. The Admiral knew that this first application of atomic energy, beyond the bombing of Hiroshima and Nagasaki, had so many state-of-the-art challenges for the engineers that either extreme schedule pressure had to be applied or else the program would drag on for years.

I was fascinated to watch the Westinghouse manager drive the program under Rickover's pressure. Each section manager reported progress against a tight schedule. In most cases, the manager really wanted to say, "Give me five years and five times the money, and I'll deliver a breadboard model." Instead, they had to explain any weekly slippage and their efforts to recover.

The whole program was described as piling one rickety card table after another on top of each other, and it worked! I had taken some Engineering in my Naval officer training, but I learned a lot more by listening. One fascinating aspect was that the design of the engine room, as well as the reactor room, had new challenges. Driving a submarine with nuclear energy was, of course, brand new, but the idea of putting into a submarine a steam turbine system that expanded with heat, required creativity on the part of the mechanical engineers. Simply to run a straight pipe from the compressor to the turbine generator would be impossible; the pipe needed enough bends to accommodate the expansion while the submarine's hull was contracting from sea pressure.

One of my many jobs was coordinating Admiral Rickover's visits to the mock-up of the *Nautilus*. This full-scale wooden model was in a part of the yard called "Siberia" and was used to run wire or pipe before actual installation. Siberia was also where engineers demonstrated to visitors how an atomic submarine would work, using a small-scale lucite model. Attending a few dozen of these dog-and-pony shows gave me a growing understanding of how the *Nautilus* really worked.

Setting up these meetings was typical of my grab-bag job description. One of my more unusual assignments was: "Don't lose Dr. Teller." Edward Teller had the dubious distinction of being known as the "Father of the H-Bomb." At that time, Teller was a member of the Reactor Safeguards Committee, a group of top experts from many disciplines. Their responsibility was community safety, recognizing that the *Nautilus* was the first use of nuclear energy since the bombing of the Japanese cities. The test site in Arco, Idaho, had been selected not for local talent but on the basis of low population density.

Electric Boat officials were of the opinion that Teller, a brilliant theoretician, could be a bit vague about his surroundings, possibly confusing New London, Connecticut, with London, England. Whether this was true or not, my job was to track Dr. Teller's every move while he was in the area.

Admiral Rickover was a regular visitor to Electric Boat. He was constantly and effectively selling his whole nuclear sub program to Congress. The groups he would bring from Washington to Electric Boat, and to demonstrations in Siberia, included important Congressmen such as the head of the Military Appropriations Committee.

Rickover was a crusty, unpleasant genius who deserves credit for the success of the *Nautilus* and the whole atomic sub program. He was also talented in developing relationships with Senators and Representatives. If he had not possessed this talent, he would not have survived the Naval establishment's reluctance to promote a Jewish captain to admiral. In effect, Rickover had been promoted by Congress, not by the Navy.

These were very exciting years. I was aboard the *Nautilus* during construction several times a week. Work that produces growing tangible results is especially satisfying. At the same time, my democratic capitalist instincts were offended by the working environment, a fundamental alienation between the "Yard" and the "Hill." The head of Electric Boat, O. P. Robinson, thought he was viewing the real world when he made surprise visits with his entourage to the Yard. The Yard, however, had a signaling system, primitive in its tools but sophisticated in its results. O. P. was being tracked and announced as if he were on radar.

Every few years, expensive strikes only made the alienation worse. A conversion to democratic capitalism would have been easy in the sense that cooperative efforts could have produced tremendous improvements with results to be shared. The organizational culture change, however, would have had to be radical and would have been difficult because the work was in a constant state of change. The Navy was not good at knowing when and how to freeze a design. Naval engineers seemed to believe that the Cold War would be won only by the latest design changes.

After a few years of work on the atomic sub program, I hit my self-development ceiling. Those had been good years, and the work had included my reorganizing a large department. I was stimulated by the creative reorganization but bored by the day-to-day running of it. Some who had been in the same department for thirty-five years were surprised that such a young manager wanted to leave.

I was able to arrange an interview with Carl Shugg, Electric Boat's new president, but he seemed unimpressed with my proposals about all the good things I could do for him. Luck was with me, however, as O. P. Robinson, Shugg's predecessor, had been requesting that Shugg find him an assistant. Shugg thought that he had a win/win opportunity—he could get rid of me and Robinson in one move. Shugg recommended me to O. P.

O. P. had lost in the struggle with John Jay Hopkins to run the corporation later to be known as General Dynamics. O. P. was then kicked upstairs from head of the boat yard to become corporate senior vice president in charge of minor matters, one of which was Electro Dynamic, small and unprofitable, but an original component of the corporation. O. P. assigned me to visit and analyze Electro Dynamic.

Electro Dynamic

Electro Dynamic built electric motors in a plant in Bayonne, New Jersey. Older than either G.E. or Westinghouse in the motor business, Electro Dynamic was, nevertheless, still small, losing money, and dismal. Some of the buildings were circa 1905. The machine shops were dark, the wood soaked with machine-cutting oil, and full of mostly sullen people. The picture was not exactly that of the 1850 London factory workers whose misery energized Marx, but it was not entirely different, either.

John Thurston, a wartime friend of the top officers of General Dynamics, was brought in to be the new general manager of Electro Dynamic in 1956. New management was overdue, and although I was the internal consultant who had been studying this sad operation for a couple of years, it would not be I, for no one in the corporate office had the courage to put a 28-year old in that position.

Thurston's first action was to terminate my involvement with Electro Dynamic. Who needed a corporate consultant hanging around? This action was rescinded a few weeks later. After Thurston had talked to the people who had developed a respect for me, and recognized the enormity of the challenge, he called me in and offered the job of plant manager. I quickly moved my family from Stonington, Connecticut, to Rumson, New Jersey, to take this opportunity to make a difference. Five years later, Thurston left to run a larger part of General Dynamics, and I became president of Electro Dynamic.

In any company needing restructure, the first priority is a great deal of listening. Listening simultaneously trains the manager, starts the process of involving the people, and raises their self-esteem. At Electro Dynamic, most of the people had high potential and were eager to improve their situation, but they were at the same time suspicious of management. Quickly, we painted the buildings, painted the machines, put in adequate lighting, and dressed the place up so much that we decided to have an open-house for all the employees' families. The pride, dignity, energy, and innovation that previously had been dormant now began to blossom.

During the next several years, Electro Dynamic revolutionized a part of the motor industry by building hi-tech motors for use in low-noise submarines. In addition to the typical horsepower and speed requirements, the U. S. Navy added specifications for airborne and structural noise levels throughout the frequency spectrum.

These motors were designed by a genius named Harris Shapiro, the son of a rabbi, from New York's Lower East Side. Sophisticated motors were manufactured and tested by a self-taught manufacturing engineer, Neil Bonner, a Bayonne high-school graduate, who combined his twenty years of shop experience with Shapiro's design theories. The marketing was done by another talent in his own field, Al Reposi, a high-school graduate from nearby Staten Island and a 20-year employee of Electro Dynamic.

Shapiro, 25 years old when I met him, must have been the world's most brilliant motor designer; Electro Dynamic's proud future was based on his brilliance. My opinion of Shapiro's brilliance was supported during a visit, in the early 1960s, to a large British motor manufacturing company, English Electric, in Bradford, England. The general manager seemed intrigued with Harris's knowledge of all types of motors, so he brought in team after team of his specialists to interrogate Shapiro. Small AC motors, large AC motors, small DC motors, large DC motors, motor generators, frequency converters—the whole thing sounded like the Olympics of motor design, and clearly the Bayonne Kid was winning every event.

Shapiro's brilliance would have been wasted, however, except that I was the right person, a self-taught democratic capitalist, who could provide the environment in which these people could use their enormous latent powers. The other prerequisite for Electro Dynamic's metamorphosis from a century of failure to become the leading hi-tech motor company was that Shapiro's brilliance was not ego-centered. His mission was to design an elegant product, and in this mood he sought and respected the contributions of Neil Bonner; Neil's brother, Jimmy; Al Reposi, and others.

At that time, many engineers took a superior attitude towards manufacturing types, many of whom, like the Bonner brothers, had no education beyond high school. The Bonners, however, collaborated with Shapiro at every step in the development of our company, and together with him they revolutionized the motor design and manufacturing process.

Radical changes were needed because of the Navy's requirements to make motors noise and vibration free. The Navy had discovered that the new nuclear submarines could be tracked by sophisticated sonar from Portsmouth, New Hampshire, to Bermuda. Worse, each sub could be identified by its unique noise signature. Admiral Rickover would not tolerate this, so he challenged the industry to eliminate this broadcasting of location and identity of his subs. In the middle of the Cold War, these nuclear subs were a critical component of U.S. military posture.

With the usual amount of trial and error, the Bonner brothers converted manufacturing to a precision process. Our operators learned how to machine to tenths of thousands tolerance and a 63-micro-inch finish, working with twenty-year-old turret lathes! In the late-1950s, the motor industry's first certified, pressurized clean-room was built at Electro Dynamic, with the assemblers decked out in smocks, gloves, booties, and hair covers. The old greasy-looking manufacturing plant now looked like an early version of the semiconductor industry.

When the first generation of motors was tested, they could not pass the frequency spectrum test. This was all new art: Navy engineers had imposed a new specification, and no one knew whether it could be met or not. Shapiro and the Bonner brothers determined that the offending frequency was caused by the bearings. Neil Bonner then went on a pilgrimage to find the perfect bearing. He could find it at none of the U.S. manufacturers, even with their premium-priced, Navy source-inspected bearings. He found it, instead, in a commercial warehouse in Hoboken, New Jersey; it was a low-priced commercial Japanese bearing. These bearings solved the technical problem, but they presented an administrative problem at the same time: Only premium-priced, Navy source-inspected bearings were allowed. By then, however, Electro Dynamic had its own andrometer and other bearing-testing equipment, so the Navy was able to ignore the paternity of the bearings by making Electro Dynamic an approved bearing-test site. The motors passed all tests with these bearings.

These superior bearings were an early indication of the emerging Japanese economic miracle that was no miracle at all but merely the application of many of the principles of democratic capitalism. Specifically, the Japanese had a cooperative environment;

good training; a strong work ethic; a well educated work force; job security; plenty of low-cost, patient money dedicated to long-term growth; and a sense of common purpose natural to their national recovery effort. With help from the United States, they also had the opportunity to do their manufacturing with the latest in equipment and processes. For example, the Japanese were the first to forge, rather than machine, the bearing races.

Al Reposi, another resident talent critical to this success story, did much more than direct the typical marketing activities. He and his sales engineers did all of that, but they also had to be intimately involved in design concepts. To solve the submarine noise problems, some Navy engineers developed a poorly informed preference for sleeve bearings as superior to ball bearings. Reposi had the subtle job of deflecting this alternative while much of the convincing evidence was still in Shapiro's head. Similarly, Reposi had to sell motors to the pump manufacturers who, in many cases, were blaming their inability to meet specs on the motor. In a team effort with Shapiro and Bonner, Reposi learned how to instruct his customers in this new technology without offending them.

With the increasing support of 800 employees and the good will of union officials in a positive atmosphere, our group built a profitable and rapidly growing business. An early disappointment at Electro Dynamic, however, was the failure to put a profit-sharing program in place. The UAW's New Jersey business agent, Manny Mann; the union president, Tony Marino; and the chief steward, Al Annunciata, had all been sufficiently interested in the idea to join me on a trip to Cambridge, Massachusetts, to learn about an MIT professor's program called the "Scanlon Plan," a plan to involve workers, increase productivity, and share in the financial improvement.

We did not implement the Scanlon Plan, however, for two reasons: The methodology of the plan was flawed (this was later confirmed by companies that tried it unsuccessfully), and UAW leaders were not yet ready to approve a cooperative effort with management. The UAW headquarters, at that time, regarded a labor/management partnership with suspicion because they thought that it would be a battle over the loyalty of the workers. This is generally not the case today. Union statesmen now recognize that to grow and prosper, unions must support the workers' involvement in generating good quality and high productivity.

All of these talented people had been at Electro Dynamic when I arrived and were just waiting for the opportunity to make their full contribution. But after working hard to build a proud company, many of us at Electro Dynamic stood on a nearby hill well into a Saturday night, April 20, 1963, watching the whole effort literally go up in smoke. By that time, Electro Dynamic's growth had required the repurchase of several adjacent buildings formerly owned by Elco, a part of the parent company. One of these buildings had been used to build PT boats, including PT-109, President Kennedy's famous boat. All was consumed in a raging fire that started at a near-by plastics factory and spread before 50-knot winds blowing from the west across Newark Bay.

The following morning, about 15 managers and foremen met at my home in Rumson to face a tough question: How do you rebuild a complicated business that has been completely destroyed? The destruction was total: fourteen buildings; all machines, except a few turret lathes; all jigs, dies, fixtures; and finally, all our drawings. We had carefully microfilmed the drawings, but we had not been smart enough to move the films off-site. When the three-story buildings caved in, the microfilm back-ups melted in their vaults.

The Electro Dynamic team re-enacted the mythology of the Phoenix's rising from its own ashes and accomplished a seemingly impossible task. Some people were assigned parts of the problem to be acted upon, and others volunteered. All were then, by necessity, completely free to work on their part of the reconstruction. Each was motivated to the fullest as part of a whole, and all performed beyond belief. Previously marginal performers responded to the challenge of common purpose and turned out to be some of the greatest heroes. Ever since, I have imagined the potential progress for society as a whole, if these seemingly simple factors could only be brought into play: A common mission for the common good, with sufficient freedom for people to make their respective contributions.

In space provided by our good neighbor, Englander Mattress, we were back in business on Monday morning after the Saturday fire. With good service from the phone company, our phones were being answered bravely, "Electro Dynamic!" as though it were simply the beginning of another ordinary work week. That morning, employees were informed that all benefits would be continued. Within five months, new motors were being shipped from a new facility. Virtually every employee had stayed with Electro Dynamic.

During this time, I had the stressful responsibility of convincing the Board of General Dynamics to rebuild E.D. For this purpose, I was invited to make my presentation to the Board in the latter part of 1963 at the company headquarters in Rockefeller Center. I was, of course, nervous; the livelihood of 800 people and their families hung on the decision.

During my presentation, Colonel Henry Crown, the largest shareholder, asked a legitimate business question: Why should the corporation not simply pick up the insurance pay-off and get rid of this small division? I like to think that it was my eloquence that resulted in the Board's decision to rebuild Electro; actually, it was Shapiro, the Bonners, Reposi, and 800 others who had built up the premier position in low-noise submarine motors. No way could large General Dynamics offend the Defense Department by pulling the plug on small Electro Dynamic!

The metamorphosis of Electro Dynamic from a century of failure to industrial preeminence is, to me, empirical confirmation of the democratic capitalist principle about the enormous potential of people. The way in which we overcame the total destruction of the fire was living proof of both the human potential and harmonizing principles.

I was 37 years old at the time, and I saw that during the eight years before—five as plant manager, three as president—these principles had been demonstrated in the remarkable conversion of Electro Dynamic from persistent failure to outstanding success, but that was nothing compared to the performance of hundreds of people functioning under extreme pressure. Many at General Dynamics's corporate office had thought the task impossible. The ordinary people at Electro Dynamic, however, accomplished the impossible through the kind of noble effort that, tragically, we usually see only in wartime. This has to be the ultimate self-criticism of the human effort at governance: Our most noble efforts often emerge only as part of the obscenity of war. Nations' leaders have historically stimulated a sense of common purpose while sending young people to kill and be killed in war, but few have succeeded in developing an equivalent sense of common purpose in peacetime.

The greatest compliment to this team's extraordinary performance was paid by Admiral Rickover himself when his organization ordered the Navy to use GE motors on an *interim* basis until Electro Dynamic could get back in business. The re-creation of this business from total destruction was an agonizing experience, but it also taught many useful lessons. Since this experience, I have never had any doubts about the enormous potential of people when they are united in a common purpose.

The parent company, General Dynamics, was an unmanageable conglomerate that had been put together by an ego-driven deal-maker. He was succeeded by CEOs and a corporate staff who had neither training nor instinct for democratic capitalism. Most of the division presidents were capable, but the corporate group failed to recognize that success of their illogical assortment of operations depended on sufficient freedom for the division managers and their people. Large repetitive errors were an inevitability in this environment, such as the ill-fated 880-990 commercial jet program. This was a corporate office plan to diversify the company away from dependence exclusively on defense work. General Dynamics had jumped on the commercial jet program late in the game. The only available customer was TWA, then dominated by the erratic Howard Hughes, who insisted on designing the plane's interior layout in a way that had no appeal to other potential customers. General Dynamics ended up with the largest corporate loss at that time in American history.

As the youngest member of the internal General Dynamics Board of Management representing by far the smallest division, I was still required to meet with other division presidents and corporate officers once a month. Stepping from the survival efforts at Electro Dynamic, in Bayonne, into the California world of jets and missiles, was a surreal experience.

I left Electro Dynamic in 1966; within a couple of years, Shapiro, the Bonners, and Reposi left to start Hansome Energy Systems, which became a successful company. I was pleased when they asked me to become a Director.

The parent company, General Dynamics, regarded Electro Dynamic as a nuisance because of its relatively small size. After I left, they brought in unqualified managers who proved that whereas it takes time and a unique combination of skills to build a good company, it takes but little time and no skill to destroy it.

In 2000, General Dynamics shut down Electro Dynamic and sold the property. Hansome Energy, who had already absorbed most of Electro Dynamic's motor business, then purchased the rest. Harris Shapiro and the Bonner brothers had died, but their legacy of democratic capitalism continued under Al Reposi as chairman, and Harris Shapiro's sister-in-law, Selma Rossen, as president.

Howe Richardson Scale Company and the Robert Morse Corp.

Bob Morse was third generation of the Fairbanks Morse family. The U. S. company was fought over in a well-known takeover battle in the 1950s. Bob then "bought" the Canadian Fairbanks Morse Company from his grandfather and proceeded to acquire pump and scale companies in the United States. His consultant recommended that he bring in a chief operating officer. I was selected.

My job was simultaneously to be president of the Howe Richardson Scale Company and Group V. P. of the corporation, which was headquartered in Montréal. The Howe Richardson part was easy—good people, good products, good markets. With the help of Walter Young, we cut staff by attrition and selectively raised prices for a quick and dramatic improvement. I passed on the president's title to Walter, and he proceeded to grow the business.

Morse talked me into moving my family to Montréal; a year later, concerned about a potential new capital gains tax in Canada, he decided to sell the business. All of the many divisions were doing substantially better under my leadership, so Bob started the sale by using me as the prize in the top of the Crackerjack box. Subsequently, Bob recognized that he might have to sell the company in pieces, so I left.

My kids know that I think self-development is everything in career building, and that every setback is an opportunity to develop one's abilities. Everyone gets dumped on by external events; some learn to whine and they become victims, some learn to control their own destiny by regarding these events as opportunities. Looking for a job can be a demeaning experience, however, and I had my share of interviews with arrogant CEOs, after having traveled considerable distances for the "opportunity." This was a period of considerable "self-development."

ADT, Inc.

When I joined ADT in 1970, the company was distracted by a recent anti-trust settlement, loss of market share, and limited technological momentum. ADT was over 100 years old, and it occupied the largest position in the central-station alarm business. ADT central stations monitored fire and burglar alarm signals 24-hours-a-day, 7-days-a-week, transmitting from commercial premises, especially jewelers, banks, and manufacturers. ADT had recently become an independent public company as a result of an antitrust action. The new Board, led by John Whitehead, co-head of Goldman Sachs, and later Deputy Secretary of State, recruited me to manage the company in its new circumstances.

Inside the dismal headquarters, a departmental organization concerned itself more with turf wars than with cooperation. I made no criticism of this situation, whether inside or outside the company. I had been through this before; so, I started off by listening and by treating the situation for what it was, an opportunity for all. I knew before I began that many good and talented people were yearning for a chance to get involved and make their contributions.

Motivating the organization was essential. Equally fundamental to ADT's future was building technological momentum. Many of ADT's hundreds of thousands of electro-mechanical systems on customer premises were old but well maintained, and they produced a stable, recurring revenue on a lease-contract basis. The whole industry, however, was ready for a step-change of technology to solid-state electronics with systems that could perform important new functions for less money. The new availability of micro-processors in 1970 was changing everything.

Kinetic management challenges require a redirection from existing momentum; static management challenges are more difficult. At ADT, I had to put various new forces in motion. ADT, at that time, was like a large ship dead in the water, as sailors say. Recognizing this, I embarked on a long-term plan to motivate the organization and grow the business.

When I joined ADT at age 44, I put most of my net worth into the purchase of ADT stock. Although the amount was modest, I instantly became the largest stockholder on the Board by a considerable amount. Buying stock in the company with one's own money gives the professional manager an ownership-feeling usually not accomplished through stock options. Options engender an ownership feeling for some, but for many, they foster a short-term attitude and a susceptibility to deal-making. During my eighteen years with ADT, I took every dollar of bonus in ADT stock. Many times, that left us "cash poor," but that is how an owner is supposed to feel!

At ADT, I spent my first two years traveling and listening. My first changes were the decentralization in two selected regions, and the appointment of a scientific advisory committee. High-tech professors on this committee stimulated ADT engineers, under the direction of Engineering V.P. Tony Grosso, to recognize the wonderful things they could do with the new electronic technology.

The decentralization was not complicated. Los Angeles and New York became the test districts in which the district managers there were made responsible for all disciplines. Sales, service, and operations had previously reported up the hierarchy to senior positions in headquarters for each discipline. An MBA from Harvard was not required to make this change, but it did take a democratic capitalist who recognized the right people, promoted them from within the company, motivated them, and left them free to make their business work locally.

Once sufficient operating momentum had been generated, ADT moved to new headquarters on the 91st and 92nd floors of the World Trade Center in New York City, where it remained until 1985. The tragedy of September 11, 2001, is especially shocking to me because the first plane hit near where my office and adjacent Boardroom had been located.

By 1977, the ADT working culture was sufficiently changed to be ready for a profit-sharing, stock-purchase plan. *Care and Share* was then implemented. With the help of previously under-utilized talent at ADT, we had redesigned ADT's product line and reorganized the company according to the principles of democratic capitalism; good growth and increased profits followed. ADT expected all employees to contribute up to their potential, and I knew that to sustain their efforts, everyone had to share in the improvements. A contest to name the new plan was held, and a woman in the Detroit office won, proposing that the more workers *cared*, the more they would *share;* hence, *Care and Share*. With the assistance of Bob Donnelly, V.P. and General Counsel, we designed and launched the plan with immediate success.

In most branches, 60% employee participation was typical, whether in union or non-union cities. This level of participation is notable because the employees had to make deductions from their wages to participate in *Care and Share.* There was no waiting period for participation; all workers were encouraged to become *Care and Share* associates from the first day of their employment, and to start thinking like owners.

From 1970, when I had joined ADT, until 1983, profits improved every year. Wall Street was always looking for either bigger gains or, preferably, a takeover of the company, for ADT was under constant attack by predators. We managers felt that we had to play defense every morning in order to play offense in the afternoon.

The Wall Street analysts' instincts were accurate: ADT could have produced much higher short-term earnings but at the sacrifice of long-term growth. Our strategy was to produce sufficient improvement to keep Wall Street reasonably quiet, if a bit sullen, and then invest incrementally above these modest profit improvements in new products and new markets. From 1970 to 1983, ADT followed this strategy, adding to stockholders' profits each year while pumping what could have been stronger profit improvement into new-growth programs. This was not exactly a unique strategy, for most democratic capitalist companies follow a similar pattern, dividing improvements between increased profits and sales growth. This, however, was before short-term earnings pressure became excessive in the 1980s.

ADT had a profitable customer base that paid a fee once a month for central-station services and the maintenance of their systems, but by 1983, ADT had to face a new challenge, for we had shot ourselves in the foot. By integrating the new technology into such effective, customer-friendly systems, we inevitably stimulated old customers using old systems to ask, "When can we get this new system called *Focus*?"

How could we not offer advanced technology to our existing customers? But if we did, we would destroy this precious recurring stream of revenue. The archaic systems with their point-to-point wiring and simple controls needed to be replaced with multiplex systems that supervised and monitored all points of protection. Later, the technology allowed two-way communication of vital information, not just back to the on-premise control but all the way to the newly automated remote central stations. ADT had the same dilemma that AT&T and IBM faced on a much larger scale. The long-term answer was an expensive plan to upgrade the old systems and provide the new features.

ADT bit the bullet and embarked on this plan, after telling stockholders that profits would be sacrificed for a couple of years. In the face of already declining profits, the boldest part of the plan was the addition of about 300 people to the sales force. We believed in the new products, both for existing customers and for new customers, and we had to honor that belief with a commitment to cover the market. By 1987, our investments were paying off in strong sales growth and profit momentum. The consolidation from a worldwide total of 166 central stations down to about 20 highly automated stations was well underway, as was the less glamorous but equally important effort to integrate the entire data system.

On May 12, 1987, I reviewed the financial prospects and the *Care and Share* plan in my remarks at the annual stockholders' meeting on the 106th floor of the World Trade Center:

> The final unique strength of ADT is a program and an environment intended to release the tremendous power of turned-on people. This is the tenth anniversary of the introduction of the *Care and Share* program, which encourages everyone to participate and contribute to the success of the company and share in the improved results. It is based on several very fundamental concepts which, happily, seem to be getting emphasis and attention in many areas of industry recently. These concepts include giving

42

proper dignity and respect to all, and recognizing that the best way to improve an operation is with the ideas and involvement of the people doing the work.

It recognizes that although improvement can be made in a fear environment, the potential is severely limited when compared to a participatory environment. While the potential is much greater, the participatory environment is much harder to attain. It becomes possible only when a philosophical base combines integrity with management skills.

A critic of the plan, based simply on earnings-per-share improvement, could recognize simple congruence with all shareholders, but might view the plan as too amorphous, too removed from individual action, to have any real motivational benefit. This is basically true and was recognized. The answer is that a *Care-and-Share* type plan takes longer, and depends on great communication and leadership skills at all levels.

For all of these reasons, we feel that the Plan is still in its early stages, even though it has been in place for ten years, and most regard it as very successful. Let me remind you of a few specifics of the Plan. We now have over 4,500 participants in the U.S. and Canada. Participants can put up to 8% of their income into the Plan. Under the U.S. 401(k), part of this is put in as pre-tax dollars. This is a good federal benefit that helps improve the abnormally low rate of savings in the U.S.

Investment options include equities, bonds, a money-market fund, and, of course, ADT stock. For every dollar an associate puts in, the Company contributes a minimum of 20 cents. When earnings per share improve 12% or more, then the more substantial sharing begins. At 15%, ADT's investment is 50 cents per dollar; at 20%, 75 cents, and at the tough target of 25%, the Company would match dollar-for-dollar. All of ADT's money goes to the Plan trustee, Bankers Trust, and is put into ADT stock.

During the ten years of the Plan, the Company has contributed over $13.5 million. Mostly as a result of *Care and Share*, associates now own about 11.5% of the Company. In addition to the earnings sharing, over $1 million in dividends is now flowing into the Plan annually.

A recent issue of *Business Week* had a cover piece on the dichotomy between management and shareholders. I'm sure you can recognize the common interest at ADT, among management-shareholders, associate-shareholders, and outside shareholders, that this Plan provides.

An additional reason that the Plan is important to ADT is the unsupervised nature of our business. We send thousands of sales people, installers, maintenance people, and inspectors out in the morning with a "Do good, avoid evil, and give ADT a good day's work!" and are regularly reminded of how dependent we are on the attitude of associates.

All of these ambitious goals for improving the quality of life for all associates are realizable, in the broadest context, in democratic capitalism. With the 200th anniversary of the drafting of the Constitution this summer, it is an appropriate time to recognize the incredible system in which we have the good fortune to operate. The powerful combination of economic and political freedom has produced the greatest gains in standard of living for the greatest number of people in history.

At the beginning of this stockholders' meeting, I made a financial commitment to improve earnings a consistent 15% a year, and then I made the even bolder prediction that ADT could do this irrespective of the state of the economy. I felt that the stockholders had been patient for several years of weak earnings while we restructured the company to take best advantage of new technology. Fairness to our stockholders required us to tell them that their acceptance of this long-term effort by management would now pay off.

Contrary to management's agenda, ADT was taken over in 1987 by the Hawley Group, who later changed their own name to the better known ADT. The new owners had the good sense to keep the management of ADT under Les Brualdi who had been a key part of management for the preceding 12 years. Under Les's direction, ADT grew rapidly and set new records with the introduction of affordable security systems for homeowners. In 1970, residential systems had been regarded as a distraction by most people in ADT; by the end of Les Brualdi's term in 1997, ADT was selling over 200,000 home systems a year. Among Les's many achievements, he kept *Care and Share* in place.

When ADT was sold in 1987 for $815 million, the employees received about $115 million of this total. ADT associates took home large checks, many over $100,000, to spouses who had never seen amounts that large before. In 1997, ADT was merged into Tyco, a U.S. company in many related businesses. ADT's value at that time, with help from the bull market and many acquisitions, was placed at $2.8 billion. When I had joined ADT in 1970, its market value as well as sales had been about $90 million. These comparisons validate the financial premise of democratic capitalism: The investment in human values at ADT produced profits and growth superior to any of its major competitors.

When Workers Become Owners

The following is the message to all ADT employees that introduced *Care and Share* in 1977:

TO ALL ADT EMPLOYEES:

The new ADT Profit Sharing and Savings Plan may be one of the most important programs in ADT's history, for you and for the Company. I'm convinced that all of us at ADT have a tremendous potential to do better. This plan is intended to encourage us to improve ADT and to reward us as these improvements are made.

Most people like to feel they are playing on a winning team. Most people like to be associated with things that are "First Class." Most people like to feel they are pursuing excellence in their lives. All of these feelings relating to personal satisfaction are available in our work if we learn to CARE, if we learn to COOPERATE, if we learn to COMMUNICATE.

ADT is a fine company now. It can be a great Company. I'm convinced that we at ADT have a unique opportunity to make a Plan such as this work successfully. We have the potential for improvement, we have opportunities to expand, and I believe we have the type of employees that will make it work!

My enthusiasm for the Plan is quite clear. But it is important for me to emphasize to each of you that this is a savings and investment decision which each of you has to make. Any investment decision includes an element of risk. I would urge you to study the Plan carefully, be sure all of your questions are adequately answered and then make a well informed decision.

July 1, 1977
Raymond B. Carey, Jr.
President

Because of the record bankruptcy of Enron in 2001, political attention has been paid to employees' concentrating too much of their net worth in their company's stock. I pointed out the risk factor in this introduction to *Care and Share*, although the plan was in addition to, not a substitute for, the company's pension plan. Every manager was also responsible annually to review each *Care and Share* account with the employee. Associates who would retire in five years were encouraged to convert their account to guaranteed income bonds. Associates were reminded that, while ADT ought to continue to prosper, the stock market could fall and pull ADT down with it.

Thousands of plans like *Care and Share* are operating successfully today, but as democratic capitalism has little visibility either among the intellectual community or in the educational process, the importance of these plans for worldwide wealth-creation is little understood. These are not "nice to have, feel-good programs"; they are an indispensable part of wealth-creation and distribution. Properly applied, they contain the answers to economic dilemmas both in mature and in developing countries.

Segue

In 1989, at the end of my career as CEO of ADT, Inc., I was convinced that I understood the template that, when competently applied, would produce superior results in a commercial situation. As this form of capitalism draws its superior strength from attention to human values, from insuring the opportunity for each to realize his or her full potential, it puzzled me that democratic capitalism enjoyed little visibility compared to the prevailing intellectual view that generic capitalism is a cruel economic mechanism in continuing tension with democracy. This myopia seemed to me to be blocking social progress. My curiosity prompted the next fifteen years of study that have now resulted in this book.

Imagine how excited I was to discover that Information Age companies depend on the democratic capitalist culture! I had been working on putting this culture in place all of my business life, and now a new Industrial Revolution had erupted, based not on manual labor and wage suppression but on cognitive power and human involvement. Utopian visions for the twenty-first century could now be grounded in economic determinism. A company could not be successful in this new age without a culture that provided modern wage earners with opportunities for individual development as well as an environment of trust and cooperation. The logic of combining this work-culture revolution with the socio-economic reality that the workers themselves were now the prime source of investment capital, meant that the workers had become the capitalists. How could the alienation between management and labor continue for long, after everyone realized that the workers and the capitalists were now the same people? With these forces in motion, the democratization of capitalism seemed an inevitability.

CHAPTER 3

The Social Development of Democratic Capitalism

The Communist Manifesto
In place of the old bourgeois society, with its classes and class antagonisms, we shall have an association, in which the free development of each is the condition for the free development of all.

Karl Marx and Friedrich Engels, 1848[10]

The Democratic Capitalist Manifesto
The other mode in which cooperation tends still more efficaciously to increase the productiveness of labor, consists in the vast stimulus given to productive energies, by placing the laborers, as a mass, in a relation to their work which would make it their principle and their interest—at present it is neither—to do the utmost, instead of the least possible, in exchange for their remuneration. It is scarcely possible to rate too highly this material benefit, which yet is nothing compared to the moral revolution in society that would accompany it; a new sense of security and independence in the laboring class; and the conversion of each human being's daily occupation into a school of the social sympathies and the practical intelligence.

John Stuart Mill, 1848[11]

John Stuart Mill (1806-1873) and Karl Marx (1818-1883) were close to agreement on the economic-political system that could create so much broadly distributed wealth that material scarcity would

---

[10] Karl Marx and Friedrich Engels, *The Communist Manifesto* (New York: Penguin Books, 1967), p. 105.

[11] John Stuart Mill, *Principles of Political Economy, with Some of Their Applications to Social Philosophy* (Fairfield, New Jersey: Augustus M. Kelley, 1987), p. 789.

be eliminated and all people would be elevated and unified. The definition and test of this social arrangement wherein each and all could reach their full potential had begun three-quarters of a century before Mill and Marx wrote their manifestos.

Society's erratic search for comfort and justice was illuminated in the late-18th century by the near simultaneous contributions of Adam Smith (1723-1790) and Thomas Jefferson (1743-1826). Smith's proposal of economic freedom through growing capitalism, and Jefferson's ideal of political freedom through growing democracy, became available to be combined in a template for the governance of social progress. The commercial application of this ideology resulted, and continues to result, in democratic capitalism. When private property and competition are combined with participatory democracy, the whole of society can reach its full potential as the sum of the greatest self-development of each individual.

Over the two centuries since Smith's and Jefferson's advocacy of complementary freedoms, democratic capitalism has been tested, validated, and refined. The society with the greatest freedom during this time, the United States of America, produced the greatest comfort and justice for the largest number of people. By the end of the twentieth century, however, corruptions from both ends of the U.S. political spectrum were causing an economic, social, and political decline; maldistribution of wealth domestically; and the failure of America as the world's economic leader. Before we Americans can reverse this decline, we must understand how the fundamentals of capitalism and democracy are being corrupted.

The legacy of the 17th-century geniuses, Galileo (1564-1642), Descartes (1596-1650), and Newton (1642-1727), was the identification of a natural order in the physical world. Following them, classical liberals were optimistic that identification of similar natural laws for civil society would lead to universal freedom, justice, and comfort. Adam Smith defined a system of industry, society, and public ethics that combined the new technology, and involved workers; propelled by this energy of economic progress, he foresaw, scarcity, exploitation, and class conflict would be eliminated. Thomas Jefferson and James Madison (1751-1836) defined and implemented a political structure that supported this economic system by promoting and protecting freedom within a civil discipline. The German Idealists, Immanuel Kant (1724-1804) and G.W.F. Hegel (1770-1831), speculated on a society that would reach ever-higher levels of development through freedoms focused by rules for moral secular conduct. Following Kant and Hegel, Karl Marx tried to bridge the British Empiricists and the German Idealists, tying social progress to an improvement in the economic system. Marx wrote:

> My view is that each particular mode of production, and the relations of production corresponding to it at each given moment, in short the economic structure of society, is the real foundation, on which arises a legal and political superstructure and to which correspond definite forms of social consciousness, and that the mode of production of material life conditions the general process of social, political, and intellectual life.[12]

With the proposed elimination of scarcity, exploitation, and alienation, the human species seemed ready to reach its temporal potential. Academia, the media, politicians, and the ecclesiastical establishments might well have embraced the new system, offering it to students and citizens by way of education. New leaders, motivated by the social morality of democratic capitalism and trained in its protocols of governance, might have converted the ideal into the real. It did not work that way, however. The predatory forces of mercantilism and imperialism, with their economic logic based on government privileges, still prevailed. Much of the world veered off in tragic pursuit of Marx's radical restructuring that derailed his mission of individual self-development in the process; meanwhile, academia, the media, the churches, and political governments failed to synthesize Marx's and Mill's contributions.

Because democratic capitalism as an integrated system never became part of either academic inquiry or public awareness, progress

---

[12] Karl Marx, preface to "A Contribution to the Critique of Political Economy," footnote 35, *Capital* (New York: Penguin Classics, 1976; written by Marx in 1859), vol. 1, part 1, chapter 1, p. 175.

for workers eventually came instead from the pressure of the trade-union movement, collectivist action by liberal government, and the trial and error of self-taught entrepreneurs. The motivation was the urge towards more freedom; the power was growing democracy; the results were better wages and working conditions and a rising standard of living.

Before 1810, for an early example, working hours at New Lanark were reduced by Robert Owen (1771-1858) from 14 hours a day to ten hours a day.[13] Years later in America, the new country, the General Congress of Labor, in Baltimore, declared in 1866:

> The first and greatest necessity of the present, to free the laborer of this country from capitalist slavery, is the passing of a law by which eight hours shall be the normal working day in all states of the American union.[14]

In the 20th century, numerous corporations went further in their democratization of capitalism by adding job security, participatory management, profit-sharing, and equity-purchasing plans.

Because democratic capitalism has enjoyed little visibility during the first two hundred years of its existence, it has had to take a variety of imperfect, experimental forms, short of the ideal. Progress was made, but productivity and innovation from a cooperative effort were limited because democratic capitalism had to be reinvented by each succeeding generation instead of being researched and then taught and learned in the universities.

Before Adam Smith issued his fundamental vision of economics, the mercantile system was unable to improve most lives. In 1756, Edmund Burke (1729-1797), still in his twenties, asked: Why has every human effort to structure society for peace and plenty been a failure? Why does the only animal capable of reason kill more of its own species than does any other animal?

---

[13] *Ibid.*, p. 411.

[14] *Ibid.*, p. 414.

It is an incontestable Truth, that there is more Havoc
made in one Year by Men of Men, than has been made
by all the Lions, Tigers, Panthers, Ounces, Leopards,
Hyenas, Rhinoceroses, Elephants, Bears and Wolves,
upon their own several Species, since the Beginning of
the World; though these agree ill enough with each
other, and have a much Greater proportion of Rage and
Fury in their composition than we have.[15]

Burke added up all of the humans killed by humans in history.
The methodology leading to his total of 37 billion was probably
flawed, and some have used it to argue that Burke's book was
satirical, but his conclusion that human history is about great failure is
tragically correct. Burke included in his litany of civil society's
failures the exploitation of the poor, and the conclusion of the
powerful, after viewing the poor in their demeaned condition, that
ordinary people are not capable of participating in their own
governance.

Burke's summary of thousands of years of human failure was
based on a battle over finite resources between the predatory few and
the exploited many. The movement from the slave-based economy of
Athens, through medieval serfdom and the wage-slavery of
mercantilism, to the educated and involved associates of modern
democratic capitalism in the Information Age, has taken 2,500 years.
Even though the democratic urge for freedom was ever growing
stronger, and the economic logic of combining democracy and
capitalism was becoming more and more clear, one must nonetheless
ask: Why has it taken so long, and why has the route been so bloody?

*Adam Smith's Vision: Society's Opportunity to Build Wealth,
Distribute It Broadly, and Eliminate Material Scarcity*

In 1776, a diminutive Scottish social philosopher, Adam
Smith, described an economic dynamic in which the new technology

---

[15] Edmund Burke, *A Vindication of Natural Society, or a View of the Miseries and
Evils Arising to Mankind from Every Species of Artificial Society* (Indianapolis,
Indiana: Liberty Classics, 1982), pp. 39-40.

of the Industrial Revolution; involved, well-paid workers; and worldwide free trade, would combine to grow wealth and spread it widely.[16] As the volume of production increased, Smith reasoned, costs would go down. Free competition would insure that this reduction in cost would be passed to the consumer. With lower prices, others could afford to buy, and that would generate more volume, still lower costs, and yet lower prices; then, more wage earners would become consumers demanding greater volume, and so on. Smith's vision was of an economic perpetual-motion machine. Smith knew that more units under production would lower the per-unit cost because the cost of tools, machinery, and set-up for production would be spread over more units.

A dramatic example in our time of Smith's commercial dynamic is the computer industry, in which each year new functions are added, the machines increase geometrically in power, and prices tumble. Another phenomenon of the Information Age is the extension of Smith's dynamic to service industries. The power of microchips and distributed processing to work stations allow, for the first time, major reductions of administrative expense, and they open up additional markets from reduced cost and price. Cost and price reduction that sustains growth in the Information Age has now moved from the factory floor to all aspects of business. Free competition and the innovative spirit of engaged and highly paid workers, just as Smith said would happen, drive the system.

Smith wrote *Wealth of Nations* as an economist to describe the interaction of costs, prices, markets, labor force, and monetary policy; he wrote as a political scientist to show that the general welfare is served by the most efficacious commercial system; and he demonstrated as a moral philosopher that capitalism, as he defined it, functions best when trust rules in the workplace, and integrity in business dealings. Adam Smith was a pragmatist who saw social benefits being derived from the energy and ambition of people who enjoy the requisite freedoms. He was a realist who recognized exploitation and class conflict in the prevailing system, mercantilism.

---

[16] Adam Smith, *An Inquiry into the Nature and Causes of the Wealth of Nations* (New York: The Modern Library, 1937).

He was an optimist who anticipated the greatest success in North America, proportionate to its greater freedoms.[17]

Adam Smith criticized the English monetary system as an economic impediment: It sacrificed growth and jobs to protect the asset value of the wealthy. In Smith's theory, money is a medium of exchange that needs to be ample, low-cost, non-volatile, patient, and free of its own influence on the economic process. Smith did not think like the mercantilists who saw workers as a cost commodity to be suppressed, as Marx later put it, "in order to extract the maximum surplus value." Smith saw workers, rather, as a vital part of the economic process, with a capacity for involvement:

> It is naturally to be expected, therefore, that some one or other of those who are employed in each particular branch of labour should find out easier and readier methods of performing their own particular work, whenever the nature of it admits of such improvement. A great part of the machines made use of in those manufacturers, in which labor is most subdivided, were originally the invention of common workmen in order to facilitate and quicken their own particular part of the works.[18]

Smith proposed the view, radical at the time, that as worker involvement improves profits, so the workers involved must share in the improved profits, if their motivation is to be maintained:

> The liberal reward of labour, as it encourages the propagation, so it increases the industry of the common people. The wages of labour are the encouragement of industry, which like every other human quality, improves in proportion to the encouragement it receives. A plentiful subsistence increases the bodily strength of the labourer, and the comfortable hope of bettering his condition, and of ending his days perhaps in ease and plenty, animates him to exert that strength to the utmost. Where wages are high, accordingly, we

---

[17] Smith, *op. cit.*, book II, chapter 11, p. 70.

[18] *Ibid.*, p. 9.

shall always find the workman more active, diligent
and expeditious, than when they are low.[19]

Smith never used the expression *laissez-faire*, although he had
studied the French physiocrats who did use it. He has also been badly
interpreted to be an apologist for greed. He was, in fact, clear about
the tension between his system and mercantilism, and he was opposed
both to the mercantilists' government privileges and to their greed.
Similarly, he anticipated the conflict between mercantilists who think
that wage suppression improves profits, and others who see the
opportunity for every worker to contribute to the success of the
enterprise and share in the improved results. Smith reasoned that
financial capitalism's only legitimate function is to support the
productive sector with low-cost, non-volatile, and patient capital. He
was emphatic that all financial machinations are a subtraction from a
nation's wealth:

> So the stock of money which circulates in any country
> must require a certain expense, first to collect it and
> afterwards to support it, both of which expenses,
> though they make a part of the gross, are, in the same
> manner deductions from the neat revenue of the
> society.[20]

These conflicts between mercantilism and finance capitalism
on one hand, and democratic capitalism on the other, continue to
permeate every aspect of political and economic life, from the mission
of government, to tax laws affecting capital formation, and to the
application of surplus, job security, and ultimately the growth-rate of
the global economy, which, in turn, affects the standard of living.
Resolution of these conflicts will determine whether the world will
grow together in economic common purpose or continue in violence.

---

[19] *Ibid.*, p. 81.

[20] *Ibid.*, p. 273.

Jefferson's Vision: A Democratic Structure to Sustain Each Citizen's Natural Rights

Thomas Jefferson and his lifelong collaborator, James Madison, drew on the radical view of Englishman John Locke (1632-1704), that each person is endowed with inalienable rights. When Locke had proposed this theory of natural rights, particularly in the second of his *Two Treatises of Government* (1690),[21] the prevailing structure was tyrannical and static. Under the hierarchy of monarchs, nobles, and gentry, the idea that serfs had individual rights was revolutionary.

Jefferson and Madison also drew heavily on Montesquieu (1689-1753), a Frenchman who described the benefits of a mixed republic in which power is diffused among legislative, judicial, and executive branches.[22] Jefferson and Madison adopted the principle, ignoring Montesquieu's caveat that such a government could be functional only in a small, homogenous society. Madison, at the Constitutional Convention in Philadelphia, fought hard for the balanced arrangement; he argued that a large country could use this principle of checks and balances of power among the three branches of government to avoid concentration of power in any one aspect of government, while counting on diversity in the large population to prevent a tyranny by the majority.[23]

Earlier, when the Anglican Church in Virginia, subsidized by the Colony, was persecuting Baptists, Jefferson and Madison had both battled successfully in the Virginia Assembly for religious freedom. They also spoke against slavery as an institution, but neither of them succeeded in breaking out of their cultural conditioning as Virginia planters sufficiently to recognize for the slave population the same inalienable rights enjoyed by their owners.

---

[21] John Locke, *An Essay Concerning the True Original, Extent and End of Civil Government,* in *The English Philosophers from Bacon to Mill,* Edwin A. Burtt, ed. (New York: The Modern Library, 1939), p. 403.

[22] Charles-Louis de Secondat, Baron de Montesquieu, *The Spirit of the Laws* (Berkeley: University of California Press, 1977).

[23] Lance Banning, *The Sacred Fire of Liberty* (Ithaca, New York: Cornell University, 1995), pp. 203-4.

While Madison toiled away at the Constitutional Convention in hot Philadelphia, May to September, 1787, Jefferson was in Paris as ambassador to France. Jefferson continued, nevertheless, to argue by letter for specificity about individual freedoms, and his emphasis was honored later when the priority of the new Congress became the passage of the first ten amendments to the new Constitution, the Bill of Rights. The philosophical legacy of Jefferson and Madison is a belief in the wisdom and energy of ordinary people, given sufficient freedom, education, and rational leadership. The corollary of this first principle is the government's mission to nurture the environment of participatory democracy by limiting the government's intrusions. At the same time, the economic first principle of government as mandated in the new country's new Constitution is that the government's economic role is "to promote the general welfare."

Jefferson viewed America of that time as a country of independent farmers. He was wary of a financial oligarchy similar to those in Europe, and also wary of manufacturing. This ambiguity was itself part of the North/South animosity that contributed later to the Civil War. Because of the dominance by finance capitalism that Jefferson and Madison feared, the government failed to control currency and credit to promote the general welfare, as prescribed in the Constitution. The mixed-republic design, with deliberate diffusion of power, did not prevent the left from abandoning Jeffersonian principles by introducing a suffocating and mistake-prone central administration. On the right, the republic's structure failed to resist the corruption of financial capitalists who began substantially to direct the government's fiscal and monetary policies for the benefit of a few.

By the turn of the 21st century, many United States citizens had lost faith in a government that had become so polarized and superficial that it was unable to address root causes. Some suggested that Montesquieu had been right, that the diffusion of power among the executive, legislative, and judicial branches was unworkable in a large state.[24] The opposite argument was that an educated citizenry can still define a long-term, non-adversarial, integrated program that does address root problems, and can elect representatives to execute that plan.

---

[24] Daniel Lazare, *The Frozen Republic: How the Constitution is Paralyzing Democracy* (New York: Harcourt Brace and Company, 1996), p. 46.

Kant's Vision: The Human Condition Improving, Energized by Growing Freedom and Supported by Ideals Common to Religion and Reason

Immanuel Kant, a German professor, spent most of his life at the University of Königsberg in East Prussia. Whereas Adam Smith, an empiricist, had described an economic and political system that could provide comfort for all, Kant, a metaphysician, reasoned about free, moral humans for whom secular perfection is both their opportunity and their obligation. He challenged the tradition in which it was assumed that the human's exclusive goal is eternal happiness, and that a static structure of serfs, nobles, absolute monarchs, and church is God-given.

In *Critique of Pure Reason* (1781),[25] Kant gave credit to Adam Smith's friend, David Hume (1716-1776),[26] for having defined the limits of reason not connected with experience, and he emphasized a philosophy oriented to the life of action. By attempting to integrate reason with experience and tradition, Kant tried to relieve the tension between science and religion. Writing before the French Revolution and the toppling of European monarchs, Kant shared Jefferson's view that the human instinct towards freedom would lead to governments that ruled by free consent of the governed. He identified the human moral agenda, the human purpose, and the rules of secular conduct that are common to reason and faith.

Kant saw freedom, disciplined by morality, as the core for human progress. The ultimate moral duty, as Kant defined it, is the categorical imperative: "Act only on a maxim by which you can will that it, at the same time, should become a general law."[27] This rational morality forced the individual to analyze how society can best organize itself. The product of human reason in control of human behavior, it is imperative: unconditioned by time and place or circumstance, it is categorical.

---

[25] Immanuel Kant, *Critique of Pure Reason* (New York: Modern Library, 1960).

[26] David Hume, *A Treatise on Human Nature* (New York: Penguin Classics, 1984, first published in London, 1739).

[27] Kant, *op. cit.*, p. 473.

Kant was not the first to have sought simple rules as the basis of social ethics. Centuries earlier when Confucius (542-479 B.C.) was asked if there were one word that could improve society, the Chinese philosopher had answered, "Reciprocity."[28] The wisdom traditions of many religions hold the same first principle of human conduct as Confucius's reciprocity and Kant's Categorical Imperative, including the Judeo-Christian Golden Rule: "Do unto others as you would have them do unto you."[29]

In 1784, Kant wrote his *Idea for a Universal History*, having been stimulated by a student's observation:

> Professor Kant's favorite idea is that the ultimate purpose of the human race is to achieve the most perfect civic constitution … and to show to what extent humanity in various ages has approached or drawn away from this final purpose, and what remains to be done in order to reach it.[30]

In his "Eighth Thesis," Kant elaborated upon "a perfectly constituted state as the only condition in which the capacities of mankind can be fully developed, and also bring forth that external relation among states which is perfectly adequate to this end."[31] He concluded that whether one approaches with an understanding of history as a natural process or an effect of providence, humans can find the way to social perfection — for any other conclusion would make "man alone a contemptible plaything."[32] Kant argued that this process would "force the states to the same decision (hard though it may be for them) that savage man also was reluctantly forced to take,

---

[28] Confucius, *The Analects* XV.24 (London: Penguin Classics, 1979), p. 15: "It is perhaps the word shu (reciprocity). Do not impose on others what you yourself do not desire."

[29] Gospel of Matthew 7:12.

[30] Immanuel Kant, *Selections, Idea for a Universal History from a Cosmopolitan Point of View and Perpetual Peace*, Lewis White Beck, ed. (New York: Scribner/MacMillan, 1998), p. 415.

[31] *Ibid.*, p. 422.

[32] *Ibid.*, p. 416.

namely, to give up brutish freedom and to seek quiet and security under a lawful constitution."[33]

In 1795, Kant in his seventies wrote *Perpetual Peace: A Philosophical Sketch*,[34] his first publication since the government of King Frederick William II had imposed a ban on Kant's theological writings. Again Kant demonstrated his capacity to move from the most detailed metaphysics to the broadest challenges facing the human species. Kant proposed that a republican form of government is a precondition to the cooperation of nations in a federation whose only purpose ought to be the protection of peace; further, he argued, peace can be assured only when morality holds hegemony over politics. Kant demonstrated his grasp of governance by describing the separation and diffusion of power inherent in the republican form. The United States of America alone among the nations had recently adopted this formal separation of powers.

Kant expressed "a certain indignation" over the mixture of folly with wisdom, and violence with peace:

> One sees men's actions on the great world stage and finds, besides the wisdom that appears here and there among individuals, everything in the large woven together from folly, childish vanity, even from childish malice, and destructiveness.[35]

In her study of Kant, Sissela Bok summarized the moral constraints that governments must adopt if they are not to face a war of mutual extermination. These Kantian constraints include prohibitions against violence, deceit, and breach of trust. Bok described the fourth constraint as a prohibition against state secrecy.[36] These seem obvious enough until compared to the still prevalent Machiavellian view that "national interest" is a political matter of survival that transcends morality.

---

[33] *Ibid.*, p. 420.

[34] *Ibid.*, p. 429.

[35] *Ibid.*, pp. 415-16.

[36] Sissela Bok, *A Strategy for Peace: Human Values and the Threat of War* (New York: Vintage Books, Random House, 1990), pp. 35, 40.

In the system of economic and political freedom, constraints against violence, deceit, treachery, and secrecy are all functional prerequisites. The dilemma suggested by Reinhold Niebuhr (1892-1971), that is, replicating the morality of individuals in the collective, explains the failure of nations to realize Kant's vision of cooperation. Niebuhr's analysis reflects the historical failure of nations to stop the violence, but Niebuhr did not address the opportunities for nations united in economic common purpose. Despite the demonstrated capacity of economic freedom to improve lives, Niebuhr pessimistically concluded that many were still destined for misery caused by economic inequity:

> Human society will never escape the problem of the
> equitable distribution of the physical and cultural
> goods which provide for the preservation and
> fulfillment of human life.[37]

A similar lack of idealism on the part of many contemporary philosophers provides tacit support for politicians who pursue policies based on the inevitability of continued violence. New philosophers, inspired by the pragmatic idealism of democratic capitalism, could instead make "national interest" become participation in interdependent economic freedom. States combined in that purpose would be the collective moral society that eluded Niebuhr's imagination. As the standard of living and the quality of life go up, the violence goes down.

Condorcet's Vision: A Summary of the Contributions of the Eighteenth-Century Enlightenment toward a Rational Order for the Organization of Human Affairs

The last philosopher of the French Enlightenment, the Marquis de Condorcet (1743-1794) was a protégé of Voltaire (1694-1778); with this type of sponsorship, he became secretary to the Academy of Sciences at a young age. A mathematician like Descartes, Condorcet

---

[37] Reinhold Niebuhr, *Moral Man and Immoral Society* (New York: Charles Scribner & Sons, 1932; renewal copyright 1960), p. 1.

combined Descartes's dedication to scientific truth-searching with Voltaire's passion for justice. Condorcet summarized the work of the 18th-century Enlightenment with his vision of human perfectibility. While in hiding during the Reign of Terror, Condorcet wrote an extraordinary document, *Esquisse d'un Tableau Historique des Progres de L'Espirit Humain*. He borrowed heavily from the work of his friend, Turgot,[38] who was both a philosopher and a statesman. If Louis XVI (1754-1793) had followed Turgot's (1727-1781) reforms when Turgot had been his minister, instead of firing him, the King might have kept both his throne and his head.

Following a life of action, dialogue, and reflection, Condorcet proposed this liberal agenda for social progress:

> Free trade, freedom of speech, freedom of press, the end of censorship, the end of slavery, the enfranchisement of women, universal free education, equality before the law, the separation of state and church, religious toleration, the adoption of a written constitution with a written declaration of the rights of people embedded in the constitution to insure the recognition of those rights, the establishment of a representative or parliamentary form of national government, and local self-government to encourage the independence and the participation of the peasants in government.[39]

Condorcet was a man of action as well as thought, having served in the French National Assembly. Condorcet's agenda for social progress also benefited from his discussions with Adam Smith, Thomas Jefferson, and Thomas Paine (1737-1809). Condorcet's wife, Sophie, translated into French Adam Smith's *Theory of Moral*

---

[38] Anne-Robert-Jacques Turgot, Baron de l'Aulne, Comptroller General of Finance 1774-1776.

[39] Edward Goodell, *The Noble Philosopher Condorcet and the Enlightenment* (Buffalo: Prometheus Books, 1994), p. 162.

Sentiments[40] and Thomas Paine's speeches to the French National Assembly.[41]

Condorcet sustained his optimistic belief in human progress despite having to hide and then be in prison. The terrors that he experienced did not undermine his belief in human potential. From his discussions with Thomas Jefferson, Condorcet was inspired by the mission of the new republic, the United States:

> One nation alone escapes the two-fold influence of tyranny and superstition. From that happy land where freedom had only recently kindled the torch of genius, the mind of man released from the leading-strings of its infancy, advances with firm steps towards the truth.[42]

In the final chapter of *Esquisse*, "The Tenth Stage, The Future Progress of the Human Mind," Condorcet laid out his blueprint for social progress based on the elements of democratic governance, "believing that nature has set no limit to the realization of our hopes."[43]

Condorcet on imperialism and free trade:

> The nations of Europe will finally learn that monopolistic companies are nothing more than a tax imposed upon them in order to provide their governments with a new instrument of tyranny. The peoples of Europe, confining themselves to free trade, understanding their own rights too well to show contempt for those of other peoples, will respect this independence, which until now they have so insolently violated.[44]

---

[40] Adam Smith, *The Theory of Moral Sentiments* (Indianapolis, Indiana: Liberty Classics, 1959, written in 1759.)

[41] Goodell, *op. cit.*, p. 157.

[42] *Ibid.*, p. 227.

[43] *Loc. cit.*

[44] *Ibid.*, p. 228.

Condorcet on the template available for emerging nations trying to improve the lives of their people:

> The progress of these peoples is likely to be more rapid and certain than our own because they can receive from us everything that we have had to find out for ourselves, and in order to understand those simple truths and infallible methods which we have acquired only after long error, all that they need to do is to follow the expositions and proofs that appear in our speeches and writings. When mutual needs have brought all men together, and the great powers have established equality between societies as well as between individuals and have raised respect for the independence of weak states and sympathy for ignorance and misery to the rank of political principles, when maxims that favor action and energy have ousted those which would compress the province of human faculties, will it then be possible to fear that there are still places in the world inaccessible to enlightenment, or that despotism in its pride can raise barriers against truth that are insurmountable for long? The time will therefore come when the sun will shine only on free men who know no other master but their reason.[45]

Condorcet on wealth distribution:

> It is easy to prove that wealth has a natural tendency to equality, and that any excessive disproportion could not exist or at least would rapidly disappear if civil laws did not provide artificial ways of perpetuating and uniting fortunes; if free trade and industry were allowed to remove the advantages that accrued wealth derives from any restrictive law or fiscal privilege; if taxes on covenants, the restrictions placed on their free

---

[45] *Ibid.*, p. 230.

employment, their subjection to tiresome formalities and the uncertainty and inevitable expense involved in implementing them did not hamper the activity of the poor man and swelled up his meager capital; if the administration of the country did not afford some men ways of making their fortune that were closed to other citizens.[46]

Condorcet on a social safety net:

Here then is a necessary cause of inequality, of dependence, and even of misery, which ceaselessly threatens the most numerous and most active class in our society. We shall point out how it can be in great part eradicated by guaranteeing people in old age a means of livelihood, by securing for widows and orphans an income which is the same and costs the same for those families which suffer an early loss and for those which suffer it later; or again by providing all children with the capital necessary for the full use of their labor, available at the age when they start work and found a family. It is to the application of the calculus to the probabilities of life and the investment of money that we owe the idea of these methods which have already been successful, although they have not been applied in a sufficiently comprehensive and exhaustive fashion to render them really useful, not merely to a few individuals, but to society as a whole, by making it possible to prevent those periodic disasters which strike at so many families and which are such a recurrent source of misery and suffering.[47]

Condorcet's vision was not a prediction of the perfect welfare state but rather a "calculus" designed to fashion a society capable and willing of helping those in need. Condorcet emphasized throughout

---

[46] *Ibid.*, p. 231.

[47] *Ibid.*, pp. 232-233.

not only the desired specifics for social progress but also the *process*, or "calculus," by which society might systematically identify problems and arrive at their solution.

Condorcet on capital formation:

> We shall reveal other methods of insuring equality, either by seeing that credit is no longer the exclusive privilege of great wealth, or by making industrial progress and commercial activity more independent of the existence of the great capitalists.[48]

At the beginning of the twenty-first century, cash to fund economic growth no longer comes from "great capitalists" but is either produced internally within the system or comes mainly from wage-earner savings and pension funds. Despite this new, democratic effect of capital, wealth is becoming more concentrated because ultra-capitalists concentrate wealth for their own benefit from OPM (other people's money). Privileges continue and wealth becomes more concentrated because Condorcet's calculus has not been refined and applied.

Condorcet on education for a full and happy life and involved citizenship:

> The degree of equality in education that we can reasonably hope to attain, but that should be adequate, is that which excludes all dependence, either forced or voluntary. We shall show how this condition can be easily attained in the present state of human knowledge even by those who can study only for a small number of years in childhood, and then during the rest of their lives in their few hours of leisure. We shall prove that, by a suitable choice of syllabus and of methods of education, we can teach the citizen everything that he needs to know in order to be able to manage his

---

[48] *Ibid.*, p. 233.

household, administer his affairs, and employ his labor
and his faculties in freedom; to know his rights and to
be able to exercise them; to be acquainted with his
duties and fulfill them satisfactorily; to judge his own
and other men's actions according to his own lights
and to be a stranger to none of the high and delicate
feelings which honor human nature; not to be in a state
of blind dependence upon those to whom he must
entrust his affairs or the exercise of his rights; to be in
a proper condition to choose and supervise them.[49]

Although much of Condorcet's vision has been realized, the
educational process in the United States and elsewhere is failing, if
Condorcet's agenda be taken to be the mission and measure of
education. Millions are not educated sufficiently to avoid a life of
dependency. Most of the rest are not educated sufficiently to fulfill
their responsibilities as citizens. Condorcet's proposition on education
should become a mission statement and challenge to all educators. A
comprehensive curriculum is lacking, although an extraordinary
delivery system using new communication technology is now
available.

Condorcet's emphasis on integration of the variables in the
social equation:

These various causes of equality do not act in isolation;
they unite, combine, and support each other, and so
their cumulative effects are stronger, surer, and more
constant. With greater equality of education there will
be greater equality in industry and so in wealth;
equality in wealth necessarily leads to equality in
education, and equality between the nations and
equality within a single nation are mutually
dependent.[50]

---

[49] *Loc. cit.*

[50] *Ibid.*, pp. 234-5.

Condorcet on freedom through education and the discipline of law:

> We might say that a well-directed system of education rectifies natural inequality in ability instead of strengthening it, just as good laws remedy natural inequality in the means of subsistence, and just as in societies where laws have brought about this same equality, liberty, though subject to a regular constitution, will be more widespread, more complete than in the total independence of savage life. Then the social art will have fulfilled its aim, that of assuring and extending to all men enjoyment of the common rights to which they are called by nature.[51]

Condorcet on epistemology:

> As the mind learns to understand more complicated combinations of ideas, simpler formulae soon reduce their complexity; so truths that were discovered only by great effort, that could at first only be understood by men capable of profound thought, are soon developed and proved by methods that are not beyond the reach of common intelligence. The strength and the limits of man's intelligence may remain unaltered; and yet the instruments that he uses will increase and improve, the language that fixes and determines his ideas will acquire greater breadth and precision and, unlike mechanics where an increase of force means a decrease of speed, the methods that lead genius to the discovery of truth increase at once the force and the speed of its operations.[52]

Condorcet and his fellow French philosophers did not seek a detailed rationalized scheme for human affairs. They hoped for a

---

[51] *Ibid.*, p. 235.

[52] *Ibid.*, pp. 235-236.

truth-searching process by which each generation could make its contribution and build society's momentum towards perfection. Condorcet outlined the building-block approach that has produced the extraordinary tower of knowledge in the natural sciences. Condorcet assumed that humans, the rational animal, would pursue the mission of perfectibility by using the same building-block approach to frame the social order. This seemed the obvious mechanism to intellectuals who were also people of affairs.

Academia, the natural place to assimilate, organize, and test the spectrum of knowledge necessary for the best conduct in human affairs, did not, however, either take up this challenge of the Enlightenment or assume the responsibility of rationally determining the best organization. This has been the great default, now compounded by the great paradox: At the most propitious time in human history, many leading philosophers in academia are not working on a truth-searching process that would lead to a world of peace and plenty; they have declared that ideal an impossible illusion.

Society's destiny thus far had headed into catch-22 circularity: When humans are not educated and trained to function within a rational order, then the inevitable folly and violence convince many that no rational order is possible. When the ideal is not clearly presented for student examination and development, the consequence is that more poorly educated citizens elect more equally poorly trained leaders whose governance by default leads the world back into the same old folly and violence.

Condorcet on the eternal contract among generations:

> Men will know that they have a duty toward those who are not yet born, that duty is not to give them existence but to give them happiness.[53]

Condorcet on women's rights:

> Among the causes of the progress of the human mind that are of the utmost importance to the general

---

[53] *Ibid.*, p. 239.

happiness, we must number the complete annihilation of the prejudices that have brought about an inequality of rights between the sexes, an inequality fatal even to the party in which favor it works. It is vain for us to look for a justification of this principle in any differences of physical organization, intellect, or moral sensibility between men and women. This inequality has its origin solely in an abuse of strength, and all the later sophistical attempts that have been made to excuse it are vain.[54]

Condorcet on war, mercantilism, and the relations of nations:

Once people are enlightened they will know that they have the right to dispose of their own life and wealth as they choose; they will gradually learn to regard war as the most dreadful of scourges, the most terrible of crimes. Nations will learn that they cannot conquer other nations without losing their own liberty; that permanent confederations are their only means of preserving their independence; and that they should seek not power but security. Gradually mercantile prejudices will fade away, and a false sense of commercial interest will lose the fearful power it once had of drenching the earth in blood and of ruining nations under pretext of enriching them. When at last the nations come to agree on the principles of politics and morality, when in their own better interests they invite foreigners to share equally in all the benefits men enjoy either through the bounty of nature or by their own industry, then all the causes that produce and perpetuate national animosities and poison nations' relations will disappear one by one; and nothing will remain to encourage or even to arouse the fury of war. Organizations more intelligently conceived than those projects of eternal peace which have filled the leisure

---

[54] *Ibid.*, p. 243.

and consoled the hearts of certain philosophers, will
hasten the progress of the brotherhood of nations, and
wars between countries will rank with assassinations as
freakish atrocities, humiliating and vile in the eyes of
nature and staining with indelible opprobrium the
country or the age whose annals record them.[55]

What a wonderful vision! Two hundred years later, however,
Condorcet's optimism is difficult to reconcile with the events of the
bloodiest, most violent century in human history, the twentieth
century; and Condorcet's optimism is difficult to sustain in view of
the apparent continuation of this bloodthirsty violence into the new
century following the new outburst of terrorism on September 11,
2001. How can the world in the grip of reciprocal atrocities find its
way towards building economic common purpose?

The French Revolution also knew something of terror. Despite
the beauty of Condorcet's vision and the specificity of his means,
most of the energy in the French Revolution went into rearranging the
power structure among the monarchy, the church, the nobles, and the
bourgeoisie, leaving the peasants to go on starving. Edmund Burke,
by then a well-known British Parliamentarian, warned that too much
infrastructure was being torn down too fast; he accurately predicted
the dire results.[56] Reforms did not give priority to a better commercial
way to improve miserable lives. In time, the Paris mobs and the
starving peasants took over, and the Revolution went from tyranny to
bloody anarchy to new tyranny. Despite this lesson, reformers since
have repeated the error, changing the political structure rather than
improving the commercial system.

Condorcet summarized on behalf of the Enlightenment an
ideal, the means to attain it, and the intellectual process to validate the
ideal and specify the means. His was a comprehensive and integral
proposal, comprehensive in that all the working parts are included,
and integral in that they are related in a logical way. Condorcet
sketched the original liberal philosophy that we now term "classical

---

[55] *Ibid.*, p. 244.

[56] Edmund Burke, *Reflections on the Revolution in France* (London: Penguin
Books, 1986, first published 1790), p. 122.

liberalism" to distinguish it from its modern distortions of so-called "liberalism." Condorcet sketched the democratic capitalist culture and protocols, including specificity on free trade, capital formation, and monopolies. If his advice on emerging economies had been followed in the 1990s, for example, then the post-Communism Russian economic disaster might have been avoided. If Condorcet's specification for broad access to capital and broad distribution of wealth had been followed in the 1990s, for a further example, then ultra-capitalism would not have become dominant in the United States.

By 1800, the Enlightenment had raised the challenge to find the rational order in human affairs, and enlightened minds had responded to the challenge with great specificity. The Scotsman Smith, the American Jefferson, the German Kant, and the Frenchman Condorcet had all made enormous contributions. In the 19th century, workmen like the Welshman Owen, and social philosophers like the Englishman Mill and the German Marx, would validate and refine the vision of a perfectible society.

Owen's Vision: A World without Scarcity, People Educated and Motivated to Reach Their Potential

Robert Owen, a poor Welsh boy, left home at ten; in his twenties, he met the owner of a Glasgow textile mill, borrowed some money, bought the mill, and married the owner's daughter. Owen then proved in practice that a commercial system based on developing the potential of each worker can produce better growth and profits than did systems that treated workers as an exploitable commodity.

Whereas Smith had speculated and Kant had philosophized, Owen actually took a final convincing step—experimental verification. Owen saw the potential in each individual, and he undertook to release latent human power through education from the earliest age, clean housing, sobriety, higher wages, and shorter working hours.

Owen was opposed to the mercantilists who made money from government privilege, while viewing urban workers as they were in their miserable social conditions, rather than seeing them as they could become. The mercantilists' priority was cost containment, so they paid leading economists to lobby Parliament in support of employing lower-cost, eleven-year-old children on the night shift. They perverted Malthus's theory of population, arguing that increased wages would increase population, thereby increasing wage competition and driving wages back down. One might as well, the mercantilists rationalized, institutionalize poverty and misery by keeping wages at a level of bare subsistence so that procreation would be limited in the first place.

Mercantilist policy precluded the involvement, innovation, and productivity of willing workers, and it did not provide sufficient spendable income to purchase products made by other wage earners in either one's own or other countries. The resulting maldistribution of wealth aborted the wealth multiplication inherent in Adam Smith's economic dynamic. Two hundred years later, this mercantilist economic impediment still continued, now called "downsizing" and "wage arbitrage."

Owen verified that investment in the workers' quality of life results in larger profits for the owners than does the mercantilists' policy of cost containment. Owen believed in job security: He paid out £7,000 in wages during the four months his company was shut down by the American cotton embargo in 1806. Social benefits included free medical services, a contributory pension fund, schools, food and clothing at cost, and social and recreational facilities. "Owen calculated that during his 30 years at New Lanark (1799-1829), more than £300,000 in profit was divided among the partners over and above the 5% per annum paid on capital invested." Owen reported: "The value of the mills increased between 1799 and 1813 from £60,000 to £114,000; profits of £160,000 were produced in the period 1809 to 1813."[57]

In the preface to *A New View of Society*, Owen described his obligation to invest both in equipment *and* people to maximize stockholder returns. With his appreciation of the workers' potential, however, he emphasized the significantly *greater* returns from the investment in people:

---

[57] J.F.C. Harrison, *Robert Owen and the Owenites in Britain and America: The Quest for the New Moral World* (London: Routledge and Kegan Paul, Ltd., 1994, first published 1969), pp. 154-5.

From the commencement of my management, I viewed
the population, with the mechanism and every other
part of the establishment, as a system composed of
many parts, and which it was my duty and interest so
to combine, as that every hand, as well as every spring,
lever, and wheel, should effectually cooperate to
produce the greatest pecuniary gain to the proprietors.
If, then, due care as to the state of your inanimate
machines can produce beneficial results, what may not
be expected if you devote equal attention to your vital
machines, which are far more wonderfully
constructed? From experience which cannot deceive
me, I venture to assure you, that your time and money
so applied, if directed by a true knowledge of the
subject, would return you not five, ten or fifteen
percent for your capital so expended, but often fifty
and in many cases a hundred per cent.[58]

Building on his success at New Lanark, Owen became an
evangelist for the development of each individual, advocating trust,
cooperation, respect, and training to allow people to participate. In
this environment, structure could be minimal, and execution could be
simpler and more effective than in the command-and-control,
adversarial approach. Owen was convinced that this value system and
its associated protocols could solve more problems for less money. He
repeatedly petitioned Parliament on behalf of working children, and
he proposed job solutions after the 1816 food riots.

In 1818, this uneducated Welshman, speaking in his working-
class accent, addressed leaders from America and Europe assembled
for a conference at Aix-la-Chapelle following the Napoleonic Wars.
Owen described the way to social progress that he had developed
while working with ordinary people in his factories. His extraordinary
vision was that through his form of democratic capitalism, humans
need no longer starve or live in misery and despair. In Owen's

---

[58] Robert Owen, *A New View of Society*, (Baltimore, Maryland: Penguin Books),
Introduction, p. 39.

Memorials, presented on behalf of the working class, his "First General Result" was a promise of universal comfort:

> The period is arrived, when the means are become obvious, by which, without force or fraud of any kind, riches may be created in such abundance and so advantageously for all, that the wants and desires of every human being may be more than satisfied. In consequence, the dominion of wealth, and the evils arising from the desire to acquire and accumulate riches, are on the point of terminating.[59]

In the "Second General Result," Owen addressed the education necessary to develop each person:

> The period is arrived, when the principles of political economy are becoming obvious, by which without disorder, force or punishment of any kind, the rising generation may be with ease and advantage to all, surrounded by new circumstances which shall form them into any character that society may predetermine. Such education will enable each child to pass the barriers of error and prejudice.[60]

Many became eager to find out about a system that eliminated scarcity by elevating people. Between 1815 and 1825, some 20,000 visitors, including Nicholas, Grand Duke of Russia, came to Owen's town, New Lanark, to view the working model. The universities, with their mission to investigate and illuminate, unify and elevate, might have recognized this coherent, workable system, and presented it to their students for consideration. The churches, concerned to feed the hungry, clothe the naked, and house the homeless, might have blessed Owen's discovery. Governments, dedicated to promoting the general welfare, might have built on Owen's capitalism as the best source of

---

[59] Robert Owen, *A New View of Society*, (New York: AMS Press, 1972), Appendix, p. 7.

[60] *Ibid.*, Appendix, pp. 16-18.

economic opportunity, the prerequisite for benefiting from other freedoms. It did not work that way, however.

Hegel's Vision: The Unified Human Spirit in the Process of Identifying and Attaining the Secular Ideal

Building on Kant's optimism about the improving human condition, Georg Wilhelm Friedrich Hegel (1770-1831), professor at Heidelberg and Berlin, developed a new philosophy of history. He believed that nature is an organic whole in the process of growth and development, and that society is being drawn upward through contradiction and struggle to higher stages of development. He recognized the human duality of being both individual and social, one and one-of-many.

Hegel described *"Geist"* (spirit), the metaphysical equivalent of Smith's "invisible hand" of commerce, as that which moves the whole towards perfection:

> That those manifestations of vitality on the parts of individuals and peoples, in which they seek and fulfill their own purposes, are, at the same time, the means and instruments of a higher and broader purpose of which they know nothing.[61]

Hegel affirmed the motivation of this *Geist*:

> The nature of spirit may be understood by a glance at its direct opposite — matter. As the essence of matter is gravity, so on the other hand we may affirm that the essence, the subject of spirit, is freedom.[62]

Like Kant before him, Hegel reconciled the tension between freedom and theological dogma by identifying the temporal human purpose and the means to attain it as common to both reason and faith:

---

[61] G. W. F. Hegel, *Introduction to the Philosophy of History, from Lectures on the Philosophy of History* (New York: Modern Library, 1960), p. 559.

[62] *Ibid.*, p. 551.

> Freedom is its own object of attainment, and the sole
> aim of spirit. This is the result at which the process of
> the world's history has been continually aiming, and to
> which the sacrifices that have ever and anon been laid
> on the vast altar of the earth, through the long lapse of
> ages, have been offered. This is the only aim that sees
> itself realized and fulfilled, the only pole of repose
> amid the ceaseless change of events and conditions.
> This final aim is God's purpose with the world; that is,
> His Nature itself is what we here call the Idea of
> Freedom, translating the language of religion into that
> of thought.[63]

Hegel, like Kant, added emphasis to the movement towards freedom that energizes social progress. This idealism was coupled with the proposition that the rules for human conduct are common to reason and religion, and prerequisite to attaining both secular and spiritual goals.

Tocqueville's Vision: A World Moving towards Freedom

Alexis de Tocqueville (1805-1859), a young French nobleman, visited America in the 1830s to observe democracy in action. France was still working its way out of the tyrannical church/state structure whose abuses had provoked the French Revolution. The United States, during the same period, was enjoying the political freedoms that had been advocated by Thomas Jefferson and James Madison. Anxious about France's future, Tocqueville wanted to observe how democracy was at work in America. Trained in the law, like Montesquieu, Tocqueville was also a political scientist who took the long view of history. He recognized the same movement towards freedom that Smith, Jefferson, Madison, Condorcet, Owen, Kant, and Hegel had seen:

> The various occurrences of material existence have
> everywhere turned to the advantage of democracy. The

---

[63] *Ibid.*, p. 554.

gradual development of the principle of equality is,
therefore, a providential fact. It is universal, it is
lasting, it constantly eludes all human interference, and
all events as well as all men contribute to its
progress.[64]

This inexperienced young aristocrat then identified a
motivation important to successful democratic governance. Although
the movement towards freedom encourages humans to produce and
innovate, humans, however, instinctively give priority to equality of
condition:

There is, in fact, a manly and lawful passion for
equality that incites men to wish all to be powerful and
honored. This passion tends to elevate the humble to
the rank of the great; but, there exists also in the
human heart a depraved taste for equality which impels
the weak to attempt to lower the powerful to their own
level and reduces men to prefer equality in slavery to
inequality with freedom. Not that those nations whose
social condition is democratic naturally despise liberty;
on the contrary, they have an instinctive love of it. But
liberty is not the chief and constant object of their
desire; equality is their idol; they make rapid and
sudden efforts to obtain liberty, and if they miss their
aim, resign themselves to their disappointment; but
nothing can satisfy them without equality, and they
would rather perish than lose it.[65]

Whereas Smith and Owen had both seen the elimination of
scarcity and the equality of opportunity achievable through the
liberation of individuals to produce and innovate, Tocqueville
anticipated reformers with new political power who would severely

---

[64] Alexis-Henri-Charles-Maurice Clerel, Comte de Tocqueville, *Democracy in America* (New York: Random House, Vintage Books, 1990; first published in 1835 and 1840), author's introduction to volume 1, p. 6.

[65] *Ibid.*, volume 1, chapter III, pp. 53-54.

damage this freedom as a source of wealth in their eagerness to redistribute wealth. Tocqueville warned against a new governmental tyranny in the name of the general welfare:

> Above this race of men stands an immense and tutelary power, which takes upon itself alone to secure their gratifications and to watch over their fate. Thus it every day renders the exercise of the free agency of man less useful and less frequent; it circumscribes the will within a narrower range and gradually robs a man of all the uses of himself. It covers the surface of society with a network of small complicated rules. The will of man is not shattered, but softened, bent and guided; men are seldom forced by it to act, but they are constantly restrained from acting. Such a power does not destroy, but it prevents existence; it does not tyrannize, but it compresses, enervates, extinguishes and stupefies a people till each national is reduced to nothing better than a flock of timid and industrious animals, of which government is the shepherd.[66]

If Tocqueville could have re-audited the U.S.A. in the 1950s, he would have found a *Federal Register* 10,000 pages long "covering the surface of society with a network of small complicated rules." By the end of the century, this bureaucratic bulk had accumulated over 90,000 pages of suffocating burden.

Tocqueville recognized two ingredients as necessary for democracy, namely education and moral discipline. He wrote of the priority of education, and he understood Jefferson's vision of sustaining religion's role in civil morality after the uncoupling of the tyrannical, or potentially tyrannical, church/state structure. A generation after Jefferson and Kant, Tocqueville saw in practice the interaction of freedom and moral discipline to which each had dedicated his life's work.

---

[66] *Ibid.*, volume 2, book 4, chapter VI, pp. 318, 319

Religion perceives that civil liberty affords a noble exercise to the faculties of man and that the political world is a field prepared by the creator for the efforts of mind. Free and powerful in its own sphere, satisfied with the place reserved for it, religion nevermore surely establishes its empire than when it reigns in the hearts of men unsupported by aught besides its native strength. Liberty regards religion as its companion in all its battles and its triumphs, as the cradle of its infancy and the divine source of its claims. It considers religion as the safeguard of morality, and morality as the best security of law and the surest pledge of the duration of freedom.[67]

Tocqueville had an optimistic view that free religion in the new American republic would be an important contributor to a secular, unified purpose. He hoped religion could help structure the new freedoms so that each citizen would be educated to be sensitive to the rights and needs of others. It did not work that way, however.

John Stuart Mill's Vision: A Superior Mode of Capitalism that Maximizes Productivity and Innovation by Purging Exploitation and Class Conflict

John Stuart Mill published his *Principles of Political Economy* in 1848, the same year in which Karl Marx and Friedrich Engels published *The Communist Manifesto*. Mill and Marx shared the view that the state's mission is to promote the general welfare, not deliver privileges to the few. They both believed in the worth and potential of each individual, that the development of society is the sum of the development of each person, and in broad wealth distribution through worker ownership. Marx observed, "The productive forces, too, have increased with the all-round development of the individual, and all the springs of shared wealth flow more abundantly."[68]

---

[67] *Ibid.*, vol.1, chapter II, p. 44.

[68] Frank Manuel, *A Requiem for Karl Marx* (Cambridge, Massachusetts: Harvard University Press, 1995), p. 158, note 2, letter from Marx to Engels.

Mill and Marx contrasted sharply with one another, however, in terms of their proposals to achieve social progress on the basis of economics. Whereas Marx, revolted by mercantilist exploitation, wanted to tear down the whole structure. Mill proposed evolutionary development within Adam Smith's theory of free markets. Marx, myopic in this view, had no interest in the contributions of Mill, whom he described as a "bourgeois economist, a mere sophist, and sycophant to the ruling class."[69]

Mill developed his theory of democratic capitalism on the basis of his study of alternative systems. He recognized that socialists did not understand that the motivation from private ownership is fundamental to a successful civil society. Mill understood the importance of cooperation in any society, but he corrected the socialists by insisting that competition is also a vital function in the free commercial process. Up to this point, Mill was affirming Adam Smith's point of view, but he went further and added other important elements. In "The Probable Futurity of the Working Class,"[70] a chapter in his *Principles*, Mill included profit-sharing, job security, and worker ownership as logical developments of Smith's economic freedom.

Mill had studied various enterprises, such as American shipping in the China trade, mining in Cornwall, and entrepreneurial efforts in France. He concluded that whenever workers are motivated to reach their individual human potential, the results are better than are results from workers in the dependent state. From this, Mill recognized in the cooperative approach the opportunity for increased profits as well as the improvement in quality of life. On the basis of this analysis, Mill wrote what amounts to a manifesto for democratic capitalism, the statement presented as the introduction to this chapter.

In the tradition of Smith, Locke, Jefferson, Condorcet, and Owen, Mill had respect for ordinary people and their potential when given opportunity through education, training, and leadership. Quality of life is enhanced by the self-esteem of trained workers doing good work, the satisfactions of working in harmony on a team, and the tangible rewards for the benefit of the spouse and children. For the

---

[69] Marx, *Capital, op. cit.,* p. 98.

[70] John Stuart Mill, *op. cit.,* book IV, chapter VII, pp. 752-794.

work environment to be cooperative and effective, Mill argued, trust and morality must prevail.

These social philosophers had all seen beneficial results from the conscious application of individual ambition when harmonized with the instinct for social cooperation. Smith had seen individual ambition as the "invisible hand" providing economic momentum; Hegel had seen each individual as both the one and part of the many. Mill now saw social harmony as improving the quality of life by starting in the workplace. All were restating the elementary truth of social organization: Everything works better, and the process is not only more productive but also more fun, when individual ambition and social cooperation are harmonized.

Marx's Vision: A Classless Society without Scarcity or Exploitation, in which Individuals May Realize their Potential

Karl Marx was born at Trier, Germany, of a middle-class Jewish family that had converted to Christianity. He studied in Bonn and Berlin and later joined German and French Socialists in their various revolutionary efforts for which he and Friedrich Engels, in their late twenties, composed *The Communist Manifesto*. Marx then fled to London where he lived with his wife and children until his death. His persistent poverty was partly relieved by the generosity of his friend, Engels.

Marx declared himself to be "the pupil of that mighty thinker," Hegel,[71] and then spent his life trying to surpass him. Hegel had undertaken to synthesize all of history and knowledge, integrating the empiricism of the English with the rationalism of the Continental intellectuals. Marx tried to combine all of this with the radical restructuring of society as proposed by the French Utopians.

In the tradition of the German Idealists, Marx espoused moving towards a state of society based on freedom and self-development, in which the development of the individual, the elimination of class antagonisms, and the broad distribution of wealth would combine in the ideal.[72] Marx favored the material world of

---

[71] Marx, *Capital, op. cit.*, Vol. 1, p. 103.

[72] Marx and Engels, *op. cit.*, p. 105.

Smith to the metaphysics of Kant and Hegel, and he disagreed with Hegel's view of social progress. Marx saw movement from one level to the next as possible only when a superior mode of production had superseded an inferior one. He labeled his process "scientific," and he called his theory "dialectical materialism." By confirming Smith's theory, proved in practice by Owen, Marx made a significant move from the earlier intellectual tradition, concluding that social progress is a product of improvement in the economic system.

Each of the following Marxian confirmations of Smith's theories is relevant today both for mature economies, in which broader wealth distribution is needed to sustain economic growth, and for emerging economies trying to improve lives through economic freedom:

- The state's mission is to promote the general welfare through the support of commerce.[73]

- Social progress depends on improving the form of commerce.[74]

- Commerce can be improved by eliminating exploitation and enhancing the individual.[75]

- Money is merely a medium of exchange; it should not be allowed to influence the commercial process.[76]

- The free economic system is inherently deflationary.[77]

---

[73] Marx, *Capital*, *op. cit.*, p. 286, note 6: "The writers of history have so far paid little attention to the development of material production, which is the basis of all social life, and therefore of all real history."

[74] Marx, *ibid.*, p. 175.

[75] Smith, *op. cit.*, p. 81, Marx, *ibid.*, p. 449.

[76] Smith, *ibid.*, p. 339; Marx, *ibid.*, pp. 253-4.

[77] Smith, *ibid.*, p. 64; Marx, *ibid.*, pp. 436-7: "Capital therefore has a tendency towards increasing the productivity of labor in order to cheapen commodities and cheapening the worker himself."

- When workers are trained and motivated, the surplus is maximized.[78]

- Broad distribution of the surplus puts money in the hands of those whose spending will maximize economic growth.[79]

- A nation's wealth is the total of its production of goods and services; financial machinations are a subtraction from this wealth.[80]

- Speculators drive up the cost of money, introduce a volatility inimical to productive growth, and divert surplus to those activities that subtract from a nation's wealth.[81]

- When governance is based on participation, administrative functions can be decentralized and minimized.[82]

---

[78] Smith, *ibid.*, book 1, chapter I, p. 9; Marx, *ibid.*, p. 387: "This power arises from co-operation itself, when the worker co-operates in a planned way with others, he strips off the fetters of his individuality and develops the capability of his species." (447)

[79] Smith, *ibid.*, p. 79; Marx, *ibid.*, vol. I, chapters 22 and 23 both relate economic growth to reinvestment, not to hoarding or speculation. Volume II is described in the introduction by the editor, E. M. Mandel, p. 17, as elaborating on the concepts of surplus value and expanded reproduction: "For economic growth to occur, part of the surplus-value produced by the working class and appropriated by the capitalists must be spent productively and not wasted unproductively on consumer goods (and luxury goods) by the ruling class and its retainers and hangers-on. In other words, it must be transformed into additional constant capital (business equipment, etc)."

[80] Smith, *ibid.*, 273; Adam Smith wrote on labor as the basis of commercial exchange. Marx wrote volume I of *Capital* primarily on labor value and the surplus value of labor.

[81] Smith, *ibid.*, p. 339; Marx, *ibid.*, p. 96.

[82] Marx, *ibid.*, introduction, quoting the 1755 manuscript of Adam Smith: "Little else is requisite to carry a state to the highest degree of opulence from the lowest barbarism, but peace, easy taxes, and a tolerable administration of justice." Marx went further than Smith to predict the decline and ultimate demise of the warrior state.

The system that Marx tried to describe would eliminate scarcity and distribute wealth fairly while abolishing exploitation and alienation. That system had been gestating for seventy-five years. In principle, it was democratic capitalism, and it might have superseded mercantilism, but Marx tried to accelerate the historical process by imposing a perfect system. Angry, myopic, disorganized, with no knowledge of governance or how to motivate people, Marx felt nonetheless qualified to reengineer the world. This idealist could never develop a consensus among his fellow revolutionaries, but he was prepared to design a classless world of unified purpose.

Even though Marx was vague both about his ideal and on how to attain it, his analysis of mercantilism was accurate. According to the cost-containment philosophy of mercantilism, wages would be constantly pressured downward in response to world competition. In the downside of a business cycle, the pressure is greater; wages go down further, and the reduction in spendable income causes further decline. This is one of the inherent contradictions in capitalism that Marx felt would cause it finally to implode in a proletarian revolution.

Marx's solution was to seize the means of production and redistribute the surplus to the workers in the belief that this would sustain buying demand. Marx did not realize, however, that collectivism produces little or no surplus. Rejecting Mill's examination of democratic capitalism, Marx missed the resolution of the contradiction: faster growth with increased productivity, innovations, the motivations from private property, and the monitoring influence of competition.

Marx dreamed of "free people" in the abstract. He did not understand freedom's daily interaction with moral discipline, intellectualized by a few like Kant, and practiced by many from their religious and ethical beliefs. Marx lumped religion together with the prevailing exploitative structure, and he threw it out in preference for his utopian dream of a classless, religionless, new world. The communistic application of Marx's collective theories smothered initiative, failed at central planning, and consequently produced little surplus. In its worst forms, communism killed, maimed, and degraded people, all in the name of noble purpose.

Marx also believed that, in each period, intellectuals support the prevailing mode of commerce. The superseding mode overlaps the preceding mode, but for as long as the existing system still has room to grow, the new mode remains in gestation. Marx was right about that: Mercantilism, despite its low level of productivity and innovation, and its loss of domestic momentum in countries like Great Britain, nevertheless continued to grow through imperialism, using superior naval and gun power to exploit the world.

Marx recognized that the spread of commerce would result in the decline of the warrior state, and this, along with the elimination of scarcity, would give world peace a chance.[83] He foresaw the spread of worldwide wealth based on more spendable income in the hands of workers resulting from the fair distribution of surplus.

All of this amounted to Marx's restatement and refinement of Adam Smith. From Kant and Hegel, Marx had absorbed the ideal of a perfect world of comfort, aesthetic pleasure, freedom, and harmony. From inside the library of the British Museum, Marx had arrived at the same beautiful vision that Robert Owen had seen from the inside of his textile factory in Scotland over a generation earlier: a world where the dominion of ignorance, violence, and fraud had been terminated.

Looking forward, however, Marx predicted that big companies would grow to monopoly size, crushing small companies in the process. This does happen, but monopolies are inherently inefficient and cannot withstand free competition. He predicted that capitalist exploitation would result in the steady decline of wages, and that workers would become more revolutionary. This did not happen. Marx believed that capitalism's investment in new technology would reduce the need for labor and further suppress wages. Marx's myopia about labor cost precluded a vision of the expansion of markets from new technology's culmination in the Information Age revolution.

Marx was also wrong about the business cycle: He thought it was caused by the anarchic nature of free enterprise, and he assumed that productivity would improve only with central planning. History has proved him wrong on both counts, and as well in his postulation that the business cycle is an inherent contradiction in capitalism. The business cycle is caused by wars, leveraged speculation, lack of free trade, and deliberate monetary policy, such as the deflation of

---

[83] Marx and Engels, *op. cit.*, p. 102.

currency for the benefit of the wealthy in Great Britain following the Napoleonic Wars. Marx did not understand the effect of the monetary policy which, according to Austrian economist Ludwig von Mises (1881-1973), causes the business cycle and had caused the emergence of Marx himself:

> When, after the Napoleonic Wars, the United Kingdom had to face the problem of reforming its currency, it chose the return to the pre-war gold parity of the pound and gave no thought to the idea of stabilizing the exchange ratio between the paper pound and gold as it had developed on the market under the impact of the inflation. It preferred deflation to stabilization and to the adoption of a new parity consonant with the state of the market. Calamitous economic hardships resulted from this deflation; they stirred social unrest and begot the rise of an inflationist movement as well as the anticapitalistic agitation from which after a while Engels and Marx drew their inspiration.[84]

Early in the 20th century, von Mises called attention to that part of capitalism needing reform: the domination of national monetary policy by the wealthy and powerful. Reformers, with the support of growing democratic power, could have modified government policies to control currency and credit for the general welfare. It did not work that way, however.

Marx's attack on exploitation and the alienation of the classes stimulated intellectual reformers all around the world to design a just society throughout the following century. Like Marx, the reformers were revolted by capitalist greed and dehumanization of the mass of workers, but they also suffered from Marx's lack of knowledge of governance, monetary policy, and how people are motivated. They assimilated Marx's attack on exploitation and his mission to eliminate alienation, but they never understood his message that social progress

---

[84] Ludwig von Mises, *The Theory of Money and Credit* (Indianapolis, Indiana: Liberty Classics, 1980, first published in Austria 1912, first translated into English 1934), p. 498.

is dependent on improving commerce, for they had inherited the intellectual tradition of loving the state and distrusting commerce.

Marx thought that statism is an unavoidable phase on the way to liberating the individual; some intellectuals viewed the state as the end product of their own design. Opposing groups defended the *status quo* and espoused a command-and-control structure to build personal wealth, control the masses, and fight wars. Those with a reformer's zeal thought of the paternalistic state as providing for the general welfare. Both were top-down; neither was democratic.

In place of the traditional state in which the few control and exploit the many, Marxists ideally substituted a state comprising an intellectual and political elite that controls production and exploits the wealthy few for the benefit of the poor. The traditional state provides selective privileges; the collectivist state polices and punishes commerce; neither serves the general welfare. In the United States, this competition over control of the state has brought about an intellectual and political gridlock.

Marx's insidious legacy has resulted in generations of professors and writers who have stimulated young minds about a world free of exploitation and class conflict through collectivist solutions, but who failed to perfect the theory of the capitalism of Smith, Owen, and Mill. What a waste! Millions of young people searching for a way to contribute to social progress have been deflected into support of unworkable socialist systems that exploit, alienate, and undermine democratic principles.

The Flawed Tradition

Most intellectuals have been conditioned by the Western cultural tradition that, since Plato (427-347 B.C.) and Aristotle (384-322 B.C.), viewed the state as the agent for social progress but was contemptuous of commerce. Plato and Aristotle worked hard at defining a just society within the constraints of the Athenian population that was over half-slave, in the Greek culture depleted by repetitive wars, and in an elitist time long before public education. They encouraged a collectivist mentality of the elite few ruling the common many. Marx's dialectical materialism, which ultimately depended on the freedom and self-development of each individual, was inconsistent with this Platonic tradition, but an awareness of this contradiction never penetrated the cultural conditioning of most collectivists.

Aristotle positioned the state as superior: "The *polis* is prior in the order of nature to the family and the individual. The reason for this is that the whole is necessarily prior (in nature) to the part."[85] His glorification of the state was coupled with contempt for ordinary people and for democracy: "For a man who lives the life of a mechanic or laborer cannot pursue the things which belong to excellence."[86] Aristotle had learned his anti-commerce bias from Plato who wrote as follows:

> First, [it is important] for the state first to keep its trading class as small as possible; second, trade should be made over to a class of people whose corruption will not harm the state unduly; third, some means must be found to prevent those engaging in such activities from slipping too easily into an utterly shameless and small-minded way of life.[87]

Aristotle was also impressed by a regulation that he discovered in Thebes, where "no man could share in office who had not abstained from selling in the market for a period of ten years."[88]

Plato and Aristotle lived in a society that was corrupted by its dependence on slavery and wars; prices and margins were micro-managed by the state; traders and money-lenders fought for a financial edge in the non-free environment. In the Greek slave society, the concept that the state might improve the general welfare through commerce, was unknown. Plato, however, was radical by including women in his plan for education. Thus constrained, Plato and Aristotle contemplated a splendid intellectual society only for the few. Thus they set in place a philosophic contempt for commerce that

---

[85] Aristotle, *The Politics of Aristotle*, Ernest Barker, ed. and trans. (New York City: Oxford Press, 1958), 1253a, p. 6.

[86] *Ibid.*, 1278a, p. 109.

[87] Plato, *The Laws* (London, England: Penguin Classics, 1970), book 11, p. 459.

[88] Aristotle, *ibid.*, 1278a, p. 109.

has been pervasive in Western culture. Plato and Aristotle promoted the idea that the contemplative life is the highest level of human potential, a congenial proposition for succeeding generations of academicians.

The writings of Plato and Aristotle were rediscovered by Europeans during the Middle Ages and became an important part of the new cultural tradition. Contempt for commerce was a common denominator between the Greek and Judeo-Christian traditions. A few centuries later, intellectuals conditioned by this contempt echoed Marx's outcry against mercantilism and his proposal for radical change. Failing to comprehend that social progress is dependent on moving to a superior mode of commerce, many intellectuals were unwilling to analyze other evolving forms of capitalism. Like Marx, they used up most of their energy in their anger at the exploitative system, rather than spending energy analyzing the options.

A Better Option

What might have been the outcome had reformers accepted Mill's manifesto instead of Marx's? At the middle of the nineteenth century, society faced an exciting opportunity: Smith had defined a system that could eliminate scarcity. Owen had proved that building on human values fosters growth and profits. Jefferson had helped establish a political structure that would sustain individual freedoms. Mill extended the commercial concept to include job security, profit-sharing, and workers' acquisition of some ownership. Mill recognized the spiritual dimension in this version of capitalism that included an improvement in quality of life that started in the workplace.

This line of thought should have produced the commercial system that works best, and the political structure to protect and maintain the idealism as practical reality. By combining commercial growth with education for all, that society could have moved with unified purpose towards comfort and satisfaction for all. New leaders, motivated by these human values and trained in appropriate protocols, could have governed society through these principles of democratic participation. Sensing unified purpose in a cooperative, trusting environment, most citizens would have exercised moral discipline as the concomitant of freedom. Once again, however, it did not work that way.

Instead, ignorance, violence, and fraud reached new and disastrous levels in the twentieth century. Hundreds of millions of people were not provided opportunity for self-development. Kant's and Hegel's theories of the potential ideal becoming the actual were reversed; instead, the worst possibilities became the real. Fascist Germany, Imperial Japan, Marxist Russia, and Maoist China committed atrocities beyond comprehension. The Jewish Holocaust was symptomatic of a worldwide return to barbarism. In the twentieth century, total war was waged indiscriminately by all warrior states against women, children, the elderly, and other non-combatants. Over Hiroshima and Nagasaki, Americans used new technology to accomplish even greater indiscriminate destruction than was accomplished with lower-tech means over London, Berlin, Tokyo, Dresden, and in numerous other sites of devastation.

Many of the intellectual community who had failed to study, refine, and present the system that works best by elevating people through commerce, now viewed the carnage and concluded that "Idealism" had been a cruel illusion and that "Progress" was a pejorative term. Marx's terrible legacy had not only spawned the collectivist systems and slowed the progress of democratic capitalism by seducing intellectual reformers but also severely damaged practical idealism in the process.

At the end of the twentieth century, there arose for many, however, a new optimism and belief in human progress. The failure of collectivism, especially in the collapse of Soviet Communism, contrasted sharply with improvement in the lives of millions all over the world, wherever the various forms of democratic capitalism prevailed. More freedom works better than less freedom. Optimism for social progress in the nineteenth and twentieth centuries had not been wrong; it was just too early.

In the view of others, the new century and the new millennium promised only the continuing clash of civilizations, more countries with economic power, terrible weapons, and memories of reciprocal atrocities. The predatory influences of war, imperialism, and speculative capitalism would continue to do social damage, despite the evidence that they had lost economic logic. Collectivism in various forms would continue to pursue its social mission in expensive and ineffective ways. The mature economies in the United States and Europe would continue to be impeded by the polarized forces of collectivism on the one hand, and by the nexus of state and ultra-capitalism on the other.

I have written this book to side with the former and work against the latter. For new and special reasons, I believe, the twenty-first century could be the first human era dominated by economic common purpose that will eventuate in a lessening and end of violence. The Industrial Revolution two centuries ago spawned the optimistic social philosophers described in this chapter. Now, a new revolution of the Information Age is spawning a new generation of optimistic and pragmatic philosophers. The new philosophers will reconfirm that material scarcity can be eliminated worldwide. They will recognize that global commerce will simultaneously shrink the world and free the individual. They will recognize that the key ingredient in the Information Age is cognitive power, and for this reason its workers must participate as educated, motivated, voluntary partners. Information Age industries to be successful must, in other words, operate on the principles of democratic capitalism. New philosophers will recognize economic common purpose through democratic capitalism as the way to satisfy universal human needs for food, clothing, shelter, education, good health, protection of the environment, and hope for a steadily improving world.

CHAPTER 4

How Democratic Capitalism Works

*But what if there were another way, one that engages people
in the business and leverages rather than destroys their
energy, knowledge, and talent? In fact, such an alternative
exists, a system that aligns the interests of employees,
managers, and shareholders for the mutual benefit of all. And
the best part of it is that it actually works.*

Charles A. O'Reilly III and Jeffrey Pfeffer[89]

An understanding of how freedom and mutual respect make
democratic capitalism work can be extrapolated to an understanding
of how the world could work, were society based on the same values.
Society grows from the exchange of goods and services by people
seeking to improve their lives. Experience shows that cooperation and
trust facilitate the exchange, competition assures the best products and
services at the lowest prices, and the system is energized by
individuals free to improve through an interdependent effort. Some
would say that the system based on trust and cooperation is natural to
humans; many would say that, empirically, it works best. O'Reilly
and Pfeffer described specific companies that were able to release the
latent power of ordinary people because they were "able to align their
purposes with the spirit of their employees, capturing their emotional
as well as intellectual energies."[90]

In democratic capitalism, the broader mission of commerce is
to eliminate material scarcity, elevate spirits, and unify people.
Government's mission is to protect life and property, and support the
best commercial system. Education's mission is to equip the
individual to participate by developing both individual and social

---

[89] Charles A. O'Reilly III and Jeffrey Pfeffer, *Hidden Value: How Great Companies
Achieve Extraordinary Results with Ordinary People* (Cambridge, Massachusetts:
Harvard University Press, 2000), p. 17.

[90] *Ibid.*, p. 8.

skills. Religion's secular mission is to support this moral commercial system in order for society to become all that it can be.

The United States of America has demonstrated the benefits of economic freedom for over two centuries. Building on this freedom, American companies lead the world in profitability. Democratic capitalists add value, build customer loyalty, involve their people, build shareholder loyalty, build supplier loyalty, and achieve superior performance. These companies had to learn the philosophy of democratic capitalism and how to apply its protocols by trial and error because this form of capitalism has received only limited examination and promulgation by education, government, the media, and religion. Despite this lack of visibility in other parts of the culture, the economic logic of democratic capitalism became more apparent at the end of the 20th century because world competition, and the needs of high-technology industry, forced recognition that higher standards could be met only by involving and motivating everyone engaged in the enterprise.

In contrast, ultra-capitalism, called the "American Model," treated wage earners as a cost commodity, and made short-term earnings the exclusive mission. By the 1990s, conventional wisdom in Business Schools and the financial press was that the outstanding success of the "American Model" was due to its efforts to maximize shareholder value, although in many cases, actions were taken at the expense of longer-term value. Frederick Reichheld, director of a Boston consulting firm and popular business lecturer, observed: "Stakeholders became a joke, both in investment circles and at business schools. The very concept was derided as an excuse for ineffective, self-serving, unaccountable management."[91] Even high-performance companies that commit to customers, employees, suppliers, and their communities, as well as to shareholders, were treated as followers of fuzzy, outmoded concepts.

The model that could be called "American" ought to be the economic system that succeeds through the synergistic coupling of democracy and capitalism. Service industries in information, computing, and telecommunications generated many of the new jobs

---

[91] Frederick F. Reichheld, *The Loyalty Effect* (Boston: Harvard Business School Press, 1996), p. 161.

in the United States in the 1990s. Most of these companies grew by releasing the power of their people, for many of them started with little more than innovative, committed people, working long hours as part of a team. The companies that lead in this extraordinary performance are not the ultra-capitalist companies; they are, instead, democratic capitalist companies who maximize surplus by elevating people. The emphasis in these corporations is vision and core values. Their mission is to serve a broad constituency of stakeholders, shareholders, customers, employees, suppliers, and communities.

In 1997, *Fortune* analyzed the "100 Best" companies to work for. In following years, many of the "100 Best" positions shifted, not because companies were abandoning their principles but because the competition was heating up. The question of which policy maximizes profits for the stockholder, whether ultra-capitalism that demands instant profits or democratic capitalism that elevates the workers as the source of productivity and innovation, was answered in the *Fortune* study:

> Investors might like to know whether a corporate culture of mutual respect also provides a competitive advantage. Last year we determined that the publicly traded companies on the list did deliver higher average annual returns to shareholders than the companies making up the Russell 3000, the index that best mirrors our list. This year's group demonstrates much the same: The stock of the 55 companies on our list that have been publicly traded for at least five years had an average annual appreciation of 25% in that period, compared with a gain by the Russell index of 19%.[92]

The charts accompanying the year 2000 *Fortune* report were just as impressive: The total stock market return of the public "best companies" compared to the S&P 500 was 35.5% versus 17.6% over

---

[92] Shelly Branch, "The 100 Best Companies to Work for in America," *Fortune*, January 11, 1999, pp. 134, 142.

ten years, 33.3% versus 18.3% over five years, and 29.8% versus 11.4% over three years.[93]

Fortune did not draw the line between democratic capitalism and ultra-capitalism in the article, but a reading of the particulars of these "best" companies shows that they are democratic capitalist enterprises whose common denominators are freedom for their employees to produce and innovate, performance bonuses, ownership opportunities, job security, meritocracy, training, and education.

While *Fortune's* "100 Best Companies to Work For" in 2001 was a new study, the conclusions were not different from the 1990 *Fortune* study of the most admired companies. Many names are prominent on both lists, such as Merck, 3M, Wal-Mart, Hewlett-Packard, Johnson & Johnson, and Berkshire Hathaway. The world's best known investor, Warren Buffet, head of Berkshire Hathaway, had not changed his message about long-term value: "Invest forever and look at stock prices about every six months." Policies of some of the most admired companies in 1990, however, now seem quaint: "At 3M, researchers spend 15% of their time on projects that will pay off only far down the road."[94] A decade later, the CEO of 3M was criticized in the financial press for not laying off enough people to improve short-term earnings. Subsequent downsizing provoked the witticism that the company had become "2M." Wal-Mart, on the other hand, did not change its mind about involvement. In 1999, *Fortune* reported:

> The nation's largest employer, Wal-Mart, engenders loyalty and enthusiasm by investing heavily in training and by promoting workers from within. Sixty percent of management started as hourly associates. It does not hurt that the profit-sharing plan is heavily invested in Wal-Mart stocks.[95]

---

[93] Robert Levering and Milton Moskowitz, "The Best 100 Companies to Work For," *Fortune*, January 8, 2001, fold-out next to p. 149.

[94] Brian Dumaine, Brian O'Reilly, Faye Rice, Patricia Sellers, Stratford P. Sherman, and Sarah Smith "Leaders of the Most Admired," *Fortune*, January 29, 1990, pp. 40-43, 46, 50, 54.

[95] Branch, *op. cit.*, p. 136.

Container Store of Dallas, Texas, was rated #1 again in 2000. The democratic spirit of this company was confirmed because "97% of the employees say that people care about each other here."[96] TD Industries, also of Dallas, was #6 for the second year:

> People at this plumbing, heating, and air-conditioning company are called "partners"—they own the company through ESOP and 401(k) plans. No surprise that 91% agree that they are treated as full members regardless of position.[97]

At the beginning of the 1990s, profits of American companies were proportionate to America's share of the world's GDP. By the end of the century, the profit percentage had doubled. In 1992, American companies accounted for 25% of the profits of the six major countries. By the third quarter of 1998, that was up to 38%! Was this impressive record being driven by ultra-capitalism or democratic capitalism? Both, but the *Fortune* study shows that superior results are produced by elevating people, while analysis shows that much of the profit of ultra-capitalism is either from dubious accounting techniques (see chapter 9) or cashing in on investment in future growth for the sake of present profits.

The economic logic of investing in people, illuminated by the *Fortune* articles, runs contrary to conventional wisdom of the 1990s. Collins and Porras challenged this wisdom, describing the common view of the most successful companies that build on vision and core values:

> Contrary to business school doctrine, maximizing shareholder wealth has not been the dominant driving force or primary objective through the history of visionary companies. Visionary companies pursue a cluster of objectives, of which making money is only one—and not necessarily the primary one. Yes, they seek profits, but they're equally guided by a core

---

[96] Levering and Moskowitz, *op. cit.*, p. 147.

[97] *Ibid.*, p. 149.

ideology—core values and sense of purpose beyond just making money. Yet, paradoxically, the visionary companies make more money than the more purely profit-driven comparison companies.[98]

Frederick Reichheld added another dimension when he traced superior performance through building the interrelated loyalties of customers, employees, suppliers, and shareholders. He encapsulated his conclusion in his subtitle, stating that mutual loyalty is "The Hidden Force Behind Growth, Profits, and Lasting Value." Within this culture, profit is recognized as indispensable, but "it is nevertheless a consequence of value creation."[99] Integrity is a repetitive theme: "Loyalty leaders tend to ignore modern management theory in favor of a code of behavior that is close to the Golden Rule, or in the case of several hugely successful companies, the Golden Rule itself."[100]

The Democratic Capitalist Culture

The first element of the democratic capitalist template is *integrity*. On a foundation of mutual trust and cooperation, *minimum structure* and *maximum freedom* become attainable, and these are the second and third elements of the template. The fourth element of the template, *competence*, embraces a proper balance between task and resources, and the capacity for decisive, effective action. These four elements of the template of democratic capitalism underlie the following common denominators in most democratic capitalist cultures.

Mission Statement: For many, writing a mission statement seems at first to be an exercise in the obvious, but then the task becomes intellectually difficult. The first draft usually seems amorphous and incomplete. Mission definition gains from the

---

[98] James C. Collins and Jerry I. Porras, *Built to Last: Successful Habits of Visionary Companies* (New York: Harper Business, 1994), p. 8.

[99] Reichheld, *op. cit.*, p. 3.

[100] *Ibid.*, p. 28.

100

involvement of all, and it results in useful ideas and a sense of participation that assures better understanding, easier accountability, and greater commitment. A good mission statement depends on rigorous examination of relative strengths and weaknesses that affect the company's ability to identify and add customer value. The mission statement emphasizes customer loyalty, employee loyalty, meritocracy, job security, and responsibility to stakeholders. The mission statement identifies the principles by which the company lives, and the vision of a future that it seeks to accomplish.

Reichheld affirmed: "New theory sees the fundamental mission of a business not as profit but as value creation. It sees profit as a vital consequence of value creation—a means rather than an end, a result as opposed to a purpose."[101] Collins and Porras described the mission statement thus: "A well-conceived vision consists of two major components—core ideology and an envisioned future. It defines what we stand for and why we exist."[102]

For the second half of the twentieth century, Hewlett-Packard was one of the most admired American companies. Its co-founder, Bill Hewlett, remarked after the death in 2001 of his partner, David Packard:

> The greatest thing he left behind him was a code of
> ethics known as the "HP Way." H-P's core ideology
> includes a deep respect for the individual, a dedication
> to affordable quality and reliability, a commitment to
> community responsibility, and a view that the
> company exists to make technical contributions for the
> advancement and welfare of humanity.[103]

Hewlett-Packard followed this code from its founding in 1938, and in 1998 it was number ten of *Fortune's* 100 best companies to work for. H-P's revenues were seven times greater than any of the other top ten, and it ranked #1 among design and manufacturing

---

[101] *Ibid.*, p. 5.

[102] Collins and Porras, *op. cit.*, pp. 220-221.

[103] *Loc. cit.*

companies. Even H-P is not protected from the conflicts in capitalism, however. The merger with Compaq Computer Corp. in 2002 became a battle between family members and the new CEO.

Reichheld pointed out the natural human values inherent in democratic capitalism: "Work that is congruent with personal principles is a source of energy. Work that sacrifices personal principles drains personal energy."[104] Reichheld's observation is consistent with my experience: Trust and cooperation, teamwork, and individual ambition in a harmonious whole produce results superior to the combination of excessive individualism and the exclusive money motive; moreover, it is more fun.

The mission statement is not a one-shot effort to be looked at occasionally; it has to be a living, breathing part of the work culture. This can be done by integrating it into management speeches, team meetings, and training programs. Visual materials used to merchandise the mission can be effective by coupling integrity with meritocracy because the unencumbered opportunity for promotion gets people's attention and helps give meaning to integrity. The commitment to integrity needs repetition in the face of a prevalent cultural perception that either immorality or amorality is the capitalistic norm. Unfortunately, many capitalists reinforce this negative perception with visible evidence of their greed and lack of principle.

Customer Loyalty: The mission statement can be complete about the value system and company vision, but if it does not emphasize the company's purpose in understanding and serving customer needs, it is committing the error of internalizing. The external democratic capitalist culture works extraordinarily well with customers and suppliers because the ability truly to listen, trust, and cooperate is as important in building customer and supplier loyalty as it is in building the loyalty of associates.

The work culture has to be constantly sensitized to relate to the customer and to fight this tendency to internalize. An example of internalizing would be engineers who become excited about all of the bells and whistles that can be added "for free" because of chip

---

[104] Reichheld, *op. cit.*, p. 29.

technology. A company's analysis might reveal that the added features would be of interest to fewer than 5% of the customers, and that complication of the learning curve and user manual would make the product less user-friendly for 95% of customers. A customer-sensitive company would either eliminate the confusing features or package them as separate, higher-priced, optional add-ons.

Just as workers become more profitable as they mature, customers also become more profitable. Customer retention becomes a passion with good companies. Some calculate the NPV (net present value) of customers by comparing the selling cost to win a new customer with the lower maintenance cost of an existing customer, someone already familiar with the products and business protocols. Most accounting systems do not reflect the costs of losing customers, even as they do not reflect the costs of worker turnover. Accurate reporting of these costs would further demonstrate the greater profitability of democratic capitalism.

Lexus, the automobile company, has set new standards for customer loyalty. An astounding 68% of its customers continue to buy Lexus. Mercedes is in second place at 42%, while other auto companies retain only 30% to 40%.[105] Lexus accomplishes this through technology and involved people. Headquarters monitors all of its dealers online, full-time, and any dealership that has customer-retention problems is soon blitzed with tested remedies. Their online monitoring is a version of the revolution in electronic commerce in which source data on defects is automatically entered into a computer and instantly becomes widespread knowledge throughout the communications network.

"Nothing happens until someone sells something" is a typical marketing-company slogan. Evangelistic sales meetings are peppered with anecdotes of heroic efforts to help out a customer. This, however, is the easy part; the hard part is educating everyone, not the salespeople only, to understand their personal impact on customer relations. For example, some companies spend generously on advertising, but they allow people, or computers, to handle the phones. Companies put the least trained at the front desk or on the phone, the first to meet customers and, therefore, the first to alienate

---

[105] *Ibid.*, pp. 232-4.

them. Similarly, it is painful to have produced an elegant product only then to suffer serious customer dissatisfaction because of sloppy billing procedures.

The measurement and analysis of customer loss or retention is an important addition to the analysis of sales growth and market share. Companies can spend heavily on improving market share without realizing that they are adding new, less profitable customers at the same time they are losing old, more profitable customers. To avoid the tendency to internalize, customer attitudes need to be routinely sampled, this effort backed with sufficient resources for quick follow-up. This discipline must be centralized because any slippage needs early feedback and may be in areas of product design or billing procedures, not within a branch's responsibility.

Worker Ownership: Associates in the democratic capitalist culture are involved and contribute individually and as part of a team to maximize the surplus. Sharing financially in the improved performance can be accomplished through profit-sharing plans and various ways to accumulate ownership. Whatever the formula, the cycle is continuous: Because associates think and act as owners, they make the surplus bigger, and then they are rewarded as a result of the improved performance that they themselves have helped produce. Employee ownership, a common feature among the 100 best companies, is the subject of chapter 5.

Training: Good training is impossible in an environment of distrust and friction but good attitudes will not last without good training. Morale surveys invariably mention better training as a priority. Since poor training and poor management go together, "poor training," mentioned in a job-satisfaction survey can be a code word for "poor management."

Democratic capitalism is built on the assumption that the potential of every individual is enormous when provided with the proper motivation and training. Most individuals function at well below their potential. Companies, schools, the government, and society as a whole function at an even lower rate because their realization of overall potential is held down by the lowest common denominator.

In democratic capitalism, training is a continuous priority, and it includes the following:

- Formal skills training.

- The use of interactive computer training that provides self-development opportunities.

- Informal training that results from team environments in which all share in the benefits of improved performance.

- Continuous leadership training that anticipates and prevents managers under pressure from reverting to top-down management by fear.

- Formal education that improves associates' cognitive, communication, economics, and other forms of learning skills that contribute to individual development.

- Good companies contribute to the continuous education of citizen-workers, an aspect of personal development upon which any democracy depends.

Intensity, the Secret Ingredient: Although the emphasis in democratic capitalism is on consensus, cooperation, and human values, effective action still requires leadership with authority, capable of decisive action. Leadership policy in democratic capitalism needs to be preceded by the involvement and cooperation of all, but ultimately it cannot be a democratic process in the political sense. A good leader, whether top management or a supervisor, will help build consensus and then merchandise the agreed-upon plan, but success depends on the leader's capacity to "make things happen." This sounds like a business slogan because it is one, and a good one, too!

When someone promoted into a position of greater responsibility based on a record of achievement and perceived qualities then fails to perform, everyone is disappointed. Knowledgeable and respected, the person in the new job may fail at leadership for lack of intensity. What is intensity? Energy? Desire?

Fire-in-the-belly? Hard to define, intensity is easy to recognize when you see it, and you see it over time.

When a leader is held accountable to a three-year plan, first failure will provoke analysis and retraining, but successive failure must result in the appointment of a new leader. In some cases, a manager most sympathetic to human values may lack the required intensity to act. This can become a weakness in democratic capitalism, if managers assume that good people working diligently is all that is required. In addition to good will and hard work, intensity is critical to continuous improvement.

Emphasis on leadership does not contradict the concept of self-supervised worker groups; it makes them possible. The leader remains invisible until the exception principle triggers his or her involvement. The communist dream of unsupervised work groups is a confession of ignorance about how people really function. After all have been given equal opportunity, extensive training, and profit-sharing motivations, significant differences in talent will nevertheless become apparent. Wealth-creation depends on meritocracy, continually moving those with the capacity to make things happen into positions of greater responsibility and authority. In an environment where all are owners, meritocracy works partly because most of those not promoted come to understand that the process was fair and that they still have opportunities for further development.

Productivity: Increasing productivity over the long term is the basis of rising wages and economic growth; consequently, it is the solution to social problems. With rising productivity, better products at lower cost are delivered to consumers; this attracts more consumers who can afford the lower prices, and this adds still more wage earners to produce the additional volume. This is a compressed version of Adam Smith's dynamic for building and spreading wealth (see chapter 6).

The last quarter of the 20th century witnessed productivity improvement stimulated by a technological revolution more profound than the late-18th-century Industrial Revolution powered by the invention of the steam engine or the late-19th-century Second Industrial Revolution powered by electric motors. This recent revolution was made possible not only by new technology but also by unprecedented participation of the workers. Here are some of its features:

- The microprocessor became ubiquitous after 1970, making decentralization and empowerment easier because information could be processed at the working level; as a result, performance standards and accountability were improved.

- Microchip technology opened large markets for products that could do new and useful things at very low cost.

- The amorphous slogan "the search for excellence" became an effort at rigorous truth-searching, finding out how to "do it right the first time." Standards of performance were developed, measured, and subjected to continuous improvement. These techniques allowed "employees to establish goals, spot failures, use standard financial-analysis techniques, evaluate trade-offs—and learn from the results."[106]

- The new standards of performance could not be met without worker participation.

- Technology and involved workers extended productivity improvements to the growing service industries.

The critical-mass effect from increasing volume has always been fundamental to lowering manufacturing costs, but it is now driving costs down in the service industries that represent over 80% of the United States economy. Productivity is a result of investment in both equipment and people, but the two kinds of investment are significantly different from each other: With training, education, and motivation, people get steadily better at what they do, whereas machines wear out.

---

[106] *Ibid.*, p. 219.

The Japanese pioneered the application of continuous-process principles to inventory control with their JIT (just-in-time) programs. They applied the same searching examination that had resulted in quantum improvements in the quality of the product and cost to produce in the uses of cash. "We've always done it that way" became a joke in companies, no longer a rationale for mindlessly perpetuating the status quo. The leading companies learned to improve the "productivity" of cash in their operations dramatically.

When the revolution in applying new technology to cash management came to retailing, I was on the Board of a large company that took more than $600 million out of inventory by rethinking its whole distribution and warehousing program, and then investing millions in the hardware and software, including a satellite network, required to do the job. The key to success, however, was capital investment combined with long-term associates eager to be trained in use of the new technology.

Job Security: A sense of job security is crucial to the democratic capitalist culture. Job security gives substance to the concepts of trust and cooperation, and it neutralizes the old industrial fear: "If I help the bosses do it better, then they will reduce the hours needed and fire me." Conversely, commitment to workers' secure future encourages involvement and participation. Worker-ownership plans are built on the basis of stable employment over a long period of time.

The introduction of new technologies and world competition are legitimate reasons for reduction of personnel. With a reasonable investment, however, workforce reduction can be accomplished through attrition, retraining, relocation, or in limited cases, generous severance. In contemporary mercantilism, the worker is still treated as a disposable cost commodity, and Wall Street celebrates this tough, soulless capitalism that fires people by the tens of thousands. The rationale for downsizing is that decisive cost-cutting management is needed in the face of world competition, although much of the downsizing is done to benefit short-term earnings.

The argument that downsizing validates Marx's theory of the inherent contradiction in capitalism, namely that pressure on profits is relieved by firing workers or suppressing wages, is partly true. An additional argument is that Wall Street analysts and the financial media have made downsizing an executive manhood check. Many large layoffs are capricious. They excite Wall Street and almost guarantee, through accounting tricks, a cosmetically better financial year following the layoffs, a higher stock price, and gains on options. Wall Street does not like attrition because it knows that immediate downsizing includes a big-bang accounting treatment that produces artificially good profits for a few years. Government policy at the turn of the century favored the large immediate write-off rather than attrition over a period of several years. This is bad accounting because it distorts true profits, and it is bad fiscal policy because it deliberately favors short-term and greedy ultra-capitalism.

Large layoffs are frequently weak in the analysis of short-term benefits versus long-term growth. R&D (Research and Development), product improvement, new markets, maintenance, new equipment, training, and community involvement are frequently sacrificed. Layoffs do not address management's failure in having added so many unnecessary employees in the first place. Layoffs also beg the question: "What will the company do for an encore?" Major cost reduction of administrative expense is a one-time improvement in profits that approaches the problem from the wrong end. A continuous-process program for sales growth approaches the problem from the correct end. Only sales growth can assure job security by assuring a profitable future for companies and a rising standard of living for countries. Finally, layoffs force unions to revert to zero-sum bargaining, in which the argument is about "more" but not about the fair share of improved performance. Reichheld pointed out the destructive effects of downsizing:

> Most companies think layoffs are a great way to raise productivity. It's true, of course, that the ratio of revenue to people will go up if you throw some of those people out on the street. But in most cases, the relief is momentary. The truth is, layoffs lower productivity; in some cases, they decimate it. Granted, some situations require layoffs for the sake of survival, and some require the short-term accounting gains

that a layoff brings. But the ultimate price of a layoff is always high.[107]

A study by the American Management Association revealed that fewer than half of the firms that downsized during a five-year period in the early 1990s subsequently increased their profits, and that only one-third reported higher productivity.[108]

According to the *Fortune* article, the wisdom of the "100 Best" companies to work for runs contrary to conventional wisdom that "job security is a thing of the past." Job security is "a recurring perk among the 100 best companies. Several have no lay-off policies, 37 have informal policies against layoffs, and 74 have never had a layoff."[109] The language in the *Fortune* article is instructive: Job security in ultra-capitalism is described as a "perk," whereas abandonment of any loyalty to workers is called the "conventional" view. *The Wall Street Journal* was even more emphatic: "The social contract between employers and employees, in which companies promise to ensure employment and guide the careers of loyal troops, is dead, dead, dead."[110]

These purveyors of "conventional wisdom" are wrong, wrong, wrong. Long-term profitability depends on the associates' desire to innovate and produce. This is possible only in an environment of trust and cooperation in which the wage earner feels secure. This has always been true, but it is even more compelling in the Information Age.

Meritocracy: Democratic capitalist companies are managed by the best and the brightest because all of the associates believe that they can go as far and fast in their careers as their talent and energy can take them.

---

[107] Reichheld, *op. cit.*, p. 146.

[108] *Ibid.*, p. 95.

[109] Branch, *op. cit.*, p. 134.

[110] Hal Lancaster, "A New Social Contract to Benefit Employer and Employee," *The Wall Street Journal*, November 29, 1994, p. B1.

The commitment to integrity assures meritocracy; meritocracy reaffirms integrity. In democratic capitalist companies, meritocracy is proactive, for the company's best interest is served when individual potential is identified early, and when opportunities and training are provided for its development. The company wins two ways: It gets superior managers and it keeps the best from leaving the company. The very best people are motivated by self-development, and unless they enjoy opportunities to learn and grow, they will leave.

After Jack Welch took over GE in 1981, GE's sales and profits went up seven times. By the turn of the century, GE was the ninth-biggest company in the world and the second-most profitable. Meritocracy is a passion at GE and the key to the company's effective participation by all.

> There's nothing egalitarian about GE's human resource philosophy. It finds the best and culls the rest—period. Sophisticated HR systems make sure that no sharp knives stay in a drawer. These include annual self-evaluations and feedback as well as a yearly, company-wide review of talent. Welch himself reviews some 3,000 people. It's not pretty, but Welch thinks a merciless push to upgrade human capital is vital.[111]

Part of Welch's genius in running GE was his ability to talk like an ultra-capitalist for the benefit of Wall Street, while, in fact, acting like a democratic capitalist in the development of GE talent. His alleged practice of firing those at the bottom, however, is overkill, in my opinion.

By contrast, I had good experience with a "Reverse Peter Principle," the principle being the theory that people are eventually promoted beyond their ability to perform. In many cases, this is the fault of the person doing the promoting; for that reason, I found that reversing the process worked well by reassigning people to jobs comfortably within their ability. Such moves need the environment of trust, but with the pride factor involved, it may not work in all cases.

---

[111] Thomas A. Stewart, "See Jack Run," *Fortune*, September 27, 1999, p. 136.

The best companies promote from within as part of their culture. Promotions from within provide new management with a detailed understanding of the business, a factor easy to underestimate. Business plans are built from the bottom up with the participation of all providing opportunities to evaluate individual performance in both planning and execution. As all wage earners are owners, they are more disposed to support the leaders who have been promoted by meritocracy.

The Continuous Process for Quality: A commercial example of the benefits of rigorous truth searching is the evolution of quality levels in manufacturing companies that are striving to be world class. Production rejects at one time were measured in parts per thousand, then in parts per million, but now world competition has pushed quality to such precision that rejects are measured in parts per billion. One who pioneered in this effort was W. Edwards Deming. His emphasis was on quality, and his method was Socratic, probing to get beyond superficial answers. Deming concluded that root problems usually cannot be discovered with fewer than five questions, digging ever deeper for final answers.

Andrea Gabor described Deming as "the man who discovered quality," and she summarized his philosophy as follows:

> A holistic vision of how companies can anticipate and meet the desires of the customer by fostering a better understanding of "the process" and by enlisting the help of every employee, division and supplier in the improvement effort. A process-obsessed management culture that is capable of harnessing the know-how and natural initiative of its employees and fine-tuning the entire organization to higher and higher standards of excellence and innovation.[112]

Deming had a single-minded mission to attain perfect quality. While oriented to quality, his organizational philosophy was one of decentralization and empowerment, in fact, democratic capitalism.

---

[112] Andrea Gabor, *The Man Who Discovered Quality* (New York: Random House, 1990), p. 5-7.

His search for excellence took him to Japan, after the Big Three motor companies in Detroit decided that they did not need him. Years later, after the Japanese had taken huge chunks of market share away from American companies with cars that took far fewer hours to produce and had dramatically fewer defects, the Big Three got serious and adopted Deming's principles. GM's Saturn plant now runs TV ads that show the assembly-line worker empowered to identify a problem affecting quality, hit the button, and shut down the line.

Deming's "Fourteen Points" call for a new philosophy that breaks down barriers among departments; empowers and trains people to think and act; and encourages cooperation, leadership, and pride in workmanship. Underlying this approach is the premise that a company will invest anything required in training, production equipment, test equipment, and supplier training, assuming an excellent eventual return. Short-term earnings are ignored; customer loyalty, not satisfaction only, is the goal. Deming's philosophy and specific advice are a significant addition to the library of democratic capitalism. Deming's points are as follows:

1.   Create constancy of purpose toward improvement of product and service, with the aim to become competitive, to stay in business, and to provide jobs.

This is captured in the popular phrase "continuous process."

2.   Adopt the new philosophy. We are in a new economic age. Western management must awaken to the challenge, learn their responsibilities, and take on leadership for change.

This challenge from Deming was offered years before the extent of the Information Age revolution was recognized. The "new philosophy" refers to the new relationship among associates, management, and capital.

3.   Cease reliance on mass inspection to achieve quality. Eliminate the need for inspection on a mass basis by building quality into the product in the first place.

In Deming's operations, inspectors are not needed because everyone builds quality into the product.

4. End the practice of awarding business on the basis of price tag. Instead, minimize total cost. Move toward a single supplier for any one item, based on a long-term relationship of loyalty and trust.

This is the "stakeholder" philosophy, in contrast to "shareholder" philosophy, that builds a two-way long-term commitment from the company to the supplier and from the supplier to the company. Loyalty and trust are synonyms for integrity, the first element in the template of democratic capitalism.

5. Improve constantly and forever the system of production and service, to improve quality and productivity, and thus constantly decrease costs.

This is Deming's restatement of Adam Smith's economic dynamic in which the growth of free markets is self-perpetuating.

6. Institute training on the job as the prerequisite to empowerment.

The routine elements of the job must be disciplined by training in order to free individuals to innovate.

7. Institute leadership. The aim of supervision should be to help people and machines and gadgets do a better job. Supervision of management is in need of overhaul, as well as supervision of production workers.

Deming's call is for a rejection of the traditional hierarchical, top-down, feudal organization to be replaced by leadership in a bottom-up environment.

8.   Drive out fear so that everyone may work effectively for the company.

Leaders, not bosses, drive out fear; full participation through worker ownership removes the basis of fear; a sense of job security drives out the greatest fear of losing one's job.

9.   Break down barriers between departments. People in research, design, sales, and production must work as a team to foresee problems of production and in use that may be encountered with the product or service.

A harmonious whole sounds simple, but many companies engage in internal turf wars that increase costs and lower quality.

10.   Eliminate slogans, exhortations, and targets for the workforce, asking for zero defects and new levels of productivity. Such exhortations only create adversarial relationships, since the bulk of the causes of low quality and low productivity belong to the system and thus lie beyond the power of the work force.

The responsibility for improvement of the whole process through investment in people and things belongs with management, not the workforce.

11.   Eliminate "management by objective" and numerical goals. Substitute leadership.

Fads like "MBO" targets posted on the bulletin board become jokes with the workers if the process investment is limited.

12.   Remove barriers that rob hourly workers of their right to pride of workmanship. Remove barriers that rob people in management and in engineering of their right to pride of workmanship.

Superior performance is coupled with elevated spirits of the workers, a fundamental of the democratic capitalist culture.

13.   Institute a vigorous program of education and self-improvement.

The opportunity for individual self-development through adult education makes for better worker-citizens.

14.   Put everybody in the company to work to accomplish the transformation. The transformation is everybody's job.

Deming completes his advice by coupling individual development with the team environment.

Six Sigma: What is Six Sigma? Is it a statistical measurement system that employs new technology to make every operation measurable and accountable? Or is it a management philosophy that believes in the involvement of all associates to produce dramatic and continuous improvement in the quality of the product and the cost to produce? It is both.

The positive impact on the quality of the product delivered to the customer, and the cost to produce that product, has been in the billions of dollars at companies such as Motorola who pioneered Six Sigma, and companies such as Allied Signal and GE who adopted it. Led by the two men who developed it at Motorola, Six Sigma is becoming an important part of Information Age business education.[113]

When Motorola pioneered Six Sigma in the 1980s, many thought that Deming had been made obsolete by a more sophisticated system. More careful examination, however, shows that Six Sigma depends on the principles of democratic capitalism and most of Deming's "Fourteen Points." Six Sigma applies Deming's simple rule: "Do it right the first time," but notably it extends the concept to the large and growing service industries. The pioneers of Six Sigma made the following claim:

Most companies operate at three to four sigma level where the cost of defects is roughly 20% to 30% of

---

[113] Mikel Harry and Richard Schroeder, *Six Sigma: The Breakthrough Management Strategy Revolutionizing the World's Top Corporations* (New York: Currency, 2000).

revenues. By approaching Six Sigma—fewer than one defect per 3.4 million opportunities—the cost of quality drops to less than 1 percent of sales.[114]

This extraordinary level of performance is dependent, consistent with Deming's philosophy, on the corporation's willingness to spend whatever is required on training and capital equipment, but Six Sigma is ultimately dependent on each individual's participation in the development of the measurement criteria, and cooperation in producing superior performance.

Wage Earner Compensation: Profit-sharing, stock purchase, stock bonuses, dividends, and capital appreciation are all additional benefits that accrue to associates when they become democratic capitalists and company owners. Through performance improvements, most wage earners can become wealthy because the potential for improvement is so great. Compensation must be competitive and sufficient to motivate workers to produce and innovate, thereby maximizing surplus. Benefits, including conventional pension plans, must also be competitive in the job market and in addition to the rewards from worker ownership.

If government fiscal policies were aligned to favor dividends, most worker-owners could receive 6 % annual dividend on their stock. Dividend income would grow each year from additional stock from payroll deduction purchases, and from stock awarded as performance bonuses. Besides this steady dividend income, wage earners could build wealth from the accumulation of stock with an annual total return of over 10%, a realistic expectation for a company in which all are involved and contributing to the improvement of performance. Associates who use all of their opportunities to build ownership over a career-long period could become relatively wealthy by retirement, as well as having received substantial dividends during their work years.

Instead of the traditional zero-sum battle between management and labor, all gain in a collaboration among all worker-owners. The plan that I designed and implemented while CEO of ADT, Inc., *Care*

---

[114] *Ibid.*, book jacket.

and Share, demonstrates this premise (see chapter 2). With this philosophy, management's job changed from worrying about whether the workers were working hard, to concern for training and cooperation among workers. This is the core of self-supervised groups: Workers help each other, and as everyone feels responsible for performance, peer pressure is continuous. The Compensation Committee of most corporate Boards addresses management compensation only. Compensation for all employees, particularly performance bonuses and stock-ownership opportunities, should be a Board and Compensation Committee responsibility. Compensation practices will continue to lack internal logic until this governance responsibility is accepted.

Executive Compensation: CEO compensation is a visible statement of a company's philosophy, whether of democratic capitalism or ultra-capitalism. To build trust and cooperation, CEO compensation must both be fair and be perceived as fair.

Compensation professionals grade jobs in a company based on working conditions, skill, financial responsibility, and educational requirements, as well as potential impact on performance. Besides the skill and responsibility criteria, an internal logic should include empirical evidence of how much of a financial increment is necessary to motivate a person to move up to the next level. For example, would a machine operator with leadership potential give up overtime pay and piece-work to take the foreman's job with all of its responsibilities for only a 5% or 10% increment in compensation? Most would not.

The combination of this logic and pragmatic judgment resulted in a structure of job grades with as many as 36 levels. The logic of this structure at the top levels worked well in democratic capitalist companies in which all felt themselves to be parts of the whole, and senior executives were respected. The internal logic of compensation has been abandoned by ultra-capitalists, however, and it has been replaced by the logic of external comparisons to other overpaid CEOs.

Ultra-capitalists care little about a harmonious whole because in ultra-capitalism excessive individualism dominates. The contribution to corporate success by the CEO and a small group of executives is assumed to be greater than the potential contribution of the whole team. Starting in the late 1970s, the multiple of base salary from the lowest wage to the highest went up from twenty-five into the hundreds. Inordinate executive compensation in the United States has resulted in unfavorable comparisons to executives in Japan or Germany, but these comparisons were based on base pay alone. Even more extreme levels of compensation were fueled by the various bonus and stock-option plans that raised CEO compensation to 300 times, or more, of that of the lowest paid.

Compensation consultants rationalized this by upgrading the CEO to "match the market" in order to "attract and retain" top-quality management. Compensation committees were an easy sell: "Matching the market" was a more compelling argument than "internal logic." Inflation was a reason for large increases when it was double-digit, but when the workforce increases were later held at around a 2% increase because of world competition and low inflation, the top group continued receiving 12% increases because "the universe has shifted," according to the compensation consultants.

Hundreds of articles addressing the subject of CEO compensation carried such titles as these: "The Boss as Welfare Cheat," "The Way CEOs Overpay Themselves Hurts the Firms They're Supposed to be Leading," and "Executive Pay Compensation at the Top Is Out of Control. Here's How to Reform It." A leading executive compensation critic, Graef Crystal, summarized his argument in his title and subtitle: "In Search of Excess, The Overcompensation of American Executives: In the Last 20 Years, the Pay of American Workers Has Gone Nowhere, While American CEOs Have Increased Their Own Pay More Than 400%. This is How They've Done It."[115]

To keep CEO compensation in context within the organization, a plan should be designed by working backwards from the Board's agreement about what the CEO ought to make over a long period for sustained excellent performance. The CEO of a very successful large company could make up to $1 million a year in salary and stock bonuses based on a CEO's earning $500,000 a year, with a

---

[115] Graef S. Crystal, *In Search of Excess: The Overcompensation of American Executives* (New York: W. W. Norton, 1991).

bonus that for top performance could match the base pay in stock. During a successful term of over ten years, the CEO can add up to $10 million to his or her net worth. Compensated this way, the CEO's interests are congruent with stockholders' interests, including those of the worker-owners.

If the stock pays a 6% dividend, the CEO can reinvest in more stock that is assumed to make steady returns in income and appreciation over 10% a year. With a pension of 60% of base pay, this CEO could retire with an annual income of several hundred thousand dollars and leave his family or charity millions of dollars in the value of accumulated stock. The congruence of the executive with the shareholders must be demonstrated by the executive's not selling company stock while managing the company. For the average person, this annual salary, build-up of net worth, and pension on retirement are astronomical numbers. They can pass the fairness test, however, if all wage earners are becoming wealthy, the design is based on professionally developed internal logic, and all associates are part of the same performance improvement plan.

Compare this scenario to the compensation history for the CEO of Bankers Trust. In the 1980s, Bankers Trust had been a proud bank, making money from prudent loans to businesses, and the competent CEO's compensation averaged less than $1 million in pay and bonuses. The next CEO moved the bank towards ultra-capitalism, tried to make money by trading in futures, and hurt the company with losses and practices that provoked lawsuits by customers like Proctor & Gamble. The CEO after that lost money in 1998, and Bankers Trust was sold to Deutsche Bank AG. This last CEO received a guarantee of bonuses of $10.1 million for each of the next five years.[116] This $55 million reward for failure is not extraordinary in ultra-capitalism; in fact, it is modest by many comparisons.

The greed infection started on Wall Street in the 1970s when the compensation of investment bankers was changed from an annual advisory amount to a percentage of deals. Merger and acquisition lawyers copied the investment bankers and departed from an hourly charge to enormous fees, with no methodology other than their wish

---

[116] Paul Beckett, "Bankers Trust's Newman to Be Paid at Least $55 Million over Five Years," *The Wall Street Journal*, February 1, 1999, p. B5.

to share in the plunder with the investment bankers. In time, corporate executives involved in mergers and acquisitions, encouraged by Wall Street, learned how to reward themselves with millions-of-dollars, whether as acquirers or acquired. Analysts responsible for providing an accurate examination of a company's performance, were rewarded by investment banking deals with the company studied. In two decades, analysts contributions to ultra-capitalism moved their compensation from five figures up to seven figures. Similarly, auditors responsible for insuring the quality of earnings were compensated for selling non-audit services. Partners' salaries moved up to the millions of dollars-per-year category.

Ultra-capitalism's demand for a rising stock price soon led to rationalizing CEO compensation on the basis of comparing it to a small percentage of increased market value of the whole company. In most cases, the market value accrued more from "irrational exuberance" in the bull market than from management performance. When the CEO's compensation is tied to the interests of Wall Street through enormous stock options, the mantra becomes: "Maximize shareholder value and pay for performance," which translates to "Get the price of the stock up."

Executive compensation consultants frequently propose new programs that have been provoked by new tax laws passed by Congressional efforts to do remote engineering of executive compensation. The result is a proliferation of new compensation instruments designed to thwart the intent of the new tax laws. This contributes to the feeding frenzy at the compensation smorgasbord: base salary, short-term cash bonus, long-term cash bonus, stock grants, stock options, phantom stock, stock appreciation rights, performance units, and restricted stock. Some Board Compensation Committees love being Santa Claus and want to award their executives all of the above; most struggle to understand how all of the elements can be integrated into a fair plan.

A plan for senior executive compensation consistent with the environment of democratic capitalism would have only three standard compensation elements: base salary, bonus in stock, and stock grants. Bonuses in stock instead of cash make the executive a true owner. Stock options, by contrast, are freebies that are usually piled on top of cash plans, and they are painless to give because they cause no profit-reducing effect on the company and no tax consequence to the executive at the time of the grant. Because corporate executives are not obliged to buy stock with their own money and hold all stock until retirement, they have little sense of true ownership. The proposal that executives buy stock, take all bonuses in stock, and hold all their stock until retirement causes some to complain that the executives would then be "cash poor," but cash poor is exactly how a capitalist should feel, for the willingness to sacrifice in order to invest is part of an owner's psyche, particularly if all the other associates are buying stock through the payroll deduction plan.

Global competition has stimulated the rise in standards of quality and productivity. Many union officials recognize a congruent interest with management in improving quality and productivity, and they cooperate in modifying work practices and converting to performance-based compensation. Excessive executive compensation, however, coupled with no concern for the workers' job security, is eroding this common ground. Union cooperation is being undermined, and this forces bargaining back to the zero-sum battle. Worker wages and benefits may improve, but worker productivity and innovation suffer.

Executive compensation is influenced by government tax laws lobbied by Wall Street in cooperation with big companies. Tax policies need to be corrected in the following ways that will democratize capitalism:

- Tax policies need to encourage executives to buy stock and take all bonus money in stock.

- Tax policies, more than they already do, need to penalize the sale of stock in the short term but favor long-term holdings.

- Tax laws need to encourage the replacement of stock options with stock grants that require a charge to earnings, that is, a reduction in profits.

- Tax laws need to encourage distribution of surplus in increased dividends by elimination of double taxation on

dividends primarily for low- and middle-income wage
earners.

Distribution of Surplus: A company's surplus can be
distributed in four ways: investment in more growth, dividends, stock
buy-backs, and acquisitions. The decision on how to distribute surplus
intersects private motives and public policy. The democratic
capitalistic distribution of surplus is reinvestment in growth and large
dividends. The ultra-capitalistic distribution of surplus for short-term
personal gain is stock buy-backs and non-strategic acquisitions. Why,
then, do tax laws favor stock buy-backs and non-strategic
acquisitions? Too many hints have already been provided: The answer
is that public policy is determined not for the general welfare but
based on the lobby power of Wall Street.

Although the tax laws clearly need to be changed to align
them with the public interest, the distribution of surplus should also
be an important part of corporate governance. The Board of Directors
as representatives of the shareholders need to review the policy
regularly and approve this distribution. Management is responsible for
maximizing profits, but they should not have exclusive authority over
use of the surplus. Evidence in support of this proposal can be found
in the hundreds of billions of dollars wasted during the last quarter of
the 20th century on stock buy-backs and non-strategic acquisitions by
ultra-capitalists.

Institutional investors have a fiduciary responsibility to
influence both corporate governance and government fiscal policy in
order to move from the stock buy-backs and non-strategic acquisitions
of ultra-capitalism to the reinvestment in growth and large dividends
of democratic capitalism. This simple clarification of mission will
have a profound effect on economic growth and the ability of the
government to provide consistent assistance for good education and
health because it will replace the boom/bust economic cycle with
strong, steady growth.

Measurement and Accountability: A company's long-term
performance is most accurately measured by adding sales growth and
cash flow to earnings per share. Sales growth measured against a
three-year plan demonstrates how well a company is managing its

123

future. Cash flow measured against a three-year plan demonstrates how well resources are being managed and is an early indicator of trouble. Strong cash flow distributed in dividends also demonstrates good management in both fast-and slow-growth companies.

Enron demonstrated, among other things, the damage caused by concentrating exclusively on quarterly and annual e.p.s. (earnings per share). Companies have been rewarded or penalized in the billions of dollars by Wall Street for producing, or not producing, a few cents in e.p.s. This simplistic passion for this imperfect measurement has driven ultra-capitalism, and, with the help of institutional investors, it has extended Wall Street's domination of the economy.

The accountability period needs to be at least three years to encourage innovation. An annual budget tends to extrapolations because time is too short to reflect the subsequent profit benefits from aggressive first-year investment. Annual budgets reflect overt or covert guidelines that contradict the philosophy of decentralization. In ultra-capitalism, budgeting guidelines in public companies are affected by Wall Street analysts' expectations, and they tend to limit investment in long-term growth.

A company's budget for multi-location operations is frequently imposed in a more top-down fashion than managers like to admit. Budgeting instructions to the "decentralized" units are frequently contradictory, asking for "your plan" but with an 8% profit-improvement "guideline." Sponsors of new products or markets, sensing limited funds for expansion, tend to understate the resources needed in order to push a project ahead. The negative result of this is the failure of many growth programs, not because the idea was bad but because the resource allocation was inadequate.

In ultra-capitalism, the original mantra was "Just give me the numbers, dammit!" with the implication that the senior officer did not care how it was done. Financial officers became heroes for their "creativity." At the beginning, they had their "drawers" in which they hid extra reserves taken from such items as bad debts and inventory write-offs to be dipped into to "smooth" earnings in a quarter that was below expectations. In time, the pressure for constantly higher e.p.s encouraged creative CFOs and managers to increase sales and profits by shipping products to a warehouse, or special deals for customers to take material they did not need until later. The only constant was the necessity to meet e.p.s. expectations, and when that could not be accomplished by more traditional tricks, many resorted to illegality.

By contrast in democratic capitalism, the control system is based on integrity and decentralization. The first three elements of the template—integrity, maximum freedom, and minimum structure—are the guidelines for designing a management control system that provides freedom for associates to make their maximum contribution. The control system is simple because it is designed for and by worker-owners to measure the vital aspects through cooperatively established standards, that is, the agreed-upon benchmarks against which performance is measured. The planning process is reiterative, starting with sufficient freedom to encourage independent and creative thinking, then proceeding through the negotiating stages among levels of management, concluding with a demanding but realistic plan.

Budgeting control systems have evolved from management information systems (MIS) into information systems (IS) that recognize worker involvement. With workstation computers, IS provides online information that affects scheduling, workloads, inventory, staff availability, and machine capacities, allowing teams to supervise themselves. Information technology is a powerful tool for decentralization and empowerment but only when integrated within the democratic capitalist culture.

Democratic capitalism's control system begins with a belief in people and their enormous potential to do better, not with the "Gotcha!" principle. Most control systems are not built on the assumption of integrity. Instead of operating on the exception principle, that is, identification of deviations against an agreed-upon norm, top-down systems try to micromanage with over-designed control methodology. An over-designed control system contradicts the philosophy of democratic capitalism, it can fail to control from the information overload, and it can suffocate individual productivity and innovation. A minimum, decentralized structure is based on the assumption that well-trained and involved people with competent leadership are pursuing a clear mission and need a minimum number of reported deviations over the longest possible time. The control system, however, must be sophisticated enough to protect against significant risk, that is, while the people are individually and team responsible, an audit process, both financial and operational, is also in place that regularly reviews and confirms the integrity of the process.

Decentralization: The broad-based control philosophy of democratic capitalism is to delegate responsibility, authority, and accountability to the level closest to the work. In a decentralized structure, people are responsible for performance and results, measured by a plan that they have helped to formulate. They are neither suffocated by detailed rules and regulations nor measured by standards imposed top-down. This is an essential difference between industry and government, and it spells the difference between high productivity in commerce and the unmeasured and unaccounted for high cost and repetitive errors of government.

The environment of integrity makes fact assimilation easier, but it must still be supported by effective fact-assimilation. In complex, fast-changing circumstances, facts can be assimilated more easily in a decentralized structure than in a centralized one. During the second half of the twentieth century, clarifying this phenomenon was one of the many contributions of Friedrich Hayek (1899-1992)[117] who persistently argued the superiority of "spontaneous order" over central control, although the momentum towards centrally planned society was so great that Hayek's argument was treated as heresy. In his last book, written in 1988 when he was 89, Hayek restated his argument for spontaneous order:

> To the naive mind that can conceive of order only as the product of deliberate arrangement, it may seem absurd that in complex conditions, order and adaptations to the unknown can be achieved more effectively by decentralizing decisions, and that a division of authority will actually extend the possibility of overall order, yet that decentralization actually leads to more information being taken into account. This is the main reason for rejecting the requirements of constructivist rationalism. For the same reason, only the alterable division of the

---

[117] Friedrich August von Hayek, *The Road to Serfdom* (Chicago: University of Chicago Press, 1989; first published by Routledge and Keegan, 1944).

power of disposal over particular resources among many individuals actually able to decide on their use—a division obtained through individual freedom and several property—makes the fullest exploitation of dispersed knowledge possible.[118]

At the turn of the century, the benefits of decentralization were a starting premise in books on "continuous process," as Michael Hammer described:

> The transition to process-centering does not occur in the rarified atmosphere of corporate boardrooms. The real action is on the front lines, where people who do the real work of the business redirect their thinking and change their behavior.[119]

Aided by Information Age technology, decentralization not only is necessary for empowerment of the people but also is the most effective way to assimilate complex, fast-changing information. Because much of the information in play is used at the working level and stays there, only a minimal amount need be chosen to be reported to another level.

A Supportive Finance Capitalism: Adam Smith specified that the success of free markets depends on money that is ample, low-cost, non-volatile, and patient. Smith also warned that speculators would deflect capital away from growth, and make money scarce, high-cost, volatile, and impatient. Smith defined the mission of finance capitalism as helping companies grow, offering advice, and lending money that meets Smith's criterion of neutrality while avoiding damage from speculators.

Investment bankers traditionally helped with long-term financing, providing new equity by offering stock or long-term bonds.

---

[118] Friedrich August von Hayek, *The Fatal Conceit: The Errors of Socialism*, edited by W. W. Bartley III (Chicago: University of Chicago Press, 1988), pp. 76-7.

[119] Michael Hammer, *Beyond Reengineering: How the Process-Centered Organization Is Changing Our Work and Our Lives* (New York: Harper Business, 1996), p. 19.

Commercial banks also provided short-term, working-capital loans for seasonal needs. British merchant banks took ownership positions in companies as well as lending them money. Had a similar policy of coupling short-term loans with long-term equity investment been in place in 1997, the Southeast Asian disaster might have been prevented because banks would have protected their long-term investment by limiting their risk on short-term loans.

The mission of finance capitalism changed during the last quarter of the twentieth century when commercial bankers and investment bankers alike converted from banking the old-fashioned way to trading in futures, making deals for enormous fees, and offering easy credit for hedge funds and high-risk projects. The money made from these activities dwarfed advisory fees and moved supportive finance capitalism towards dominant ultra-capitalism.

With hundreds of billions of dollars of pension and 401(k) money pouring in, Wall Street became the leading edge of ultra-capitalism. The bankers were energized by deals and speculation, and the institutional investors felt that their fiduciary responsibility was emphasis on short-term earnings and, in effect, support of ultra-capitalism. Corporations split into two groups: those few companies, big and small, that were so good that they could both grow the business and keep Wall Street happy, and the majority who were forced to subordinate business plans to the expectations of Wall Street (see chapter 8).

Some companies have reintroduced retainers into their relationship with investment bankers, instructing them that the scope of their annual advisory fee covers all potential deals and is related to hours spent on task. Advisory fees have an expectation of creativity and, occasionally, long working hours, but they are premised on a willingness to pay for good service. Many companies disenchanted with Wall Street, however, have now decided that investment bankers frequently add little value, and that in-house company staffs can do the work as well and save money besides.

Democratic capitalism depends either on free banking or banking regulated to provide low-cost, ample, non-volatile, and patient capital. Banking in the ultra-capitalist culture claims to be "free," but this is a fiction because banking is subsidized, insured, and regularly bailed out by the government. The invisible hand of Adam

Smith's baker and butcher pursuing personal interest and providing social benefit cannot be applied to finance capitalism. The invisible hand in finance capitalism, dominated by speculation, is a fist of individual greed that causes social damage, not economic growth. Because of a fundamental confusion about the disciplines required for free markets to function properly, an economic downturn will prompt the critics of capitalism to call for government intervention, but unless the reformers do their homework, the intervention will not include reform of fiscal, monetary, and regulatory policies consistent with Smith's insightful specifications.

Auditors: The report of a company's annual financial results is required by law to be approved by independent auditors. This external review is intended to assure the integrity of the figures and protect the stockholders. Problems that most seriously affect a corporation's financial integrity frequently involve balance-sheet values based on substantial subjectivity. These can take years to develop, and they tend to give the auditors a vested interest in an optimistic view of their resolution. The practice in auditing firms of rotating their managing partners does not adequately address this question.

Improved governance and lowered risk could be accomplished simply by changing the outside auditors every five years. The Audit Committee of the Board should be responsible for soliciting bids and selecting the new auditors, keeping management in an advisory role. Changing auditing firms, however, is an unpopular concept because the executives of companies develop a comfortable rhythm with auditors of long standing, and some rely on them to validate their tricky accounting.

In the last quarter of the twentieth century, auditors built up consulting businesses that were larger than the audit service itself. Selling consulting services to a company being audited can be a conflict of interest. The separation of auditing and consulting into different companies would not be necessary, however, if the auditors were changed every five years, and consulting for that client during that period were excluded.

I first penned the advice offered in the lines above years before Arthur Andersen and other audit firms disgraced themselves and failed the shareholders at Sunbeam, Cendant, Waste

129

Management, and most spectacularly at Enron. The need for reform should be evident, but citizens shall have to use their democratic power to counteract the lobbying that has traditionally and successfully resisted reform.

Instead of changing auditors every five years, the half-measures that will emerge from the Enron investigation may include giving to the Audit Committee of the Board more responsibility in the hiring, firing, and direct management of the outside auditors. As popular as this idea is likely to become, we need only remember that the Audit Committee of the Enron Board disgraced itself as thoroughly as the auditors at Andersen. The reform that I am proposing, namely changing auditors every five years, is fail-safe, that is, it provides an inherent protection and does not depend on oversight.

Internal Auditors: More important than the outside auditors is the quality and power of the inside audit department reporting directly to the CEO. This is the department that assures that company integrity takes precedence over short-term financial results. A strong internal audit department audits both the financial and operational process in order to assure the CEO and the Board that the requisite disciplines are in place and functioning. The internal auditing department gives the "all is well" signal and allows the CEO to sleep well.

In a democratic capitalistic environment of maximum freedom and decentralization, the internal audit department provides the minimum structure for freedom to function properly. When the CEO treats violations quickly, severely, and visibly, the CEO's relationship with this department can demonstrate that the commitment to integrity is real and not merely a bulletin-board slogan.

The internal audit department with but a few highly talented people examines and reports on significant violations to both the CEO and the Audit Committee of the Board. The Audit Committee also meets several times a year in private with the internal audit manager, at which time the Audit Committee makes certain that no constraints are placed on the internal audit department's freedom to go anywhere and examine anything. Although whistleblowers do not fit the image of the democratic capitalist culture, they can be helpful by identifying problems for the internal audit department, if the matter cannot be handled by the whistleblower's direct supervisor.

Because internal audit department personnel visit many operations, they can foster a learning and teaching opportunity by finding local best practices and then promulgating them throughout the company. They can also serve as the nucleus of a blitz squad to analyze troubled operations and recommend action. They do not have to be a large department because they can deputize managers from other locations to provide specific help. This is a win/win opportunity because it brings the best and the brightest to the problem and at the same time gives special recognition to this experienced talent. Through this process, internal auditing can not only confirm integrity in the process but also be a positive source of training and improved disciplines.

Industrial Truth-seeking: The first element in the template of democratic capitalism is a commitment to integrity that assures that the thought process is non-adversarial and non-politicized. In ideal democratic capitalist epistemology, conclusions are arrived at by consensus in a group that is sufficiently diversified through different kinds of cultural conditioning without which the examination can slip into group euphoria, miss critical points, and produce flawed programs.

The epistemological process in industry is reiterative and cumulative, productive of steadily improving information because programs are tested, providing the experimental verification that the hard sciences (math, physics, chemistry, biology) accept as one of the final components of ascertaining truth. Truth-seeking in commerce is also a closed-loop system in which information on failure or success is cycled back to those who made the assumptions and designed the program. The designers then have the opportunity to use these data to analyze the reasons for failure or success. The epistemological process in both government and academia, though not in science, usually lacks experimental verification, a closed-loop feedback, and a penalty for failure.

In my experience, the truth-seeking process was arrived at by trial and error. In my studies, I found that what my colleagues and I reinvented was close to the dynamic, collaborative, and cumulative process described by Francis Bacon (1561-1626) (see chapter 10).

Democratic Capitalism Works

Democratic capitalism works best because it builds on natural human attributes. These include the human urge for freedom, the instinct for social cooperation, the desire for mutual respect, and the hope for a peaceful, better life. Satisfying these aspirations and achieving these values make democratic capitalism work, and they are the same values that could make civil society work well. Whether from a religious perspective that interprets the divine plan for life on earth as one of public morality, or from a humanistic definition of a rational and practical order in human affairs, the value system that supports social progress is clear and consistent.

Democratic capitalism is built on society's best values, but society's record of securing a world based on these values is one of persistent failure. Why? Apparently the predatory forces have been too strong, and the mistakes of untrained leaders have been too large and too frequent. These same values now have a more pragmatic opportunity to become the dominant values because they are economically determined, that is, they have been demonstrated as the best way to provide proper food, clothing, shelter, education, good health, and hope for the world. These values are also economically determined for Information Age industries that can compete successfully only within a culture based on these values, that is, where highly motivated, educated, self-starting individuals are free to contribute in an environment of trust and cooperation.

Is economic determinism a true force in history and society? Can what works best irresistibly move the whole world to peace and plenty?

If commerce is the foundation of society, and if the most effective form of commerce, democratic capitalism, is inherently moral, does it not follow that this form of capitalism can and should be a stimulating source of social morality? Democratic capitalism presents the economic and social logic that can neutralize the predatory forces that have impeded social progress through concentrated wealth and violence among nations and people. The protocols of democratic capitalism are available to train leaders to avoid mistakes. Examination of the ideal and the means of democratic capitalism confirms the attainability of the ideal and the pragmatism of the means. Does this mean that that democratic capitalism needs only understanding and democratic support?

While this proposition has a syllogistic logic, it is contrary to both historic experience and to present-day intellectual conditioning; consequently, many will reject it without subjecting it to proper exam, test, and refinement. Perhaps the success of democratic capitalism will have to come from presenting it to a new generation. My personal experience presenting democratic capitalism to forty-eight Carey Scholars, bright college students who graduated from high schools in the Bronx, New York, has confirmed for me that young people respond well to a workable ideal.

Older generations are conditioned by two theories: the modern liberal view that government must control the destructive forces of ill-defined generic capitalism, and the traditional view that the culture should provide the ethical context within which capitalism is grudgingly tolerated. The first is the same faulty epistemology that ignored Mill's contributions but allowed Marxism to do its incredible damage; the second is hypocrisy, and young people are quick to recognize it as such. Both views are premised on economic illiteracy and the centuries-old intellectual conditioning that demeans commerce. Proponents of both views have failed to do their homework. A broad-based, widespread, careful examination of the potential of democratic capitalism is still ahead of us.

Democratic capitalism, when fully visible, will find broad support for several reasons: First, it appeals to the basic human urges for freedom, a better life, self-esteem, and mutual respect. Second, it is an interdependent experience: As each gains, all gain. Third, its economic logic should appeal to all, including the most agnostic pragmatists. A large number of people yearn for a moral society, and a large number of pragmatists yearn for what builds wealth best. Both the moralists and the pragmatists should be impressed that integrity and wealth creation need not be mutually exclusive, for the power of democratic capitalism lies in combining both.

CHAPTER 5

Worker Ownership: The Democratization of Capitalism

> *Our founding fathers knew that the American experiment in individual liberty, free enterprise, and republican self-government could succeed only if power was widely distributed, and since in any society social and political power flow from economic power, they saw that wealth and property would have to be widely distributed among the people in the country. Could there be anything resembling a free enterprise economy, if wealth and property were concentrated in the hands of a few?*
>
> Ronald Reagan[120]

Universal use of profit-sharing and ownership plans advances democratic capitalism in an interdependent way. Ownership motivates associates to maximize surplus, that is, to create wealth. Ownership then insures broad distribution of wealth that will stimulate more economic growth both in the United States and worldwide. Ownership provides the motivation for participation, productivity, and innovation only when it is part of the democratic capitalist culture.

In democratic capitalist companies, large or small, public or private, everyone has an opportunity to share in the profits and become an owner. Worker ownership is a natural extension of the democratic capitalist culture built on individual development in a harmonious whole. As each individual reaches full potential, enormous productivity and innovation are released, thereby maximizing performance of the cooperative whole. All associates share in the improved performance by accumulating ownership. This caring and sharing, caring about the work one is doing, sharing in the resulting improved performance sustains motivation, and it cycles

---

[120] Cited by Joseph R. Blasi, *Employee Ownership: Revolution or Ripoff?* (Cambridge, Massachusetts: Ballinger Publishing Co., 1988), p. 5.

surplus to those whose spending and saving have the most beneficial multiplier effect on the economy.

The culture prerequisite to worker ownership is built on the democratic capitalist template of *integrity* fundamental to the trusting, cooperative environment; *maximum freedom*, possible only in this environment; *minimum* but sophisticated *structure* to manage risk; and the *competence* to move from mission to effective execution.

The democratic capitalist culture is based on a profound belief in the capacities of people when provided with the right circumstances. The culture necessary for each to enjoy the freedom to learn, to grow, to contribute, and to share, however, is not easy to attain, for it is contrary to the traditional hierarchal organization in which fear is the managerial tool of control and command. Managers at all levels need to be motivated by the spirit of democratic capitalism and trained in its protocols.

President Ronald Reagan demonstrated his understanding that a democratic republic depends on diffused political power, which, in turn, depends on diffused economic power (see quotation at the beginning of this chapter). Despite this philosophical understanding, government policies during and since the Reagan Administration moved the American economy in the opposite direction.

- Instead of diffusing economic power, wealth is concentrated in record amounts and record percentages.[121]

- Taxes have been shifted from capital to labor.

- Finance capitalism has been deregulated at the same time that market disciplines were suspended.

- Lobby power and campaign financing preempt the voting public in influencing the political agenda.

---

[121] Jeff Gates, *Democracy at Risk: Rescuing Main Street from Wall Street* (Cambridge, Massachusetts: Perseus, 2000), pp. 25-6.

- New privileges, obtained by lobby power, and government errors have allowed ultra-capitalism to dominate the world economy.

- A worldview of America as an arrogant country, promoting a greedy and short-term capitalism, contributes to social tensions and world violence.

- The scandals in companies, such as the bankruptcy of Enron in 2001, demonstrated greedy and short-term ultra-capitalism to shocked citizens.

- Momentum towards democratic capitalism, worker ownership, and economic common purpose throughout the world, has been slowed, stopped, and in many cases reversed by the domination of ultra-capitalism.

Incredibly, this rise of ultra-capitalism through the concentration of political and economic power, has gone on at the same time when wage earners became the prime source of new capital through pension funding and 401(k) savings. In the final quarter of the twentieth century, labor and capital became one in the United States: Ownership of public companies by the people's retirement savings increased from under 15% to over 50%. More direct forms of worker ownership grew during the same period as employee stock-ownership increased from a few hundred to 11,000 plans, representing over nine million employees. Internationally, approximately 100 multinationals provided employee ownership, in addition to the wave of privatization of companies from state ownership to worker ownership in countries moving towards economic freedom.

Since the time of Karl Marx, the dream of reformers that workers would own the means of production, has become a reality through evolutionary, not revolutionary, means. Workers are, however, still limited in their participation in the financial rewards from this new capitalism and in the use of their vote as stockholders.

When the financial structure is changed to worker ownership but the work culture is not changed to democratic capitalism, the effort will fail and give worker ownership a bad name. In the 1990s, for example, United Airlines was a failing company that solved its problems by getting the pilots and mechanics to give up wages in exchange for ownership. United Airlines management failed, however, to change the culture that had caused the problems in the first place. Consequently, by 2002, the company was in more financial trouble, exacerbated by union friction among the pilots, the mechanics, and the flight attendants. Critics pointed to United Airlines as a failure of worker ownership, but it was, in fact, a failure of management to change the work culture.

Throughout the three centuries of the Industrial Revolution, capitalism has failed to reach full potential because capitalists have invested mainly in physical assets and not in people. As a consequence, capitalism and democracy have struggled with an inherent tension. In the Information Age, however, investment in people is no longer merely a choice, but a necessity for success is dependent on the release of cognitive power in motivated, involved, contributing, and sharing associates. In Information Age industries, democracy and capitalism must be synergistic. As Peter Drucker, corporate consultant and philosopher, expressed it: "If the feudal knight was the clearest embodiment of society in the early Middle Ages, and the *bourgeois* under capitalism, the educated person will represent society in the post-capitalist society in which knowledge has become the central resource."[122]

Democratic capitalism benefits society by maximizing surplus and distributing it broadly. It benefits society in another way because the educated, moral, independent-thinking, contributing associate has the same character profile as an effective citizen. This is not to suggest that democratic capitalism benefits only democratic countries. Economic freedom can work either under democratic or authoritarian governments, though not under totalitarian ones. In the last two decades of the twentieth century, Singapore, under the authoritarian leadership of Lee Kuan Yew, demonstrated this viability of economic

---

[122] Peter F. Drucker, *Post-Capitalist Society* (New York: Harper Business, 1993), p. 211.

freedom by moving from being a third-world economy to being one of the wealthiest.[123] Singapore demonstrated that it is easier for an authoritarian government to improve lives through economic freedom than for a struggling economy to attain instant democracy. Within the sequence an important logic inheres: Economic freedom, competently applied, eventually leads to political freedom, but the opposite is not the case.

Governments, whether authoritarian or democratic, can support economic freedom and spread ownership plans through fiscal, monetary, and regulatory policies. Capital-gains taxes and double taxation of dividends need to be eliminated for low- to middle-income wage earners, and corporate taxes need to be modified to encourage the spread of ownership plans. The low-cost, ample, non-volatile, patient capital needed to support ownership plans can be assured by the government's taxing and controlling speculation, allowing market disciplines to function, controlling the lending of short-term "hot money," and cooperating globally in a stable international monetary system. Ownership plans and the whole economy share the need for steady growth, and both are damaged by the boom/bust cycle.

With modest changes to the existing capitalistic structure, these profit-sharing and ownership plans can eliminate the traditional problems of the maldistribution of wealth. Wage earners can earn increasing wealth through improved performance and the cumulative effect of patient investment. For example, "At the Lowe's companies, sales managers routinely retire with $1 million, and truck drivers with $500,000."[124]

The economic arguments for worker ownership, detailed in chapter 6, are summarized here as follows:

- The supply side is enhanced by the productivity and innovation of wage earners who are motivated by profit-sharing and ownership.

---

[123] Lee Kuan Yew, *From Third World to First: The Singapore Story: 1965-2000* (New York: Harper Collins, 2000).

[124] Jeff Gates, *The Ownership Solution: Toward a Shared Capitalism for the 21st Century* (Reading, Massachusetts: Addison-Wesley Longmans, 1998), p. 57.

- Wealth distributed broadly through profit-sharing, dividends, and equity appreciation, is recycled into spending that is beneficial to the demand side. Wage earners buy the commodities with the greatest multiplier effect.

- Broad wealth distribution through profit-sharing, dividends, and equity appreciation improves wage earners' savings, and supports the supply-side with patient capital for investment in more growth.

- Broad wealth distribution through profit-sharing, dividends, and equity appreciation, provides the spendable income for reciprocal purchases necessary to make free trade a universal benefit.

- Broad wealth distribution is key to eliminating social tensions.

Ways for wage earners to become worker-owners include the following:

- *ESOPs (Employee Stock-Option Plans):* These plans allow wage earners to acquire equity with borrowed money, based on beneficial tax treatment for both the company and the lending bank. ESOPs have been frequently used in financial restructuring, but they are not conceptually limited to this use.

- *Stock purchase*: Payroll deduction to buy stock, usually with the company matching a portion of the wage earner's purchase.

- *Stock purchase plus profit sharing*: Payroll deduction to buy stock in which the company matches the wage earner's purchase, based on a performance improvement formula. This is more motivational than a simple company match because it focuses the associates' attention on improvement of performance.

- *401(k)*: Savings plans that allow wage earners to save in pre-tax dollars. This feature can be integrated with other types of plans.

- *Defined-benefit pension plans:* This was the original pension mandated by ERISA in 1974, requiring the company to take cash out of the company to fund specific future benefits.

- *Defined contribution pension plans:* The company and the wage earner put a specific amount of money into the plan, and decisions on a range of investment opportunities are made by institutional investors.

- *Stock options*: Shares given by companies for the recipient to buy at some time in the future, usually at the price at the time the option is given. Stock options incur no cost to the company, and the employee has no tax consequence until the option is exercised; consequently, there is little discipline in how many shares are given.

- *Stock grants*: The company gives the employees stock as part of their compensation or profit-sharing, but, contrary to stock options, the grant is disciplined because it is an expense deducted from profits, and it is considered taxable income for the recipient.

All of these have a potential to democratize capitalism, but the simplest, quickest, and most universal way is for wage earners to become owners by buying shares through a profit-sharing and stock-purchase plan. (The *Care and Share* plan that I designed and implemented while CEO of ADT Inc. is described in chapter 2.) This type of plan generates the greatest motivation because it requires individual financial sacrifice that builds a true feeling of being an owner.

Pension money, ESOPs, profit-sharing, and 401(k) savings can be lumped together as an enormous opportunity, properly designed, to democratize capitalism. This opportunity, however, is not being realized; on the contrary, the capital is being put at the disposal of ultra-capitalism. Jeff Gates described this dichotomy in capitalism: "$17 trillion now resides in the hands of U.S. money managers who respond solely to values denominated in financial terms."[125] This phenomenon may be the ultimate contradiction in capitalism. The conflict between capital and labor should have ended when labor became the prime source of capital; however, ultra-capitalists for their own short-term purposes are still able to control the workers' money.

The changes required for the benefit of profit sharing and stock-purchase plans are a significant reduction in capital-gains taxes for long-term holdings, and elimination of double taxation on dividends for the participating wage earners. Both changes would accelerate the use of these plans and help to position dividends as a key component of better wealth distribution. Stimulated by more favorable tax treatment, institutional investors would then pressure companies to pay large dividends. Such a payout is possible when the priority use of surplus cash is reinvestment in growth and dividends, and not stock buy-backs and non-strategic acquisitions.

Experts properly caution that basic pension benefits must be secure, and that employees should diversify their investments. The Enron debacle in 2001 devastated the employees' savings and called attention to the necessity for investment diversification. Worker-ownership plans, however, should be in addition to, not a substitute for, basic pensions.

Karl Marx and John Stuart Mill: Differing Views on Worker Ownership

By the mid-nineteenth century, capitalism had demonstrated its ability to improve lives, but it was functioning at only a fraction of its potential. In 1848, Karl Marx identified the reason: Capitalism had enormous productive capacity to eliminate material scarcity worldwide, but capitalism's distribution of surplus was so

---

[125] Jeff Gates, *Democracy at Risk, op. cit.*, p. xiii.

142

concentrated that most people did not have the money to buy what capitalism could produce. Marx believed that a change in the mode of production, moving the relationship between capital and labor from alienation to cooperation, would produce a new leap forward in the economic system's capacity to produce wealth.

Marx pointed out that in an economic decline, the flaw of concentrated wealth accelerates the downward cycle because lost jobs and wage cuts further reduce demand. Marx believed that worker ownership is the solution because workers would be motivated to maximize surplus that would then be distributed broadly. Marx felt that this superior economic system would supersede capitalism only, however, after the existing economic, political, and cultural infrastructure had been torn down.

John Stuart Mill, also at mid-nineteenth century in London, proposed the same idea, worker ownership, as the method of balancing capitalism's demand with supply. Mill, however, had a better understanding of the management of change than did Marx, and grafted his refinements onto the existing system of private property and competition. By combining management skills with more productive workers in a new work culture, Mill foresaw the same goal, but he avoided Marx's structural mistakes that later caused such tragic results.

Mill improved the definition of democratic capitalism that Adam Smith had formulated and Robert Owen had validated by careful examination of socialism and other cooperative efforts. Mill supported socialist reform of mercantilism, the existing system that demeaned the worker, but he parted with the socialists over any abandonment of competition: "While I agree and sympathize with Socialists in their aims, I utterly dissent from the most conspicuous and vehement part of their teachings, their declamations against competition."[126] Mill was similarly adamant that private property is fundamental to any successful economic system.

---

[126] John Stuart Mill, *Principles of Political Economy with Some of Their Applications to Social Philosophy* (Fairfield, New Jersey: Augustus M. Kelley, 1987), p. 791.

Marx and his friend, Engels, published the *Communist Manifesto*[127] in 1848, the same year that Mill published his *Principles of Political Economy*. Marx and Mill agreed on the theory that society would progress only by moving to a superior economic system based on worker ownership. Marx's and Mill's features in common included the opportunity for the fullest individual development, a harmonious whole, maximum surplus through greater productivity and innovation, broad wealth distribution to sustain motivation, and broad wealth distribution to sustain economic growth and prevent economic decline.

Integration of worker ownership into democratic capitalism through modifying the economic-political structure, as outlined by Mill, was the practical alternative to Marx's revolutionary approach. Based on competition and private property vital to capitalism, Mill offered a manifesto (see introduction to chapter 3) that coupled the power of capitalism to eliminate material scarcity with the elevation of the spirit attendant to, and necessary for, that accomplishment. Mill recognized, however, that a simple cooperative of worker-owners would lack the managerial skills needed for success, and that the most effective reform would combine the motivations of ownership and cooperation with the experience and skills of managers, united in a new culture.

Mill saw the opportunity for the enterprise to reach its full potential when wage earners reached their full potential. He knew that this synergistic realization would require a change in the nature of leadership, from top-down to bottom-up, and a change in attitudes, from fearful to cooperative. Mill foresaw that these changes could be expedited when the workers gained an opportunity to share in continuous improvement through profit sharing and opportunities to become part owners:

> That the relation of masters and work people will be
> gradually superseded by partnership, in one of two
> forms: in some cases, association of the laborers with

---

[127] Karl Marx and Friedrich Engels, *The Communist Manifesto* (New York: Penguin Books, 1967), p. 105.

the capitalists, in others, and perhaps finally in all, association of laborers among themselves.

The first of these forms of association has long been practiced, not indeed as a rule, but as an exception. In several departments of industry there are already cases in which everyone who contributes to the work, either by labor or by pecuniary resources, has a partner's interest proportional to the value of his contribution. It is already a common practice to remunerate those in whom peculiar trust is reposed, by means of a percentage of the profits; and cases exist in which the principle is, with excellent success, carried down to the cause of mere manual laborers.[128]

Mill's proposals were extrapolations of the existing structure. In Mill's vision, no tearing down was called for, but rather an evolutionary restructuring that would release the enormous latent power of the people. Mill's theory of capitalism is made up of three components: wage earners who are owners, managers who are wage earners, and capital. The difference between Mill's nineteenth-century proposal and twenty-first century capitalism is that now the wage earners have also become the source of capital. Capital is no longer derived from a separate class of people but is produced, usually, internally to the operation, and is available from the wage earners' savings and pension money as patient capital for investment in the job-growth economy.

In democratic capitalism, the managers are not a class apart; they are the aristocracy of talent and virtue, the product of meritocracy. Those once dichotomized as "workers and owners," "employees and employers," "labor and management," are now all "associates" in a cooperative effort, sharing in improved performance. Mill outlined this worker ownership arrangement in these words:

The existing accumulations of capital might honestly, and by a kind of spontaneous process, become in the

---

[128] Mill, *op. cit.*, p. 764.

end the joint property of all who participate in their
productive employment, a transformation which, thus
effected, (and assuming of course that both sexes
participate equally in the rights and in the government
of the association) would be in the nearest approach to
social justice, and the most beneficial ordering of
industrial affairs for the universal good which it is
possible at present to foresee.[129]

Reformers, excited by Marx's angry attack on capitalism,
defaulted on their responsibility to synthesize Marx's contributions
with Mill's alternative. They assimilated Marx's attack on the whole
existing infrastructure, but they did not assimilate Marx's axiom that
social progress depends on movement to a superior economic system.
The bloodiest century in history, the 20th, was the result of this
intellectual confusion.

A less revolutionary movement towards the democratization
of capitalism took place in the United States in the late-nineteenth
century, stimulated by greater personal freedoms. The Knights of
Labor, for example, had a vision of workers leaving the wage-slave
condition and becoming educated and dignified participants in the
industrial process. The Farmers' Alliance, in 1877, similarly tried to
help farmers become entrepreneurs, proclaiming their democratic
purpose to "more speedily educate ourselves in the science of free
government." The leaders believed that citizen-farmers, properly
educated, could then construct "a grand social and political palace
where liberty may dwell and justice be safely domiciled."[130] Both the
Knights and the Alliance failed, however, because they were opposed
by the powerful mercantilists who regarded workers, in fact, as wage-
slaves, and by politically powerful finance capitalists who regarded
cooperatives as subversive.

The Labor Movement was forced to abandon its cooperative
idealism. Unions led by Samuel Gompers, instead, improved the
distribution of wealth through hard and frequently bloody bargaining.

---

[129] *Ibid.*, pp. 791-2.

[130] Lawrence Goodwyn, *Democratic Promise: The Populist Movement in America*
(New York: Oxford University Press, 1976), p. 33.

By the 1920s, however, visionaries became convinced that there were better ways to couple democracy and capitalism to improve both the creation and distribution of wealth. Congress took positive action in activating that potential synergy when they passed the Revenue Act of 1921, which gave tax-favored status to stock-bonus and profit-sharing plans.[131]

ESOP (Employee Stock Ownership Plan)

The promotion of worker ownership through tax policies was lost during the 1920s in the speculative excitement of the bull market, then lost again for another decade during the Great Depression of the 1930s, when the concern became economic survival. Worker ownership came alive again from 1973 to 1987, when Senator Russell Long (D., Louisiana) promoted the passage of 15 different worker-ownership laws favoring the use of ESOPs.

Louis Kelso, an advisor to Long, was dedicated to a version of democratic capitalism. Kelso, aided by his wife, Patricia Hetter Kelso, invented ESOPs, which were described in 1991 in Kelso's obituary as follows:

> The employee ownership plan, known as ESOP, was invented to democratize access to capital credit. In human terms, it is a financing device that gradually transforms labor workers into capital workers. It does this by making a corporation's credit available to the employees, who then use it to buy stock in the company. The earnings of the company itself are used to pay for the stock. The company's reward from an ESOP—in addition to a motivated workforce of worker owners—is the low-cost financing of its own capital needs.[132]

---

[131] Joseph R. Blasi, *op. cit.*, p. 8.

[132] Alfonso A. Narvaez, "Louis O. Kelso, who advocated worker-capitalism, is dead at 77," *The New York Times*, February 23, 1991, p. B10.

Mortimer Adler, a philosopher and instigator of the *Great Books* program at the University of Chicago and other Liberal Arts colleges, had long been a student of democracy and alternative political arrangements, but like most academicians, Adler was unaware of democratic capitalism. After he met Kelso, Adler recorded his shocking discovery:

> I slowly came to realize that political democracy
> cannot flourish under all economic conditions.
> Democracy requires an economic system which
> supports the political ideals of liberty and equality for
> all. Men cannot exercise freedom in the political
> sphere when they are deprived of it in the economic
> sphere.[133]

Adler had it almost right: It is economic freedom that can improve lives and then lead to political freedoms. Adler, however, discovered what the intellectual community has been missing for too long, thus his epiphany is central to understanding why the world is one of folly and violence, and not one of peace and plenty. The "thinkers," the intellectual community, have concentrated on changing the world through the political structure and the culture instead of discovering the superior economic system and helping align the political structure and culture in its support. In this persistent default, they have ignored Marx's signature concept that social progress depends on movement to the superior economic system. Adler apparently did not connect Kelso's manifesto with Marx's, so he did not propose a more careful examination by the intellectual community of this crucial axiom.

Like many managers who discover the power of democratic capitalism through trial and error, the Kelsos and Adler did not acknowledge walking in Marx's footsteps when they identified the potential synergy between democracy and capitalism. In the *Capitalist Manifesto* that Adler and Kelso co-authored, they proposed ways for workers to borrow money in order to become capitalists and enjoy the

---

[133] Louis O. Kelso and Mortimer Adler, *The Capitalist Manifesto* (Westport, Connecticut: Greenwood Press, 1958), preface written by Adler, p. x.

benefits of ownership. Kelso was an investment banker; consequently, he thought in terms of leveraged buy-outs; and he designed a plan to enable the employees to borrow the money to purchase ownership in their company. In Kelso's plan, profit-sharing is not used as a way to build equity; only borrowings are used for that purpose. For this reason, ESOPs give a measure of motivation but not so strong as worker ownership that requires a financial sacrifice to buy ownership through a payroll deduction plan. Kelso's legacy is kept alive by CESJ (The Center for Economic and Social Justice), founded in 1984 by Norman Kurland, who participated in the first meeting between Louis Kelso and Senator Long in November, 1973.[134]

Senator Long became evangelistic about employee stock ownership, and he challenged Congressional interest:

> Employee ownership should and would broaden and expand ownership; encourage capital formation and innovative corporate finance; improve labor/management relations, productivity and profitability in firms; help the economy accommodate developments in technology, the spread of transfer payments, and inflation; and create an economic democracy.[135]

In 1975, Senator Jacob Javits (R., New York) supported the concept of worker ownership to "improve the financial condition of working Americans and at the same time improve the productivity of American industry."[136] Tax benefits were subsequently approved by Congress for ESOPs and for banks lending money to ESOPs.

ESOPs enjoyed other bi-partisan support. Republicans, such as President Reagan, interpreted the intentions of the American Founders as an economic system based on broad distribution of wealth that would prevent economic and political power-concentration.[137]

---

[134] See website: www.CESJ.org.

[135] Blasi, *op. cit.*, p. 18.

[136] *Loc. cit.*

[137] Gates, *The Ownership Solution, op. cit.*, p. 5.

Democrats, such as Hubert Humphrey, connected ownership and job growth: "Capital and the question of who owns it and therefore reaps the benefit of its productiveness, is an extremely important issue that is complementary to the issue of full employment."[138]

Jeff Gates, who was counsel to Russell Long's Senate Finance Committee, documented support for worker ownership from Republicans, Democrats, Martin Luther King's widow, and Russian Premier Mikhail Gorbachev, the author of *Perestroika*. This broad support validated in 1998 the appeal of worker ownership, and it dramatizes the thirst for a "third way" between raw capitalism and inept socialism. This ideological support is extraordinary in a polarized and grid-locked country, where political opposites seem incapable of truth-seeking or combined action for the common good. The following quotations—lifted from the jacket of Gates's book, *Ownership Solution*[139]—span the political spectrum, lending further optimism that the country and the world are aware of the need of, and are ready for, ownership solutions that democratize capitalism:

- "Expansion of ownership and greater access to capital will both strengthen and spread democracy and market economies throughout the world." Republican Jack Kemp, former Senator and Presidential candidate.

- "Broad-based personal ownership can strengthen communities and make global sustainable development possible." Democrat Dick Gephardt, Majority Leader, U.S. House of Representatives.

- "Worker ownership focuses on the central issues that have to be addressed if the twenty-first century is to transcend the simplistic dilemma of capitalism versus socialism and create a new, sustainable civilization." Mikhail Gorbachev, former Russian premier and author of *Perestroika*.

---

[138] *Loc. cit.*

[139] *Ibid.*, book jacket.

- "Ownership is a *sine qua non* of sustainable development." James D. Wolfensohn, President of the World Bank.

- "Long-term, sustainable development requires a balancing of economic, social, fiscal, and environmental goals. Broad-based capital ownership can help achieve them." Bill Bradley, U.S. Senator 1979-1997, and unsuccessful candidate for President in 2000.

- "Somewhere in between unbridled capitalism and the welfare state, there has to be a more just and equitable economic system which provides genuine opportunities for all citizens, while preserving incentives for investment ... a creative yet credible strategy for empowering working people with a more vital interest in private enterprise. If capitalism can indeed have a human face, the reforms proposed merit careful consideration." Coretta Scott King, founder of the King Center and widow of Martin Luther King, Jr.

In the 1970s and 1980s, most of the bi-partisan support for worker ownership concentrated on ESOPs, not on profit-sharing and stock-purchase plans. Inevitably, clever people took advantage of the tax breaks that were legislated, and applied them to refinance failing or troubled companies. Some owners used ESOPs to take cash out of the companies and leave the workers holding the bag. These events resulted in a loss of confidence in ESOPs and worker ownership in general. One book on the subject was subtitled *Revolution or Rip-Off?*[140] and one magazine article said it all in the title: "Employees left holding the bag, the deals looked wonderful when companies decided to sell out to their workers. But many employees lost their equity, jobs, pensions, and more. Now they're suing."[141]

Stories of failing ESOPs are reminders that even democratic capitalism cannot succeed when management lacks skill, and when products and markets are mismatched. Democratic capitalism works

---

[140] *Blasi, op. cit.*

[141] Anne B. Fisher, "Employees Holding the Bag," *Fortune*, May 20, 1991, p. 83.

best when it is applied as a coherent whole; financial motivation alone will not work when the rest of the corporate culture is not dedicated to the development of the individual in a harmonious whole. In retrospect, although many experiences validated the enormous power of worker ownership, some ESOPs failed because they involved too high a rate of change. When too many of the business variables are in a state of flux, the demand for management skills goes up exponentially.

Another route to worker ownership is the gradual accumulation of equity through profit-sharing and stock-purchase plans with no radical change in the financial structure, but a significant change in the corporate culture. Profit-sharing, stock-purchase plans, and ESOPs, however, are not mutually exclusive; they can each democratize capitalism under different circumstances. Success of any such program should encourage greater use of the others.

Profit-Sharing and Stock-Purchase Plans

The most universal, safest, long-term way for employees to accumulate ownership, and for capitalism to be democratized, is for workers to *buy* stock with their own money and *earn* more through performance bonuses. Using the 401(k) feature that allows deductions from pre-tax dollars, a worker purchases company stock through a payroll deduction, along with other investment options. While many plans are available in which the company matches part of the employee's money, the plan most consistent with the democratic capitalist culture does the matching based on a performance improvement formula. In these plans, the associates make their contributions, both individually and as part of a team, and then they share in the results. The feeling of ownership from stock purchase, along with sharing in improved group performance, motivates the associates to maximize the surplus, and this then is distributed broadly. Both the creation and distribution of wealth are optimized.

This democratization of capitalism depends on a trusting and cooperative work culture that can be sustained only by a fair sharing of the improvement produced. Profit-sharing and stock-purchase plans make clear whether the financial motivation and the work

152

culture are consistent. If they are not, employees typically will not sign up to give up part of their paycheck. The total of the payroll deductions can also be a significant source of low-cost equity capital for the company's growth. Alternatively, if the company does not need growth capital, it can buy stock on the open market and prevent dilution. Over years, substantial equity and dividend income can be produced from seemingly small payroll deductions. Worldwide use of these plans would allow workers in even low-wage countries to build significant savings and dividend income. This addition to spendable income for reciprocal purchases can help make free trade the route to peace and plenty that it should be and not a source of friction that it has become because of the corruptions of ultra-capitalism.

ERISA

During the 1970s, Washington squandered a unique opportunity to democratize capitalism and have an enormous positive effect on wealth creation and distribution. The opportunity was to couple the interest in worker ownership of Senator Long's committee with the flow of funds provoked by ERISA (Employees' Retirement Income Security Act), the 1974 law that required companies to fund future pension benefits fully. "Full funding" means that companies could no longer pay these obligations out of future earnings that might not materialize: The managers were required to take the cash out of the company and invest it for the future pensioners.

About 100 billion dollars a year, half-private/half-public, was now looking for an investment opportunity. The largest part of it ended up on the stock market, a money dump that upset the normal buy/sell dynamic sufficiently to initiate and sustain the longest-running bull market in history. When this flow of funds began to move to Wall Street, average corporate stock prices were 10 times earning per share. At the market peak in 2000, this P/E ratio had quadrupled to over 40, but because so many companies were cooking the books, the actual P/E ratio was substantially higher. This bull market, in turn, caused the short-term earnings pressure that allowed ultra-capitalism to dominate the economy. Another result of this government error is in the future: When pensioners begin to draw this money out of the market to live on in their retirement, the ebb tide of funds will reverse the stock-buy pressure to a stock-sell pressure, with a negative effect on market values.

Those in Congress excited by worker ownership apparently did not make the connection that ERISA funds could have flowed more directly into worker ownership. For example, a new financial instrument could have been offered, a 6% convertible preferred stock, that allowed workers to buy ownership with their pension money; enjoy an annual return of 6% to be spent, saved, or reinvested in more stock; and a chance to contribute to, and benefit from, the long-term appreciation of the stock. The companies could have either used reinvested dividends for long-term growth investment or they could have paid more dividends. In this fashion, ownership plans would have spread rapidly by the attraction of an annual 6% return plus the longer-term appreciation. Dividends would thus have taken their place as an important part of broad wealth distribution. It did not work this way, however.

Unfortunately, the connection of worker ownership and the new, enormous flow of pension money was not made by government planners; instead, most of the annual flow of 100 billion dollars of new cash went to Wall Street and helped build the dominance of ultra-capitalism. In effect, no-cost internal capital used for growth or dividends was extracted from industry through the efforts of the Wall Street lobby and delivered to the stock market. Only a part of it was recycled back into the job-growth economy.

At the beginning of the 21st century, the debate about privatizing part of Social Security ignored the reality that a FICA Social Security payroll-deduction dollar can be used only once, either as an investment for the future benefit of a younger person or as a payment to a retired person. Betting part of Social Security money on Wall Street could also upset the economy the same way ERISA did, with another blow torch of excessive liquidity that distorts the market's buy/sell dynamic, pushing values to artificially high levels and with very little returned to the real economy. The alternative was still open, however, to design a new financial instrument that balances income, appreciation, and security for more direct investment in the job-growth economy.

Other countries have demonstrated the benefits of using Social Security money as an investment, not as a source of funds for general government purposes. For example, Chile privatized their Social Security with impressive results. The average Chilean worker, who earned only one-half of an American counterpart's income during similar careers, nonetheless enjoyed pension benefits double the American level.[142] The retirees' money, instead of being used by the government as a not-well-understood subsidy for more spending, was used as investment capital to energize the economy and provide jobs. *The Wall Street Journal* reported on Chile's having pioneered this private system in 1980:

> A fully funded private pension system based on savings and investment rather than taxing and spending. In most of the world, trade liberalization is cast as a battle between capitalists and employees, between "global elites" and the "common man." In Chile, however, market-invested retirement funds mean that every employee is a capitalist and has a visible stake in an internationally competitive economy. For 13 years, under three different governments, economic growth has averaged 7% a year.[143]

The U.S. government's record of economic error is a long and unhappy one. If the same rules legislated in ERISA, that is, the necessity to put funds away now to pay future benefits, had been applied at the beginning to Social Security and government employees' pensions, an enormous additional flow of funds would have been available to fund job-growth while democratizing capitalism. Social Security would not need to be saved, had the government followed the same practice at the beginning that it forced on industry. Instead of putting the money into investments to pay future benefits, the government spent it on current costs. Instead of building up a huge fund to pay the huge future retirement obligations

---

[142] Peter Ferrara and Michael Tanner, *Common Cents, Common Dreams* (Washington D.C.: Cato Institute 1998), pp. 31-5.

[143] José Piñera and Aaron Lukas, "Chile Takes a Bold Step toward Freer Trade," *The Wall Street Journal*, January 15, 1999, p. A11.

of government employees, including the military, the money will now have to come, instead, from future tax revenues.

Stock Options

The broad use of stock options became popular particularly in Information Age companies. Many regarded this expansion of stock options as a manifestation of a more democratized capitalism. Already in the 1980s, I regarded the proliferation of stock options, however, with dread, for I had experienced the bad things that could happen in a bear market. I opposed this proliferation on the two Board Compensation Committees on which I served, but I was in the minority. My argument was that stock options were being given to people who combined little financial sophistication with a trusting attitude: "If the company is giving it to me, it must be good."

My concerns were well founded. After the stock market decline in 2000-2001, *The New York Times* reported 25 cases of personal bankruptcies filed by Microsoft workers. Behind the figures were stories of personal tragedy:

> Some people who were experienced engineers and programmers yet naive about the stock market turned their options into stock and then borrowed against those shares to pay their taxes. The high-risk practice, known as a margin loan, is more often a tool of speculators aiming to buy additional stock without additional money. As the stock fell, these workers' shares were sold, leaving them broke.

> One mid-level Microsoft employee said that a broker at Solomon Smith Barney, the firm hired by Microsoft to administer its option program, pushed him to take these risks. At the peak, his shares were worth about $1.5 million, but, when the stock began to dive, the firm began selling shares out of his account to pay off the loan. Finally, most of his stock was gone and he owed $100,000 in taxes, more than he made in a year and more than he had. His only remaining asset was a

modest Seattle home, which he and his wife feared
they would lose.[144]

Stock options are a counterproductive compensation device at
all levels of corporations. Employees ought never to be financially
destroyed by the downside of any corporate compensation plan. At
the executive level, stock options became the coupling device with
Wall Street that motivates executives to go to extremes for short-term
earnings or deals that rain money on all of the deal-makers but that
leave the downsized parched and dry. Stock options helped create the
environment in which executives faked profit improvement and
disgraced the word "capitalism." Stock options are a poor way to
democratize capitalism.

Stock Grants

An effective alternative to stock options is stock grants
because grants incur a charge to earnings and tax consequences to the
recipient at the time that they are given. This financial pain disciplines
the quantity of grants provided, and in contrast to stock options,
grants remind everyone that "there are no free lunches." The
argument used by promoters of stock options, such as Senator Joseph
Lieberman (D., Connecticut), that options are critical to the success of
start-up companies by helping to attract the requisite talent, does not
survive examination because these companies are not making money
anyway and the expense of stock grants only adds to their tax loss for
the benefit of future profit. Similarly, the use of grants instead of
stock options to attract highly talented people would require the
company to take over much of the individuals' tax obligation in the
form of a signing bonus. In each case, some pain goes with the gain,
and that is what provides the missing discipline. Other alternatives,
according to *Business Week,* include "restricted stock, which converts

---

[144] Gretchen Morgenson, "Some Suffer Tax Hangovers from Microsoft Option
Spree," *The New York Times*, April 18, 2001, p. 1.

into common stock over time, and performance shares—grants based on meeting certain goals." [145]

Worker Ownership around the World

The massive privatization plan in Russia in the 1990s is an example of good concept (democratize capitalism) but terrible execution. The country's assets were stripped and a corrupt few were made enormously wealthy (see chapter 7). The workers lost their new equity either from failing companies or through sale to the new oligarchy. Eastern Europe had a more mixed experience: 300 companies with 80,000 employees were privatized in Hungary; 1,500 companies with 350,000 employees in Poland; and 91% of all privatized companies in Slovenia gained employee ownership. A study of 299 companies during the 1990s identified a 17% boost in productivity from profit-sharing plans. [146]

Interest of the European Commission in worker ownership has been marked by a series of PEPPER reports. PEPPER stands for "Promotion of Employee Participation in Profits and Enterprise Results." These reports highlighted 57% of French, and 40% of British, companies that had profit sharing schemes.

At Kent University in May 2001, representatives of many countries participated in an International Seminar on Employee Ownership. The meeting was organized by Capital Ownership Group (COG) whose stated mission is to "forge a coalition that will promote broadened ownership of productive capital in order to reduce inequality of income and wealth; increase sustainable economic growth; expand opportunities for people to realize their productive and creative potential; stabilize local communities by improving living standards; and enhance the quality of life for all." [147]

John Logue reported on one of the best known success stories of worker ownership, the Mondragon experience in Spain:

---

[145] Robert D. Hof, "Stock Options Aren't the Only Option," *Business Week*, April 14, 2003, p. 60.

[146] David Erdal, "Employee Ownership Models in Europe: The Search for Best Practices," paper delivered at "Ownership for All" conference, Capital Ownership Group, Kent State University, May, 2001.

[147] *Loc. cit.*

In the Basque region of Spain, the Mondragon cooperative industrial group does $3 billion of sales, 47% export; the retail group does $4 billion in sales; and, its bank has more than $7 billion in assets. This worker owned group was started in the mid-1950s by a priest in a technical school. It has become the seventh largest, closely-held business in Spain, employing 53,000 people.[148]

The Ohio Employee Ownership Center (OEOC), associated with COG, experienced the conflict among competing forms of capitalism first hand in their work in Russia, where they introduced the advantages of employee involvement by training both workers and managers in 1990. The Russian oligarchy, however, abetted by bad advice from U.S. experts, chose instead the greedy opportunities in ultra-capitalism and took their country down in one of the worst economic disasters of the twentieth century (see chapter 7).

Gongyun Situ, an economist from Nanjing University in China, presented a paper at the COG International meeting on the extensive experiment with ESOPs and cooperatives formed around China's TVES (Township and Village Enterprises). China plans for more ESOPs as part of their enormous privatization of state industries. The TVES are a little understood part of China's movement to economic and political freedom:

> More than 600 million rural voters in 31 provinces, municipalities, and autonomous regions have taken part in the elections to the Village Committees in the last ten years. The voter turnout averages 80%.[149]

The Chinese ownership story is typical of start-up failures and successes, but China has demonstrated the patience and determination to make economic freedom work that was lacking in early efforts in

---

[148] *Ibid.*

[149] George Matthews, "China: Struggle for Basic Democracy," *The Times of India*, November, 2002, p. 1.

Russia. China provides an important test of worker ownership, not only because of this patience and determination but also because they have avoided many of the structural problems of ultra-capitalism that destroyed the economies of the Southeast Asian countries in 1997 (see chapter 7).

Also at the COG meeting, Jay Choi, Project Director, Korean Desk of Union Network International, described similar successes and problems in South Korea. The total number of ESOP companies in South Korea reached 1,546 in 2000. The unions were worried about ESOPs because of the almost total concentration of the workers' net worth in a single company. Choi made her report before "Enron" became a household name and called attention to the "too many eggs in one basket" problem.

Worker Ownership: the Way to Democratize Capitalism

In the last quarter of the 20th century, many managers found that world competition forced a reevaluation of the whole working culture. A *Fortune* article reported:

> So it has come to this: You've automated the factory,
> decimated the inventory, eliminated the unnecessary
> from the organization chart, and the company still isn't
> hitting on all cylinders and you've got an awful feeling
> you know why. It's the culture. It's the values, heroes,
> myths, symbols that have been in the organization
> forever, the attitudes that say, don't disagree with the
> boss, or don't make waves, or just do enough to get by,
> or for God's sake, don't take chances. And how on
> earth are you going to change all *that*?[150]

DuPont CEO Edgar Woolard discovered what all democratic capitalists understand: "Employees have been underestimated." He concluded with the democratic logic, "You have to start with the

---

[150] Brian Dumaine, "Creating a New Company Culture. More managers are doing just that to boost their competitiveness. A few have found some common keys to success, notably that change begins at the bottom," *Fortune*, January 15, 1990, p. 127.

premise that people at all levels want to contribute and make the business a success."[151]

The National Center for Employee Ownership (NCEO) reported over 10,000 ESOP plans in place in the United States along with growth abroad in the early 1990s, when politicians again discovered the promise of worker ownership. Congressman Dana Rohrabacher (R., California) enthused:

> Employee ownership is freedom's next step. A force in society to be applauded by those who believe in individual rights, free enterprise and democratic government.[152]

As worker participation grew, it became more apparent that it was a change in management that was required to make it work. The right culture depended on management who had a natural respect for the ordinary worker.

Business executives, politicians, and journalists have rediscovered the powerful coupling of democracy and capitalism. They have reaffirmed the original liberal principles of the American Founders. They have awakened to the fundamental mission of the nineteenth-century Populist Movement, the Farmers' Alliance, and the Knights of Labor. Capitalists and Congress people have become aware of the good effects promoted by new tax laws in the early 1920s and later in the 1970s. Bi-partisan thinkers have realized that the diffusion of economic power is vital to the diffusion of political power and deserves support by Republicans, Democrats, and independents.

A just and comfortable society depends on a growing economy based on optimum wealth creation and broadest possible distribution. The historical tension between capital and labor has obscured the opportunity for broad-based ownership to create more wealth and distribute it broadly. Worker-owners are motivated to innovate and produce for personal gain and as part of a team; hence, wealth is maximized. As owners, they share in this maximized

---

[151] *Loc. cit.*

[152] Dana Rohrabacher, *Human Events*, February 2, 1991, p. 11.

surplus, then they recycle their financial rewards back into spending that sustains economic growth, and into saving that provides patient capital for greater growth.

Worker ownership succeeds because it is built on the human duality of individual ambition and the instinct for social cooperation. The requirement of leadership is to provide the education and training necessary for individual development and the trusting, cooperative environment necessary to develop team spirit. Combining the needs, drives, and effects of the individual with the social in human interaction focused on work, releases the latent power that can move the whole towards realization of full potential.

Worker ownership is the best way to create and distribute wealth because it is freedom based. It satisfies the universal urge for freedom and comfort. It provides individuals with a wider opportunity to control their lives. Worker ownership encourages a sense of personal responsibility in the recognition that one can make a difference, both as an individual and as part of a team.

Emerging economies can expedite their progress by early adoption of worker-ownership plans. Just as they can skip generations of obsolete communications infrastructure by moving to fiberoptics, wireless, and internet, so their economic system can skip generations of alienation between capital and labor by moving quickly to democratic capitalism. Even in low-wage countries, significant ownership can be accumulated over time to the benefit of the workers and the whole economy alike.

The problem of alienation between capital and labor should no longer be with us. The wage earner, through pension plans, 401(k) savings, and stock-purchase plans, is now the major source of new American capital. Labor and capital are now largely one! In addition, the Information Age has enhanced the capacity of capitalism to feed, clothe, shelter, educate, and provide good health care and hope to the world. Competitive demands in the Information Age for involved, educated, and contributing associates will finally result in their demanding full partnership and a full share.[153]

---

[153] Peter Drucker, "Beyond the Information Age Revolution," *The Atlantic Monthly,* Oct. 1999, p. 57.

Despite these positive developments, the fatal flaw of traditional capitalism, concentrated wealth, shockingly persists. More than two billion of the world's six billion population live in poverty. Wealth is concentrated in record percentages in the United States, and although most people are living better, a sense of unfairness is building social tensions. Japan's economy has been starved for decades by the lack of adequate consumer demand at the same time that large corporations have amassed tens of billions of dollars in cash. Europe's economy does not distribute surplus to the wage earner; instead, they tax and redistribute from 50% to over 60% of their countries' national production. Modest changes in the tax laws in all of these countries would encourage the spread of ownership plans and the greater distribution of surplus in dividends directly to the people. Wealth distributed in ownership plans motivates people to maximize the surplus; wealth redistributed through taxation, by contrast, demotivates people and reduces the surplus. In the United States, wealth is still concentrated because government policies are dominated by Wall Street and designed for the privileged few, not to promote the general welfare. For example, hundreds of billions of dollars have been spent by corporations buying back their own stock, most of this repurchase without economic benefit, and a similar amount wasted making acquisitions to hype short-term earnings.

Democratic pressure by institutional investors is needed to get corporations to pay large dividends and to get the government to eliminate the double taxation penalty on dividends. Tax-free dividends for low and middle-income wage earners would return the surplus to the benefit of the economy. Large dividends would be a strong inducement for the spread of profit-sharing, stock-purchase plans, and ESOPs that maximize surplus and then distribute it broadly to raise domestic demand and make free trade a universal benefit. Many would reinvest their dividends in more stock, thus providing low-cost, patient capital for economic growth. Finally, this priority for large dividends would relieve the stock market's frantic pressure for short-term earnings by valuing companies highly for large dividends as well as for fast growth.

This democratization of capitalism is now both possible and urgent! Why, then, is it not presented in the Business Schools as a coherent and integrated whole?

Since 9-11 and the Iraq War, people have searched for an alternative to an increasingly violent world. Economic common purpose based on broad wealth distribution through forms of worker ownership is that alternative because only when the standard of living throughout the world is steadily going up, will the violence go down.

CHAPTER 6

The Economic Logic of Democratic Capitalism

The body of economic knowledge is an essential element in the structure of human civilization; it is the foundation upon which modern industrialism and all the moral, intellectual, technological, and therapeutical achievements of the last centuries have been built. It rests with men whether they will make the proper use of the rich treasure with which this knowledge provides them or whether they will leave it unused. But if they fail to take the best advantage of it and disregard its teachings and warnings, they will not annul economics; they will stamp out society and the human race.

Ludwig von Mises[154]

The Warnings

Austrian economist Ludwig von Mises (1881-1973) proclaimed the benefits of free markets along with issuing passionate warnings that the benefits would be wasted unless the principles were observed. One example that Mises delineated was the deliberate devaluation of currency by the government of Great Britain after the Napoleonic Wars. The government and the financial establishment conspired to slow economic growth by choking off the supply of money. The bankers and politicians knew that this action would hurt most of the people through unemployment, lower wages, and higher prices for food, but it accomplished the mission of restoring the asset value of the wealthy to pre-war levels.

The human injustice of this action is obvious; the economic principles violated were the neutrality of money and broad distribution of wealth. In 1912, Mises commented on this brutal practice:

---

[154] Ludwig von Mises, *Human Action* (Chicago: Contemporary Books, third revised edition, 1966; first published by Yale University Press, 1949), p. 885.

165

Calamitous economic hardships resulted from this deflation; they stirred social unrest and begot the rise of an inflationist movement as well as the anti-capitalist agitation from which, after a while, Engels and Marx drew their inspiration.[155]

Marx's theory, that society is dominated by class conflict, was confirmed by this type of greedy action of the wealthy class against poor people. Marxism drew its strength from these actions, but then Marxists proceeded to make their own egregious mistakes that set the stage for the 20th-century catastrophes that Mises had warned about in 1912.

In this chapter, I present the positive economic aspects of democratic capitalism and free markets, but I begin by mentioning these negative events and warnings because violations of economic principles have become worse and now threaten society's unprecedented opportunities in the 21st century. An understanding of democratic capitalism and free markets is available from a synthesis of Smith, Marx, and Mill. This theoretical work, however, is the easy part, for history demonstrates that lack of an understanding of the impediments, and the concentration of power that protects them, have prevented necessary reforms. An educated citizenry must do more than understand; they must also organize democratic action to purge these two persistent errors:

- Government policies, lobbied by ultra-capitalists, that result in flagrant concentration of the world's wealth, provoking social tensions and new forms of terrible violence.

- Reformers who do not understand these violations of free-market principles and do not use available democratic power to correct them.

---

[155] Ludwig von Mises, *The Theory of Money and Credit* (Indianapolis, Indiana: Liberty Classics,1980; first published in Austria 1912, first translated into English, 1934), p. 98.

The power nexus between the government and finance capitalism provided special privileges to the few that stimulated Mises's criticism of the establishment, which is notable because he is generally regarded as a conservative economist. He knew, however, that economic freedom functions poorly when wealth is not broadly distributed; he understood the need for neutral money; and he knew that governments that do not understand their relationship to the free market will persist in providing privileges that give money an undue influence, contrary to the principle of the need for neutral money.

In 1998, the world's best-known speculator and philanthropist, George Soros, warned of potential catastrophes from unsupervised financial markets. He stated bluntly: "Market fundamentalism is today a greater threat to open society than totalitarian ideology."[156] In 2003, the world's most respected investor, Warren Buffet, used his letter in the annual report of his company, Berkshire Hathaway, to warn that derivatives, a favorite tool of ultra-capitalists, are "time bombs and financial weapons of mass destruction, carrying dangers that, while now latent, are potentially lethal."[157]

The Wall Street Journal took Buffet seriously and leapt into print with a lead editorial defending ultra-capitalism's money tree, arguing that derivatives are "miracles of financial engineering," adding arguments by that great defender of derivatives, the Chairman of the Federal Reserve Board, Alan Greenspan. The smug headline in the middle of the article declared: "Every great investor makes an occasional mistake"[158] (see chapter 7).

Resolution of this debate will help determine the direction of the world in the 21st century. American citizens are pivotal in the direction that will be taken. Citizens must do their homework and decide which argument they accept and take action on it. Will American citizens respond to the combined wisdom of one of the greatest philosopher-economists of the 20th century; one of the

---

[156] George Soros, *The Crisis of Global Capitalism: Open Society Endangered* (New York: Public Affairs, Perseus Books Group, 1998), p. xxii.

[157] Warren Buffet, "Avoiding a Mega-Catastrophe," *Fortune*, March 17, 2003, p. 82.

[158] Editorial, "Derivative Thinking," *The Wall Street Journal*, March 11, 2003, p. A14.

wealthiest, most socially sensitive speculators; one of the wealthiest men in America with a reputation for common sense and the long view? Or will Americans continue to abandon the field to the defenders and protectors of ultra-capitalism?

The Alternative

The alternative to ultra-capitalism is the economic system originally defined by Adam Smith and now refined by two hundred years of trial and error. Smith's vision was of a self-sustaining dynamic for economic growth based on private property, competition, involved workers, and the increased productivity of the Industrial Revolution. Three-quarters of a century after Smith, the reason that capitalism was functioning at only a fraction of its potential was identified by Karl Marx and John Stuart Mill: People did not have enough money to purchase what capitalism could produce. Both Marx and Mill proposed that profit-sharing and ownership participation would motivate workers to maximize the surplus which, then, would be broadly distributed to those whose spending and saving would have the most beneficial effect for *steady* economic growth. This refinement of capitalism by Marx and Mill completed the economic logic of free markets.

In contrast to the impediments from ultra-capitalism, democratic capitalism operates on the economic and social logic that can free the twenty-first century of material scarcity and violence. The economic opportunities for better food, clothing, shelter, health, and education result in social opportunities for freedom, knowledge, hope, and justice. This interdependent experience can unify people and motivate them to develop greater individual skills in a more harmonious whole, adding to the momentum for social progress.

Unity within a nation may grow slowly, but it will grow steadily from the realization that the lives of individuals, their families, and future generations can be made better through economic freedom. Religious, ethnic, and nationalistic sources of violence will gradually recede over longer periods of time as this same realization spreads throughout the world. Momentum to attain the full economic potential of comfort for the greatest number of people, and the social potential for peace, will be sustained by the universal urge towards freedom and a better life.

During the two centuries after Adam Smith wrote his inquiry into the wealth of nations, economic freedom has demonstrated the capacity to eliminate material scarcity, but it has functioned at considerably less than its potential because the conditions for success prescribed by Smith have not been met. World economic growth has been slowed and social tensions caused because wealth has continued to be too concentrated in the hands of the few, easy credit for speculation has been too available in the mature countries, and too little spendable income has been available in the rest of the world.

At the end of the twentieth century, however, new developments should have democratized capitalism and positioned the world's economic system to reach far greater potential in the twenty-first century. The failure of communism to improve lives was contrasted with the demonstration in many emerging nations of the dramatic success of economic freedom; the dawn of the Information Age released the cognitive power of people, a phenomenon possible only in the democratic capitalist culture; and wage earners, through their pension funds and savings, became the a major source of new capital in America.

Despite these favorable developments, however, democratic capitalism has not been adopted either domestically or globally as public policy and general practice. Several mistakes by the United States government thwarted this unprecedented opportunity and, instead, escalated the traditional impediment of wealth concentration into a dominant influence that damages both economic and social opportunities. An extraordinary volatility in international currency and interest rates resulted from the American government's floating the dollar in 1971 without an alternative stabilizing mechanism or control of speculation with borrowed money. This was followed in 1974 by a further U.S. government action that coupled the excessive volatility with excessive liquidity. A new law, ERISA, required present funding of future pension benefits and effectively took about $100 billion a year out of the economy and delivered most of it to the stock market with only a part of that sum recycled into the economy. In addition to the volatile and impatient money that these mistakes caused, the government in the last quarter of the 20th century compounded the problem by deregulating finance capitalism at the same time it was abrogating the market disciplines upon which free markets depend.

Instead of a new era of democratic capitalism, these mistakes ushered in the age of ultra-capitalism in which workers were treated as cost commodities, speculators with borrowed money became more powerful than central bankers, and Wall Street wrote the rules. Instead of leading the world towards economic freedom, the United States government encouraged the gravitational pull of speculation and short-term and greedy ultra-capitalism. As a result, the U.S. leapt into the bubble economy of the 1990s, many emerging economies had their economic momentum reversed with dire social consequences, and the United States became an economic imperialist with a cop-of-the-world attitude that provoked acts of violence and a growing populist revolt.

The optimism of the early 1990s, that the twenty-first would be the first century when humans learned how to stop the violence, receded and began to disappear. I have already cited in the introduction to chapter 1 Yale Professor Paul Kennedy's warning that the twenty-first century presents challenges that can be met only by educated citizens and wise leadership.[159] I cite Ludwig von Mises, in this chapter, to the same conclusion: The fate of the world is tied to the ability of citizens to organize their society based on sound economic principles. Both observers of society are emphatic that ignoring this opportunity could lead to catastrophic results. These warnings have been ignored, and as was tragically demonstrated on 9-11, the twenty-first century has had a terrible beginning. We still have time to save ourselves, but the dangers are growing more threatening, and the time is growing shorter.

Reform of the American system is vital to realizing the world's opportunity for economic and social advances. This can be accomplished by a return to the theories of economic freedom stated by Adam Smith. This time, however, the government must control

---

[159] Paul M. Kennedy, *Preparing for the Twenty-first Century* (New York: Random House, 1994), p. 349.

currency and credit for the benefit of general welfare, not for the privileged few.

Efforts at reform are complicated, however, by a political right that supports leveraged speculation with volatile and impatient money, while the political left ignores reform of macroeconomics in favor of microeconomic intrusions into the free market. The resulting gridlock has produced what I call the "Great American Inversion": Monetary matters that should be controlled are freed; commercial matters that should be free are controlled.

Penetration and resolution of this political-economic paradox is the obligation of American citizens who must influence the universities and schools to educate the next generation concerning democratic capitalism. Action is required, also, by institutional investors, those who manage and invest the collective wealth of the workforce in pension and retirement funds. The institutional investors are potential agents of change who can most immediately and forcefully redirect the economic system from ultra-capitalism to democratic capitalism, and turn the world away from more folly and violence and towards peace and plenty.

The Way to Peace and Plenty according to the Economic Logic of Adam Smith

Adam Smith expressed this belief in free markets:

Little else is required to carry a state to the highest degree of opulence from the lowest barbarism but peace, easy taxes, and a tolerable administration of justice; all the rest being brought about by the natural course of things.[160]

Human history had been dominated by a frequently violent struggle over scarce resources. Adam Smith foresaw elimination of this material scarcity by way of a self-sustaining dynamic for economic growth from a combination of private property, competition, involved workers, increased productivity from the

---

[160] Adam Smith, *An Inquiry into the Nature and Causes of the Wealth of Nations* (New York Modern Library, 1937), p. xiii.

Industrial Revolution, consumers with a free choice in spending their money, and producers with free choice over what to produce and at what price to sell. In this dynamic, costs would go down, competition would assure that lower costs were passed on in lower prices, the lower prices would attract new consumers now able to purchase, the added volume from these additional consumers would require more wage earners and provide the critical mass to reduce costs further, these lower costs would be passed along to new consumers, and this would require another round of more wage-earning producers. At each stage, the consumers who had the affluence to purchase at the earlier higher prices would then have money made available for other purchases or savings. In this fashion, wealth would spread worldwide, providing jobs, producing better products, and improving the quality of life. Strong, stable, economic growth would then generate tax revenues for governments to invest wisely in education, health, the environment, and other matters not directly addressed by the free market.

Smith foresaw the energy released by free markets naturally building and spreading wealth. Smith proposed that an "invisible hand" is at work within the commercial enterprise that results in a positive effect in society that the business persons probably does not have in mind when conducting business. The pursuit of profit and excellence in a given business thus redounds to the general good of society in which each entrepreneur "neither intends to promote the public interest, nor knows how much he is promoting it, and he is in this led by an invisible hand to promote an end that was no part of his intention."[161] Smith mentioned this "invisible hand" only once in his *Wealth of Nations,* placing more emphasis on the "natural course of things" energized by involved, well-paid workers, competition, private property, and a government that did not intrude in the process but did assure a supply of nonvolatile, patient capital to allow the "invisible hand" to do its good work.

Smith's dynamic is the core of democratic capitalism and free markets. When the culture and politics are properly aligned in its support, then the world will be well on the way to peace and plenty. The cultural assimilation of this ideal for social progress depends on

---

[161] *Ibid.,* p. 423.

presentation to students beginning at the earliest age. Smith's dynamic of work and wealth is not so complex that it requires years of study, but time and hard work is needed to understand the impediments; moreover, enthusiasm for this economic ideal needs to be instilled in open minds in order to inspire a hope for social progress and a will to sustain democratic reform.

The success of Smith's radical vision was premised on commerce free of government intervention, and a monetary system protected from speculators. A low-cost, ample, non-volatile, and patient monetary system could be the product of free banking, as practiced in Scotland at the time of Smith, or by government regulation supported by market disciplines that assured that banks that make too many imprudent loans would go out of business or be severely punished.

Adam Smith published *The Wealth of Nations* in 1776, the same year that Thomas Jefferson and the Founders wrote the American *Declaration of Independence*. Smith felt that America had fashioned the best arrangement of economic and political freedoms for his vision to become a reality. He was correct, for during the next two centuries, the United States demonstrated to the world the power of freedom harnessed in the coupling of democracy and capitalism. Michael Novak, one of the first to present democratic capitalism effectively, commented as follows on the American experience:

> In 1776, the time of the *Wealth of Nations*, the embryonic U. S. had already shown the world that the poverty of the poor is not irremediable. In the colonies, a beneficent system was enabling millions of the poor to rise steadily from poverty, supported by the charity of the public. In this way, the example of the U.S. changed history. No longer could the poverty of millions simply be dismissed as an unalterable fact of human existence, perhaps even willed by God ("The poor ye shall always have with you" was long used as an excuse.) The U.S. thus became the first developing nation. What made it so, Smith saw, was its system. The people who came here had worked just as hard in Europe. They had been just as virtuous. But here the

new political economy did not frustrate their work and their good habits. What was the new system? It was democratic in its political part and capitalist in its economic part. Its unprecedented liberties were both political and economic. These together opened up liberties of conscience, information, and ideas. Democratic capitalism signals that the polity and the economy need each other, support each other, gain from each other.[162]

At the beginning, the momentum from economic freedom in the United States was primarily agricultural. Jefferson made the Louisiana Purchase to provide land for his favorite citizens: independent, educated, hard-working, virtuous farmers. Jefferson had a distrust of manufacturing because he had viewed it only in its mercantilist phase in Europe. The wage-slaves of mercantilism living in poverty did not fit his profile of citizens in the new democratic republic. Smith understood Jefferson's theory of political freedom, but Jefferson did not understand Smith's theory of economic freedom that could raise the quality of life for manufacturing workers. Freedoms in America were, nonetheless, sufficient to allow manufacturing to grow, but many years would pass before the associates of democratic capitalism, who matched the profile of Jefferson's independent farmers, could displace the wage-slaves of mercantilism.

The Supply-and-Demand Logic of Democratic Capitalism

The unique socio-economic symbiosis of democracy and capitalism is apparent in the positive effect on both the supply side and the demand side of the economic equation. The supply side, the production of goods and services, depends on ample, low-cost, non-volatile, patient capital, a high savings rate, educated workers, fair regulation, no non-democratic privileges, and taxes designed for the benefit of the general welfare. The demand side, the consumption of products and services, is supported by full employment and broad

---

[162] Michael Novak, "A Phrase with a Ring," *Forbes*, August 7, 1989, p. 56.

wealth distribution. Democratic capitalism supports both sides of the economic equation with an economic logic that eliminates material scarcity, and a social logic that improves the quality of lives in these ways:

- Supply-side production is improved with the productivity and innovation of involved wage earners who are motivated by profit-sharing and ownership.

- Broad wealth distribution from profit-sharing, dividends, and equity appreciation is recycled into spending that is beneficial to the demand side because wage earners buy the commodities with the greatest multiplier effect for *steady* economic growth.

- Broad wealth distribution from profit-sharing, dividends, and equity appreciation improves wage earners' savings; this supports the supply side with patient capital for more growth through investment in equipment, facilities, and human capital.

- As growth and profits are maximized, more wealth is produced, benefiting the demand side by increased spending.

- Worldwide job growth follows Adam Smith's economic dynamic when motivated workers combine their efforts with new technology to reduce the cost to produce. Competition insures that this cost savings is passed on to the consumer in lower prices. New consumers can then afford to buy, thus adding more sales, which requires more wage earners to produce more goods, which generates more spendable income, and this causes another iteration of cost-reduction through economies of scale.

- Reciprocal purchases, the *sine qua non* of free trade, are made possible by broad wealth distribution in all countries by way of profit-sharing, ownership opportunities, and large-dividend income inherent in democratic capitalism.

- A more efficient government structured on the principles of participatory democracy and utilizing Information Age technology, could substantially reduce personal income taxes. If corporations and speculators, instead of being privileged by the government, were fairly taxed by the government, the tax burden would be lifted from wage earners, small business owners, and entrepreneurs. Part of this wealth returned to the people would be spent to the benefit of the demand side, and part of it would be invested to the benefit of the supply side.

- The greatest self-development of each in democratic capitalism depends on high-quality, continuous education. Education and training bring more people into the work force, converting many who might otherwise receive tax dollars through public welfare into tax-paying wage earners. The wages of these new workers add to the demand side; the capital freed by lower taxes then becomes available for growth investment, strengthening the supply side.

- Investment in environmental and physical infrastructural needs can help the supply side. Wages associated with this area of investment will build demand. Cooperatively planned environmental investment can raise economic living standards as well as the quality of life.

- When finance capitalism is subordinate to democratic capitalism, capital flows to investment in economic growth and is not deflected and wasted in speculation. This redirection of capital benefits the supply side while the additional investment in growth adds to the demand side.

- Inflation is neutralized in democratic capitalism because incremental compensation is based on productivity. The resulting lower cost of capital for growth benefits the supply side in general and stimulates growth in whole industries, such as house construction.

- The supply side will make its own demand through worldwide economic growth and full employment as eventually billions more people become wage earners and consumers.

- With modest deficits, full employment, low inflation, low interest, and balanced trade, all possible with democratic capitalism, nations can agree on a harmonizing mechanism to stabilize currencies. The elimination of volatility in the international monetary system can minimize the deflection of capital into speculation. Financial stability then provides the supply side with the necessary component for long-term investment in economic growth.

- Restraint of short-term bank loans for long-term investment and control of leveraged speculation will help eliminate economic crises, such as those in the Southeast Asian countries in the late 1990s. Avoiding these crises will eliminate the extreme currency devaluation that leads to the competitive wage devaluation among countries that severely hurts the demand side.

- The spreading affluence and broad education inherent in democratic capitalism can help moderate ethnic and religious animosities. The common purpose of a better standard of living and a better quality of life for all can finally defeat the greatest enemy of social progress, war, thereby benefiting both the supply and demand sides while offering society a realistic opportunity to reach its full potential.

- The benefits of economic freedom are available to all cultures because they can be provided under either democratic or secular authoritarian governments.

- When the government controls currency and credit for the general welfare, the economically and socially damaging boom/bust cycle will be eliminated.

- The cycle in which economic distress helps cause wars, and wars help cause economic distress, will be broken.

- As the ideal of world peace and plenty becomes realistic through economic common purpose, the world can demilitarize, thereby freeing trillions of dollars for investment in education, training, environmental needs, and aid to poor nations for better health and economic growth.

The Economic Logic of the Broad Distribution of Wealth

What is the difference between Tanzania and Goldman Sachs? One is an African country that makes $2.2 billion a year and shares it among 25 million people. The other is an investment bank that makes $2.6 billion and shares it among 161 people.[163]

Adam Smith and, later, Karl Marx and John Stuart Mill all emphasized that broad wealth distribution is a critical necessity for the success of economic freedom, for these reasons:

- People cannot be motivated to produce and innovate unless they share in the improved results.

- Maximum economic growth can be attained only when wealth is distributed to the wage earners who purchase the commodities that energize Adam Smith's economic perpetual-motion machine.

---

[163] John Miklethwait and Adrian Wooldridge, "It Could Happen Again," *Forbes ASAP*, August 21, 2000, p. 186.

- Broad wealth distribution, necessary to spread wealth to all parts of the world, allows people to make the reciprocal purchases upon which the success of free trade depends.

- Broad wealth distribution helps unify people and reduce the social tensions that cause war and violence.

- Diffusion of economic power is fundamental to the diffusion of political power that is prerequisite to an open, democratic society.

Despite the clarity of this logic, the most persistent impediment to worldwide economic growth throughout history has been the inequitable distribution of wealth. For most of this time, a zero-sum battle has been fought between those who held the capital and those who performed the labor. Those with the capital had the mercantilist idea that their return on capital would go up as their cost of labor went down, and they accomplished this through capital investment and wage suppression. Industry copied the hierarchical and fearful, top-down organizational structure from government and the military, thereby precluding the release of the productivity and innovation of the people. Mercantilists ignored the advice of Smith, Marx, and Mill, and the evidence of Robert Owen (see chapter 3), that profits are maximized by elevating people when they are motivated to reach their full potential and rewarded on the basis of improved performance.

The realization that elevating people means elevating profits was arrived at from different directions. Owen had demonstrated it at New Lanark a generation after Adam Smith; some found it by studying the *Communist Manifesto,* which says: "We shall have an association, in which the free development of each is the condition for the free development of all;"[164] some found it in W. Edwards Deming's "Fourteen Points" which emphasize that industrial excellence is attained only by the participation of all in a cooperative environment. Most managers who found it were self-taught

---

[164] Karl Marx and Friedrich Engels, *The Communist Manifesto* (New York: Penguin Classics, 1985, originally published in London, 1848), p. 105.

democratic capitalists in companies like those honored by *Fortune* as the "100 Best" (see chapter 4), self-reliant people of commerce who had to reinvent democratic capitalism by trial and error because neither the public schools nor the Business Schools were teaching it.

Adam Smith distinguished between, on the one hand, wage earners' purchases that energize the wealth-creation dynamic (the so-called "multiplier effect"), and on the other hand, the purchase of luxuries by the wealthy that have little multiplier effect. The former generate the additional volume that drives costs and prices down, consistent with Smith's economic dynamic; the latter lack this critical-mass effect.

Smith also warned that the demand side would be damaged by hoarding, or passive investment, in contrast to the later theory of aggregate demand put forward by David Ricardo (1772-1823) and Jean-Baptiste Say (1767-1832), who stated that whether money goes to the wealthy, to the poor, to the middle class, to consumption, or to savings, all of it eventually goes back into the economy. This proposition has been favored by the wealthy who have found it useful in their lobbying for lower taxes, claiming that more wealth for the already wealthy will help the economy.

Jean-Baptiste Say, French businessman and professor, is credited with the free-market law of aggregate demand. John Kenneth Galbraith commented: "Say's law held that out of the production of goods came an effective (that is, actually expended) aggregate of demand sufficient to purchase the total supply of goods. No more, or less."[165]

David Ricardo, Say's English contemporary, made his money as a stockbroker and then, with the encouragement of J.S. Mill's father, wrote on economic matters. He is remembered for the "Iron Law of Wages," that, according to Galbraith, "established that those who worked were meant to be poor and were not to be rescued from their poverty, and from this controlling law would come the commitment to the inevitable misery of those who live under capitalism."[166]

---

[165] John Kenneth Galbraith, *Economics in Perspective: A Critical History* (Boston: Houghton Mifflin Company, 1987), p. 75.

[166] *Ibid.*, p. 85.

Just as Adam Smith has been badly translated as an apologist for greed, so also have other contributors to economic lore been similarly badly translated. For example, Say also celebrated the entrepreneur's stimulation of economic improvement, and Ricardo predicted that capital investment in technology would improve the standard of living of the workers. Neither thinker is well remembered for these more optimistic contributions.

John Maynard Keynes commented on the opportunistic interpretation by the wealthy and powerful of Say's and Ricardo's "laws":

> That its teaching, translated into practice, was austere and often unpalatable, lent it virtue. That it was adapted to carry a vast and consistent logical superstructure, gave it beauty. That it could explain much social injustice and apparent cruelty as an inevitable incident in the scheme of progress, and the attempt to change such things as likely on the whole to do more harm than good, commended it to authority. That it afforded a measure of justification to the free activities of the individual capitalist attracted to it the support of the dominant social force behind authority.[167]

Economists agree on little, including the multiplier effect. Is it not clear, nevertheless, that $100 million of surplus distributed in $1,000 packages to 100,000 workers will generate a multiplier effect much greater than the same amount in $1 million packages distributed to 100 millionaires? This "law" of the broad distribution of wealth, however, is contrary to the "law" of aggregate demand. The additional money distributed to wage earners energizes Smith's economic dynamic because it adds volume, provides jobs, drives prices down, generates more jobs, and sustains the economic dynamic of spreading wealth. The amounts expected to trickle-down from the millionaires are spent by them, instead, either on luxuries and stock

---

[167] John Maynard Keynes, *The General Theory of Employment, Interest, and Money* (New York: Harvest/HBJ, 1964; first published in London, 1935), pp. 32-3.

portfolios or, as Smith put it, the money spent by the rich goes into services that "vanish in the act of performance." The flaw of the trickle-down theory is that it produces, in fact, not much more than a trickle. Only a small portion reaches the level of job production needed to activate Smith's economic perpetual-motion machine.

During the 1930s, Henry Ford's economic epiphany is a dramatic example of how broader wealth distribution had an energizing effect on the economy. Ford viewed the supply/demand equation as his black Model T's were rolling along the assembly line. His revelation came when Ford realized that he could make hundreds of thousands of these cars, but only if his own workers could afford to buy them. Ford raised his employees' wages to the extraordinary level of $5 a day not because he was either a social philosopher or a Professor of Economics but because he was a pragmatist. His action was Adam Smith's "invisible hand" in action. Whatever the motivation, Ford's action of enlightened self-interest followed sound economic and social logic: When wages go up, consumer demand goes up, the economy goes up, and social tensions go down.

In the late 1990s, the Japanese government spent heavily trying to energize Japan's economy; at the same time, they also raised their sales tax from 3% to 5%, a regressive tax that hurt consumer demand. During Japan's strong economic growth, few companies recognized the importance of domestic demand and broad wealth distribution. Few Japanese corporations incorporated profit sharing and ownership opportunities that would have built demand and the domestic economy. The Japanese tried to grow their economy mainly through exports in selected and subsidized industries. At the beginning of the new century, Toyota was sitting on $19 billion of surplus cash that could have gone to the workers in wages, profit-sharing, and dividends, had Toyota been as sharp as Ford. Instead, in 2001, Japan changed the law to allow Toyota to use this surplus to buy back stock in order to prop up the stock market. This is an example of how latter-day American-style ultra-capitalism, instead of Ford-style capitalism that benefits the worker, has spread the economic infection around the world. The Japanese would be better off today if they had imitated Ford and learned about broad wealth distribution.

The Economic Logic of the Capitalism that Combines Income from Large Dividends, Long-Term Appreciation in Stock Value, and Security for the Wage-Earner's Retirement Money

The rewards of capitalism should be balanced among income, appreciation, and security. When the priority use of surplus cash is large dividends, second only to reinvestment in growth, then the investor will take a longer view of appreciation, and capitalism will be relieved of the bad practices associated with exclusive concern with the short-term price of the stock. This more patient view of the price of the stock will reduce the volatility of the market, and this, in combination with a good annual return in dividends, will improve the safety of the investment.

Dividends have historically been an important part of the rewards of capitalism. With their steady recycling of the surplus of capitalism, they have built consumer demand and sustained steady economic growth in contrast to the wild swings and damaging effects caused by exclusive concern with the stock price. Financial analyst A. Gary Schilling described the historical pattern: "The impact of higher dividends is hard to ignore: For the 46 years through December 1991, the Dow Industrials rose 6.1% per year in price but delivered an 11.2% total return with dividends included."[168] Financial analyst Robert J. Schiller commented as follows about the importance of dividends:

> Dividends historically represent the dominant part of the average return on stocks. The reliable return attributable to dividends, not the less predictable portion arising from capital gains, is the main reason why stocks have on average been such good investments.[169]

Dividends are wonderfully flexible because they can be spent, saved, or reinvested in more stock. In the twenty-first century, because the major source of capital is now broadly based in pension

---

[168] A. Gary Shilling, "Dividends Back in Style," *Forbes*, May 27, 2002.

[169] Robert J. Shiller, *Irrational Exuberance* (New York: Broadway Books, 2000), p.13.

funds and 401(k) savings, the money recycled to the economy in dividends can be an even more important part of wealth distribution, spent with a strong multiplier effect on economic growth, or saved in patient capital reinvested for companies to grow on. Only start-up, fast-growth companies that need all of their cash to grown on are exempt from the obligation to pay large dividends.

With the annual influx of cash from pension funding and 401(k) savings, and the efficiencies of the Information Age, the U.S. economy at the turn of the century was awash in cash. For example, IBM had used over $44 billion to buy back stock during the decade of the 1990s. Despite this strong cash flow, companies did not significantly increase their dividends because Wall Street does not favor dividends. Wall Street makes commissions when investors buy or sell a stock, not when a company increases or pays a dividend. Wall Street favors "churning," buying and selling as often as possible; and Wall Street believes that dividends do not help the price of the stock. The short-term effect on the price of stock, however, should not be the question; rather, the focus should be on whether larger dividends generate a better long-term return for stockholders, encourage the use of the stock market as a source of new equity capital, encourage the spread of employee ownership plans, and accelerate the growth of the domestic and world economies.

From the early 1980s to the turn of the century, the dividend yield dropped from over 6% to under 1%. Wall Street's low priority for dividends was demonstrated also by a drop in the percentage of earnings paid out in dividends, which "fell from a postwar average of 50% to 30% in the third quarter of 2000."[170] Dividends have the following positive benefits:

- Dividends of 6% reward wage earners for buying a share in ownership, and through these ownership plans, dividends further democratize capitalism.

- Large dividends, combined with a conservative estimate of long-term appreciation, provide opportunity for secure

---

[170] Shilling, *op. cit.*, p.170.

double-digit return for wage earners' pensions and 401(k) savings.

- Large dividends recycle surplus money to the economy, build domestic demand, and sustain *steady* economic growth.

- Dividends can be reinvested in more stock, which is *patient* capital for further economic growth.

- Large dividends, extended to emerging economies through profit-sharing and ownership plans, add spendable income for reciprocal purchases upon which free trade depends.

- Large dividends can bring the stock market into a more healthy balance by reducing exclusive concern with stock price.

- Large dividends give appropriate attention to high-quality, slow-growth companies. Expectation that all companies, at all times, will grow sales rapidly is unrealistic.

Besides these positive benefits, large regular dividends neutralize the following corruptions of ultra-capitalism:

- The balance of income and appreciation moves capitalism away from the single-minded focus on quarterly and annual e.p.s. that has corrupted companies' long-term programs as well as the integrity of the financial reports.

- Large dividends move the stock market away from causing volatility and impatience in money, both contradictions to the needs of the free market.

- The stock-market speculation craze will be changed over time to interest in investment and long-term growth by the payment of large dividends.

- Stock buy-backs and non-strategic acquisitions artificially affect the buy/sell balance by reducing the total amount of stock in the market. Distribution of surplus in dividends eliminates this distortion and, through more equity financing, adds stock to the market further normalizing the buy/sell equation.

- A conversion of the stock market from speculation to investment will reduce the extreme P/E ratios that stimulate companies to acquire other companies for the short-term earnings spurt.

- A conversion of the stock market from speculation to investment will eliminate the extreme swings that always favor the wealthy few in the up direction and hurt the many in the down direction.

- A conversion of the market to investment, and away from speculation, will encourage more issues of new stock for growth capital.

A shift to large dividends would, therefore, result in numerous benefits that would further democratize capitalism and neutralize the damage from ultra-capitalism. The shift could be rapid and effective. The actions required to achieve this shift are as follows:

- A change in the tax laws to eliminate the double taxation penalty on dividends.

- A change in tax laws to give additional benefits in both dividend income and capital gains for low-and-middle-income wage earners in ownership plans.

- Additional benefits in the tax laws on dividends and capital gains for pension and 401(k) savings.

- A change in capital gains tax law to penalize further short-term gains and reward long-term holdings.

- Recognition by institutional investors that their fiduciary responsibility requires support of the combination of income, appreciation, and security that begins with large dividends.

- An understanding of democratic capitalism that can energize a populist lobby to implement these specific reforms, and counteract the lobby power of Wall Street.

In early 2003, both the world's most powerful man and the world's wealthiest man made moves to democratize capitalism through the distribution of surplus in larger dividends. President Bush proposed to Congress that it eliminate the double taxation of dividends, and Bill Gates, founder of Microsoft, declared the first dividend payment in his company's history. President Bush had been impressed with arguments favoring more dividends, but typical of his Administration he packaged the tax relief in a way that benefited primarily the wealthy.

Microsoft, an Information Age industry leader, is so strong that they can support investment in growth and still accumulate a cash pile of $43.4 billion with another $1 billion a month flowing in. The conditioning by Wall Street has been so anti-dividend, however, that high-growth companies like Microsoft have been embarrassed to declare dividends, fearing that the action would be construed as an admission that they were slowing down. For example, the financial press commented that the new Microsoft dividend "does not seem to be a concession that the hi-tech growth company is slowing down." Later in the article, Microsoft's CFO "bridled at any suggestion that the dividend decision meant Microsoft was shifting to a slow-growth track."[171]

Because of this Wall Street pressure to use cash for stock buy-backs or as a stimulus for mergers, capitalism in the latter part of the 20th century lost the proper balance among income, appreciation, and security. Trillions of dollars that could have sustained economic

---

[171] Steve Lohr, "In a Surprise, Microsoft Says It Will Pay a Dividend," *The Wall Street Journal*, January 17, 2003, p. C1.

growth or added to wage earners' retirement money was wasted. This exclusive concentration on the short-term price of the stock drove the bubble economy, caused another damaging, unnecessary boom/bust cycle, and set the tone for social tensions.

The Twenty-First Century Potential for Greater, Steadier Economic Growth

The ideal and the means of an economic system that can eliminate material scarcity, elevate spirits, and unify people have been validated over the past two centuries. The world, however, still functions at a fraction of its economic and social potential due to a lack of understanding of the impediments that block economic freedom, and the lack of public will to eliminate the impediments. According to the theory of democratic capitalism, the means to eliminate the impediments begins with the involvement of educated, independent-thinking, motivated associates who become engaged in improving their companies, or by the actions of the same people who, as citizens, vote for elected representatives who will run the country in ways that promote and complement the benefits of democratic capitalism. In any form of governance or commerce, participation releases the enormous potential of the people to produce, innovate, and cooperate. No part of the world lacks this potential, neither the most disease-ridden parts of Africa devoid of infrastructure nor those nations fractured by sectarian groups full of hatred and violence.

The economic potential of democratic capitalism is not a matter of one- or two-percent improvement; it can be ten or fifteen percent or even more, as Robert Owen described it! (see chapter 3). Until very recently, however, optimism for growth like this has been contrary to the view taken by most economists. Basing their growth projections on economic history, they concluded that mature economies, such as the United States, could grow at only a 2.4% annual rate, half from growth in the labor pool, half from productivity. At the same time, economists were struggling to find a new rationale and method of measurement to explain the productivity surge resulting from the Information Age revolution.

The selective historical review of many economists led them to assume that the potential of people, companies, nations, and the world would continue to be suppressed by the same suffocating principles that had resulted in the historical failure to reach anything more than a fraction of full potential. Visionaries then, more than economists, are needed to extrapolate the productivity and growth from Information Age industries and the democratic capitalist culture to the system as a whole.

If world leaders in the twenty-first century give priority to planning for a continuation of violence rather than for economic common purpose, then further violence is inevitable. Similarly, if fiscal and monetary policy-makers assume that the same level of potential will be reached in the future that was reached in the past, then society will never reach its full potential. Stronger growth can insure full employment, a rising standard of living, adequate surplus to invest on behalf of those people who are not supported by the economy, and funds to pay for protection of the environment. None of these ends can be accomplished if the means are not in place to make them happen. At every level of society, the question is this: Shall we extrapolate the foolish and violent past, guaranteeing that we will repeat it, or shall we plan carefully to reach the ideal? Those who regard "planning" as a threatening expression must recognize that the planning implied in democratic capitalism fosters an environment that frees the system and frees the people.

The opposite argument of some protestors and demonstrators, that somehow the ill effects of "globalization" and ultra-capitalism can be defeated if we hunker down, keep it small and inefficient, and resist the juggernaut of worldwide economic interdependence, is the least likely ideology of all to achieve success. Ultra-capitalism will not be defeated by throwing sand into the machine; it will be defeated only by presenting a superior form of commerce.

Maximizing economic growth is fundamental to any government's effort to protect and enhance the commonwealth. However, in the United States, maximum economic growth has historically been seen as a source of inflation. Inherent in this fear of inflation is a rejection of the concept that such growth and rapidly rising compensation could be productivity based and not inflationary. The cruel paradox is that the government has not promoted democratic capitalism by favorable tax policies; consequently, productivity has been limited. Economists then use low productivity, much of it the result of the adversarial zero-sum battle between capital and labor, to predict future limited productivity.

Government programs cause inflation that then provoke other programs that slow growth in order to fight inflation. This was dramatically demonstrated when President Johnson's "Guns and Butter" program caused inflation, followed by Fed Chairman Paul Volcker's scorched-earth fight against the inflation that Johnson's policies had caused. The consequences of the extraordinarily high interest from these uncoordinated government actions included the bankrupting of several South American countries on floating interest rates, and decimation of the whole S&L industry that was borrowing high-cost short-term money to invest in long-term low-return mortgages (see chapter 7).

Fiscal and monetary policy continues to allow leveraged speculation that regularly devastates the economy, followed by policies that further slow the economy. The economic history of the United States is one of swings from speculation to recession caused by the speculation. The government's mistake in not controlling speculation causes economic distress, and then the government adds to its mistakes by trying to fix the banking system with actions that further slow the economy and hurt ordinary people.

Citizens must, therefore, come to understand the importance of these targeted growth rates. A *steady* 3.5% GDP growth rate will raise the standard of living for all, and fiscal and monetary policies should be designed to meet this target. At the end of the 20th century, however, well-known economists such as Alan Blinder were still lecturing the unsophisticated about the realities that cause slow growth. Blinder, former Vice-Chair of the Federal Reserve, scolded optimistic CEOs who insisted that the United States economy could grow over 3% annually. Blinder and most economists at that time pointed out that 1.2% improvement in productivity plus 1.2% increase in the labor force had to add up to no more than 2.4%, but their argument reflects historical patterns that have none of the dynamics of the Information Age. In 1997, Blinder described non-economist CEOs in these terms:

> They did not want harsh realities intruding upon and
> ruining their dreams. Based on some simple arithmetic

that I will display shortly, mainstream economists are exceptionally united right now around the proposition that the trend growth rate of real gross domestic product (GDP) in the United States, the rate at which the unemployment rate neither rises or falls, is in the 2 percent to 2.5 percent range.[172]

Professor Blinder thus decreed that the United States and the world could not begin to reach greater economic potential. Many of the unsophisticated CEOs who had been predicting fast growth, however, were involved with explosive growth in Information Age industries. They knew from experience with their own operations that the world now had opportunities for growth and improved productivity never before seen.

The 1.2% labor-pool growth limit proposed by most economists seems to have more logic to it than does the 1.2% productivity figure, but it still has room to grow. Many who have been effectively disenfranchised by the lack of good education represent an opportunity both for our society to honor the democratic promise to these citizens and to add to the labor pool at the same time. In the United States, an investment in education and training of this group represents a large overdue bill that neither political party is willing to address in its totality.

Many traditional economists were wrong about productivity because they looked only in the rear-view mirror. That the assumption of a 1.2% growth in the labor pool might be historically accurate is no argument in favor of its being canonized as a rigid rule. Countries such as Germany and Japan experience limited growth because their populations are not growing, and because they limit immigration. America, by contrast, is a multicultural, open society whose job opportunities and personal freedoms are magnets to people from other countries. Other factors also will predictably add to the labor pool: longer life spans, flexible work time, and technology that allow people to work at home.

---

[172] Alan Blinder, "The Speed Limit, Fact and Fancy in the Growth Debate," *The American Prospect*, September-October, 1997, p. 57.

By the beginning of the twenty-first century, many economists had gone to the other extreme exaggerating the productivity potential from the Information Age:

> Until recently, some Fed officials have suggested that they felt the gross domestic product couldn't safely grow faster than about 3.5% to 4% a year. The new data seem to indicate that, for the foreseeable future at least, the economy could grow 4% to 4.5%, or possibly higher. The Commerce Department said Friday that the economy grew at a 5.3% annual pace in the 2000 April-to-June quarter.[173]

This important subject is clouded by the government's inability to keep score on the Information Age without using its technology. On October 28, 1999, the Commerce Department changed the score all the way back to the Carter Administration:

> Productivity growth from 1981, when Reagan took office, to 1989, when he left, was 1.6%, far faster than Carter's 0.8% rate. Productivity rose at a 1.7% rate in Bush's term, and in the first four years of the Clinton administration, it rose at a 1.8% rate before soaring by an estimated 2.8% in 1998 and 1999.[174]

Business people who had predicted high growth proved right, whereas many economists were proved wrong, both arithmetically and philosophically because they had ridiculed the business executives instead of listening and learning. The effect of Information Age technology is profound, but the learning curve slows productivity for a few years before increasing it. The radical restructure of entire administrative, financial, distribution, and warehousing systems takes time, costs money, and works poorly unless the operations people are

---

[173] Jacob Schlesinger, "Fed Signals Comfort with Faster Growth," *The Wall Street Journal*, August 28, 2000, p. C1.

[174] Michael J. Mandel, "How Most Economists Missed the Boat," *Business Week*, November 15, 1999, p. 102.

retrained in technique and attitude. Capital demands, the availability of people with the requisite technical knowledge, and the ability to manage change, can spread a restructuring effort over five years.

Unfortunately the government's inability properly to measure GDP growth leaves a potential range from 2.4% to over 5%, a range too broad for policy determination. The economists and government officials that have been underestimating for years now are overestimating productivity. The surge of real productivity resulting from the Information Age revolution is wonderful, but the measurement of output-per-hour of all non-farm business can be inflated by downsizing, movement to low-wage countries, extensive use of part-timers, overtime, and outsourcing. The numbers also obscure the increasing maldistribution of wealth because productivity has improved partly because real wages in manufacturing went down for two decades.[175]

Despite the confusion in economists' scorekeeping, an extraordinary opportunity is emerging: The United States economy can, I affirm, grow 3.5% per year in a non-inflationary, *steady* fashion. With the economy growing at this steady rate, unemployment will be minimal, and tax revenues will be sufficient to take care of those on the margin of the economic growth.

The Economic Logic of Free Trade

The dynamic for sustained economic growth described by Adam Smith includes private property, competition, motivation for workers to maximize surplus, and the broad distribution of wealth. The same fundamentals support the economic logic of free trade that can be the interdependent experience that improves lives and unifies people in a nation or across national borders. In developing countries, wages at barely a subsistence level, by contrast, can neither stimulate domestic demand nor provide for the reciprocal purchases upon which free trade depends.

The United States government has free-trade experts who promote exciting targets for world trade through the World Trade

---

[175] Jeff Gates, *Democracy at Risk* (Cambridge, Massachusetts: Perseus Publishing 2000), p. xiv.

Organization (WTO). Robert Zoellick handled the trade talks at both NAFTA and the Uruguay round meeting during 1989-1992 while at the State Department, and he later became the United States Trade Representative whose mission was to achieve free trade around the world. "He pressed Congress to enact the Trade Act of 2002 which re-established the vital trade authority ("fast track") that had lapsed for eight years."[176] In November 2000, Zoellick helped launch the Doha Development Agenda at Doha, Qatar, that includes specific and aggressive targets for free trade expansion. For example, farm tariffs between 2002 and 2010 are targeted to be reduced as follows: United States from 6% to 2%; Europe from 28% to 8%; Japan from 46% to 8%; South Korea from 62% to 14%; and India from 115% to 20%.[177]

The U.S. proposal in 2002 would free the world of all manufacturing tariffs by 2015. This proposal would eliminate the barriers between developing countries that pay 20% tariffs on manufactured goods. The *Economist* enthused: "By eliminating barriers to the farm and manufactured-goods trade, the income of the developing world could be boosted by over $500 billion." America also proposed greater free trade for the growing service industries that in 2002 represented 80% of the U.S. economy but only 20% of world trade. "The World Bank had pointed out that eliminating services barriers in developing countries alone would yield them a $900 billion gain."[178]

These are exciting and attainable goals, but they are dependent on governments' giving priority to the world's economic growth, not wars and the power-plays of geo-politics. Their attainment also depends on adoption of democratic capitalism and the purging of ultra-capitalism. Ernesto Zedillo, the former President of Mexico, commented on this urgency:

> Commitments to free trade by all WTO members and more enlightened leadership from the U.S. and the EU are the essential ingredients for avoiding the collapse of the Doha

---

[176] "Unleashing the Trade Winds," *The Economist*, December 7, 2002, p. 27.

[177] *Ibid.*, p. 28.

[178] *Loc. cit.*

round. Preventing this disaster is in everybody's best interest.[179]

When Adam Smith and his good friend, David Hume, described the benefits of free trade, they were responding to positive experiences after the tariff walls had been eliminated by the unification of England and Scotland in the early eighteenth century. They were also reacting, on the other hand, to the protectionism that had caused food riots. Both Smith and Hume rejected the British concept of managing imports and exports with the Colonies in order to maintain a favorable trade balance, a policy that governments favored in order to hoard hard currency to fund the next war. Smith's and Hume's advice was largely ignored; not until 1840 was the Corn Law repealed, a cause for continued misery and repetitive food riots.

Free trade, as viewed by Smith and Hume, is an extrapolation of the basic economic dynamic that benefits consumers by lowering prices. Free trade can lead the world to peace and plenty, but only if all of the components are in place, in order, and at work: workers with profit-sharing and ownership; free consumer choice; free producer choice; no tariffs or subsidies; private property; competition; low-cost, ample, non-volatile, patient capital; and resolution of the current paradox: Trade that should be free is controlled, and money that should be controlled is free.

Since World War II, the United States has traded foreign access to the U.S. market for political hegemony. That is, market access is granted in exchange for a continued American military or political presence in many parts of the world. This intrusion into free trade may have been defensible in the face of Russia's pretensions to world domination, but post-Cold-War continuation of this policy damages the momentum of economic freedom and heightens international tensions. What started as a protection for world democracy has mutated into a new form of imperialism, and many people abroad, both friends and enemies, resent the policy. This policy has also contributed to a current account deficit, an excess of

---

[179] Ernesto Zedillo, "Will the Doha Round Implode in 2003?" *Forbes*, February 3, 2003, p. 29.

imports over exports, that is setting new records in the new century, an additional threat to the U.S, economy.

In the early 1980s, the United States shifted from being the world's largest creditor nation, to whom others owed money, to being the largest debtor nation, owing money to other countries. Since then, the U.S. has spent increasingly more on imports and military presence abroad than it has earned on exports. This deficit was financed by other countries, particularly the Japanese and Europeans, by buying U.S. assets such as real estate, stocks, and government bonds. The current account deficit that had concerned some when it was still under 1% of the GDP, swelled in 2002 to over $450 billion—over 4.5% of the GDP. In early 2003, the Fed was between a rock and a hard place because efforts to stimulate the economy were the opposite of those needed to defend the dollar, weakening because of the enormous current account deficit.

Managed trade has further resulted in a hollowing out of the American manufacturing base, the degree of which damage we shall not be able fully to assess for years to come. Some greet this change positively, making the argument that the American economy has moved from a manufacturing economy to an information economy. The argument that the Information Age has displaced America's dependence on manufacturing is, however, superficial. Eamonn Fingleton has demonstrated that manufacturing is still the basis of a strong and enduring economy.[180] Fingleton describes complex, multi-million-dollar manufacturing equipment needed to produce electronic components in large volume, and he points out that movement of this type of equipment to other countries has a weakening effect on American competitiveness because we lose not only manufacturing but also manufacturing know-how.

Other nations' use of managed trade has allowed first Japan and then other Asian nations to build successful economic momentum primarily through export sales. A further result of this policy has been a wealthy Japan pouring capital into the United States at the same time that the Japanese people were paying many times the world price

---

[180] Eamonn Fingleton, *In Praise of Hard Industries: Why Manufacturing, Not the Information Economy, Is the Key to Future Prosperity* (New York: Houghton Mifflin Company, 1999).

for rice, thanks to the Japanese government's subsidies of rice farmers in Japan and tariff control over the import of foreign rice. Managed trade has contributed to a decade-long Japanese recession due to weak domestic consumer demand.

Chalmers Johnson, president of the Japan Policy Research Institute, commented on the danger of building an economy exclusively on export sales:

> To base a capitalist economy mainly on export sales rather than domestic demand, however, ultimately subverts the function of the unfettered world market to reconcile and bring into balance supply and demand. Instead of producing what the people of a particular economy can actually use, East Asian export regimes thrived on foreign demand artificially engineered by an imperialist power.[181]

Some movement of American manufacturing to lower-wage countries is a positive event in raising the world's standard of living, but only if the wages are high enough in the emerging economies to buy products from other countries, including America. When managed trade prompts the government to subsidize the movement of manufacturers out of the U.S., free trade is corrupted. Likewise, when other countries subsidize selected companies so that they can undersell their competitors to the U.S. market, free trade is corrupted.

While the United States' trade policy for goods and services has been dominated by political expediency at home and political hegemony abroad, at the same time, a campaign to eliminate any controls of finance capitalism has been conducted at the highest level. Specifically, President Bill Clinton and Secretary of Treasury Robert Rubin were both involved in convincing nations to eliminate all cross-border controls of capital in the 1990s, at the same time that market disciplines of this capital were being suspended. No protocols were in place to control the lending of hot money, and the speculators with borrowed money were more powerful than the central bankers. The

---

[181] Chalmers Johnson, *Blowback: The Costs and Consequences of American Empire* (New York: Metropolitan Books, Henry Holt and Company, 2000), p. 196.

unintended consequence of this action was the reversal from economic growth to economic decline in countries from South America to Southeast Asia.

The United States presumes to be the world's free-trade leader; however, in addition to managing trade for political hegemony, it contradicts many of the components of successful free trade by imposing thousands of tariffs, paying hundreds of billions of dollars in subsidies, and maintaining a money flow that is high-cost, very volatile, and very impatient. Daniel T. Griswold commented in a Cato report as follows:

> America's engagement in the global economy has been oversimplified into a battle between isolationists and free traders, whereas the ultimate struggle is between those who support a truly free market and those who favor government intervention, such as tariffs, subsidies and bailouts in the international marketplace. Protection and subsidies alike deny Americans the freedom to spend and invest their resources as they choose. They diminish our national wealth by diverting resources to less productive but politically favored sectors of the economy. Subsidies undermine support of an open economy by tainting the cause of free trade as just another favor for big business.[182]

Griswold estimated that the total annual cost to the U.S. economy from various trade barriers in the 1990s was between $15 billion and $70 billion. Tariffs restrict American purchases of sugar, peanuts, textiles, clothing, shoes, steel, and a lot more, and the hidden tax is passed on to the American consumer.[183] Corporate welfare and government-to-government bailouts are chiefly the work of the Exchange Stabilization Fund, the IMF (largely dominated by the United States), the World Bank, OPIC (Overseas Private Investment Company that insures investments), and the Export-Import Bank. During the last quarter of the twentieth century, a large percentage of

---

[182] Daniel T. Griswold, *Free Trade, Free Markets: Rating the 105th Congress* (Washington D.C.: Cato Institute, Feb. 3, 1999 #6), p. 1.

[183] *Loc. cit.*

these hundreds of billions of dollars came from the American taxpayer and were used to subsidize American companies who moved manufacturing from the United States to other countries.

These various corruptions of free trade have damaged the opportunities for a world of peace and plenty. They have resulted in a polarized and superficial political debate that makes focusing on root-cause solutions difficult. Cato counted only 25 members of the House of Representatives and only 12 Senators in 1999 who were supporters of trade that was truly free of this kind of lobbied control and political tampering. The rest were "internationalists," like President Clinton, who mixed free markets with government intervention; "isolationists," like Patrick Buchanan, who combined xenophobia and protectionism in a political package; and thorough "interventionists" who favored full government "solutions."

In 2002, two events demonstrated the degree to which the United States had compromised itself in its world leadership toward free trade. The first was a politically motivated new tariff protection for "Big Steel"; the second, new agricultural subsidies. Laura D'Andrea Tyson, Dean of the London Business School and former chair of President Clinton's Council of Economic Advisors, called the farm subsidy a "$200 billion disaster with substantial collateral damage to the nation's foreign policy and national budget."[184]

As long as Europe, America, and Japan subsidize agriculture in their countries, they are taking away the best opportunity for poor countries to join in the world's economy and improve the lives of their people. The on-going debate over how much rich nations give in foreign aid is important, but the elimination of agricultural subsidies is more urgent and can be more productive. Among other benefits, the elimination of agricultural subsidies would purge another example of an uncaring and hypocritical United States. A *New York Times* editorial was emphatic on this subject:

> Continuing on the present perverse course will feed
> social instability and environmental devastation
> throughout the developing world. It will mean

---

[184] Laura D'Andrea Tyson, "The Farm Bill Is a $200 Billion Disaster," *Business Week*, June 3, 2002, p. 26.

increased illegal immigration to fill agricultural and other jobs in richer countries, instead of increased jobs and incomes in the third world. Any serious effort to combat extreme poverty, promote third world development, and share the benefits of globalization more fairly must begin with a radical assault on agricultural subsidies. It must begin now.[185]

Another root problem of globalization is wage arbitrage. The world has grown smaller and industry has become more mobile. Companies can easily move to parts of the world where wage differentials are 50:1 or larger. Countries vary in their standard of living from around $41,000 per person per year in Switzerland, to less than $1,000 in China, and only a few hundred dollars in most African countries. These numbers represent the country's GDP divided by its population. In time, free trade can raise levels in all countries, but it will fail if the mercantilist philosophy of wage suppression prevails. William Greider pointed out that free trade fails when workers in poor countries do not have sufficient spendable income over bare subsistence to make the reciprocal purchases upon which free trade depends, and that "raising wage incomes at the bottom as rapidly as possible offers a dual benefit to the overall system: increased consumer demand for the global surpluses and also, necessarily, a slower pace of new development and industrial migration."[186]

The solution is found in democratic capitalism's maximization and distribution of surplus, that is, profit-sharing and ownership opportunities applied on a global scale. This is no longer an argument about class struggle between those who own the capital and those who do the labor. The stock of global corporations is now largely held by the people who work for the companies and by their retirement funds invested by their money managers. Protestors in the streets opposed to globalization should join with other stockholders and advise their money managers to pressure corporations to extend profit-sharing,

---

[185] Editorial, "The Hypocrisy of Farm Subsidies," *The New York Times*, December 1, 2002, p. 8.

[186] William Greider, *One World, Ready or Not: The Manic Logic of Global Capitalism* (New York: Simon and Schuster, 1997), p. 168.

ownership opportunities, and large dividends to the emerging economies.

The question remains, however, when stockholders will be educated sufficiently to exercise their democratic voting prerogative to democratize capitalism, or when will money managers be sufficiently enlightened to influence global corporations to see what Henry Ford saw in the 1930s. Long-term world economic growth depends on workers with enough spendable income to enjoy more comforts domestically, and to add their purchases to the world's economy.

By the early 1990s, the world seemed poised to move steadily toward economic common purpose and away from violence because economic freedom, including free trade, had demonstrated that lives can be improved. Unfortunately, much of global capitalism was still dominated by ultra-capitalism. Adding the visible feeding-frenzy in executive compensation to this domination, it is not surprising that a populist revolt is building momentum against generic global capitalism. The opportunity for a world of peace and plenty through free trade remained at risk because although the protestors recognized the social damage from the domination of the world economy by ultra-capitalism, they had not yet focused on the potential for broad wealth distribution inherent in democratic capitalism. At the WTO meeting in Seattle in late 1999, 50,000 protestors represented 1,000 NGOs (non-government organizations). Confirming that their protests can be described as "populist," the majority of Americans questioned felt sympathetic to the protestors in Seattle. The protestors were mobile, well organized, and well represented at subsequent WTO, IMF, and NAFTA meetings in Washington, D.C.; Davos, Switzerland; and Quebec City, Canada. They were protesting lethal finance imperialism and neo-mercantilism. Part of my mission in writing this book is to present protestors with an alternative to their rejection of generic capitalism. That alternative is democratic capitalism.

The Economic Illogic and Catastrophic Potential in Ultra-Capitalism

The critical-mass theory works when building and selling products and services because the mission is better quality, new functions, and lower cost. The increased volume drives down the cost and price, which opens up new markets among consumers now able to purchase at the lower price. This is the core concept in the creation and spread of wealth in a free economy. According to classical economics, a free market will reflect changes in supply and demand and through this process find equilibrium. This search for equilibrium is actually improved by Information Age technology because changes in supply and demand can be more quickly assimilated.

Belief in the capacity of the free economic system to self-correct is known as "market fundamentalism." *Laissez-faire* adds the concept to market fundamentalism that the government should not intrude into the process. From the beginning of capitalism, however, government has failed to intrude properly to control currency and credit for the general welfare; instead, it has intruded improperly by providing special privileges to finance capitalists. Now with the advent of ultra-capitalism, the government has dramatically extended its intrusions into free markets through the "liberalization of capital markets," extending the concept of free markets and market fundamentalism, or *laissez faire,* to financial services. This extension to financial capitalism is in contradiction to the system outlined by Smith and in rejection of Smith's warnings about speculation and the bad habits of the "prodigals and projectors." Smith specifically warned that lack of supervision of speculation would limit the government's ability to control excessive liquidity: "The over-trading of some bold projectors was the original cause of this excessive circulation of paper money."[187]

Adam Smith was clear about the government's responsibility to keep finance capitalism subordinate to the job-producing economy. Smith recognized the distinction between short-term loans for working capital and fixed capital invested patiently for income and long-term appreciation. According to Smith:

> The returns of the fixed capital are in almost all cases much slower than those of the circulating capital; and, such expenses even when laid out with the greatest prudence and judgment, very seldom return to the

---

[187] Smith, *op. cit.*, p. 288.

undertaker till after a period of many years, a period
far too distant to suit the convenience of a bank. Fixed
capital ought to be borrowed upon bond or mortgage or
such private people as propose to live upon the interest
of their money, without taking the trouble themselves
to employ the capital.[188]

Had Smith's advice been followed, the flow of hot money in
and out of the Southeast Asian countries in the 1990s would have
been controlled, and the immeasurable economic and social damage
that it caused would have been lessened, at least, and possibly
avoided.

Smith proposed that although investments must be patient, the
investor will nonetheless be rewarded by significant annual return on
the investment, whether interest or dividends. Smith's proposal for a
combination of income and long-term gain stands in sharp contrast to
the practices of ultra-capitalism wherein the stock price dominates.
The impatient capital of ultra-capitalism frequently moves from one
stock-market sector to a more favored sector, always churning
commissions. Much of the capital stays in the stock market and is not
invested for economic growth.

Smith described the nation's wealth as the total of building
things, growing things, and selling them, less the costs of managing
money: "Every saving in the expense of collecting and supporting that
part of the circulating capital, which consists in money, is an
improvement of exactly the same kind."[189]

Smith emphasized the economic dynamic in which additional
sales volume drives down costs and prices, thereby adding additional
buyers who are then able to afford the purchases. This critical-mass
phenomenon has been easier to observe in manufacturing in which
development costs, administrative costs, machinery cost, and the cost
to set up machines are spread over more units, thereby reducing the
per-unit cost. In the larger service industry, this phenomenon is harder
to observe, but it is nonetheless an exciting part of the Information
Age revolution. With microprocessors and new communications

---

[188] *Ibid.*, p. 291.

[189] *Ibid.*, p. 276.

technology, the enormous administrative costs in service can be dramatically reduced. More volume now has the same dynamic identified by Smith by amortizing service-industry costs, such as software, satellite networks, training and restructuring of administration and distribution. Service companies also discover that sophisticated management systems, such as *Six Sigma* (see chapter 4), are applicable to service with possibly even greater returns. The microprocessor that encourages decentralization and distributed processing has the same applicability in service industries where virtually every operation can be measured and made accountable. Like similar effects in manufacturing industries, these improvements depend on the involvement and cooperation of the associates and for that reason work best in a democratic capitalist environment.

Ultra-capitalism contradicts classical economics by the gross violations of economic principle enumerated at the beginning of this chapter. Financial services also contradict classical economics because they do not use increased volume to lower costs and improve services. One exception to this is the emergence of discount brokers, but generally, finance capitalism, with its mission of making money on money, prices its services not on costs but as high as tacit agreement among competitors with the same mission will allow. This assertion can be confirmed by the entire pricing philosophy in investment banking, and more specifically in the credit-card industry with their usurious rates, ever-rising banking charges for ATMs, and in the mutual fund industry that contradicts Smith's dynamic by increasing its fees as its volume of business goes up. *Business Week* reported on this phenomenon in the mutual fund industry from 1993 to 2001:

> Big brand-name funds are a potential toxic waste site for the baby boomers' retirement hopes. Twisting the knife in the wound, big fund companies are charging investors royally for lackluster results. They take $1.54 in fees for every $100 invested in equity funds, up nearly 14% since 1993.[190]

---

[190] Mara der Hovanesian, with Lewis Braham, "The Mutual Fund Mess, Lousy Returns, Lumbering Giant Firms, Too Many Funds—Can the Industry Right Itself?" *Business Week*, Special Report, December 17, 2001, p.102.

These are the pricing practices that fund the growth and dominance of ultra-capitalism. In a country with many more stockbrokers than steelworkers, these practices replace Smith's economic perpetual-motion machine for the creation of wealth with an economic dynamic that results in greater concentration of wealth.

William C. Field, a bank industry analyst, reported the sleight of hand by which bankers in 2002 captured the lower-cost money that the government, through the Federal Reserve, had made available to help the economy. The 4.1% spread between banks' borrowing and lending rates made some exclaim: "It's like a gift!"[191] The recovery money, had been intended to help ordinary people and stimulate the economy; it was, instead, diverted by ultra-capitalists to increase bank profits and boost the value of stock options.

George Soros attacked market fundamentalism as a generic concept, but he knew where the real problem is: "The potential for disequilibrium is inherent in the financial system."[192] Soros added:

> Market forces, if they are given complete authority even in the purely economic and financial areas, produce chaos and could ultimately lead to the downfall of the global capitalist system. This is the most important practical implication of my argument in this book.[193]

The reason for this is rarely mentioned: Market disciplines required to supervise the system and allow it to seek equilibrium, have been suspended by the United States government.

The competition for currency and credit between the job-growth economy and speculation has always been tilted in the direction of speculation. Speculation has a time and amount preference, that is, it has the appearance of a greater return in a shorter time. For this reason, without government regulation, currency and credit will naturally gravitate towards speculation and high-risk

---

[191] William C. Field, "Banks Heap Windfall from Falling Rates," *Bloomberg News Service* (Asbury Park Press), February 17, 2002, p. 1.

[192] Soros, *"The Crisis of Global Capitalism," op. cit.*, p. xxiv.

[193] *Ibid.*, xxvii.

adventures. As Adam Smith expressed it, the speculators would preempt the available capital: "Sober people, who will give for the use of the money no more than a part of what they are likely to make by the use of it, would not venture into the competition."[194]

Many examples can be cited of the deterioration of finance capitalism into greater risk and more corruption. Every speculative event, from the S&L scandal, to the junk bonds of Michael Milken, to LTCM (see chapter 7), to Enron (see chapter 9), to the IPO craze, has followed the same pattern. In each case, early profits raise expectations for higher profits from a constantly rising base of comparison. As the pressure for bigger profits grows, ultra-capitalists slip into greater risk and sometimes criminal behavior.

Milken was a financial innovator who discovered that the risk of default of a certain type of bond was not so great as commonly thought. These bonds called "high-yield bonds" by their supporters, and "junk bonds" by Milken's competitors and critics, were promoted by Milken as an effective way for companies to obtain growth capital. Milken became famous when he "earned" $550 million in 1987, based on a profit formula that he had negotiated with Drexel, the parent firm.[195] In order to show constantly improving results, Milken was caught in the upward pressure, and his bonds were increasingly used for unfriendly takeovers to the extent that Milken's annual conference became known as the "Predators' Ball."[196] Milken became involved with the infamous Ivan Boesky in alleged insider trading and became the scapegoat for the excessive greed of the 1980s. Although most of that generation of greedy players got away with it, Milken ended up in jail.

One of the proud accomplishments of finance capitalism was the financing of the many new Information Age ventures, but this financing was not protected from the corrupting influence of ultra-capitalism. In 2002, some of the best-known names in investment banking were being investigated by the government for providing

---

[194] Smith, *op. cit.*, p. 339.

[195] Daniel Fisher, *Payback: The Conspiracy to Destroy Michael Milken and His Financial Revolution* (New York: Harper Business, 1995) p. 24.

[196] Connie Bruck, *The Predators' Ball: The Junk-Bond Raiders and the Man Who Staked Them* (New York: Simon & Schuster, 1988).

large amounts of limited stock to big investors in exchange for the investors' willingness to keep buying at higher prices after the initial offering. This was a modern version of the "pump and dump" techniques that the few have used for centuries to take money from the many on the stock market. *Wall Street Journal* reporters described the technique applied to IPOs (Initial Public Offerings):

> Some securities firms coerced investors who got hot IPO shares into placing orders for the same stocks at higher prices on the first day of trading, as a condition of getting the IPOs. That practice, known as "laddering," contributed to the huge one-day run-ups in many IPOs during the tech-stock mania.[197]

During the 1970s, under the direction of John Whitehead and John Weinberg, Goldman Sachs was the standard of integrity in the investment banking industry whose mission was "excellence" in support of world economic growth. By the end of 2002, Goldman Sachs was one of the companies that settled with SEC regulators over a "litany of misconduct that had burned investors."[198] At the same time that Goldman Sachs was buying off a more detailed examination of Wall Street corruptions through a group settlement, they were trying to sustain earnings improvement by increased speculation in derivatives. According to *The Wall Street Journal*, falling profits pushed Goldman managing directors to direct their traders to "step up your game and increase your risk."[199]

Speculation with the firm's money in volatile markets such as currency already represented 25% of Goldman's reported profits. Once the mission changed to maximizing short-term profits, then the tendency was towards increased risk because earning profits the old-fashioned way was becoming difficult. This same pattern was

---

[197] Randall Smith and Susan Pulliam, "Two More Wall Street Firms Are Targeted in Trading Probe," *The Wall Street Journal*, April 25, 2002, p. 1.

[198] Patrick McGeehan, "Wall Street Deal," *The New York Times*, December 21, 2002, p. C1.

[199] Gregory Zukerman and Joanne Craig, "High Rollers: In a Risky Period, Goldman Depends More on Riskier Bets Using Firm's Own Cash," *The Wall Street Journal*, December 17, 2002, p. 1.

followed by LTCM in 1998, an experience that demonstrated that companies taking increased risk with a great deal of borrowed money can threaten the whole system, especially now that the government is the protector, not the regulator, of the money industry.

The S&L industry got out of control after the government extended deposit insurance to multiple locations and increased the insured amount to $100,000 with no limit on multiple locations. Prodigals and projectors took over much of the S&L industry, but major investment bankers aided in the process. Merrill Lynch, among others, scanned the country daily on their computers to determine which S&L was paying the highest interest. This was usually an indication of high risk or a troubled Thrift trying to double its bets and get even, but that apparently did not bother Merrill who made hundreds of billions of dollars by brokering the transfer of people's money from savings accounts to high-paying CDs (Certificates of Deposit).[200] Much of this money was subsequently lost when the Thrifts went broke. In ultra-capitalism, the pattern never changes: The bankers go for quick profits and do not worry about the quality of the investment; then, in time, the people are hurt.

In all of these cases, the government structure allowed currency and credit to flow into speculation under the banner of "deregulation" and "free markets." The government assumed—in error—that the economic logic of supply and demand that can find equilibrium in commerce also applies to finance capitalism. In the globally interdependent financial markets, however, equipped with new technology that makes possible trading huge amounts in seconds, ultra-capitalists need more supervision at the very time that the supervision is being suspended. Economic principles are being violated as never before in world commerce in ways that threaten to pull down the whole system. The new mode of production, democratic capitalism, with the capacity to distribute wealth broadly and resolve the inherent contradiction in capitalism, is being displaced by ultra-capitalism that concentrates wealth in record amounts. Consider the words of billionaire speculator Soros:

---

[200] Stephen Pizzo, Mary Fricker, and Paul Muolo, *Inside Job: The Looting of America's Savings and Loans* (New York: McGraw-Hill, 1989), p. 11.

Communism abolished the market mechanism and imposed collective control over all economic activities. Market fundamentalism seeks to abolish collective decision making and to impose the supremacy of market values over all political and social values. Both extremes are wrong. What we need is a correct balance between politics and markets, between rule making and playing by the rules.[201]

Leveraged Speculation and the Business Cycle

According to the classical theory of economics, the interaction of wages and prices in an environment of competition and private property, free of government intervention, would find equilibrium within the natural forces of the market. The proper role of government in this context is to maintain a legal infrastructure upon which free markets could function well. Smith qualified his free-market system, however, with a requirement for ample, low-cost, non-volatile, patient money. Smith indicated that this could be achieved either through free banking or through government control when all of the market disciplines are in effect. In either case, Smith warned of the gravitation towards speculation, and the necessity for money to remain neutral and without influence on the process. John Kenneth Galbraith summarized classical economics two centuries after Smith:

Prices adjusted to marginal costs; costs, including that of labor, adjusted downward as necessary to ensure the employment of available plant materials, and—above all—workers. Say's law ruled. Demand was adequately sustained by what was paid out in wages, interest and profits; prices moved to accommodate to any interruption in the return flow of purchasing power.[202]

---

[201] Soros, *op. cit.*, p. xxvii.

[202] Galbraith, *op. cit.*, p. 179.

Galbraith's definitive understanding resonates clearly: "Money was still seen in these years as a largely neutral intermediary that facilitated the exchange process."[203]

Many felt that the Great Depression in the 1930s signaled the demise of classical economics. According to classical economists, wages were supposed to drop far enough to restart the economy when products became so cheap that people would buy. This was a theory that had no relevance in the real world of the 1930s. The 25% who were out of work had no wages to spend, no matter how cheap products became, and working people could barely live on the little they were making, having nothing left over to sacrifice to economic theory. Recognizing this, both the government and the unions opposed further wage cuts. What had failed, in fact, was not classical economics but the government's obligation to keep money neutral. Easy credit and leveraged speculation, rampant during the 1920s, had caused the economic devastation, and that was no more Adam Smith's fault than it was the fault of the workers out of work or those barely getting by.

John Maynard Keynes understood this. Less troubled by economic technicalities than many, he tried to solve with psychological solutions a psychological problem, a problem of public feelings that had resulted from an unnecessary economic problem. People were in such a state of shock, Keynes believed, that they needed a counter-shock from government spending, the device known as "priming the pump."

Both supply and demand are sensitive to attitude. If the mood is positive and optimistic, the supply-siders will invest in new plants, and the consumers will spend. If speculation is not controlled, then capital is deflected away from further supply-side investment in growth and towards speculation. After the speculative climax occurs, followed by a crash, the demand side suffers psychological damage, and people stop buying. President Franklin Roosevelt's understanding of this damage to both supply and demand was expressed in his famous dictum in 1932: "We have nothing to fear but fear itself." His words of encouragement were calculated to prompt the supply-siders

---

[203] *Loc. cit.*

to invest in growth and the demand-siders not to be afraid to go to the stores and spend.

Most reformers in the 1930s leapt at the opportunity to discredit free-market capitalism. They were conditioned by Marx's description of "the inherent contradictions in capitalism," and they were excited by the emergence of Communism and Socialism that would need their type of intellectual leadership. These ideological trends and influences kept the reform-minded economists and other leaders from a more complete examination of the causes of the Great Depression. This was the beginning of the superficial debate that continues to the present, one extreme defending the privileges to concentrate wealth, the other espousing government micromanagement of the economy.

No such contradiction inheres in Smith's classical economic theory of capitalism. As long as leveraged speculation remains under control, and wealth is broadly distributed, wild swings of the business cycle that severely damage the economy are held in check. Modest changes in supply and demand of an economy wherein money is in fact neutral, can be accommodated by wage reductions, not the draconian wage reduction allegedly needed to end the Great Depression, but rather wage reductions in the salaries of well-paid associates. People who enjoyed profit-sharing and dividend income during an up market would expect less of both during a down market.

The world had been devastated by the Crash of 1929 and subsequent government errors. The government had allowed leveraged speculation to go on for years on Wall Street. When the bubble burst, the government exported the market spasm on Wall Street to an economic disaster on Main Street by making three monstrous errors: a retroactive tax hike as high as 63%; shrinkage of the currency by 30% in two years; and passage of the trade-protectionist Smoot-Hawley Act that exported the depression worldwide.

After the depression had been started by bad financial practices, the government followed the additional bad advice of finance capitalists to salvage as much of the wealth of the wealthy as possible while doing enormous harm to the ordinary people. In a depression or recession, the problem is a falling volume of work; bankers, however, look only at the balance sheet and take action to return their reserves for loan losses to conservative levels. Unfortunately, these actions curtail lending to good companies, making the problem worse because they further slow down the volume of work. This same banker's instinct to tighten credit in an economic crisis was at the root of the damage done by the IMF in Southeast Asia in the late 1990s (see chapter 7).

Much of the pump-priming did not work well, and only the production demands of World War II were sufficient to pull the country out of 18% unemployment in the late 1930s. This fact of history does not bother the latter-day collectivists who allege two nostrums from the 1930s, that the Great Depression demonstrated the inherent contradictions in capitalism, and that classical economics came to an end. On the other hand, argue the collectivists, the New Deal and the Keynesian revolution demonstrated the benefits of government economic planning. Both the nostrums and conclusions are historically incorrect, but the analysis was, and still is, congenial to academicians because it fits their cultural conditioning of distrust for generic capitalism and trust in government. This is one of many examples of a truth-seeking process that has become flawed through superficiality and political polarization.

The media are the midwife in this process of misunderstanding economic reality, for the journalists and television commentators treat a stock-market crash not as an isolated financial spasm but as an event with an important bearing on the total economy. From this mixture of economic illiteracy and hype, the media screams the news on TV and in large headlines every time the stock market declines. This barrage of financial "news" conditions ordinary investors to the erroneous impression that the stock market has an important function within the general economy. To the contrary, the stock market's function in ultra-capitalism is liquidity and speculation, but it has little to do with funding economic growth. Were the stock market to shut down tomorrow entirely, democratic capitalism would have no problem funding its own growth. During the 1990s, industry was putting more capital into the stock market in stock buy-backs and mergers than it was taking out in new capital for growth! In a financialized economy, capital flows from industry to the stock market, not from the stock market to industry. In a democratic capitalist economy, well balanced among dividend income, stock appreciation, and security, the stock market would become, again, an important source of new capital for growth.

Defenders of the stock market will properly point to IPOs to refute my outrageous statement. They are correct to the extent that new ventures have been well funded, but much of the IPO capital goes to venture capitalists, not to companies for growth. IPOs have been an important source of funding for new ventures, as well as an instrument for extreme speculation. In general, however, the idea that the stock market is a source of growth capital is exaggerated, for its true mission is to make money on money.

During ultra-capitalism's final quarter of the twentieth century, the linkage between government and finance capitalism became the dominant axis running through the economic system. Included in this were abrogation of market disciplines, allowance of extreme leverage for speculators, and rejection of any oversight for new speculative instruments called "derivatives." From these corruptions emerged LTCM in 1998, Enron in 2001, and many more, who became poster-boys for ultra-capitalism (see chapters 7 and 9). Most people are not aware of the size, speed, and threat of this new aggressive and greedy form of capitalism. They do not realize the financial power that ultra-capitalists wield: In a world where only a few nations measure their annual GDP in the trillions of dollars, ultra-capitalists trade over a trillion dollars every day in the currency markets alone.

The business cycle of boom and bust is really a leveraged speculative cycle. Speculation on borrowed money drives values up, motivated by greed, then after values reach artificially high levels, the down cycle is motivated by fear and, further exacerbated by the lender's demands that the borrower pay back the money borrowed. This repetitive pattern has gone on since the beginning of the republic because the finance capitalists write the rules, well-lobbied or well-compensated politicians enact the laws, and the people are inadequately educated to insist on democratic correction. Macroeconomic policy continues to be designed by Wall Street because the political left has never understood the process and does not know how to use democratic power to reform it.

The Silence of the Experts

My assertion that most severe economic dislocations are caused by leveraged speculation cannot be confirmed by studying most books on Economics. Economists have the urge to treat their discipline as though it were a hard science like math or physics. Perhaps they find instabilities in business, rather than in speculation, more attractive because the former are more susceptible to being described with mathematical models. Speculation, by contrast, depends more on psychology than it does on mathematics, more on perception than reality. Although Adam Smith's warnings about the dangers from the prodigal speculators have been echoed by contemporary economists, including John Maynard Keynes, I find that textbooks on economics contain little analysis of speculation with borrowed money and its effects. The examinations of M1, M2, M3 money supply are endless, and most of them are obsolete by the time the books are in print. Those same books, however, contain very little about the damage from speculation and nothing that I can find about the government's responsibility to control it.

For example, in the 1,000-page textbook, *Economics*, by Samuelson and Nordhaus, only two pages are given to a discussion of speculation. The section is titled: "Why stabilization by speculators can increase utility," followed by explanations about how arbitrage and hedging help discipline commerce. The following two paragraphs from this section on "speculative bubbles" comprise the examination of the negative effect of speculation:

> Having seen how ideal speculation can increase economic welfare, we must note the possibility of less happy outcomes. From time to time, investors lose sight of fundamentals and fall prey to rumors, hopes, and fears. Sometimes, speculation gets caught in the grip of a mass contagion, like the inexplicable dancing crazes that swept medieval villages, like the Dutch tulip mania that sent the price of a single bulb higher than that of a house, like the South Sea Bubble in which companies sold stock at fabulous prices for enterprises which would "later be revealed."

> While economic science may have difficulty
> explaining why "rational" investors would buy into
> such speculative bubbles, history documents numerous
> cases. Moreover, such destabilizing speculation serves
> the economy poorly. Destabilizing speculation leads to
> a deterioration in economic welfare.[204]

The operative words here are "economic science" and Samuelson's indication that economists have difficulty forcing real-world events into a scientific explanation. The alternative is to accept that some people are greedy and irresponsible, and that some government structure must be designed to minimize the damage that speculators can do to the economic system. To me it is obvious that structuring the system ought to begin with control of speculation with borrowed money because that is where many of the greedy people concentrate their energies. Most economists, however, give more emphasis to how speculation "disciplines the system" than to how it violates the neutrality of money by its very lack of discipline.

John Maynard Keynes put speculation into context after first using it to make his own fortune. His observation seems to have anticipated ultra-capitalism: "Speculators may do no harm as bubbles on a steady stream of enterprise. But the position is serious when enterprise becomes the bubble on a whirlpool of speculation."[205]

In John Kenneth Galbraith's effort to put economics into perspective, he too did not provide much analysis of leveraged speculation. He did give thorough attention to what happened after the Crash of 1929, but he failed to give sufficient attention to what happened before the Crash or to ask why it happened. Galbraith pointed out that studies of business cycles had been a specific line of inquiry and teaching that had achieved neither general agreement nor integration with other economic disciplines. The causes of business cycles, according to some of these studies, included sunspots, with or without their effect on agriculture. Galbraith did summarize the

---

[204] Paul A. Samuelson and William D. Nordhaus, *Economics* (New York: McGraw Hill, 13th edition, 1989; first published in 1948), p. 600.

[205] Keynes, *op. cit.*, p. 159.

influence of leveraged speculation, but without sufficient examination of its causes or follow-up recommendations for preventing it:

> More probably, the cause was the recurring speculative episodes of the previous century—periods of expansion based on easy borrowing from the unduly accommodating banks of the time, with the inevitable contraction when loans were called or when notes came for redemption in the hard money that was not there.[206]

With these few words, Galbraith left the topic of speculation there and returned to the more popular subject of the voiding of classical economics by the Great Depression. New theories and Schools of Economics, whose names were often prefixed with "neo" and "post," were launched from this shaky platform, institutionalizing the conclusion that free markets could not self-correct, and that classical economics had been disproved by the Great Depression. This conclusion is superficial and unacceptable because, I believe, more profound examination will identify leveraged speculation, not an imbalance between manufacturing supply and demand, as the original cause of the Crash, followed by egregious government errors that escalated a well-deserved stock market correction into the undeserved Great Depression.

Failure of the Federal Reserve Board

The reason that economic freedom has functioned at but a fraction of full potential for over two centuries in America has been the inability of the government to direct money to the job-growth economy and away from those who speculate with borrowed money. This failure to control speculators with borrowed money has also undermined the economic leadership of the United States around the world. Easy credit from the regulated banks has fueled every boom part of the repetitive cycles. Tightened credit by the banks after the

---

[206] Galbraith, *op. cit.*, p. 194.

boom climaxed has hurt ordinary citizens in every bust part of the cycles. The Federal Reserve Board was organized in 1913 to prevent this repetitive damage to strong and steady economic growth. The Fed failed in this mission in 1920, spectacularly in 1929, and equally spectacularly in the 1990s.

In this latest cycle, the lost opportunity was particularly tragic because many emerging economies were moving toward economic freedom for the first time. The failure of the Fed in the 1990s was notable because the chairman publicly proclaimed that he could have done nothing to prevent the cycle. Alan Greenspan tied this inability to interest rates, and to a certain extent, he was correct: Control of interest rates alone cannot prevent the destructive boom and bust of the business cycle. What else might he have done?

Other more effective tools, if the government would only use them, include these: regulation of the banks to raise reserves, when assets, such as stocks and real estate, move up from real to artificial levels; increase in brokers' margins and all other borrowing sources, thereby to deleverage speculation; and taxes that incrementally punish short-term trading but reward long-term holdings. Fundamentally, the government has to accept its Constitutional responsibility to control currency and credit for the general welfare, and to follow Adam Smith's advice to know where the money goes. A fortune in taxpayers' money is spent in the lame effort to measure the money in circulation, but little is spent trying to identify whether that money is going to the job-growth economy instead of to those whose mission is to make money on money. This default has come about because those who make money on money also make the rules.

In 1999, the Fed chairman expressed his concern over "excessive exuberance" in the stock market, accurately identifying the stock market's excesses, rather than the traditional whipping boy, a rise in factory workers' wages, as a source of potential inflation. Greenspan's action, however, was to raise the interest rate, an action that penalized ordinary people who buy things on credit and take out mortgages on their homes, rather than curtailing the speculators. Why did Greenspan not recommend, instead, a policy requiring speculators to bet with 60% or 75% of their own money when speculating on stocks? In 1999, loans to speculate on stocks were at a high level:

"Margin debt as a percentage of total market value is 1.6%, which is the top of the range for post-war cycles."[207]

Chairman Greenspan made his disagreement with Adam Smith clear when he stated his belief that the government's macroeconomic policy for "price stability" should address the balance between supply and demand in the economy, but not intrude in the amount of money available for speculation. Greenspan wrote Congressional Representative Jim Leach (R., Iowa), Chairman of the House Banking Committee, to clarify comments that Greenspan had made during the semi-annual Humphrey/Hawkins testimony to Congress, a report required by the 1978 Act that modified the Full Employment Act of 1946. Greenspan explained: "The Federal Reserve is concerned about imbalances between aggregate demand and supply and their implications for inflation and sustainability of the expansion."[208] Having thus abandoned classical economic theory and free market principles, the chairman went on to protect leveraged speculation: "With regard to margin requirements, studies suggest that changes in such requirements have no appreciable and predictable effect on stock prices."[209]

I disagree with this statement because I believe an examination will confirm that every speculative cycle in economic history has been fueled by easy credit. Greenspan's statement is expressive of the attitude of government in its allowance of privilege to ultra-capitalists that is the root cause of their dominance of commerce, and of such scandals as LTCM and Enron. Greenspan's statement was also evidence of the tendency to protect, not regulate, ultra-capitalism. Greenspan's defense of leveraged speculation also suggests his rejection of the move by the SEC, shortly after its formation in the early 1930s, to raise the amount of one's own money to purchase stock from 25% to 50%. Was Greenspan unaware of the compelling evidence of how the rising amount of money for speculation helped cause the Crash of '29 ?

---

[207] Martin Sosnoff, "Don't Get Greenspanned," *Forbes*, September 6, 1999, p. 27.

[208] Joseph Rebello, "Greenspan Denies the Fed Is Acting to Deflate Markets," *The Wall Street Journal*, March 31, 2000, p. A6.

[209] *Loc. cit.*

Greenspan's mission to protect the stock market was demonstrated in 1998 when a drop in the market triggered drops in the interest rates, even though the economy was cruising along at a 3% growth rate. These changes moved the bubble market into a higher gear. John Cassidy, a leading business journalist, described these contradictions of free markets this way:

> Greenspan demonstrated the primacy of Wall Street interests in the Fed's deliberations. His actions added to the growing belief that the Fed would always be there to bail out investors if anything went wrong and this made investors even more willing to take risk.[210]

Then Cassidy went on to examine the real mission of the Fed:

> The very reason that the Fed was founded in 1913 was to prevent a repeat of the speculative busts that had become increasingly common in the previous half century. Sometimes they [speculators] succumb to greed and the herd mentality. In these instances it is up to the Fed chairman, invested with the intellectual and political authority of his office, to try to restrain them. Greenspan could have tried to limit margin lending which the Securities Exchange Act of 1934 empowered him to do.[211]

Cassidy might have added that the subject of limiting stock speculation on margin had at least gotten attention: Senator Charles Schumer (D., New York) and others proposed that margin requirements should be raised to 60% or higher,[212] but the Wall Street lobby quieted them down.

Instead of jerking interest rates and currency supply around with counterproductive results, the U.S. government ought to

[210] John Cassidy, *Dot.con, The Greatest Story Ever Sold* (New York: Harper Collins, 2002), p. 189.

[211] *Ibid.*, p. 265.

[212] *Loc. cit.*

concentrate on policies that limit borrowing for speculation on one hand, and encourage dividends and the spread of worker-ownership plans on the other. These policies in combination with the inherent growth and productivity in the Information Age, could bring the U.S. GDP growth to a *steady* 3.5% without inflation, and bring the emerging economies back close to double-digit growth. The economic and social consequences from a *steady* 3.5% growth domestically, and double-digit growth in the emerging economies, would be enormous, but the possibility is nonetheless realistic. The difference between steady growth and the wild swings of speculation is the difference between a society powered by economic momentum reaching the ideal or one functioning at only a fraction of its potential.

By 2003, some encouraging signs could be seen. A few powerful and financially sophisticated people were disagreeing with Chairman Greenspan, people who could influence the government in the future finally to meet its Constitutional obligation. *Business Week* described two schools of thought in debate over the future of the Fed, the "inflation-targeting" school of economists still trying to make Economics into a hard science, and a promising new school called the "anti-bubble" school, people who take the position that the government could have done much more to prevent the bubble of the 1990s. Those who took this view of government's responsibilities included Stephen P. Cecchetti, former research director of the Federal Reserve Bank of New York and an economist at Ohio State University; Henry Kaufman, well-known Wall Street economist; Lawrence B. Lindsey, President Bush's economics advisor; William C. Dudley, chief economist at Goldman Sachs & Co.; and Andrew Crockett, general manager of the Bank for International Settlements, the central bankers club in Basel, Switzerland.[213] This imposing group wanted the next Fed in varying degrees to "act against excesses in all asset markets, such as unwarranted run-up in stock prices, a housing bubble, or even an overvalued currency."[214]

Frequently ignored in the "business cycle"—which is really a "government mistakes cycle"—are the damaging indirect effects. For

---

[213] Rich Miller, "The Future of the Fed," *Business Week*, December 16, 2002, pp. 95-104.

[214] *Ibid.*, p. 97.

example in 2003, cities like New York and most States were facing large fiscal deficits that provoked cuts in service. They had all overspent in the heady days of the bubble economy, engaging in the inefficiencies that always accompany such euphoria. Another insidious example of the residual effect of the boom/bust cycle was the number of companies with under-funded pension plans. General Motors, for example, reported a $19.3 billion shortfall even after charging $2.6 billion to earnings in 2002. IBM charged $4 billion to earnings in 2002, trying to catch up on their pension-funding obligations.[215] These pension problems hang like a black cloud particularly over the potential profitability of airlines, steel, and autos.

One might ask how this problem had developed in view of the mission of ERISA in 1974 to protect pensions. The answer is that most companies chasing short-term earnings during the bubble economy had used paper gains on the stock market to hype earnings. As the stock market rose, the companies kept upping the estimate of what they could earn from the pension money. At the same time, those companies were lowering the dividend contribution to the annual total return, thereby increasing their risk. Pension funding and insurance is heavily government regulated, but the government allowed companies to up their inflated estimates to 10 or 11%, and now they are forced to pay the piper. Contributing factors later included the low interest rates and government regulation that denied tax deduction during the bubble economy for some companies that wanted to fund their obligations more aggressively. The core problem, however, is the boom/bust cycle and its inevitable damaging aftereffects. The cause of a shortfall as high as $300 billion in American industry for defined benefit plans alone, was described this way in an article in *The Nation:*

> It's rooted in a flawed structure that aggravates the boom-and-bust cycle. During a boom, the pension fund soars and no contributions are needed to maintain fund solvency. But when times are bad and the employer faces cash ebb, the actuaries insist there must be more

---

[215] Mary Williams Walsh, "Many Companies Fight Shortfalls in Pension Funds," *The New York Times*, January 13, 2003, p. 1.

dough on the table. Companies hide the unpleasant
truth by fancy accounting. When they can no longer do
this. They cut investment programs. This financing
regime is dangerously pro-cyclical; that is, it
encourages booms and aggravates recessions.[216]

This scandal is but another example of how badly Congress
with the help of the lobbyists do financial engineering. The usual
mistaken product is *ad hoc,* politicized, and superficial. The needed
comprehensive, integrated, long-range, fiscal, monetary, and
regulatory program has never been addressed.

The Economic Illogic of an American Government Gridlocked between "Tax and Spend" Collectivists and Protectors of Ultra-Capitalism

During the 20th century, collectivism grew in the United States
as the percentage of the nation's wealth taken in taxes and
redistributed by the government grew from 3% of the GDP to over
30%. Thus the minimalist approach to government specified by both
Smith and Jefferson for the effective coupling of democracy and
capitalism was abandoned. During the latter part of the century, this
abandonment of free-market principles and participatory democracy
was paralleled by the government's protection of ultra-capitalism that
combined insurance, subsidies, and bailouts with deregulation.

After the advent of the New Deal and the Keynesian
Revolution during the 1930s, most agreed that the government,
through the Federal Reserve, was responsible for the overall policies
that determine the performance of the economy. The policy that
emerged, inflation-fighting, did not address the regulation of currency
and credit for the economy. In fact, the policies encouraged excessive
liquidity, suspended market disciplines, and ended up protecting and
promoting ultra-capitalism instead of regulating it. The free-market
fundamental of neutral money had become a dim memory.

---

[216] Robin Blackburn, "The Great Pension Crunch: How the Crisis is Destroying
Jobs—and What Can Be Done about It," *The Nation*, February 17, 2003, p. 24.

In theory, macroeconomics is the responsibility of government, but microeconomics, the rest of the elements of free markets, is supposed to be left, *laissez-faire* fashion, to the free market to sort out. This has been the theory though not the practice. The political left and the political right have combined in a steady proliferation of new laws that, in the words of Alexis de Tocqueville (1805-1859), "cover the surface of society with a network of small complicated rules."[217] (See chapter 3.)

Politicians of both major parties, at all levels of government, discovered how easy it is to get media attention by proposing a new law for every hurt, or perceived hurt, of society. The resulting rules have usually been intended to accomplish a desirable mission, such as worker safety, assistance to the disabled, or prevention of sexual harassment, but in most cases, the profusion of bureaucratic regulations has violated free-market concepts and failed to produce cost-effective results. For example, instead of promoting ways to make the workplace safe, and relying on the economic motives of reducing lost time and insurance costs, laws have been passed to micromanage such matters as which shoes to wear and which ladders to use. This pattern has gone on so long and is so pervasive that it has changed the nature of industry in the United States. Companies have steadily gone to outsourcing and the use of temporary employees in order to avoid inefficient regulation and reduce the bureaucratic cost of full-time employees. This trend is contrary to the democratic capitalist culture that builds long-term relationships between a company and its associates. Peter Drucker commented on this phenomenon as follows:

> Even more onerous than the costs of complying with employment laws are the enormous demands that the regulations place on management's time and attention. Between 1980 and 2000, the number of U.S. laws and regulations regarding employment policies and practices grew by about 60%, from 38 to 60. The regulations all require managers to file multiple

---

[217] Alexis de Tocqueville, *Democracy in America* (New York: Random House, 1990, first published, 1835 and 1840), p. 319.

reports, and they all threaten fines and punishment for noncompliance, even if the breach was unintentional. Then there is the constant, and constantly growing, threat of lawsuits: Between 1991 and 2000, the number of sexual harassment cases filed with the Equal Employment Opportunity Commission more than doubled, from about 6,900 a year to almost 16,000 a year. And for every case filed, ten or more were being settled in-house, each requiring many hours of investigation and hearings, as well as substantial legal fees.[218]

Instead of reforming the macroeconomic policies that concentrate wealth and hurt economic growth at home and abroad, the political left uses its energy in a way that suffocates the system. Since the New Deal, people on the political left have convinced themselves that their mission is to tame the wild instincts of capitalism. In practice, these collectivists have ignored the macroeconomic policies that cause economic disasters; instead of targeting the underlying causes of economic malaise, they concentrate on proliferating microeconomic laws. These "tax and spend" Democrats, as the Republicans call them, have wasted taxpayers' money on many poorly designed plans, and they have impeded wealth creation in the process. John Stuart Mill called these kinds of laws the "authoritative interference of government"; and for these, Mill had a simple solution:

There is another kind of intervention which is not authoritative: where a government, instead of issuing a command and enforcing it by penalties, adopts the course so seldom resorted to by government and of which such important use might be made, that of giving advice, and promulgating information.[219]

---

[218] Peter F. Drucker, "They're Not Employees, They're People," *Harvard Business Review*, February 2002, p. 73.

[219] John Stuart Mill, *Principles of Political Economy with Some of Their Applications to Social Philosophy* (Fairfield, New Jersey: Augustus M. Kelley Publishers, reprinted 1987, first published in London, 1848), p. 942.

The collectivists have abandoned macroeconomic policy to the control of Wall Street, satisfied that the reform of capitalism was being accomplished by suffocating it with detailed rules. In doing this, the collectivists demonstrated their lack of understanding of participatory democracy as the alternative to authoritarian behavior by the government. The political right, meanwhile, loudly complained about the inefficiencies of "Big Government" while successfully lobbying that same government for privileges for their own legalized stealing. The result is political gridlock that places reform responsibility on the rest of the culture—the universities, the institutional investors, democratic capitalists, the unions, civic groups, and religious groups. Reform will come through the political process, however, only after the people have elected a new breed of politicians, economically more literate politicians who are willing to run on a platform of democratic capitalism.

The political left concentrates political power while the political right concentrates both wealth and political power, but the two parties come together in support of the Federal Reserve in its fight against inflation. Inflation is a real threat to all people, but only a relative one. If the goal is zero inflation, then the policies will favor the creditor class. If the inflation rate is in the 2%-3% range, then the debtors are favored. At this rate, a modest amount of wealth is redistributed to those who have not enjoyed the wealth-producing privileges that have resulted in record wealth concentration. If democratic capitalism were the prevalent system, a debate about inflation policies would be unnecessary because in democratic capitalism, surplus is maximized in a non-inflationary way by motivated associates and then broadly distributed to associate-owners: Each gains and all gain. Ultra-capitalism is fundamentally a zero-sum game in which the standard of living of the many is sacrificed for the benefit of the few, and then extreme inflation-fighting is offered to protect the economy when, in fact, its priority is mainly to protect concentrated wealth.

For many years, the Fed's inflation-fighting mission was based on the economists' belief in the "Phillips Curve," a theory according to which inflation and unemployment move in an inverse ratio: As more people lose their jobs, the risk of inflation goes down. In time, the economists replaced the Phillips Curve with the more sophisticated sounding "Non-Accelerating Inflation Rate of Unemployment" (NAIRU). The new term helped institutionalize the ugly concept of government's responsibility to keep enough people out of work so that inflation would not erode the asset value of the wealthy. Inflation fighters always point to protecting the elderly on fixed income as the rationale for their actions. Policy requires, however, that Social Security benefits for most people in this group be indexed to inflation.

Karl Marx worried about a deflationary force in capitalism: The pressure on costs would be unrelenting and cause a downward pressure on wages. Marx concluded that this would get worse in an economic downturn, at which time the further reduction of demand caused by growing unemployment would exacerbate the downward wage spiral until it imploded in a proletarian revolution.

Today's hi-tech industries are an extreme and contrary example of price deflation that benefits consumers. Rather than putting excessive pressure on profit margins, the lower prices in these industries are compensated by productivity, rising demand from lower prices, and growth from new products. This is benign deflation in contrast to Marx's malign deflation, and it dramatically exemplifies Adam Smith's dynamic for wealth creation. This phenomenon is not well understood as yet because many assume that higher productivity automatically means higher corporate earnings. This is a popular view for those praying for another bull market. Higher productivity long-term usually improves corporate earnings, but according to Smith's dynamic, it first reduces prices, adds volume, and spreads wealth.

Benign deflation based on Information Age productivity was not understood by the government's inflation fighters for many years. They did not realize how much the reduction in the cost to produce and the price to buy compensated for the traditional inflationary forces in an expanding economy. In 1997, however, the chairman of the Federal Reserve faced reality and loosened interest rates and currency a bit because the real world kept contradicting NAIRU. Government policy-makers believed in a NAIRU with 6% unemployment, below which they supposed inflation would be triggered and the Fed would be obliged to slow the economy. At the beginning of the new century, real inflation was about zero, and

The Economic Logic of Democratic Capitalism

unemployment had dropped to under 4%, a dramatic example of how persistently wrong and damaging government policies had been.

Chairman Greenspan was given credit for recognizing new productivity levels. He had, however, been under persistent pressure from Information Age executives. Felix Rohatyn, one of the country's best-known investment bankers and former ambassador to France, also applied pressure on the Fed. He met at different times with President Clinton, Secretary of the Treasury Rubin, and Chairman Greenspan. The CEOs and Rohatyn insisted that the Information Age economy could grow much faster without inflation,[220] and they succeeded in persuading the government to recognize new economic realities and to modify policies.

With a lot of help from the media, the Fed chairman has been deified for his expert control of the economy. This erroneous perception has hidden the extent of gridlock in American government most of which is beyond the control of the Fed. In this gridlock, one part of the government grabs the philosophy of free markets that builds and spreads wealth and applies it to the protection of ultra-capitalism that does the opposite by concentrating wealth. The collectivists, on the other hand, persist in top-down government solutions to social problems despite ample evidence during the 20th century that central planning works poorly. While the right perverts the philosophy of market fundamentalism and successfully uses it for their greedy purposes, the left is left without a workable philosophy or a practical agenda.

Republicans on the right criticize "tax and spend" Democrats for their unworkable "Big Government" solutions, while Democrats on the left whine about the unfair distribution of wealth and the many social problems not addressed. Both sides sustain their enthusiasm by their accurate criticisms of what is wrong with the other side. Both are devoid, however, of any understanding of the synergistic combination of democracy and capitalism that can accomplish the goal of the right: the maximization of wealth, and the goal of the left: the broadest distribution of that wealth that can improve all lives.

---

[220] Bob Woodward, *Maestro: Greenspan's Fed and the American Boom* (New York: Simon & Schuster, 2000), pp. 149-51.

The Structure Needed for Economic Freedom to Function Worldwide

Adam Smith described the spread of wealth around the world as the "natural course of things" when free trade prevails. Smith expected that governments would exercise their responsibility by keeping money stable and patient and so expedite the process and protect free markets from the speculators. During the last quarter of the twentieth century, the power to improve lives through this natural course of things was demonstrated many times in the experiences of countries that moved from tyranny to economic freedom. During the same period, economic freedom demonstrated its power to improve lives, whether the government structure were democratic or authoritarian.

The international structure required to support economic freedom is more complex than in Smith's day, but now, as then, tariffs and subsidies need to be eliminated, and ample, low-cost, non-volatile, and patient capital at the international level as at the national level must be assured. At the beginning of the 21st century, the international structure was too weak to withstand the greedy demands of ultra-capitalism. A large reform task looms before the international community of commerce, and this task demands democratic understanding and the exercise of will to correct the effects of unnecessary, repetitive economic and social disasters caused by the world's bankers.

For free markets to function properly, money must be no more than a medium of exchange. This facilitating function of money is crucial if the "spontaneous order" is to work. Within the classical theory of economics, supply and demand will spontaneously find equilibrium when freed of government intrusions. All commerce thrives on money of known predictable value, but global commerce, with its many currencies, is particularly dependent on this stability. Economic growth also depends on patient money, that is, money that can be invested in building companies for growth and gain over many years into the future. During the last quarter if the 20th century, however, worldwide transactions on the electronic casino traded in currency futures, interest rate futures, and various derivatives in amounts dwarfing the total of all commercial transactions. Money, with all of its derivatives, is now a tradable commodity in its own right, no longer a neutral tool of commerce.

The currency volatility that encourages speculation was initiated when the American President, Richard Nixon, floated the dollar in 1971. For the first time in commercial history, no monetary stabilizing medium was in place. The idea that international currencies would sort themselves out with the same spontaneous order that works in free markets for goods and services, seemed to have a logic to it, but that logic depended on prudent lending practices, an ability of countries to harmonize their economic fundamentals within a conservative range, and government regulation of leveraged speculation. After 1971, these conditions no longer prevailed; at the turn of the millennium, they continued to be unmet; consequently, lethal monetary instabilities took over world commerce (see chapter 7).

After the demise of Communism, many were excited about a world moving towards free markets. U.S. government officials took the lead in encouraging emerging economies to remove all cross-border controls of capital. These controls had been erected to prevent the precipitous flight of capital, but now, the experts argued, world economic growth would accelerate to everyone's benefit if capital were free to seek its best investment opportunity. This is good theory, but only if money remains nothing more than a medium of exchange, investment capital is patient, and the objective is not speculation but investment for economic growth that builds companies and countries.

Lee Kuan Yew, the builder of modern Singapore, commented on the structural imperfections that allowed Southeast Asian countries to be blind-sided by ultra-capitalism:

> The G-7 finance ministers had pressed the Asian economies to liberalize their financial markets and free capital movements. But they did not explain to the central bankers and finance ministers of the developing countries the danger inherent in today's globalized financial markets, when massive amounts can flow in or out at the touch of a computer button....What began as a classic market mania with funds flowing exuberantly into East Asia became a classic market

panic when investors stampeded to get their money out.[221]

As a result of this structural imperfection, the economic momentum in these nations, which was improving the lives of millions, was dramatically reversed, and the good feelings associated with a rising standard of living were displaced by social chaos and violence. This economic devastation was the result of the "liberalization of capital markets" promoted by the U.S. Treasury Department and the U.S.-dominated IMF during the 1990s. This policy was freedom without the requisite structure, and it was designed by ideologues who had neither the experience nor the training to understand large-scale management of change. The ensuing catastrophe became one of the worst examples of unintended consequences of the twentieth century. At root it was a process failure in seeking truths about the proper organization for world commerce.

A spontaneous order in commerce works only when the rule of specific law prevails to expedite the process. In other words, the "order" can be "spontaneous" only when everyone is playing by the same set of agreed-upon rules that are fair, reasonable, and practiced. An international structure needs legal foundation and protocols to prevent over-lending of hot money, market disciplines free to monitor the process, and extensive deleveraging and taxation of speculation. Global capitalism depends on countries' limiting economic nationalism, and their willingness to harmonize their fundamentals within a reasonable range. The economic fundamentals of nations include limits to deficit spending, low inflation, low interest rates, low unemployment, moderate current account deficits, and ample foreign reserves. The European Union is a test case of how to harmonize these fundamentals.

This long and complex subject is of little interest to most citizens, and for that reason, it has lacked resolution on the basis of majority wisdom. These imperfections in the global monetary system will continue to damage the world's economy during the twenty-first century unless and until enough citizens become interested and

---

[221] Lee Kuan Yew, *From Third World to First: The Singapore Story: 1965-2000* (New York: Harper Collins, 2000), p. 346.

educated. To date, unfortunately, the rules have been heavily influenced by those who make enormous amounts of money on the very volatility that must be eliminated.

Despite the example of the Marshall Plan after World War II, the United States failed in the late-twentieth century to provide leadership to improve the many desperate economies of the world. The most promising economies had positive momentum reversed by the hot money and leveraged speculation of ultra-capitalism (see chapter 7). In the very poor countries, money was wasted because it was either poorly directed, or world agencies underestimated the investment in time, money, education, and training to turn the corner from a nation's being an economic liability to becoming a participating member of the world's economy. Besides the waste from poorly designed programs, the mature economies' agricultural subsidies deprived poor nations of their best opportunity to improve their economies by exporting their produce.

The United Nations has targeted .7% of mature economies' national income to be invested in foreign aid, and some countries exceed that target. The United States "increased" its budget for foreign aid in 2003 to .11% of national income, an "increase" that left the U.S. commitment still at the second-lowest level of aid since World War II.[222] By contrast, the planned American military expenditure was over twenty-five times foreign aid, and that was without paying for new wars. Not only that, but most of the "foreign aid" continues to be used more for political hegemony than to help other nations rise from misery.

The desperate circumstances of more than one-third of the people of the world demands humanitarian attention premised not on sentimentality but on the recognition of inescapable interdependence. Helping to energize their economies can respond to the humanitarian need, but adding wage earners and consumers to the ever-upward process of world economic growth is, in the long run, the more efficient way to express humane concern.

---

[222] Jim Vandetter and David Rogers, "Bush Seeks $5 Billion Foreign Aid Boost Over Three Years to Quell Charges of Stinginess," *The Wall Street Journal*, March 15, 2002, p. A12.

The spread of the benefits of economic freedom can be accomplished only by cooperation among governments and global corporations. "The five hundred largest corporations account for 70% of world trade."[223] In a democratic capitalist culture, these corporations would be agents for positive change, but if the wealthy nations and global corporations do not accept the long-term economic-moral logic of such an investment, the results will be grave. Economic freedom will not spread, new markets will not open, and in our increasingly interdependent would, the infections of disease and sectarian violence will spread.

Certain structures must be put in place by world leaders and global corporations in order to avoid these tragedies, and certain policies must be practiced to allow economic freedom to spread its benefits around the world. They include the following:

- Capital for growth in all countries must be made available based on long-term return consistent with the nature of the investment. World bankers from the mature economies have violated this basic banking principle by lending short-term money, hot money, to be used in long-term investments. The debt/equity ratio that has long been used to examine the quality of company's balance sheets must be applied to assure that whole countries do not incur a disproportionate amount of short-term debt. Global banks have chased short-term profits, ignoring that countries were putting the money into risky ventures, overcapacity, and speculation. When the financial-trouble alarm goes off, this money flees the country, and its flight exacerbates economic decline.

- International financial agencies need to assist emerging economies to overcome the numerous, predictable weaknesses in their financial infrastructure. World financial leadership, however, has exploited these weaknesses instead of compensating for them and helping

---

[223] Robert D. Kaplan, *The Coming Anarchy: Shattering the Dreams of the Post Cold War* (New York: Vintage Books, 2000), p. 81.

countries correct them. The BIS (Bank for International Settlement), the central bankers organization in Basel Switzerland, for example, wrote new rules in 1988 in an attempt to modify the relationship of capital to loans on the basis of the risk, but these detailed rules did not work very well, and in fact encouraged the inflow of hot money. World bankers would support economic growth better with general rules that require a mix of short-term and long-term money on the part of investors. The longer-term capital would give a more fail-safe guarantee that the quality of the investments was being carefully examined.

- Some have recommended that subordinated debt become a more significant part of bank's capital structure. The lenders of this debt know that if the bank gets into trouble they are repaid last. Consequently they examine risk carefully and reflect it in their interest rate they charge. "For a bank judged by the market to be well capitalized and extremely safe, the rate would be low; for a bank judged to be under capitalized and risky, it would be too high."[224]

- When national crises arise, world financial agencies need to require that short-term money be converted immediately into long-term loans or equity. This policy would also force bankers at the time of the original investment to examine the quality of the loans carefully. A "best effort" functional agreement of this sort would work better than a set of technical rules, except that this sort of policy flies in the face of the money-making opportunities of the BIS's constituencies and receives little attention from either the reformers or the protestors. Ultra-capitalists would object that such a protocol would slow down world growth, but the Southeast Asian countries so devastated by ultra-

---

[224] "Safety First: How to Handle Bank Regulation," *The Economist*, May 3, 2003, p. 20.

capitalism in 1997 were high savings economies that had
limited need for foreign money.

- An international monetary structure must monitor the
  system through market disciplines. The United States has
  led in promoting the benefits of "free" capital while
  contradicting the concept with subsidies, insurance, and
  bailouts. Loans in a free market must be monitored by a
  fear of failure; take away that fear, and the result is too-
  easy credit for increasingly risky projects and speculation.

- The BIS must assure that capital goes to the job-growth
  economy and not to speculation. In the late-twentieth
  century, highly leveraged speculators demonstrated their
  superior power several times to defeat the best efforts of
  central bankers to defend a national currency under attack.
  Because sophisticated investors and bankers knew of this
  uneven power, even the threat of a speculative attack was
  enough to cause them to flee a nation's currency, turning
  the threat into a self-fulfilling prophecy.

- This precipitous movement of capital in and out of a
  country ruins the opportunity for *steady* economic growth
  and must be controlled by international agreement.
  Besides the ways of improving the quality of lending
  described above, both transaction taxes on the daily
  worldwide electronic trade of $1.7 trillion, and taxes that
  penalize short-term gains and reward long-term holdings,
  could be levied to deleverage speculation.

- Governments must devise a structure that assures stable
  international currency. For 2,500 years, world commerce
  was expedited by currencies stabilized either by a standard
  of precious metals, usually gold or silver, or by the
  willingness of a country, such as Great Britain or United
  States, to convert currency. Neither of these approaches is
  practical any longer; consequently, stability must come
  from the spontaneous order of free markets. Whether

nations use fixed, pegged, or floating currencies, however, no system can ultimately withstand the effects of volatile and impatient capital caused by ultra-capitalism. Only after the now-prevailing speculative volatility and impatience is purged shall international monetary stability return. At that time, an international peg based on the dollar, yen, and euro could be adopted, and economic fundamentals could be appropriately harmonized.

- A coalition comprising multinational corporations and the governments of wealthy nations, sponsored by the United Nations, could implement policies that help poor nations develop their legal and physical infrastructure. This global economic coalition must accept responsibility for the broad education and job training of leaders and citizens in many nations. The reality that programs may take a generation or more for success must be recognized and funded on that long-term basis.

At the end of the twentieth century, most of the world was eager to move towards economic freedom. To be successful, however, any freedom requires an appropriate discipline. Tragically, the United States and the other G-7 nations did not put the structure in place. The United States, in fact, made the same grievous mistakes on the international level that it was making at home by allowing ultra-capitalists to dominate commerce and write the rules. The global problem is essentially the same as the domestic problem, and so is the solution: We must align fiscal, monetary, and regulatory policies in support of democratic capitalism with the corollary intention of purging the corruptions of ultra-capitalism.

Summary of the Economic Logic of Democratic Capitalism

Democratic capitalism, not communism, is the next great stage in the evolution of economic-political systems. Marx traced this evolution from the slave society of Athens to the serfdom of the European Middle Ages to the wage-slaves of Industrial Revolution capitalism. The next evolutionary step, Marx predicted, would be communism. In this prediction, Marx recognized that Smith's vision of the capacity of free markets to eliminate material scarcity had been confirmed, and that the pressure of economic determinism would then shift to the mode of production, that is, the relationship between capital and labor. Marx correctly foresaw that the future would evoke a new mode of economics, one that melded the interests of capital and labor, that would improve production, and would eliminate the inherent contradiction of concentrated wealth. Marx correctly judged that society could not fully benefit from capitalism's capacity to produce (the supply side), if people did not have the capacity to consume (the demand side). Up to that point, Marx got it right. Then, in order to introduce communism, Marx proposed to tear down the whole existing infrastructure and throw out the crucial components of private property and competition. That is where Marx got it wrong.

John Stuart Mill recognized concentrated wealth as the same flaw in capitalism that Marx had seen, but Mill proposed an evolutionary solution instead of a revolutionary solution. Like Marx, Mill saw that if workers could participate as owners, they would be motivated to maximize the surplus, which could then be distributed broadly. Therefore, Mill proposed the introduction of worker-ownership, integrating that highly motivating factor with private property, competition, and trained management. Mill got it right!

Marx compared his evolutionary theory of human development to Darwin's evolution of the species, but then he contradicted himself by presenting instead a revolutionary way to move to the next stage in the mode of production. Mill's evolutionary proposal was brilliant, whereas Marx's proposal for radical structural change was tragically wrong. Generations of reformers then ignored Mill and kept repeating Marx's terrible error.

Marx's second signature concept was that social progress depends on moving to a superior economic system rather than depending on the political structure or the culture for progress. According to Marx's sense of priority, politics and culture become modified to support the economic system. Ironically, communism failed as an economic ideology because it could not get past the imperfections of the political structure intended to expedite its introduction. Marx was right in his theory that social progress depends on movement to a superior form of commerce, but revolutionaries and reformers after him made the mistake of resorting to politics to change commerce, rather than changing the political structure to support the superior form of commerce. In effect, Marxism contradicted Marx.

During the 20th century, the world was split between those who, on the one hand, wanted to protect traditional capitalism and its privileges, and the collectivist reformers, on the other hand, who either ignored or inverted Marx's own axiom that social progress depends on movement to a superior economic system. Communism, various forms of socialism, and the many forms of collectivism failed to deliver on their social contract because a state structure for central planning works poorly, and the people are not motivated to participate.

By the end of the 20th century, however, the evolutionary process had dramatically changed the mode of production. In many companies, workers were buying ownership and obtaining more stock through profit-sharing programs. "Workers" had become "associates," and the traditional "labor *versus* management" dichotomy was disappearing. Under this new mode of capitalism, the worker-owners' retirement savings and their pension funds became a major source of investment capital. Incredibly, however, even though the mode of production had evolved according to Marx's vision, the fatal flaw of concentrated wealth had become worse.

The reason for this anomaly is that those with wealth and power assiduously protected both, while reformers with democratic power available to change the system continued to pursue collectivist solutions. In the United States, the situation at the beginning of the 21st century was as follows: A democratic political structure to filter and reflect the will and wisdom of the majority was in place; the mode of production had evolved to couple the interests of capital and labor; democratized forms of capitalism had confirmed many times over its superior ability to maximize and distribute wealth; and Information Age industries to be able to function properly demanded the democratic capitalist culture. The United States was, therefore, positioned again to be the "light on the hill," showing the world the way to peace and plenty.

It has not worked that way, yet. Despite this unique opportunity in human history, neither the American political structure

Democratic Capitalism

nor the culture supports democratic capitalism as the means to reach the ideal, although experience has validated the means and confirmed the attainability of the ideal. In this confusion, the political process remained polarized and gridlocked, the theorists on the left were wallowing in ideological uncertainty, the theorists on the right were wallowing in righteous certainty, the protestors were picketing the wrong targets, the liberal reformers were searching for a new identity in all the wrong places, and the ultra-capitalists were counting their money.

CHAPTER 7

The Rise of Ultra-Capitalism

Volatilities gave electronic speculation what it needed to feed on and flourish beyond the wildest expectations. The consequence is a massive, revolutionized, and largely unregulated financial sector armed with the latest high-tech weaponry and pursuing profits on any battlefield, straining the stock and bond markets, plucking loot from any debacle, shooting the economic wounded, and outgunning the "real economy" in its transactions by huge ratios. This leap in the importance of spectronic finance is hard to overestimate.

Kevin Phillips[225]

If Phillips's words seem extreme, he has sophisticated company. George Soros, one of the world's wealthiest speculators, likened the financial forces in global capitalism to massive tectonic plates rubbing against each other, "often creating earthquakes, crushing minor currencies in the process."[226] Soros also used the metaphor of a giant wrecking ball swinging from country to country, knocking over the weaker ones.[227] The enormous economic and social damage to Indonesia in 1998 from this new force has been compared to a drive-by shooting.[228] I call it ultra-capitalism.

What did the world's presumed economic leader, the United States, do about this? Nothing. Congress held hearings on the 1997 Asian economic problems. Soros was invited to make his recommendations. Nothing happened because those in government

---

[225] Kevin Phillips, *Arrogant Capital* (New York: Little Brown and Co., 1994), p. 99.

[226] George Soros, *The Crisis of Global Capitalism* (New York: BBS Public Affairs, 1998), p. xxi.

[227] *Ibid.*, p. 136.

[228] A series with contributions from ten correspondents in eight countries, "In an Entwined World Market, No Man (or Nation) Is An Island," *The New York Times*, February 17-18, 1999, p. A8.

with the responsibility and the knowledge to propose the needed reforms had a higher loyalty to Wall Street. So many ultra-capitalists were making so many hundreds of billions of dollars from the monetary volatility in global capitalism that solutions to root causes were not pursued.

A powerful financial oligarchy is nothing new. What is new, however, is its capacity to damage global economic momentum severely. What is new is the sad picture of countries successfully improving the lives of their people through economic freedom but then being set back by the imperfections in global finance. Positive economic momentum takes years to produce; reversal of this momentum can happen in weeks, and result in social chaos and frequently violence.

In the early 1990s, the world seemed to be moving toward a common ideology of economic freedom, powered by the growth, productivity, and unifying capabilities of the Information Age Revolution. Communism and socialism had failed to produce a superior social contract, but in contrast, economic freedom was improving lives wherever it was competently applied. Democratic capitalism seemed prepared to eliminate material and cultural scarcity; a world of peace and plenty seemed to be both an opportunity and an obligation for society.

Southeast Asian nations—Malaysia, Thailand, South Korea, and Indonesia—were examples of the momentum from this common purpose. All had dramatically improved the lives of their people by adopting many of the principles of democratic capitalism. Stronger economic growth had generated new jobs, but the Asians had also kept their economic fundamentals in reasonable shape: Inflation was under control, government deficits were modest, and the balance of trade was favorable. Indonesia, the world's fourth-largest nation in population, and the largest Muslim nation, had reduced the number of its 211 million people under the poverty line from 40% to 10% over several decades. Was it an imperfect process? Yes. Was there "crony capitalism?" Of course, but the mission of improving lives was being accomplished.

By the end of 1997, however, all four of these Asian economies were in shambles. Currency was devalued as much as 70%; wages were cut 40%; unemployment, prices, and interest rates were all rising; government deficits were growing bigger; virtually no new money was available for business; even lines of credit for operating successful businesses were cut.

Quickly, the uplifting sense of common purpose was replaced by confusion and dangerous social tensions. Government leaders who had been proud of their nations' successes were now disparaged at home and abroad. Those leaders who had espoused the common ideology of free markets now became angry critics of the immorality of currency speculators and the economic imperialism of the West. Indonesia's Suharto, the architect of dramatic improvement in Indonesia's standard of living, was driven from office with the help of the media.

When economic freedom is the norm, an economy can run itself, with little required of governments except civic order, a stable medium of exchange, and capital prepared to invest in long-term growth. Instead, the world's economy had been damaged by ultra-capitalism, accompanied by great instabilities in the medium of exchange, and impatient capital demanding quick returns.

The world's economic leader, the United States, was largely responsible both for causing and failing to correct these situations. The U.S. government made mistakes during the 1970s that caused excessive liquidity and volatility, and then coupled bank deregulation with the suspension of market disciplines. U.S. government officials helped convince emerging economies to remove all cross-border capital controls—a good idea in theory, a bad idea under the compromised circumstances.

To free the world economy to grow and improve all lives, governments, led by the United States, need to take action on these root-problems that hurt global capitalism:

- Control speculation through taxation and by limiting the amount that can be borrowed.

- Allow market disciplines to monitor the process by stopping subsidies, large-risk insurance, and bailouts.

- Regulate world banking to limit damage from "hot" or short-term money rushing in and out of the countries.

- Develop a new currency-stabilizing mechanism by harmonizing economic fundamentals in selected countries.

The U.S., the best example in history of the benefits of economic freedom, has also been the worst example of a government's allowing repetitive economic damage through its unwillingness to control leveraged speculation. This failure of leadership caused the panics of 1818, 1834, 1857, 1873, 1907, 1920, and 1929, the Great Depression, the Savings and Loan debacle, the Bond Massacre of 1994, the failure of Long-Term Capital Management in 1998, the bankruptcy of Enron in 2001, and the turn-of-the-century slow-down of the world's economy. The same failure of leadership infected emergent economies, resulting in the South American and Mexican crisis of 1982, the Mexican crisis of 1994, the Asian crisis of 1997, and it contributed to the Russian debacle in 1998.

The inherent contradiction in capitalism, according to Marx, is pressure on profit margins relieved by downward pressure on wages. According to his theory, in an economic downturn, both pressures are magnified until the system implodes in a proletarian revolution. Marx was partly right, but the greater cause of the boom/bust cycle is government's unwillingness to control speculation with borrowed money. Contrary to Marx, the inherent contradiction is not in the economic theory of capitalism but in government's failure to manage currency and credit to benefit the general welfare. The fault lies with politicians, their errors of judgment, and their willing response to the lobbying from ultra-capitalists for too easy credit.

Until the Industrial Revolution in the eighteenth century, society remained feudal, with static classes and limited freedom. Capital for commerce was provided by a few wealthy people; labor was manual, provided mainly by slaves and serfs. With the new technology of the Industrial Revolution, productivity increased by several thousand times, although capital held by only a few was still dominant. Adam Smith, and later J. S. Mill, described how to maximize surplus through involved workers' sharing in improved performance; most of industry, however, remained feudal, for return on capital was adequate, even when workers were more wage-slaves than participants. Because Mill's theory of broad wealth distribution through workers' accumulation of ownership received little visibility, democratic capitalism had to be developed by the trial and error of entrepreneurs willing to experiment with capitalism by improving it through democratic participation.

In the 20th century, visionary companies combined new technology with involved workers motivated by performance bonuses and opportunities for ownership participation. Democratic capitalism thus gained momentum until the last quarter of the century when ultra-capitalism spread globally and became dominant. Ultra-capitalism included mercantilism that treated workers as a cost commodity, and finance capitalism that speculated with borrowed money causing investment capital to be impatient and the medium of exchange very volatile. Wall Street and institutional investors adopted ultra-capitalism and demanded short-term profits. Many CEOs were seduced to ultra-capitalism by multi-million dollar salaries and multiples of those millions from enormous stock options.

The Information Age Revolution paralleled the growth of ultra-capitalism and demonstrated productivity many times greater from cognitive power than did the Industrial Revolution from manual labor. Information Age industries, further, demand as a competitive necessity the culture of democratic capitalism in order to release the cognitive power of their people.

At the beginning of a new millennium, it is unclear whether society will benefit from the extraordinary opportunities of the Information Age and democratic capitalism, or whether the malign influences of ultra-capitalism will destroy the world's economic momentum. This choice to be made between these competing forms of capitalism is every citizen's responsibility: The choice is for either a twenty-first century of peace and plenty through worldwide economic common purpose or more folly and violence from a continued concentration of wealth and power.

The History of Economic Conflict: Cooperative Commerce versus Making Money on Money

Throughout history, leaders from government, religion, and elsewhere in the culture have recognized the threat to society from money that was not neutral, stable, and patient. The threat to cooperative commerce by those with the exclusive mission of making money on money goes back to the beginnings:

1000 B.C. and earlier: Barter was used for commercial exchange but was usually limited to two-party transactions.

1000-650 B.C.: Various items were used as a medium of exchange, including cattle, stones, and women; none was either divisible or easy to handle.

600 B.C.: First coinage was introduced with various denominations, based on the perceived value of precious metals. This was to be the basic system for next 2,500 years.

Old Testament: "Unto a stranger thou mayest lend upon usury, but unto a brother thou shalt not."[229]

New Testament: Jesus warned: "No man can serve two masters; for either he will hate the one and love the other, or else he will stand by the one and despise the other. You cannot serve God and Mammon."[230]

Rabbinic Literature: "The love of gold will not be free from sin, for he who pursues wealth is led astray by it."[231]

299-400: Roman emperors paid for war by debasing currency. Coin of the realm was recalled, melted, and reissued with lower precious-metal content.

632: In the Koran, Islamic law encouraged patient capital through equity investment but prohibited impatient capital through interest-bearing loans.

---

[229] Deuteronomy 23:20.

[230] Matthew 6:24.

[231] Ecclesiastes 31:5.

789: When Charlemagne became Holy Roman Emperor, he forbade making money on money in his *Admonitio Generalis.*[232]

1200: Anselm of Canterbury considered high interest an offense against the fourth commandment: "Thou shalt not steal."[233]

1213: Cardinal Robert Courçon presented his summa to the Council of Paris, emphasizing labor as the basic value and condemning the making of money on money as a corruption of the commercial process. "The Council ordered each Christian, under pain of excommunication and censure, to work either spiritually or physically and to earn his bread by the sweat of his brow." Courçon concluded: "All usurers, all rebels, and all plunderers would disappear, we would be able to give alms and provide for the churches and everything would return to its original state."[234]

1300: Dante Alighieri in his allegorical poem, the *Divine Comedy*, described people realizing their potential in a world of peace and justice based on a commercial order. Under Dante's scrutiny of the evils contaminating the commercial process, he found a natural law at work and reserved some of the greatest tortures in hell for the financial predators who transgressed this law.

Dante speaks to Virgil:

"Go back a little further," I said, "to where
you spoke of usury as an offense
against God's goodness. How is that made clear?"

Recalling the Old Testament, Virgil replies:

"Near the beginning of *Genesis*, you will see

---

[232] Jacques LeGoff, *Your Money or Your Life: Economy and Religion in the Middle Ages* (New York: Zone Books, 1988; published in France, 1986), pp. 24-25.

[233] *Loc. cit.*

[234] *Loc. cit.*

that in the will of Providence, man was meant
to labor and to prosper. But usurers,
by seeking their increase in other ways,
scorn Nature in herself and her followers."[235]

1694: King William III of England established the Bank of England, and provided privileges for the wealthy and powerful in exchange for their funds to fight wars with France.

1695: John Locke, physician, philosopher, statesman, humanist, and expert on distribution of wealth and monetary matters returned to England after the Glorious Revolution of 1688. Locke promoted individual freedom through his theory of inalienable human rights and also advised governments on the need for monetary control. Locke was concerned about coin-clipping because lightweight coin was circulating at higher value than its metallic value, and a provision for surrender of lightweight coin at high value enriched the fast-moving, well informed, urban speculator to the detriment of the rural, work-preoccupied farmer.[236] Locke described the conflict in capitalism:

> This is evident, that the multiplying of brokers hinders
> the Trade of any Country, by making the Circuit,
> which the Money goes, larger, and in that Circuit more
> stops, so that the Returns must necessarily be slower
> and scantier, to the prejudice of Trade: Besides that,
> they Eat up too great a share of the Gains of Trade, by
> that means Starving the Labourer, and impoverishing
> the Landholder.[237]

1776: Adam Smith assimilated lessons learned over the centuries of the development of capitalism. Smith then anticipated the conflict between the job-growth economy that benefits the many, and

---

[235] Dante, *The Inferno,* John Ciardi, trans. (New York: Mentor Press, 1954), pp. 106-7.

[236] P. H. Kelley, ed., *Locke on Money* (New York: Oxford University Press, 1991), p. 34.

[237] *Ibid.*, p. 241.

privileges for speculation that benefit the few. He warned of the dangers from the "prodigals and projectors" who would make money high-cost and volatile, and would deflect it from job growth.

1789: Alexander Hamilton, George Washington's Secretary of the Treasury, successfully lobbied for payment of war debts at par, and assumption of $21,500,000 of state debts. An incidental effect was profits derived from speculation by those who had anticipated this law and bought up revolutionary soldiers' scrip for 20 cents on the dollar. This was the first use of "insider information" in the new republic.

1790: Thomas Jefferson, Washington's Secretary of State, battled with Hamilton over a United States central bank. Jefferson thought banks were invented "to enrich swindlers at the expense of the honest and industrious."[238]

1792-1845: Scotland's economy flourished with free banking. As no central bank existed, private banks could issue their own money, virtually without bank regulation.[239] The market punishment for bad loans was quick, visible, local, and severe.

1805: President Jefferson opposed the National Bank and favored State banks as a means of diffusing the power of financial capitalism. He exhorted his Secretary of the Treasury, Albert Gallatin: "It is the greatest duty we owe to the safety of our Constitution to bring this powerful enemy to a perfect subordination."[240]

1806: Capitalists successfully lobbied for a growing body of law, resisting shorter work days and supporting imprisonment for union activity.[241] The courts outlawed strikes in Philadelphia in 1806, and in New York in 1810.

---

[238] Charles Sellers, *The Market Revolution: Jacksonian America 1815-1846* (New York: Oxford University Press, 1991), p. 46.

[239] George Seligman, *The Theory of Free Banking* (Totowa, New Jersey: Rowan and Littlefield, co-published with the Cato Institute, 1988), p. 7.

[240] Sellers, *op. cit.*, p. 62.

[241] *Ibid.*, p. 54

1812: President James Madison failed in his effort to control finance capitalism because he was forced to negotiate privileges for the bankers in exchange for their funding the War of 1812 when the country was nearly bankrupt. Subsequently, the postwar boom escalated into speculation, much of it on borrowed money. The Panic of 1818-19, the first speculative cycle in the United States, was the result. Madison described finance capitalism as "parasitical."

1814: John Taylor, a Virginia planter and U.S. Senator, defended democracy against the financial oligarchy, describing the fiscal policy originated by Hamilton as one that would produce "a peasantry, wretchedly poor and an aristocracy, luxuriously rich and arrogantly proud." Taylor felt that privileged capital would "in the case of mechanics, soon appropriate the whole of their labor to its use, beyond bare subsistence." Taylor warned about two threats to private property: "The first, by which the poor plunder the rich, is sudden and violent; the second, by which the rich plunder the poor, is slow and legal." Taylor concluded that the political process was biased because "we farmers and mechanics are political slaves because we are political fools."[242]

1830s: Andrew Jackson tried hard to democratize capitalism but he lacked the tools of economic understanding. Jackson engaged in a fierce battle with the head of the Bank of the United States, Nicholas Biddle, and vetoed the National Bank Act passed by Congress with a message that chided the powerful and wealthy for lobbying Congress to add more personal wealth (see introduction to chapter 9).

In Jackson's "Farewell Address," he warned that the "great bone and sinew of this nation" was threatened by "gradual consuming corruption, which is spreading and carrying stock jobbing, land jobbing, and every species of speculation." Jackson pinpointed the problem: Concentrated wealth also means concentrated political power. In some cases, money corrupts politicians; in most cases, it moves the agenda away from the general welfare.

---

[242] *Ibid.*, pp. 119-122. Taylor was in Congress during Jefferson's Administration and later in Madison's. He published *An Inquiry into the Principles and Policies of the United States*. See Eugene T. Mudge, *The Social Philosophy of John Taylor of Carolina* (New York: AMS Press, 1968).

Jackson pointed out that although the people were the democratic majority, they did not have the cohesion and organization to prevail: "The agriculture, the mechanical, and the laboring classes, from their habits and the nature of their pursuits...are incapable of forming extensive combinations to act together. They have but little patronage to give to the press." By contrast, Jackson charged, "Exclusive privileges enable corporations, wealthy individuals, and designing politicians to move together with undivided force...to engross all power in the hands of a few."[243]

Jackson won his battle by killing the Bank of the United States, but he lost the war when the State banks that he favored discredited themselves by providing the easy credit for speculation that caused the economic disaster of 1837. Like Jefferson and Madison before him, Jackson was a reformer who recognized corruption of democratic principles by finance capitalism but lacked the financial sophistication to design effective reforms.

1860s-70s: After the Civil War, dominant finance capitalists persuaded Presidents Andrew Johnson and U.S. Grant to control currency in a deliberate devaluation to restore the asset value of the wealthy to pre-war levels. This technique, copied from the British, caused unemployment, dropping wages, and rising prices in the economic disaster of 1873. Later, Ludwig von Mises would blame economic calamities in England after the Napoleonic Wars and the emergence of Marx on this same brutal practice[244] (see chapter 3).

1888: The Farmers' Alliance organized cooperative warehouses in order to resell at advantageous prices and buy supplies at wholesale with borrowed money. The bankers refused to lend money to the cooperatives, even with good collateral. "The agrarian reformers attempted to overcome a concentrating system of finance capitalism that was rooted in the Eastern commercial banks."[245] The Alliance

---

[243] *Ibid.*, pp. 345-347.

[244] Ludwig von Mises, *The Theory of Money and Credit* (Indianapolis, Indiana: Liberty Classics, 1980; first published in Austria, 1912), p. 498.

[245] Lawrence Goodwyn, *Democratic Promise: The Populist Moment in America* (New York: Oxford University Press, 1976), Introduction, p. xvii.

was also unsuccessful in its effort to get the government to lend money directly from the Treasury.

1896: The Populist Party was defeated. Their platform, including seeking democratic capital, became obscured by William Jennings Bryan's "Cross of Gold" platform, a political argument between gold and silver interests. The Populist Movement declined for lack of reform focus.

1873, 1884, 1893, 1907: Widespread money panics occurred at the height of the crop season when large amounts of money were needed to bring crops to market. This seasonal need could not be met except by paying out limited reserves, causing the whole money supply to contract.[246] When the surge of demand hit New York banks, their choices were either to draw on reserves at higher rates or form syndicates to pool resources and meet demand or borrow gold from Europe to support more lending. Eventually they did none of this, which resulted in local farmers' banks not having liquidity to make loans. This uncertainty caused people to take their money out of the banks, and that in turn caused bank runs and bank failures. At root, the system did not have the flexibility to fund short-term working-capital needs of the most basic industry, agriculture.

1913: Financial panics spawned the Federal Reserve. The Fed was founded to provide the liquidity needed to prevent a repetition of the bank panics, and to prevent the damaging boom/bust cycles by representing the public interest. Roger Lowenstein described this responsibility as follows: "The Federal Reserve System was created, in 1913, for many reasons, but the underlying one was that people no longer trusted private bankers to shepherd the financial markets." From the beginning, however, Lowenstein added: "The Fed is supposed to regulate banking but not to shelter banks."[247]

---

[246] Seligman, *op. cit.*, p. 14.

[247] Roger Lowenstein, *When Genius Failed: The Rise and Fall of Long-Term Capital Management* (New York: Random House, 2000), p. 85.

1928-32: President Herbert Hoover's Republican predecessors had done little to control the leveraged speculation that caused the Crash of 1929. After the crash, Secretary of the Treasury Andrew Mellon followed the time-honored ceremony of regaining "fiscal integrity" by hurting people. Mellon behaved like an avenging angel, shrinking currency 30% in two years and instituting retroactive tax increases as high as 63%. These actions converted Wall Street's overdue stock-market correction into Main Street's Great Depression. The protectionist Smoot-Hawley Act then exported the Depression to many other countries.

The Crash of 1929 is an example of the government's willingness to encourage speculation with easy credit. In that crash, brokers' loans, that is, stock bought "on margin," or borrowed money, went from $1.5 billion in 1923 to $6.0 billion in December 1928. Anyone observing this pattern could have seen the train wreck coming. New borrowings were collateralized by rising values; the sickness fed on itself for years. Banks were borrowing from the government at 5% and then lending at 12%. Corporations were pumping surplus cash into the stock market rather than into either growth or dividends. After the crash, the margin calls demanding that the loans be repaid, fed the downward spiral. As the values plummeted, the borrowers had to come up with more cash, which forced them to sell more, which continued the downward spiral.

A few years later, John Maynard Keynes viewed the catastrophic economic damage done by the stock market crash of 1929, and he put speculation and the motivations of Wall Street into perspective:

> Speculators may do no harm as bubbles on a steady stream of enterprise. But the position is serious when enterprise becomes the bubble on a whirlpool of speculation. When the capital development of a country becomes a by-product of the activities of a casino, the job is likely to be ill-done. The measure of success attained by Wall Street, regarded as an institution of which the proper social purpose is to direct new investment into the most profitable channels in terms of future yield, cannot be claimed as one of

the outstanding triumphs of laissez-faire capitalism —
which is not surprising, if I am right in thinking that
the best brains of Wall Street have been in fact directed
towards a different object.[248]

1930s: After the damage had been done, the government established
the Securities and Exchange Commission (SEC) to prevent future
calamities. Among other moves, the SEC raised margin requirements
to 50%. The speculators now were required to use their own money
for one-half of their bets. By the end of the century, however, the
amount of leverage allowed for speculation was close to 100% in
unregulated hedge funds, the borrowings were in trillions of dollars,
and new laws added opportunities for more leverage.

1932-44: President Franklin Delano Roosevelt in 1936 bragged that
he had neutralized the privileged financial oligarchy during his first
Administration; he planned to complete his mastery of them in the
second. He failed, however, for the usual reason: The government
needed the finance capitalists to fund preparation for World War II.

   FDR reluctantly instituted bank deposit insurance of $5,000
per account to stop bank panics, but he warned that the practice was
an abrogation of market discipline that could cause economic
catastrophes. By the 1980s, deposit insurance had been raised to
$100,000 per account with no limit on how many bank locations
where the speculators might borrow another federally-insured
$100,000. FDR was right, the Savings-and-Loan catastrophe was the
result, and the taxpayers paid for the government's mistake and the
speculators' greed.

1963-1968 : Despite the bipolar tension between the United States
and the U.S.S.R., the world after World War II made economic
progress. The relationship between freedom and improving lives was
becoming clearer, interest rates and inflation were low, and the dollar
was stable. Times were good for long-term investments. Hundreds of
millions of people around the world were improving their lives. Then,

---

[248] John Maynard Keynes, *The General Theory of Employment, Interest and Money*
(New York: Harvest/HBJ Book, 1964; first published in London, 1936), p. 159.

Democrat President Lyndon Johnson caused severe inflation by funding, mainly by deficit spending, both his expansion of the Vietnam War and his "Great Society." The subsequent inflation-fighting drove interest rates up as high as 20%.

1971: Republican President Richard Nixon caused instabilities in the international monetary system that opened up the world's electronic monetary casino. Because of American economic weaknesses in 1971, foreigners were cashing in dollars for gold so fast that the reserve was disappearing. Nixon, forced to "close the gold window" and "float" the dollar, allowed market forces to determine the dollar's value relative to other currencies. As a result, for the first time in commercial history, no mechanism was in place to stabilize currency. According to Joel Kurtzman, "It created enormous arbitrage possibilities and set the stage for the invention of a myriad of new financial products."[249] It also uncoupled the "money" economy from the "real" economy and put them badly out of balance:

> The new neural network of money made its debut
> rather abruptly on Sunday, August 15, 1971, although
> most people did not recognize its appearance for at
> least a decade. It came into being more out of
> expedience than careful planning, when Richard M.
> Nixon, then President, was saddled with a forecast of a
> recession occurring just months before the Presidential
> election of November, 1972. Nixon was also faced
> with a trade balance that had suddenly climbed to a
> negative $4 billion, an inflation rate of nearly 5
> percent, an unemployment figure of just under 5
> percent, and billions of dollars in expenditures to
> support the war in Vietnam. Nixon's critics charged
> that he was mismanaging the economy, and they
> demanded action. Nixon froze wages and prices for 90
> days, tried to make it illegal for unions to strike,

---

[249] Joel Kurtzman, *The Death of Money: How the Electronic Economy Has Destabilized the World's Markets and Created Financial Chaos* (New York: Simon & Schuster, 1993), pp. 50-51.

imposed a 10-percent surtax on imported automobiles and other products, and proposed a cut in income taxes. He also said, to quote the day's vernacular, that he had "closed the gold window."[250]

After Nixon abandoned the world's currency-stabilizing mechanism, the international economy was launched into new and uncharted financial waters. The premise that market forces would discipline the system proved to be invalid because market forces had been compromised by deposit insurance, bank subsidies, and bailouts. Nixon, a Republican, took action in other areas of the economy that contradicted free market principles with unsuccessful efforts to control prices and wages. A less visible effect of Nixon's actions was the beginning of ultra-capitalism, a perversion of capitalism in which impatient and volatile money changed industry's goals from long-term and patient to short-term and greedy. Ultra-capitalists began to demand any action, including breaking up companies, that would produce short-term gains. Kurtzman explained:

> Selling off portions of a company, borrowing money in the capital markets and then paying it out to stockholders as dividends, even using profits not for new investment but to purchase a company's own shares of stock, all became common practices used by companies to keep their stock prices high. The era of long-term investing ended sometime in the 1970s.[251]

1974: The Employees' Retirement Insurance Security Act (ERISA) was signed into law by President Gerald Ford to protect pensions. A worker's money would be available on retirement because it was "funded," that is, cash was taken out of companies, given to trustees to be invested, later to be paid on retirement.

Before ERISA, companies assumed that most of the pension money would be funded out of future earnings; consequently, current cash was used to grow the business. In effect, ERISA took no-cost

---

[250] *Ibid.*, p. 50.

[251] *Ibid.*, p. 136.

growth capital out of companies and invested it primarily in the stock market. Creative financial engineering to direct this workers' money to democratize capitalism, however, was not done. For example, basic pensions could have been insured with the pension money directly invested in companies through a preferred stock paying a 6% annual dividend. A large dividend, plus long-term appreciation, could have given the wage-earner a secure double-digit return.

ERISAs enormous flow of cash, excessive liquidity, hit the stock market at the same time that the benefits of the Information Age revolution were becoming apparent. Arbitrage on the instabilities in the international monetary market, new speculative instruments called "derivatives," and new unregulated institutions called "hedge funds" were being mixed into the financial formula. In combination, they began to drive the bull market to record levels. The world's economy was becoming more and more dominated by ultra-capitalism. Senior government officials in the Treasury Department and the Fed became more involved in protecting finance capitalism rather than pursuing the original mission of regulating it for the common good. Is this not the ultimate contradiction in capitalism when the worker's money is used by ultra-capitalism to concentrate wealth for the few?

Ultra-Capitalism Was Launched during the Last Quarter of the Century and Came to Dominate both the U.S. and World Economy

The foregoing sketch of the tortuous path of capitalism and the many bumps in its road brings us to the final quarter of the 20th century, a time when many believed that economic freedom was ready to unite the world, but other successors to the money changers of history were busy bringing ultra-capitalism into dominance. This was certainly a turning point, for the 21st century will see either the refinement of capitalism through democratic principles or the collapse of capitalism through its concentrated excesses that have already caused instabilities within capitalism itself and world violence.

Ultra-capitalism was the result of the combination of excessive liquidity (from ERISA), excessive volatility (from floating the dollar), and then the contradiction in deregulating banking at the same time that market disciplines were suspended. Each of the four contributing factors was supported by the lobby power of Wall Street, though not in an integrated way. Ultra-capitalism was the unintended consequence of the lack of an integrated policy that could actually control currency and credit for the general welfare. The lobby power of Wall Street sucked ultra-capitalism into this vacuum.

During this time, the struggle between different forms of capitalism was not apparent because most reformers regarded capitalism as a generic monolithic system; democratic capitalism was hardly on the radar screen of economists and interpreters of the culture. Ultra-capitalists were concerned only with short-term earnings, and they treated workers as a cost commodity, an expendable object fit for layoffs. Mergers and acquisitions were a rewarding way for bankers, lawyers, and executives to make large amounts of money. Benefiting from slippery accounting rules, mergers themselves became a way to improve short-term earnings. In this climate, Wall Street measured CEOs in terms of their actions in large and quick downsizings. Wall Street, most of the financial press, and even the Business Schools celebrated ultra-capitalism, calling it the "American Model," that form of capitalism with exclusive interest in building stockholder value. The time frame was always short-term, and the interests of other "stakeholders" were ignored. In this environment, in fact, the word "stakeholders" itself became a pejorative expression.

Information Age industries, although interested in stock price and stock options, depended on the involvement and contributions of their associates. Many traditional companies also built on the loyalty of wage earners and customers. Some of these companies downsized because of global competition, but they did it through attrition, retraining, generous severance, and with a view to maintaining the spirit of cooperation and trust. This part of global capitalism was building momentum on the fundamentals of democratic capitalism: corporate integrity, employee participation, profit-sharing, ownership, job security, and associates who were independent thinkers, educated, and involved.

At the same time, the relationship between government and finance capitalism in the U.S., the world's most successful economy, was growing stronger. Wall Street became transactional and speculative; compensation for investment-banking partners became routine in the $10-to-$50-million a year bracket. Many corporate executives were seduced by the big bucks into ultra-capitalism, choosing short-term profits, downsizing, and deal-making, while matching the multimillion dollar compensation of Wall Street. Kevin Phillips described this new influence of ultra-capitalism:

> Back in the early 1970s, before the global economy was hooked up to supercomputers and changed to the megabyte standard, the financial sector was subordinate to Congress and the White House, and the total of financial trades conducted by American firms or on American exchanges over an entire year was a dollar amount less than the gross national product. By the 1990s, however, through a twenty-four-hour-a-day cascade of electronic hedging and speculating, the financial sector had swollen to an annual volume of trading thirty or forty times greater than the dollar turnover of the "real economy," although the latter was where ordinary Americans still earned their livelihoods.[252]

Deal-makers thrived in this environment. Smart financial people figured out how to make money with OPM (Other People's Money). A company would become targeted for takeover, and in many cases the company's assets would be leveraged to finance the takeover, that is, used as collateral for the borrowed money. The institutional investors supported ultra-capitalism without polling their constituency, for deals always meant a quick win on their investment and a better position on their national ranking.

Most of the deal-makers had an accountant's love of cost-cutting. The complexities of building for the long term were of less interest to deal-makers who discovered that one-dimensional management was all that was required. Shortly after a takeover, the word would go out to cut people, and "downsize" became the familiar expression. Downsizing is easy to do, and it always improves results in the short-term, particularly when tax laws allow the downsizers to

---

[252] Phillips, *op. cit.*, p. 98.

pull in expenses from future years, thereby making increasing profits in following years almost a certainty.

Kevin Phillips also described the history of economic self-contradiction in which the financial part of capitalism became dominant. He traced the history, since the sixteenth century, of Spain, the Netherlands, and then Great Britain, as robust, growing economies that came to be progressively infected and diminished by "financialization." Phillips applied his historical view to the American situation:

> This national transformation was no accident. Economic circumstances had begun souring for Americans in the 1970s, and in the 1980s the United States electorate had embraced new leaders who unleashed the third of America's Republican-led capitalist booms in which income and wealth were realigned upward. Some of these same economic forces worked to the detriment of ordinary Americans by encouraging speculation, shifting tax burdens, and redistributing income.[253]

During similar financialization phases over the centuries in various countries, taxes were shifted to the middle class, manufacturing declined, financial services grew, and capital became more concentrated. The satisfaction of building and selling things morphed into the excitement of making money on money.

LDCs, the First Victims of Ultra-Capitalism

Throughout the 1970s and 1980s, the economic failure of the less developed countries (LDCs) demonstrated the need for an international monetary policy that is long-term, integrated, and protected from the *ad hoc* actions of politicians. This was the presumed mission of the Bank for International Settlements (BIS),

---

[253] Kevin Phillips, *Boiling Point: Republicans, Democrats, and the Decline of Middle-Class Prosperity* (New York: Random House, 1993), pp. 32-3.

located in Basel, Switzerland, that was the formal medium of communication for the powerful central bankers of the G-7 industrialized nations.

The LDC failures contained many lessons that, if learned, would have prevented future economic damage. In the 1970s, South American countries and Mexico were excited by great growth potential at the same time that New York banks were awash in petrodollars from Arab countries. South America's growth was financed with short-term money and impatient capital; worse, loans were made on a floating interest rate, and, even worse, much of it was lent directly to national governments (politicians), not to companies (business people). Greedy bankers chased profitable loans and ignored fundamental banking principles, such as not lending short-term money for long-term investment. Why were the loans on a floating rate? Bad banking had placed the risk on the economically weak countries that were trying to improve the lives of their citizens, instead of placing the risk on the banks that were trying to make more money on money. A long-term investment in improving the lives of desperately poor people should not be undertaken with short-term money with an interest rate that could rise out of sight, as it did.

The effect on the world's economy from rising American inflation caused by the deficit funding of Johnson's "Guns and Butter" programs, prompted the world's central bankers to gang up on Paul Volcker and insist on action in the late 1970s as soon as he became chairman of the Fed. Volcker then conducted a scorched-earth attack to reduce inflation, and in the process drove the cost of money up to 20%. An unintended consequence of this high interest rate was the bankrupting of several of the LDCs because their interest rates "floated" up. After the economic damage to the LDCs, the U.S. government and the International Monetary Fund (IMF), which had failed to put the necessary structure in place and so contributed to the problem, then reacted with credit-tightening actions that hurt people through lower wages, higher prices, lost jobs, and curtailed government assistance.

The common denominators in the South American debacles were over-lending of short-term money and excessive liquidity that encouraged investment in risky projects or speculation. This short-term hot money then fled the troubled country when the economy reversed. International banks had no protocols to measure the total of short-term debt being accumulated by countries, including the ability to relate this debt to the amount of patient capital invested. This debt/equity ratio, vital in viewing the level of a company's financial risk, was ignored in whole countries. This miss is an important example of freedom without the requisite discipline. The freedom was of free capital roaming the world, promoted by the U.S. and enabled by the dismantlement of cross-border capital controls. The lack of discipline was the absence of a structure that would have prevented too much hot money from coming in, and too much hot money leaving too fast.

Walter Wriston, head of Citibank at that time, stated the faulty rationale for imprudent lending: "Countries do not go bankrupt." Despite Wriston's misplaced optimism, countries did go broke, and several large New York banks, including Citibank itself, went technically bankrupt. All of the tricks to prevent the full damage of bad loans to banking profits were invoked. For example, a typical subterfuge was to lend more money to an already broke LDC so that they could pay the interest. When the interest went unpaid, the loan was designated "non-performing," and the rules required that the loan be written off, that is, a reduction in the bank's profits.

At the same time, many big banks were also hyperventilating over bad real estate loans they had made. Underlying these speculative, bad-banking actions, the banks' basic business, commercial loans, was also declining. Competition from the finance arms of big corporations was taking this business away. For example, General Electric's aggressive CEO, Jack Welch, had learned how easy it is to make huge profits in financial services.[254] The United States government, instead of staying on the sidelines and watching free-market forces in action, decided to save commercial banks through deregulation. The government changed the mission of commercial bankers from making prudent loans to speculation, just as the government had changed the S&L industry's mission from providing low-cost mortgages to speculation.

---

[254] Jack Welch with John A. Byrne, *Jack: Straight from the Gut* (New York: Warner Business Books, 2001), pp. 234-5.

Most commercial bankers had not been trained for speculation. If they had wanted a higher-risk career, they could have become investment bankers. A well-run conservative bank, such as Bankers Trust, which had been successful at lending money for commerce, became a not-very-good currency trader, and ended up being sued by Proctor & Gamble. The biggest bank, Citicorp, was near bankruptcy several times from bad loans and speculation under the same leadership, but the government bailed it out each time. The combination of deregulation together with the abrogation of market disciplines pushed the bankers toward ultra-capitalism, that is, towards an economy in which the desire to make money on money goes up, while the sensitivity to the quality of the loans goes down.

The government, through the Federal Reserve, suspended the effects of competition and ignored the mistakes of bankers by feeding the banks a spread between the cost to borrow at 3% or less, and the return on Treasury Bonds at 6% or more, a spread so large that bankers only whispered about it. Some called it "Greenspan spread." This weaning process brought banks back to health at the taxpayers' expense and further desensitized the bankers to the negative effects of imprudent loans. This experience was early evidence that the government's true mission was *protecting* finance capitalism, not *regulating* it. Little democratic debate over this shift of the banking mission was heard, whether in the halls of Congress or elsewhere. All of a sudden, it seemed, one's friendly, conservative banker who formally had carefully fed capital into the job-growth economy, had become an enthusiastic high-stakes player in the world's electronic monetary casino.

The Hunt Caper

One of the more bizarre episodes in the history of ultra-capitalism's domination of currency and credit was the silver round-up by rich Texans, Bunker and Herbert Hunt. The Hunts tried to corner the silver market, presumably as the ultimate hedge against inflation.

Silver had been selling for $6 an ounce in early 1979; by November, it was up to $18.77; then it topped at $52.50 in January 1980. This movement exposed the plan by the Hunts and some Saudi

Arabian associates to corner the market. The Hunts had been accumulating silver since 1973.

> They ended up controlling some two-thirds of all silver in the United States. In doing so, they borrowed nearly $1.8 billion from banks and brokerage firms at rates as low as 5% to buy silver-future contracts on margin. The collateral for the loans was the loftily priced silver assets themselves. In February and March, 1980, Hunt borrowings accounted for an astonishing 9% of all new U. S. bank credit."[255]

The same inflation-fighting high interest rates of 1980 helped get the Hunts in deep trouble. Silver prices plunged to $10.40 an ounce by the end of March, 1980. The Hunt's potential default threatened to topple their main broker, Bache Halsey Stuart Shields, and possibly the giant bank, First National of Chicago.

This presented Chairman Paul Volcker of the Federal Reserve with a difficult choice. The speculators, and those who lent them money, should have been punished quickly and severely by the discipline of free-market forces, but lacking government control of leveraged speculation, the dollar amounts had grown so huge that potential failure triggered a concern over the entire financial system. The government came to the rescue when Volcker worked over the weekend to help bail out the Hunts, "giving his blessing as godfather to a thirteen-bank consortium for a new $1.1 billion, ten-year loan to enable the Hunts to repay their short-term debt."[256]

The Hunts were hurt financially, but their $2 billion in losses did not affect their lifestyle. Some in Congress criticized Volcker for having bailed out the Hunts. This event further sensitized the banking system to the idea that if a potential failure is big enough, then it carries a *de facto* taxpayer guaranteed bailout. This unstated policy was far from Adam Smith's ideal of free banking in which people who take stupid risks, and banks that make stupid loans, are punished

---

[255] Steven Solomon, *The Confidence Game: How Unelected Central Bankers Are Governing the Changed Global Economy* (New York: Simon & Schuster, 1995), p. 144.

[256] *Ibid.*, p. 145.

quickly, severely, locally, and visibly by the natural actions of the free market. Steven Solomon summarized the Hunt escapade as follows:

> It touched a raw nerve in the bosom of democratic capitalism that politicians were only too glad to deflect onto central bankers. It was hard to explain to the democratic body politic why rescuing big financial institutions, because of their unique ability to spread contagion, served the public good while the government failed to intervene to save ordinary businesses employing thousands. In the United States, this tension always threatened to reawaken the barely dormant, passionate political divisions that had fought over money since the founding of the republic.[257]

Ronald Reagan Freed That Which Should Be Controlled, and Controlled That Which Should Be Free

The S&L scandal is a case study for all citizens to learn how the government fails to control currency and credit for the general welfare but does control deposit insurance for the benefit of the speculators. President Ronald Reagan made speeches about how a democratic republic's success depends on diffusion of both economic and political power (see chapter 5, introduction), but then his Administration moved in the opposite direction, concentrating wealth and power. An early example of this misdirection was the deregulation of the Savings and Loan industry. Reagan proudly described this deregulation in 1982 as the most important financial legislation in fifty years, not realizing that he was initiating an economic catastrophe.

A member of the Congressional staff and an industry lobbyist added the fine print to the law that escalated federal deposit insurance to $100,000, with no limit on the number of locations at which speculators might borrow. President Reagan was not in the habit of studying the details. The Secretary of the Treasury, the former head of Merrill Lynch, was pleased to anticipate a profitable shift of the

---

[257] *Loc. cit.*

peoples' money from savings accounts to certificates of deposit that would benefit Wall Street.

Republican President Reagan's mistakes can be traced back to Democrat President Johnson's mistakes in the 1960s when his inflationary policies resulted in interest rates that later rose to 20%. These actions were the direct cause of the Savings and Loan debacle, for the S&Ls were in the impossible position of borrowing high-cost, short-term money to invest in low-return, long-term mortgages. Congress tried to fix the problem with deregulation that caused worse problems. Later, Congress tried to rectify the damage caused by bad deregulation, going so far in the other direction that financially sound banks were forced out of business. Later, these banks successfully sued the government. Each of these mistakes by politicians was paid for by the taxpayer.[258]

Reagan was determined to "get the government off peoples' backs." He was convinced that "the government was the problem, not the solution." He then proceeded, like Presidents before and after him, with badly designed programs that failed in their mission, gave deregulation a bad name, and further confused people about the proper function of government. The source of the confusion lay in applying the concept and practices of *laissez-faire* to the monetary function. *Laissez-faire* could be applied to free banking, but that is not a practical alternative. The Founders had understood, and experience demonstrates, that control of currency and credit is a prime government obligation that must be part of the structure, not part of *laissez-faire* economic freedom.

While the Reagan Administration was misapplying the theory of *laissez-faire* to deregulate the banking industry, the government was at the same time protecting the banking industry. In 1984, the government actually bought the Continental Illinois Bank for $5.5 billion. Unable to get the other banks to bail Continental out, the government nationalized it, and within two years wrote off $1.2 billion in bad loans.[259] This event was the formal beginning of the

---

[258] Stephen Pizzo, Mary Fricker, and Paul Muolo, *Inside Job: The Looting of America's Savings and Loans* (New York: McGraw-Hill, 1989), p. 325.

[259] William Greider, *Secrets of the Temple: How the Federal Reserve Board Runs the Country* (New York: Simon & Schuster, 1987), p. 631.

"too big to fail" policy, the notion that once economic blunders get big enough to threaten the entire financial structure, then the government steps in to clean up the mess.

Two years earlier, much smaller Penn Square Bank in Oklahoma had failed. Many of its bad loans had been "floated upstream" to Continental Illinois and so contributed to Continental's downfall. Penn Square, however, had been allowed to fail after a battle among the Fed, the U.S. Comptroller, and the head of the FDIC (Federal Deposit Insurance Corporation), William Isaac, who argued: "If we bail this thing out, what kind of signals are we sending to the financial system? That you can engage in the most shoddy banking practices and, in the end, the government will bail you out?"[260]

Bill Isaac carried the day, that time, so Penn Square disappeared, but he had delayed the capitulation to the "too big to fail" government policy for only two years when the government bailed out Continental Illinois. America now had the worst of both worlds: The profits of big banks were privatized for the few, and their losses were nationalized and made the responsibility of the taxpayer. This ultra-capitalist corruption cost American taxpayers hundreds of billions of dollars directly, but that was small in comparison to the economic damage at home and abroad by bankers desensitized to the quality of loans.

Advice from an M&A Expert

The conventional wisdom in ultra-capitalism is that takeovers are provoked by entrenched, poorly performing management. This may be true occasionally, but the compelling motivation for takeovers is money. Deals are extremely lucrative to all involved—bankers, lawyers, accountants, CEOs of takeover companies, and even the CEOs of the companies taken over. In ultra-capitalism, deals need only this logic: "If it can be financed, it should be done."

From the earliest days of the takeover craze in the 1970s, Marty Lipton was one of the most famous mergers and acquisitions (M & A) lawyers. Lipton had made money from the process by collecting $20 million fees, but later he criticized the system, not as

---

[260] *Ibid.*, p. 498.

an efficient reallocation of resources, but rather as merely a new way to make lots of money without regard to the social impact. In 1987, Lipton published his thoughts from an earlier lecture.[261] From his profound experience in many deals, Lipton could separate the superficialities from the realities. The following were his major points:

- Takeovers are driven by speculative financial considerations, not by intrinsic business reasons.

- Some managements may be deficient, but, as a group, they pursue socially beneficial objectives such as expanding the enterprise, improving productivity, and cultivating planning, research, and development.

- Financial corporatism has none of these objectives.

- Institutional investors, managers of pension funds, dominate the market. They are graded and compensated on annual performance.

- Tax and accounting rules favor takeovers: Interest is tax deductible, dividends are not; acquisition costs, including premiums, can be capitalized and amortized over many years.

Lipton wondered how much the job sector might have been improved if the $139 billion that financed mergers and acquisitions in 1985 had been invested in new products, new markets, and automation. Lipton believed that the laws gave special privileges to the takeover artists. To level the field, he proposed elimination of double taxation on dividends, elimination of tax deductibility on junk bonds, no two-tier bids, all financing in place before announcement of a takeover, no voting rights for short-term equity, a legal limit of 10% of junk bonds as a percent of S&L assets, and a graduated capital-

---

[261] Martin Lipton, "Corporate Governance in the Age of Finance Corporatism," *The University of Pennsylvania Law Review*, volume 136, number 1, November, 1987.

gains tax on securities held for less than five years, starting with 60% on gains made in less than a year. Most of his proposals bounced off the walls of Congress, built up over the years by ultra-capitalism's lobbying.

The Plaza Accord Misfires

In New York in 1991, President George Bush and Secretary of the Treasury Jim Baker addressed the growing trade imbalance between the U.S. and Japan, seeking a stronger yen and a weaker dollar in order to reduce U. S. imports from Japan and increase U. S. exports. The communiqué issued from that meeting said that a 10-12% downward adjustment of the dollar was "manageable," or around 215 yen to the dollar. By the summer of 1992, the yen was under 80!

This wild ride of the yen demonstrated why politicians should not disrupt free-market forces with non-integrated solutions. The drop of the yen in this case demonstrated the fundamental instability of the system.

Countries with their currency pegged to the dollar, such as Thailand, were ignored in the process, despite the large dislocations that were caused to that economy.

After the Plaza Accord, the Japanese reduced their interest rate to less than 3% in order to fund the productivity improvements that were then necessary to protect their export sales from the stronger yen. Later, they took the interest rate to almost zero. The unintended consequence of this low-cost Japanese money was the over-funding of Asian economies, resulting in too much money put into too many poor investments. With politicians destabilizing the world economy through these kinds of capricious actions, and with this level of volatility, no currency system, whether fixed, pegged, or floating, can work well.

The United States supported various financial inducements for U.S. companies to move operations to other countries. In addition, ultra-capitalism's wage arbitrage became a standard practice constantly seeking the country with the lowest available wage rate. In some cases, the depressed rates had been caused by currency devaluation, itself provoked by ultra-capitalism.

The trend from manufacturing to financial services has historically preceded an economic decline. The 1998 yearbook of the Organization for Economic Cooperation and Development (OCED) shows the U.S. beginning to lose ground:

> With a per capita income at last count of just $27,821 a
> year, the United States trailed no fewer than eight other
> nations. These include Japan, Denmark, Sweden,
> Germany and Austria, all of which devote a larger
> share of their labor force to manufacturing than the
> United States. Switzerland, with the highest per capita
> income, $41,411, had a high level of manufacturing.[262]

After nearly a half-century of government inducements for American manufacturing to move to other countries, mainly for reasons of political hegemony, President Bush tried to rectify the damage by ignoring free market forces and tweaking the currency.

Alligators Lurking in the Swamp

While manufacturing was declining, ultra-capitalism was on the rise. The "prodigals and projectors" had a new toy called "derivatives"—puts, calls, options, and futures of all types. A derivative is a financial instrument by which a speculator bets on the future value of another, underlying financial instrument. Carol Loomis described them as "alligators lurking in the swamp." The alligators have been multiplying: $1.6 trillion in 1987, $7.4 trillion in 1991, $16 trillion in 1994, and over $100 trillion in the new century.[263] These numbers can be compared to the entire U.S. GDP of about $10 trillion. Derivatives have given the speculators new ways to bet, new ways to leverage their bets, and new ways to avoid banking regulations.

---

[262] Eamonn Fingleton, *In Praise of Hard Industries: Why Manufacturing, Not the Information Economy, Is the Key to Future Prosperity* (New York: Houghton Mifflin Company, 1999), p. 7.

[263] Carol J. Loomis, "The Risk That Won't Go Away, Like Alligators in a Swamp, Derivatives Lurk in the Global Economy. Even the CEOs of Companies that Use Them Don't Understand Them," *Fortune*, March 7, 1994, p. 40.

After the Crash of 1929, a new statutory provision, "Regulation T," limited the amount that brokers could lend for the purchase of stock to 50% of the total investment. Derivatives, however, are bets on the *direction* that stocks will go; therefore, they are not subject to Regulation T. Joel Kurtzman described this new and uncontrolled phenomenon:

> Conceptually, these abstract products are often outgrowths of real products that have been traded on the futures markets for years. But when they go electronic, they do it with a twist. Rather than trading a contract today for a bushel of wheat to be delivered next year, these new products are usually contracts to take delivery on a financial product. Instead of buying wheat on the futures market, the new products that are traded are contracts to buy stocks, specific ones or all the stocks on the entire stock market, in some cases, and even such esoteric items as foreign currencies and future interest rates. Future contracts on interest rates did not exist in 1971. They did not really get into the market until the late 1970s when Citicorp invented them in Tokyo.[264]

Roger Lowenstein, like Kurtzman, lamented the lack of regulation of derivatives. They both saw the sheer volume of trading as a threat because so much damage could be done so fast. Lowenstein pointed out another feature of these derivatives, the disclosure problem that makes it increasingly difficult to read financial statements and learn the facts:

> The Street has been using equity swaps to get around Regulation T for almost a decade, but in recent years the scale of the business had soared. The first modern swap was engineered in 1981, by 1990 there were $2 trillion worth of interest rate swaps, which are just one type of derivative. By 1997 the total was $22 trillion.

---

[264] Kurtzman, *op. cit.*, p. 128.

One offshoot, largely unintended, of this tremendous growth was that banks' financial statements became increasingly obscure. Derivatives weren't disclosed in any way that was meaningful to outsiders. As the volume of deals exploded, the banks' balance sheets revealed less and less of their total obligations. By the mid-1990s, the financial statements of even many mid-sized banks were wrapped in an impenetrable haze.[265]

The banks did not care; they were making too much money. The government did not care; the Federal Reserve Board was encouraging the free flow of capital by *protecting* the process, not *regulating* it. Lowenstein added:

With regard to derivatives, the policy-making arm of the Fed took a *laissez-faire* approach starting with Greenspan, who was enamored with the seamless artistry of the new financial tools. In public debates, Greenspan repeatedly joined forces with private bankers, led by Citicorp's John Reed, who were fighting tooth and nail to head off proposals for tougher disclosure requirements. Even as hedge funds increasingly used swaps to dodge the Fed's own margin rules, Greenspan cast an approving eye. Incredibly, rather than trying to extend some form of margin rule to the derivative world, Greenspan proposed to eliminate the margin rules entirely. His 1995 testimony to Congress read like a banker's brief. At its heart was a beguiling single idea: That more trading (and hence more lending) was always good because it bolstered "liquidity."[266]

The Fed explained that they did not have to control derivatives because the banks, being regulated, did that for them. This statement would be funny if the problem were not so serious. The banks were—

---

[265] Lowenstein, *op. cit.*, pp. 103-4.

[266] *Ibid.*, pp. 105-106.

and still are—a part of the problem, not its solution. According to Lowenstein:

> Save for the Fed, the only ones who could restrain
> derivative lending were the banks. But Wall Street
> never polices itself in good times. The banks' own
> balance sheets were steadily ballooning; by the late
> 1990s, Wall Street was leveraged 25 to 1.[267]

Greenspan did not heed Adam Smith's warning to beware of the "prodigals and projectors" who would deflect capital away from job growth and the general welfare and deliver it to the speculators. In his advocacy of "liquidity," Greenspan ignored the overheating of South American economies in the 1980s with petrodollars, and the "excessive liquidity" from ERISA that helped propel the bull market. The Fed's position did not anticipate the Asian crisis of 1997, in fact, it helped cause it. Ultra-capitalism had been given easy credit, market disciplines had been abandoned, repetitive crises had occurred, and the government that had in effect designed the flawed system kept on bailing it out instead of either fixing the system or letting market disciplines apply their corrections.

A democratic republic succeeds only by reflecting the will and wisdom of the people. The derivatives casino would be quickly shut down if the majority understood this corruption of capitalism. The only thing certain is that when this abrogation of government responsibility to control currency and credit for the general welfare results in an economic decline, it will be the people—remote and uninformed—who will be hurt.

The Federal Reserve's Mission: To Serve Main Street or Wall Street?

In the latter part of the twentieth century, the Federal Reserve Board effectively supported the growth and dominance of ultra-capitalism through deregulation, abandonment of market disciplines, excessive liquidity, and excessive volatility. This observation is a contrarian view at a time when the long-time Chairman of the Federal

---

[267] *Ibid.*, p.106.

Reserve is deified by most, crediting him for continued economic success. In 2002, however, when the market and economy slid into decline, his sainthood was questioned but not yet in a way likely to identify root causes of the world's economic woes. He was successful only in the sense that his mistakes were not visible for a long time, and he did eventually recognize the radical impact of the Information Age.

Greenspan's presumed function was to prevent inflation, with a subsidiary function, "not to upset the markets." His focus on inflation appropriately moved from the traditional worry about a rise in factory-workers wages to asset inflation in the stock market. Greenspan's inflation-fighting tool was his power to raise or lower interest rates. An increase can, for example, trade off a reduction in inflation with a slowing of industries like home-building. When Greenspan became worried about stock market inflation, however, the obvious question is why he did not limit the amount of money speculators could borrow from their brokers to buy stock. The equally obvious answer is because that action would have been unpopular with Wall Street and contrary to Greenspan's liquidity obsession.

The structural arrangement of government and the Federal Reserve Board was based on the perceived tension between government's urge to exercise control over money, and the capitalists' not trusting government to follow that urge in a way that finance capitalists could approve. Central banks, including the Federal Reserve, were established to bridge this tension between government and finance capitalism. Steven Solomon analyzed this relationship between democratic national policy and finance capitalism:

- Central banks arbitrated an unspoken marriage of convenience between two disparate regimes that constituted democratic capitalism, the democratic nation-state polity and market capitalist economy, to make the rules of the game by which society's wealth was produced and managed. Since the sixteenth century, these two overlapping, though at times opposing, forms of social organization evolved together through uneasy and shifting *modus vivendi*.

- The logic of capital was to maximize profit, regardless of national borders, political rights, social equity, or environmental consequences, and to seek to preserve the value of the capital it accumulated. The primary purpose of the democratic liberal state, by contrast, was to ensure liberty, equity, defense, and economic welfare for its citizenry. The disparate logics of capital and the democratic state converged on one crucial common goal, economic prosperity, and its prerequisite, a stable and friendly political economic environment for capitalist enterprise. Each of the main models of democratic capitalism, Anglo-American *laissez-faire*, European liberal social welfare, Japanese neo-mercantilist capitalism, provided this with varying divisions of responsibility and power between the market and governmental realms.

- One of the main fulcrums of prosperity that had to be managed was the special role of money and finance. Governments naturally preferred to exercise the state monopoly over money freely itself. But private capitalists did not trust them and possessed a veto: abstention from lending. Central banks evolved as a medium of compromise from this historical tension, especially from the mid-nineteenth century, when the paper money and credit revolution had assisted "financial capitalism" to dominate the heights of the market economy.[268]

Solomon's description of the tension between the liberal state and private bankers is useful to an understanding of the proper role of finance capitalism in support of the job-growth economy. Unfortunately, the tension was historically resolved in favor of Wall Street because the government needed capital to fight wars, and the

---

[268] Solomon, *op. cit.*, pp. 32-3.

politicians who were supposed to be representing *Main Street* let *Wall Street*, instead, write the rules.

Abetting this Constitutional failure during the 20th century was the persistent ignorance of reformers who convinced themselves that they were controlling the appetites of capitalism when, in most cases, they were missing the mark with small suffocating laws. This combined failure of the political left and political right resulted in the impediment of concentrated wealth that has now escalated into ultra-capitalism that threatens both the national and the world's economy.

Solomon's analysis is penetrating and useful, but I cannot be true to democratic capitalism without challenging his conventional wisdom that the maximization of profits and welfare of the citizenry are based on "disparate logics." This premise, unexamined by so many, limits visibility of the complementary logic of democratic capitalism.

The need for correction of these persistent failures is now clear. The voting public must elect a new breed of political representatives who will design comprehensive, integrated, long-term, fiscal and monetary policies, not to protect the special interests of the ultra-capitalists but to promote the general welfare of all of the citizens. Now that the people are the main source of new capital, the government can no longer be held hostage to Wall Street as the main source of capital.

In Ultra-Capitalism, Even Bonds Are Speculative Instruments

In the 1980s, traders in government bonds became more important as the deficit grew, and something as prosaic as government bonds became a speculative commodity. The politicians made political moves to pressure the Fed on interest rates, and they took action to effect the value of the currency, both moves being characteristic of traditional economic nationalism. The bond traders then used increased volatility to turn these instruments over every few weeks instead of every few years. Speculators love this rapid turnover and brokers churn more commissions out of the increased turnover. Brokers also can make money by guessing right, not on fundamentals, but on what they perceive the Fed will do with interest rates. For example, if the Fed moves rates up, the bond market can either respond positively to a movement against inflation or it can respond negatively, assuming that the Fed is concerned about more inflation. The speculator guesses which one, and then bond derivatives are bet like casino chips. Al Ehrbar described this speculative adventure on margin:

> Consider this somewhat simplified example. An institution puts up $100,000 in cash to buy $10 million of treasury bonds yielding 6.2% and, here's the leverage, borrowing the other $9.9 million at a rate of 3.5%. It collects $620,000 in interest on the bonds, pays $346,500 in interest on the loan and winds up netting $273,500 a year on its $100,000 investment, unless long-term rates head up, that is. When that happens, the institution gets a margin call to put up another $100,000 for each drop in bond prices, and it can quickly become a net loser, even if the carry remains rich.[269]

Interest rates, controlled by the Fed, kept coming down in the early 1990s for the political reason of "helping the economy," and then the Fed began to raise interest rates to "fight inflation." This government-induced volatility first provoked many to refinance homes and then later stopped them from refinancing homes. What on the surface looked like a straightforward transaction, borrowing money to buy a home, became another casino chip called "mortgage-backed securities." When the refinancing of mortgages slowed to a crawl, reflecting both saturation and the slowing action of the Fed, the mortgage-backed securities took a dive. Over-leveraged companies, such as Askin Capital, which had been using exotic techniques, went broke. Then, following another of Wall Street's formulas: "Sell what you can, not what you should," $20 billion in 10-year T-bills were sold in March and April of 1994 to offset the new risk in mortgage-backed securities. The average life of mortgage-backed securities was stretching out, and they suddenly became longer-term bonds which are riskier because they are more sensitive to changes in interest rates.

---

[269] Al Ehrbar, "The Great Bond Market Massacre, A Perilous Rise in Leverage," *Fortune*, October 17, 1994, p. 77.

Nervous traders on margin tried to average out the maturities on their holdings, that is, the mix of 5-, 10-, 20-, and 30-year bonds. In this circumstance, the bond traders could not sell enough ten-year mortgage-backed securities, so they did the next best thing and sold ten-year government bonds. Now, all of a sudden, a sell pressure was on ten-year government bonds. "What's happening? Where did this come from? How do I get out? At what loss? The phone's ringing, they want me to cover my margin. Maybe this is a free-fall; I'd better dump!" Sophisticated investors such as George Soros diversified their government bonds in many countries but still took a beating in this bond massacre.

The signals in a speculative cycle are frequently clear, but as the process wears on, the numbers get bigger, and the greed grows stronger. In the Great Bond Market Massacre of 1994, bondholders worldwide suffered more than $1 trillion in losses. Ehrbar detailed that primary government dealers' net borrowing, secured by Treasury bonds, increased from under $50 billion in 1990 to almost $200 billion in 1994. The crash was caused, as usual, by too much money on loan for speculation. The media, as usual, searched for some explanation other than leveraged speculation, including the Federal Reserve's rate increase or even a political assassination in Mexico. The real logic, however, never changes: When margin calls go out, and the cash is not there, values plummet. The bond massacre was a liquidation unrelated to economic fundamentals in either the U.S. or Europe.

The bond massacre of 1994 resulted in visible casualties. Hedge-fund managers lost heavily, life-insurance companies lost $50 billion, other insurance companies lost $20-25 billion. Rep. Henry B. Gonzalez (D., Texas), Chair of the House Banking Committee, held hearings in April, 1994, on the dangers posed by hedge funds using large credit lines for speculative purposes. Gonzalez maintained that hedge funds now needed extra scrutiny because of their ability to disrupt markets. Despite Gonzalez's urgings, no significant change in the control of leveraged speculation was forthcoming from Capitol Hill, for Wall Street, not Main Street, was still the favored route.

The Mexican Crisis of 1994

The 1994 economic crisis in Mexico was a repetition of the earlier one in South America and in Mexico in 1982, and it should have been another warning for the Asian crisis to come in 1997. The root causes in all of these cases were the same, as follows:

- No international disciplines to control the amount of short-term loans. "Hot money" stimulates economic growth beyond prudent levels. In every case when there is an oversupply of money, the result is increasingly risky projects and speculation, and Mexico in 1994 was no exception. When the economy weakens because of the effect of imprudent loans and speculation, the currency sharks are attracted. The lenders of hot money, corporations, and the well-informed wealthy, sensing the attack, then flee the currency, creating a self-fulfilling prophecy: The currency goes into free-fall. Cross-border capital controls previously prevented hot money from precipitous flight out of a country, but they had been taken down in most countries at the urging of U.S. officials.

- No international monetary structure was in place to balance the hot money and patient capital needed for long-term growth of a country. The result was excessive liquidity in hot money, too little patient capital, and no protocols to move short-term money into patient capital in an emergency.

- Bankers in the U.S., motivated by short-term earnings and stock prices, made profitable but risky loans, knowing that they were protected by the government from a bad-loan calamity. They expected the government to bail them out, as it had done many times in the past. This abrogation of free-market disciplines makes a mockery out of the expression "free movement of capital."

- Nations leading the world economy had not structured a new stabilizing mechanism for international currency after the dollar was floated in 1971. Commerce hates instability; speculators live off of it.

- In 1994, New York banks were buying *tesobonos*, Mexican bonds denominated in dollars. For the U. S. lender, *tesobonos* were a hedge against changes in the value of the *peso*; for the Mexican borrower, they were available money without a currency-risk premium. When the Mexican economy crashed in 1994, the United States government bailed out the bankers with $50 billion of the taxpayer's money.

The Mexican economy was severely damaged. Wages dropped, prices went up, social tensions were exacerbated, civil war broke out in Chiapas, and students occupied and shut down a university in Mexico City. The bankers and politicians later described the Mexican bailout as a success story, but in 2001, Henry Kissinger commented on the sustained damage to the people: "The poorer segment of the population never regained during the recoveries what they had lost during the cycle of crises.... In Mexico, wages are still below the level preceding the 1982 crisis."[270]

Asian Tigers Caught in a Trap in 1997

After the demise of Communism, many believed that the world would become a better place as economic freedom improved lives and spread around the globe. Economic freedom was expected to eliminate material scarcity, and economic common purpose was expected gradually to reduce the hatreds and violence. The people in Thailand, Malaysia, Indonesia, and South Korea demonstrated that this was an attainable opportunity, for they were enjoying a better life through forms of economic freedom. Concerning Indonesia, Paul

---

[270] Henry Kissinger, *Does America Need a Foreign Policy?* (New York: Simon & Schuster, 2001), p. 226.

Blustein, recipient of the Gerald Loeb Award in business journalism, reported as follows:

> Indonesia's per capita income in 1970 had been two-thirds that of India and Nigeria, but by 1996 it had risen to $1,080, four and a half times that of Nigeria and triple that of India. Life expectancy at birth in Indonesia was sixty-five by the middle 1990s, compared with forty-nine a quarter century earlier; the adult illiteracy rate had fallen to 16 percent from 43 percent; the infant mortality had shrunk to 49 per 1,000 live births from 114.[271]

This extraordinary performance in providing new freedoms and new human rights to the people of the world's fourth largest nation had begun in 1966, when Suharto gave the responsibility for economic planning to Widjojo Nitisastro, a man of intellect, honesty, and energy. Widjojo, a Ph.D. graduate of the University of California, understood the fundamentals of economic freedom: He quelled triple-digit inflation by restraints on government spending; he pressed Suharto to open the economy to foreign investment and trade; and he convinced Suharto to ease up on heavy government regulation.[272] The result of this infusion of new economic freedom was an average growth of 7 percent from 1979 to 1996; stable prices; and millions of people better educated, in better health, with more freedom of choices, and enjoying a better quality of life in general.

Promoters of human rights, democracy, and improvement in the human condition around the world should carefully study not only Indonesia's performance and the theory and application that supported it but also the similar improvements in the other three countries of Southeast Asia. Among the lessons learned will be the realization that economic freedom is so powerful that it can improve lives despite continued imperfections in both the political structure and culture. Once the freedom genie is out of the bottle in the economic sphere, then the other freedoms will follow, in time, and be

---

[271] Paul Blustein, *The Chastening: Inside the Crisis that Rocked the Global Financial System and Humbled the IMF* (New York: Public Affairs, 2001), p. 90.

[272] *Ibid.*, p. 89.

attained, just as it has happened in other countries. The success story in these Asian countries up to 1997 was a confirmation of Marx's axiom that social progress depends on moving towards a superior economic system. Many human-rights activists, who want to start with changes in government and improvements in human rights, fail to make this crucial connection between progress in attaining human rights by achieving economic momentum first.

What, then, caused the Asian crisis of 1997? Joseph E. Stiglitz, Chair of President Bill Clinton's Council of Economic Advisors and later Chief Economist at the World Bank, was quite clear in his opinion:

> The countries in East Asia had no need for additional capital, given their high savings rate, but still capital liberalization was pushed on these countries in the late eighties and early nineties. I believe that capital account liberalization was *the single most important factor leading to the crisis.*[273]

These Asian countries were caught in an ultra-capitalist "capital crisis" that was treated as a "liquidity crisis" by the IMF and the U.S. government. A capital crisis is a new phenomenon, the product of ultra-capitalism's excessive liquidity and volatility. This crisis should be prevented, but if it does occur, the cure is the opposite of that for a liquidity crisis because the economy has to be brought back up to speed and not slowed down further. The IMF's slow-down policies and actions in Southeast Asia were the opposite of what was needed.

The causes of the Asian crisis were the same as those described for the 1994 Mexican crisis: excessive liquidity, excessive volatility, bank deregulation, and suspension of market disciplines. The rush of short-term money from international bankers overheated the Asian economies, resulting in speculation and the funding of questionable projects. The consequent economic weakness might have been corrected by a modest tightening and a slower growth rate;

---

[273] Joseph E. Stiglitz, *Globalization and Its Discontents* (New York: W. W. Norton, 2002), p. 99.

however, because of the superior power of ultra-capitalism's currency speculators, hot money fled the countries; national currencies went into free fall, some dropping 70%; and economic progress was reversed. Previously successful businesses that had provided jobs and paid the bills suddenly had the cost of those bills multiplied by four. Many good companies could not pay at this level and went out of business. The unifying force of a rising standard of living was displaced by the disuniting effects of unemployment, falling wages, and higher prices that resulted in social unrest and sometimes violence.

The IMF had been trained and conditioned over the years in "liquidity crises," a situation in which a country's imports exceed their imports, that is, they are spending more than they are earning. From the beginning in Bretton Woods in 1944, the IMF's mission was to be a lender of last resort and to keep world prices stable. Following this mission, the IMF would lend countries money while insisting on actions that would bring income and expense into balance by slowing growth and spending less.

The threats of currency speculators and the readiness of hot money to take flight combined to initiate a downward spiral that was just the opposite of the sort of crisis that the IMF knew how to handle. The Indonesian economy spiraled downwards as its currency declined, and the more the currency declined, the more the money fled, provoking further currency attacks and deeper economic declines. In this capital crisis, not only were controls lacking on the amount and type of money coming in but also no mechanism was in place to stop its outward flow. The simplest way to stop the downward spiral would have been a conversion of short-term money to long-term debt, but amazingly, this approach was opposed by the IMF and the U. S. Treasury Department. They called it "an infringement on economic freedom." I call it "amazing" because of the policies self-contradictory hypocrisy: The structural corruptions in ultra-capitalism regularly destroy the benefits of economic freedom, and yet the constituted authorities nonetheless defend them on the faulty basis of "free capital roaming the world."

While the IMF and the U.S. Treasury Department were applying the wrong "liquidity crisis" solutions to the "capital crisis," at the same time they seemed determined to change the politics and

281

culture of troubled nations. They helped in removing Suharto, the architect of Indonesia's amazing improvement, and they agitated for more democratic elections. The record of these nations, such as Indonesia, in improving lives was outstanding, a model for any emerging economy. Despite this, the ideologues of the "liberalization of capital markets" ignored the record and applied the wrong solutions. The common denominator between the IMF and the U.S. Treasury Department in all of these tragedies was their promotion of opening up foreign markets to Wall Street services, which they did as a condition of their assistance before, during, and after the crisis.[274]

Ethnic and religious differences had receded as causes of social turmoil during the time when the Asian economies were growing rapidly and the quality of life for most of the people was improving. Conversely, when the economies reversed, the residual animosities came to the surface. This clash of cultures was highlighted in Hong Kong , September 1997, by a battle of words between Malaysian Prime Minister Mahathir Mohammed and global speculator George Soros, a debate between a Muslim Prime Minister declaring the immorality of currency speculation versus a Jewish-Hungarian-American speculator. The Prime Minister declared currency trading to be "unnecessary, unproductive, and immoral." Mahathir then proceeded to put back capital controls, ignored IMF advice, and had a faster recovery than the other nations who went along with the IMF.[275] Soros had written extensively about the instabilities in global finance capitalism that can lead to economic damage, sentiments that in many respects agreed with Mahathir's polemic; consequently, Soros's response to the Prime Minister was limited.

Many of the popular media are economically illiterate and add their disinformation to this economic confusion. American experts predicted that Asian countries would become more short-term profit oriented and lay off more workers. The effect of the crisis would be an emphasis on cost-cutting rather than on growth. Workers would be dumped as the route to greater profits, and any sense of social contract would be dumped with them. Incredibly, a crisis *caused* by ultra-

---

[274] *Ibid.*, p. 207.

[275] *Ibid.*, p. 93.

capitalism would be corrected by *more* ultra-capitalism, if you believe the media.

A few weeks after the September 11, 2001, attack on America, the "talking heads" on ABC's *Sunday Morning News* were using Indonesia, the world's largest Muslim country, as an example of American generosity to Muslim countries because of the IMF bailout.[276] No mention was made, however, of the ultra-capitalist policies promoted by the U.S. and the IMF that had precipitated the crisis and devastated Indonesia's economy in the first place, consequently making it a more friendly location for the training of terrorists.

Other parts of Western-style capitalism being adopted in Asia are more useful: greater disclosure, better governance, elimination of crony capitalism, improved debt/equity ratios, audits by independent accountants, and more outside Directors on Boards. None of this, however, addresses root-problems. The advice to make better disclosure is especially ironic because ultra-capitalism, with help from the chairman of the Federal Reserve, has successfully resisted better disclosure on derivatives in the United States for years.

The apologists for ultra-capitalism argue that a currency attack by speculators is a useful discipline. The scandal is that the mature economies, led by the United States, have let the international monetary system get so out of control that the final insult to the injured victims is to describe the extraordinarily leveraged speculators as providing a "discipline." Real discipline will come only from purging the excessive volatility from the system.

How can these crises be avoided? I propose solutions consistent with democratic capitalism throughout this book, and I repeat them here:

- The global economy, like the American economy and all national economies, requires a structure in place to monitor the amount and type of money flowing into countries.

---

[276] Cokie Roberts, on "Sunday Morning News," ABC, October 7, 2001.

- Through agreements and protocols from the BIS and the G-7 nations, the power of speculators must be checked.

- Taxes that discourage short-term speculation must be imposed.

- Investment for long-term growth must be rewarded by further reduction in capital gains taxes.

- The flow of capital must be controlled so that risk is accurately reflected in bank reserves.

- The rising value of artificial assets must not be used to collateralize easy credit.

- International banks must be regulated by rules and policies that result in high-quality loans for the world's economic growth.

A Russian Disaster: 1998

The collapse of the young, post-communist, Russian economy had several causes. The all important price of crude oil in early 1997 dropped almost by half; the nervous international bankers moved their focus from Asia to Russia; the IMF and the U.S. government again treated a capital crisis as a liquidity crisis, as they had done in Asia; and Russia lacked the necessary infrastructure for economic freedom to function.

The latter problem is ironic because the Russians and their American advisors made the same fundamental error in the transition to economic freedom that the Marxists had made. In both cases, the people in charge lacked understanding of the management of change and how to refine an existing structure to support new economic practice. In 1917, the Marxists, had followed Marx's advice to tear down the political and cultural structure; early in the 1990s, the American advisors urged the Russians to try "shock therapy," ignoring the lack of minimum structure. Economic disasters were the result in both cases.

The confusion between a capital crisis and a liquidity crisis had a special twist in the Russian disaster. A Wall Street leader, Goldman Sachs, proposed a conversion of short-term money to long-term as the best solution, namely, to convert the GKO, short-term Russian bonds, voluntarily to Eurobonds.[277] A Wall Street firm was actually recommending that the door be closed to capital flight. The proposal failed because, under pressure from the White House, the IMF pumped more money into Russia, and the bondholders took this as confirmation that Russia was "too big—and too nuclear—to fail." The bondholders were also quite happy with their 30-50% return.

Following American advice, Russia selected ultra-capitalism instead of democratic capitalism in the effort to move from tyranny to economic freedom, and they failed disastrously. Fareed Zakaria commented: "Russia's downward spiral is partly the result of mistakes made by Washington a decade ago. What can be done now? Not much."[278] The results of "one of the greatest peacetime economic and social disasters in history"[279] was that Russia's GDP fell in 1998 to half of what it had been in 1989; life expectancy in Russia declined, the only industrial country with such a trend; 70% of Russians fell to living below or just above the poverty line; and capital investment in Russia dwindled to only 10% of what it had been ten years before.[280] The Kremlin's own studies identified hundreds of billions of dollars lost to the Russian people through corruption. Russia, as the U.S.S.R., had once been a world superpower; after the collapse, Russia's national budget was $2.9 billion, a total less than New York City's budget. The mayor of New York City had more money to spend than did Vladimir Putin.[281]

Russia's economic failure caused these additional concerns:

- For the first time in history, a fully nuclear-ready country had been destabilized.

---

[277] Blustein, *op. cit.*, p. 264.

[278] Fareed Zakaria, "Lousy Advice Has a Price," *Newsweek*, September 27, 1989, p. 40.

[279] "Robbing Russia," *The Nation*, October 4, 1999, p. 4.

[280] *Ibid.*, p. 5.

[281] *Loc. cit.*

- Anti-Western sentiment had never been so strong or widespread in modern Russia as it was at the end of the twentieth century.[282]

- The economic catastrophe, in combination with pushing NATO into three countries contiguous with Russia, gave the enemies of freedom in Russia a strong position.

- Because of the economic breakdown, the possibility of nuclear disasters increased because nuclear missile sites and nuclear submarines could neither be maintained nor decommissioned properly.

- Russia's desperate need for hard currency increased the potential for sale of nuclear, biological, and chemical weapons to other nations.

- "The worst American foreign policy disaster since Vietnam and its consequences more long-term and perilous."[283]

Successful governance follows this sequence: civil order, first; then, economic freedom; followed by political freedom. Both the U.S.S.R's tyrannical structure and civil order had been torn down without a replacement. The American ultra-capitalists recommended, as usual, eliminating all cross-border controls. Foreign countries were thus encouraged to pump money in, while corrupt Russians were as quickly taking the capital out. The capital flight is estimated to have been between $150 billion and $200 billion. *The Nation's* editorial does not equivocate:

> It's probably wrong to think of it as capital flight, think of it rather as a chronic hemorrhaging of Russia's natural resources. That could hardly have happened

---

[282] Stephen F. Cohen, *Failed Crusade: America and the Tragedy of Post-Communist Russia* (New York: W. W. Norton & Company, 2000), p. 32.

[283] *Ibid.*, p. 9.

without the knowledge and complicity of Western governments, central banks, and finance houses.[284]

Fareed Zakaria pointed out a clever way to spot the evidence of capital flight:

> In all, more than $200 billion has leaked out of Russia, most of it to Switzerland. The Palace Hotel in St. Moritz is a reliable indication of the national origins of surplus cash. In the 1970s, it translated its menus into Arabic; in the 1980s, it was Japanese; today, it has them printed in Russian.[285]

Zakaria added that one did not see any Chinese on the menu at The Palace because China's currency is non-convertible, a national policy that prevents the flight of capital that drained Russia. Free-floating capital, with no border controls, is a nice theory supported by the IMF and the U.S. Treasury Department. It may well become the norm some years in the future, sometime after all nations have their structures in place to support economic freedom, and when the international community has standardized banking, stabilized currencies, deleveraged speculation, and put international free-market disciplines in place.

The Rise and Fall of Long-Term Capital Management[286]

The $3.6 billion bailout of Long-Term Capital Management (LTCM) in 1998 gave new meaning to leveraged speculation and took ultra-capitalism into dangerous new territory. LTCM was an unregulated hedge fund located for tax reasons in the Cayman Islands. The very wealthy could put up a minimum of a million dollars to participate in LTCM's extremely leveraged speculation and receive as much as a 40% return on their money in a year! LTCM claimed that

---

[284] *"Robbing Russia," loc. cit.*

[285] Zakaria, *op. cit.*, p. 40.

[286] Subtitle to Roger Lowenstein's *When Genius Failed, op. cit.*

the investments were "hedged" and "market neutral" because they used enormous amounts of borrowed money to bet, not on the direction of the market, but rather on such speculations as interest-rate spreads on bonds of different maturities returning to their historical norms. In time, however, the pressure for constantly rising profits made LTCM "go directional," that is, a purely speculative bet that a financial instrument, say Russian bonds, would go one way rather than the other. Banks that were regulated, subsidized, and insured with taxpayers' money loaned LTCM the money.

LTCM was a spin-off from Solomon Brothers after the 1991 scandal in which senior people admitted having falsified bids for Treasury securities. This had taken place in John Meriwether's department, but Meriwether's boss, John Gutfriend, took several months to inform the Fed. Warren Buffet, Solomon's largest shareholder, took over. The bond trader was fired, and, later, Meriwether and Gutfriend left. After leaving Solomon, Meriwether set up LTCM in 1993 with, at one time, 25 Ph.D's, including two Nobel-Prize winners in Economics, on the payroll. *Forbes* reported:

> John Meriwether seemed to have a magic touch. What he really had was nerve-wracking leverage. With returns like that, no wonder the Chairman of Merrill-Lynch and dozens of others at the firm invested in Long-Term Capital. But, adjusted for the risks, how good really were those returns? It's the old story: financial genius is a short memory in a rising market. Without leverage, the bet is hardly worthwhile: You would make $5,000 on a $1-million trade when the discrepancy is eliminated. But introduce the Archimedes principle and the picture changes. Suppose that you were able to buy $1-million worth of Treasuries on $10,000 in margin. Now that $5,000 profit is not just 5% on your money, it is 50% on your money.[287]

---

[287] Robert Lenzer, "Archimedes on Wall Street," *Forbes*, October 19, 1998, p. 53.

In 1998, however, Meriwether went directional, but he bet the wrong way. Instead of converging, the yields on the Treasuries spread further, but LTCM's esoteric models built by those PhD's had not included the possibility of a whole government's defaulting on bonds, as Russia did in 1998.

Again, instead of taking action to prevent the disease or let the speculators die, the government stepped in to nurse the source of infection. On October 1, 1998, the Chairman of the Federal Reserve, Alan Greenspan, and the head of the New York Fed, William McDonough, appeared before the House Banking Committee to defend their role in saving LTCM. Committee Chair Jim Leach (R., Iowa) questioned whether the Fed action precluded an offer to purchase LTCM from Warren Buffet and Goldman Sachs, which would have resulted in tossing out all the principals of LTCM. The Fed bailout left them in place, bloodied and bruised, but still able to maintain their 10% ownership, and enjoy a bonus in the hundreds of thousands of dollars for the year.

The chairman of the Federal Reserve Board admitted to the House Banking Committee that the Fed was powerless to control hedge funds; he assured the elected Representatives that, instead, the hedge funds were "controlled through the banks who are regulated."[288] To the contrary, however, the sources of LTCM's funds, namely the New York banks and investment banks, neither knew what LTCM was doing with the money nor how much had been borrowed from other sources. Roger Lowenstein registered his amazement at Greenspan's attitude and inaction, even tracing it back to Greenspan's participation in the Ayn Rand cult that regarded any government regulation as part of armed coercion. Lowenstein exclaimed:

> Incredibly, [Greenspan] again downplayed the risks posed by rogue investors such as hedge funds. The Chairman's credibility seemed to know no bounds:

---

[288] "Excerpts from Greenspan's Remarks before Congress," *The New York Times*, October 2, 1998, p. C3.

"Hedge funds are strongly regulated by those who lend the money," Greenspan asserted.[289]

Lowenstein continued:

Regulators limit the amount that Chase Manhattan and Citibank can lend, so that their loans do not exceed a certain ratio of capital. The regulators do this for a good reason: Banks have repeatedly shown that they will exceed the limits of prudence if they can. Why, then, does Greenspan endorse a system in which banks can rack up any amount of exposure that they choose, so long as that exposure is in the form of derivatives? The Fed's two-headed policy, head in the sand before a crisis, intervention after the fact, is more misguided when viewed as one single policy. *The government's emphasis should always be on prevention, not on active intervention.*[290]

In the1990s, hedge funds multiplied at a rate that further exemplified the financialization of the economy. *Forbes* estimated that Wall Street firms, on which the Fed was counting to monitor the hedge funds, were grossing over $2 billion a year on hedge-fund business and bringing a good part to the bottom line. This does not count the revenue that hedge funds were generating for other parts of the firms. *Business Week*, usually sympathetic to finance capitalism, this time issued a warning:

Who's watching the hedge funds? The lessons are clear. More disclosure is an absolute necessity in this age of leverage and global capital. Hedge funds are no exception. Someone must also be watching. The banks, certainly, must take an active role in monitoring their loans, as well as the kind of derivative transactions they support. But LTCM's wild ride shows that banks

---

[289] Lowenstein, *op. cit.*, p. 178.

[290] *Ibid.*, p. 231.

have a difficult time monitoring themselves, much less others. Federal regulators, as a consequence, must accept the fact that the public holds them responsible for the nation's financial stability.[291]

The government's practice of insuring and subsidizing risk was extended by way of LTCM to wealthy private investors who had used every possible artifice to avoid paying taxes. The Fed's argument before Congress, that no private funds were used in the bailout, is specious. What if the banks lost money in the bailout? The taxpayer would, one way or the other, make up the losses. This massive bailout extended the governments too-big-to-fail bank policy to an unregulated hedge fund for wealthy private investors, a dangerous precedent that added to the large library of non-democratic privileges that have allowed ultra-capitalism to grow and dominate.

Representative Bruce Vento (D., Minnesota), a member of the House Banking Committee, put his finger on the problem, pointing out the gap between free-market theory and practice, a double standard: one for Main Street and another for Wall Street.[292] Vento made a nice speech that probably played well in progressive Minnesota, but the Congressman did not acknowledge Congress's own responsibility, that it ought to resist the lobby-power of finance capitalism and commission a long-range integrated plan to control currency and credit for the general welfare. In his epilogue, Lowenstein concludes:

In December, fifteen months after he lost $4.5 billion in an epic bust that seemed about to take down all of Wall Street and more with him, Meriwether raised $250 million, much of it from former investors in the ill-fated Long-Term Capital, and he was off and running, again.[293]

---

[291] Editorial, "Who's Watching the Hedge Funds?" *Business Week*, November 9, 1998, p. 186.

[292] "Fed Chief Defends U.S. Role in Saving Giant Hedge Fund," *The New York Times*, September 25, 1998, p. C3.

[293] Lowenstein, *op. cit.*, p. 236.

Ultra-Capitalism: Quality of Earnings Declines along with Integrity

One by-product of ultra-capitalism's domination of the economy has been a steady erosion in the integrity of financial results reported to stockholders. In theory, the value of stocks should be based on actual corporate and expected corporate earnings. For over a 60-year period, the multiple of earnings had been around 15 times. During the bull market of the 1990s, it rose to over 30 times for "old economy" stocks, and up to infinity for dot.com companies who had no earnings. In mid-2002, after the stock market had fallen dramatically, the average multiple on trailing earnings was still around 30. The Dow Jones would have to drop to around 7,700 from its peak of 11,722 in January 2000 to fit the 60-year profile, which it did.

During the quarter-century of ultra-capitalist dominance, many companies crossed the line from aggressive interpretation of accounting rules to improve earnings to outright illegality in their frantic effort to improve reported earnings. Names such as Cendant, Sunbeam, Enron, Worldcom, Tyco, Imclone, and several others became better known for their lack of integrity than they had ever been for their good products.

In March of 2003, HealthSouth leapt into this Hall of Shame by admitting that they had been cooking the books to the tune of $1.4 billion since 1999. CEO Richard Scrushy had not been tricky at all: He just told his people flat out what the earnings had to be and later said that honesty in accounting would have to wait until he sold his stock. This mindset of a CEO corrupted by ultra-capitalism was demonstrated by Scrushy's boast in his letter to shareholders for 2001: "We celebrated another year of fulfilling Wall Street's expectations maintaining our record as the *Fortune 500* company with the second-longest streak for meeting or exceeding analysts' expectations."[294]

Before ultra-capitalism, most companies would not provide short-term profit estimates because they were naturally subject to so many outside effects. In 2003, the times were changing: Several

---

[294] Simon Romero, "The Rise and Fall of Richard Scrushy, Entrepreneur," *The Wall Street Journal*, March 21, 2003, p. C4.

major corporations were refusing to give any estimates on quarterly earnings.

In addition to outright criminality, ultra-capitalism adopted its own form of relativism, that is, a clever presentation of earnings purged of selected components. Anyone experienced in running a business is aware of annual, non-repetitive surprises that used to be routinely assimilated into the reported earnings as part of the real world. Now they were being designated differently. A front-page feature article in *The Wall Street Journal* described the phenomenon in the title and subtitles:

> Moving target. What's the P/E Ratio? Well Depends on What is Meant by Earnings. Terms like "Operating," "Core," "Pro Forma," "Earnings Before Bad Stuff" leave investors muddled.[295]

The article reports that the Standard & Poors' 500 stock index had an overall P/E ratio of 22.2 in mid-2001, and then continues:

> While that is well above the long-term historical average of 14-15, it strikes some pros as reasonable in view of factors such as low interest rates and a chance for a profit comeback...but there's a catch. In recent years, P/E ratios have become increasingly polluted.[296]

The article goes on to calculate that the unpolluted average ratio was 36.7 times, an astronomically high level in face of declining corporate earnings.

Companies in their frantic search for the earnings improvement that Wall Street demands, label certain expenses as "special" or "one-time" or "exceptional" or "non-cash." Wall Street analysts who made their performance bonuses primarily on rising stock values, passed on these phony reports to the public as real. Besides faking numbers, many good companies learned how to

---

[295] Jonathan Weil, "Moving Target," *The Wall Street Journal*, August 21, 2001, p.1.

[296] *Loc. cit.*

produce earnings during the bubble by becoming speculators. Kevin Phillips reported:

> Microsoft found the business of selling put options on their own stock a terrific way to make money... . Dell, in some fiscal quarters, made more money selling options than computers.[297]

Populist Revolt

At the turn of the century, the number of protestors against global capitalism was growing and their voices were becoming louder. Wherever international agencies met—Seattle, Washington; Davos, Switzerland; Washington, D.C., or Quebec City, Canada— protestors gathered in the thousands, and sometimes the protests became violent. Most of the protestors and Non-Governmental Organizations (NGOs) shared the view that global capitalism is exploitive and greedy.

Many of the CEOs and bankers at the Davos meeting, for example, had been rewarding themselves with many millions of dollars in personal compensation. Most refused to recognize that their compensation feeding-frenzy bore a negative relationship to the protestors only a few miles away, who, with symbolic irony, attacked a McDonald's restaurant. When the same demonstrators tried to storm the Davos meeting rooms, they were held back by police. About two months earlier in September 1999, some 50,000 protestors representing 1,000 NGOs had been present at the WTO meeting in Seattle. Their disturbances virtually shut down the meetings. Hundreds of widely divergent agendas were represented whose only unifying force was their distrust of the WTO and "globalization."

What the protestors failed to grasp, however, and what their fury obscured, is that no social theory or practice of economics can achieve what they desire other than a refined and democratized global capitalism. The economic ideology that can improve all lives, unify people, and stop the violence is not "no capitalism" but democratized

---

[297] Kevin Phillips, *Wealth and Democracy* (New York: Broadway Books, 2002), p. 155.

capitalism. If, then, protestors' energy could be focused on the democratization of capitalism around the world, they would find themselves no longer barred by the police from the meetings but, rather, leading a new non-violent revolution. The protests in Seattle, Davos, and other locations should be a wake-up call for real reform, but if the protests remain unfocused, they will do damage and add to the violence.

One of the NGOs at Seattle, a French group, showed a deeper understanding of the problems by promoting a "Tobin tax," the tax on international speculation proposed in 1979 by Professor James Tobin, Nobel-Prize winner in Economics from Yale. A win/win idea, the Tobin tax on the $1.7 trillion traded daily on the world's electronic monetary casino, over 90% of which is speculation, would dampen speculation and provide hundreds of billions of dollars to help economies get going, address environmental problems, and fund massive health and education needs.[298]

President Clinton Favors Rules-Based Trade While His Officials Deny It

President Bill Clinton had pushed for the WTO meeting in Seattle in November, 1999; then on January 30, 2000, the President, accompanied by five Cabinet Secretaries, appeared at the World Economic Forum in Davos, Switzerland, with this message: "We have got to reaffirm unambiguously that open markets and rules-based trade are the best engine we know to lift living standards, reduce environmental destruction, and build shared prosperity."[299] In so saying, the President was correct and summarized it well. The key words were "rules-based trade," but whose rules? The standard of living had been going up nicely in the Southeast Asian countries, but for lack of proper rules that progress was reversed.

Clinton and Secretary of Treasury Rubin advocated the promising global movement to free markets. With the encouragement of the Wall Street lobby, they also pushed for open markets for

---

[298] http://www.reedweb.org/iirp/factsheet.htm

[299] Jane Perlez, "At Trade Forum, Clinton Pleads for the Poor," *The New York Times*, January 31, 2000, p. 8.

financial services and elimination of all cross-border capital controls, all wonderful concepts and, in fact, part of the route to a world of peace and plenty. The devil, however, is in the details: Clinton and Robert Rubin did not address the stabilization of world currency and the standardization of banking protocols that would have controlled the lending of hot money and kept it in proportion to long-term, patient capital. Neither did they address the growing opportunities to borrow that were making the speculators more powerful than the central bankers. Nor did they address the abrogation of market disciplines that had muted the sense of risk in lending money. Also ignored were the wage levels in emerging economies, so low that spendable income necessary for reciprocal purchases that make free trade work was unavailable. Finally, they did not acknowledge that without the right structure in place, pulling down the cross-border controls made emerging economies vulnerable to attack by the peddlers of hot money and then the speculators.

Clinton's cry for a new "international financial architecture" went unheeded by his own key officials. Treasury Secretary Rubin, before his retirement in 1999, did not pursue solutions to the volatility that would have involved harmonizing economic fundamentals with those of other countries. Rubin feared losing control over such political levers as interest rates. As reported in *The Nation*:

> Although Rubin echoed some of the President's rhetoric, calling for a new financial architecture, he dismissed out of hand Tony Blair's call for a powerful global central bank, he scorned German suggestions for coordinating leading currencies, and he squelched talk about capital and currency controls. His reforms looked a lot more like patching the plumbing than like new architecture. In Cologne, Rubin squired through a reform program that reflected Wall Street's caution: Instead of a new Bretton Woods, there was a new fund for the IMF to provide help for countries prior to a crisis, and instead of capital controls or taxes on short-term speculation, there were calls for more disclosure and banking guidelines so that investors could police themselves. The debt forgiveness for the poorest

nations demanded by Jubilee 2000 became partial debt relief, to be meted out only after three years of painful adherence to IMF conditions. Enforceable labor rights were reduced to a new ILO (International Labor Organization) declaration against the worst forms of child labor.[300]

Like his presidential predecessors, Clinton talked the global economics talk, but he did not know how to walk the walk in practical economic terms. The wisdom of the politician was, unfortunately, limited to a mission statement without specificity on how to implement it. The juxtaposition, on the one hand, of the politician with a vision of improving lives through free trade, and on the other hand, a representative of Wall Street resisting reform, demonstrates the depth of the problem. Clinton, a Rhodes Scholar and "policy wonk," still did not have adequate understanding of the requisite rules to put his vision in place. Rubin, apparently an intelligent and patriotic man, was so conditioned and limited by his years of experience on Wall Street that he believed in the wrong rules. His were the rules, however, that violated Clinton's mission and became the *de facto* laws that dominate and impede the world economy. Neither man understood the structure required to make economic freedom functional.

America at the turn of the millennium, positioned to lead the world to peace and plenty through economic freedom, flunked the responsibility, instead, and led towards more folly and violence. In 2003, the world was consumed by violence and was preparing for more violence. This threatening and unnecessary situation highlights the warning of Ludwig von Mises cited in the introduction to chapter 6. If world leaders fail to improve lives and unite the world in economic common purpose, "They will not annul economics, they will stamp out society and the human race."

---

[300] Robert L. Borosage, "The Global Turning," *The Nation*, July 19, 1999, p. 20.

Ultra-Capitalism Finishes the Century with a Awesome Display of Political Power

In 1999, ultra-capitalists beat back reformers' efforts to exercise reasonable control of derivatives, and they successfully lobbied the repeal of the Glass-Steagall Act. This Act had been passed in 1933 to separate commercial banking and investment banking to eliminate a conflict of interest. Soon after the repeal of Glass-Steagall, Citigroup and other monster financial services companies demonstrated why the Act had been a necessary part of government structure to regulate banking. Citigroup, acting as commercial bankers, provided Enron with billions of dollars of loans so that Citigroup, acting as investment bankers, could get the billions of dollars of deals that Citigroup helped Enron negotiate. In time, the loans turned into bad loans and the deals turned into bad deals (see chapter 9). The financial motivation to ignore the quality of the loans in order to obtain the profitable deals resulted in the easy credit that allowed Enron to happen. Easy credit, which had caused economic disasters since the beginning of the republic, was now coupled with derivatives, and that added new ways to bet, new ways to borrow, and new ways to duck regulations.

Disturbed by the collapse of hedge fund LTCM, Brooksley Bonn, Chair of the Commodities Futures Trading Commission (CFTC), recommended that Congress consider regulation of derivatives. On November 9, 1999, the President's "Working Group on Financial Markets" issued its report recommending to Congress that it bar the CFTC from regulating derivatives. The committee included the chairman of the Federal Reserve, heads of the Treasury Department and the Securities and Exchange Commission, and the new head of CFTC. Bonn's lonely democratic voice was silent, for she had resigned. This event also illustrates the confusion of government where so many agencies are responsible for different aspects of the monetary system. In the confusion, the government remains unwilling to control leveraged speculation.

Derivatives are defended as a way for companies to hedge their businesses against changes in interest rates and currency. This defense is weak because it diverts attention from the root causes of volatility. Take away the volatility and little reason remains for companies to justify expensive hedging. Neither does this defense address the use of derivatives for speculation at multiples many times greater than their use as a business hedge.

Representative John Dingell (D., Michigan), the ranking Democrat on the House Commerce Committee, commented: "After six months of study, the working group has basically concluded that we should get rid of almost all regulation of these products and let the good times roll." Disagreeing with the committee, Dingell added: "Proposals for the creation of totally unregulated institutional markets are dangerous follies."[301]

Democrats frequently issue such warnings after another triumph of the Wall Street lobby, but the warnings never become serious efforts at comprehensive reform. The dominance by finance capitalism only grows stronger, demonstrated by the elimination of restrictions on ultra-capitalism's merging of different financial services. Confidence in the lobby power of ultra-capitalism was so great that the Citigroup merger of enormous size was already a *fait accompli* when President Clinton signed the Bill, late in 1999, rescinding Glass-Steagall. Most of the debate in Congress about the new law was about privacy in banking and priority lending to low and middle-income borrowers. Little or no discussion took place about adding hundreds of billions of dollars of potential obligations onto the taxpayers to bail out the enormous financial services corporations that this Bill encourages. No discussion at all addressed the effect of the repeal to condition bankers further to ignore the quality of loans. The repeal of Glass-Steagall substantially adds to the "too big to fail" rule; now, it is "the *really* too big to fail" rule.

By 2002, Citigroup had hired both Robert Rubin and Stanley Fisher, the prime drivers behind the "liberalization of capital markets" while Rubin had been Secretary of Treasury and Fisher was the top American at IMF. Rubin became the chairman of Citigroup's Executive Committee, and Fisher became the vice chairman of the Board. Rubin "earned" about $16 million in 2001 plus options, the year in which Citigroup was a major source of the easy credit that

---

[301] Michael Schroeder, "New Derivatives Regulation Is Opposed," *The Wall Street Journal*, November 10, 1999, p. C1.

allowed Enron to happen, and the year that Citigroup's Smith Barney was successfully sued for misleading small investors.

Rubin retired from government just weeks before Glass-Steagall was rescinded. His move provoked a letter from a coalition including the Center for Community Change, The Association of Community Organizations for Reform Now, The Greenlining Institute, The New York Public Interest Research Group, and Ralph Nader. The letter to the Office for Government Ethics objected to Rubin's move as "turnstile behavior with an undeniable appearance of impropriety." The coalition had fired its pop-gun; the Wall Street lobby remained nuclear armed.

In 2000, ultra-capitalism capped its amazing political performance by successfully passing the Commodities Futures Act. Not satisfied with merely avoiding control of derivatives, this Act, with heavy lobbying by Enron, further extended the use of borrowed money to speculate. With this new law, Congress is effectively allowing speculators to buy stock futures for 10 cents on the dollar. In 1933, the SEC reduced the amount that speculators could borrow from brokerage firms from 90% of the bet to 50%. The 2000 Commodities Futures Act effectively brings leverage opportunities back to 90%!

Derivatives: The Climax of Ultra-Capitalism

The rise of ultra-capitalism traced in this chapter has climaxed in derivatives whose daily trading dwarfs all commerce. These speculative ventures, free of regulation, are traded in amounts and at a speed that threatens the free-market system. Unprecedented violations of economic principles by derivative traders may be examined according to the following three categories:

- Disclosure: The use of derivatives makes examination of reported earnings and balance-sheet values a futile effort. Earnings can be faked by estimates of future values that are not subject to either regulation or oversight. The total amount of borrowed money reported on the balance sheet is also a fiction because of new ways to hide debt. Derivatives themselves are unregulated, but they also provide further opportunities to get around existing regulations.

- Integrity in Financial Reporting: Wall Street's enormous capacity to reward or punish companies for modest changes in quarterly earnings puts pressure on many executives to make favorable judgments of future value in the "mark-to-market" procedure. Self-serving and contradictory judgments are made on values many years into the future by both parties to the trade but are not reconciled, regulated, or audited.

- Neutral Money: The free-market theory of Adam Smith, classical economics, holds that money and credit—liquidity—must be neutral in its effect on commerce. Too little liquidity slows economic growth, too much liquidity encourages speculation and overly risky projects. Derivatives significantly increase liquidity without any control of where the money goes. Lacking control, excessive money and credit always gravitate to speculation.

Mark-to-market procedures applied to derivatives can be contrasted to standard accounting practice in which inventory is valued either by the cost when produced or by the market value at the time the financial report is being prepared, *whichever is less.* In other words, a mark-to-market procedure has been used in traditional accounting, but it was designed to have a conservative effect in reporting true value only. If ten widgets cost $100 when they were produced, but declined in value and could be sold at the time of the financial report for only $80, accounting rules require that the inventory be "marked" to the "market" value of $80. The traditional double-entry accounting rules would require a reduction in the inventory value of $200 and a reduction of current earnings of $200, as well. Then, when the company closes the books for the year and prepares the annual report, the rules require that the outside auditors validate the integrity of the reported figures. One of the many ways that they do this is by going to various locations in the company actually to count and value widgets.

Contrast this conservative accounting practice to the wonderful world of derivatives, in which beauty is in the eye of the beholder only, and the "market" value can be "marked" at whatever level both parties to the trading transaction independently feel they need as a way to meet profit targets. No rules control these judgments or reconcile contradictory forecasts, neither is there any audit to confirm that the resulting profits are fairly stated.

This seemingly magic opportunity to fabricate profits by the mark-to-market technique was generously employed by Enron at the end of each quarter when their traders produced a report of earnings that would please Wall Street by "cranking the dials." This was Enron's own expression for effecting the appearance of greater profit by raising the estimate of future value to be brought into current earnings (see chapter 9).

Ultra-capitalists treat "liquidity" as a self-validating concept, like "integrity," but whereas one cannot have too much integrity, free markets work only if there is enough but not too much money. Many times in our economic history, we have suffered from liquidity problems because the government did not properly "control currency and credit for the general welfare." Liquidity problems became so repetitive during the latter part of the 19th century that the Fed was established in 1913 in an attempt to eliminate them. The private system could not even provide the money that farmers needed to plant in the spring, pay their bills for a few months, and then pay back their loans at harvest time in the fall. The rigidities of the gold standard and mistakes by New York bankers regularly starved the local banks for funds, which caused customers to panic and run with their money. They had discovered that fractional reserve banking meant that if a lot of depositors wanted their money at the same time, not everyone would be able to get all of their money because all of the money was not in the bank at the same time. Common sense dictated that the government prevent "runs on the bank" through the new Fed by providing sufficient liquidity to meet any demands.

Adam Smith made it clear that liquidity could be either good or bad. If too much liquidity were available to the "prodigals and projectors" with which to speculate and engage in high-risk adventures, then it would be bad liquidity; if however, liquidity were available to "sober people" to invest in economic growth, it would be good (see chapter 6). In 1920, however, the Fed demonstrated that it did not know the difference between bad and good liquidity when it overfed the speculators and caused a boom/bust cycle. This, however, was just a warm-up for the Fed's repetition of the same act with the excessive liquidity that caused both the Crash of '29 and the bubble economy of the 1990s. Excessive liquidity—the bad kind—in each case can also be described as easy credit from too willing bankers who allowed too much leverage with too much borrowed money for speculation.

Excessive liquidity in each of these cases was followed by too little liquidity when the bankers, after all of the bad loans they had made, tried to put their balance-sheet reserves-to-loans-outstanding back into the shape required by government regulation. This could also be called locking the barn door after the horse has been stolen. In this process, bankers limit the lending of money to credit-worthy companies just when the money is most needed both by the companies and by the economy.

Brooksley Bonn, while head of the CFTC (Commodities Futures Trading Commission)), tried to get oversight of derivatives (see above page 298), but she was successfully resisted by senior government officials, including the chairman of the Fed, Alan Greenspan, and the Secretary of Treasury, Robert Rubin. They outmatched Ms Bonn with very clear positions on derivatives at the Congressional hearings on the collapse of LTCM. Greenspan said: "Regulation of derivatives transactions that are privately negotiated by professionals is unnecessary." Rubin added: "New rules or regulatory oversight on derivatives could increase legal uncertainty in a thriving global market place."[302]

Greenspan, Rubin, and others who have mistakenly translated Adam Smith and usurped free market principles for the benefit of financial services, have done enormous damage to the world's economy by believing and promoting the concepts that there can be neither too much deregulation nor too much liquidity. One of their

---

[302] David Barboza and Jeff Gerth, "On Regulating Derivatives: Long-Term Capital Bailout Prompts Calls for Action," *The New York Times*, December 15, 1998, p. C1.

defenses against regulation of hedge funds and derivatives is that such regulation would simply drive the hedge funds out of the country. This suggestion, instead, reminds us that the rules must be international which is presumably the mission of the BIS (Bank for International Settlement), based in Basel, Switzerland. This mission, however, needs American support, but the same senior government officials who have successfully resisted efforts to get control of derivatives and hedge funds at home have also successfully resisted efforts by other G-7 nations to write rules that would bring needed stability to the international monetary system.

The derivatives threat to the free market can be neutralized by the government's giving the same type of oversight and regulation to the derivative market that they give to banks, the stock market, and the commodities market. New rules will follow from this oversight that will place necessary controls on faking profits from future estimates, require reports of significant changes in reserves to reflect risk, and call for new types and levels of disclosure from banks and hedge funds alike. Appropriate changes in tax policy will curb speculation by means of transaction taxes and additional taxation of short-term gains. With America's influence in the world's economy, these domestic changes could be exported to the international scene, but other ideologues of the liberalization of capital markets, such as former Secretary of Treasury Robert Rubin, have actually opposed efforts by other countries to write rules that could purge volatility and bring monetary stability (see above, p. 296, 297).

An Economist, Religious Leader, Famous Speculator, and Respected Investor Warn of the Threat from Ultra-Capitalism

Two distinct groups have called attention to the corruptions of ultra-capitalism with its devastating effect on economic growth and social cohesion. One group is made up of wise, concerned citizens of the world who represent different parts of the culture, including economists, religious leaders, socially sensitive speculators, and investors. The other group numbers in the tens of thousands of protestors and demonstrators who regularly take up their placards and shout their slogans at meetings of the WTO, the World Bank, and IMF. Unfortunately, the two groups are not well integrated. The protestors waste democratic power by spending more time training in how to conduct street confrontations with the police than they appear to spend studying the wisdom of the other group. The twenty-first century will be another one of folly and violence, unless these groups learn how to couple wisdom and protest in effective reform.

The Economist: Judy Shelton warned in 1994 about the threat from instabilities in the international monetary system to the new opportunities for world economic growth. An economist at the Hoover Institute, at that time, Shelton captured the dichotomy between the greatest opportunity in human history for a world of peace and plenty on the one hand, and on the other, the threat involved in the inability of governments to agree on, and put into place, an international monetary system. Shelton commented:

> At a time when the transition to a post-communist world holds out the prospect for an international marketplace of free trade and entrepreneurial initiative, offering new levels of economic prosperity for a growing number of participants, the lack of an orderly global currency system threatens to destroy the vision. The international monetary system currently in existence is no system at all.… Global currency arrangements have deteriorated into a high-stakes poker game where the exchange rates are determined on the basis of the latest bluff between government officials and speculators.[303]

Shelton advocated a system that would support the extraordinary opportunity for stronger world economic growth with a medium of exchange that is stable, and investment capital that is patient. Whereas Keynes's 1936 warning about the domination of commerce by speculation had come after leveraged speculation almost destroyed the world's model of a democratic economy (see chapter 6), Shelton's warning in the face of growing ultra-capitalism could have

---

[303] Judy Shelton, *Money Meltdown: Restoring Order to the Global Currency System* (New York: The Free Press, 1994), pp. 103-4.

prevented leveraged speculation and monetary instabilities from upsetting whole economies and moving the world away from the universal benefits of free markets. Since 1994, however, Shelton's advice, like others', has been ignored, and the worsened condition of the world reflects that lack of response for needed reform.

The Religious Leader: In 1991, Pope John Paul II, in his encyclical, *Centesimus Annus,* addressed the question of how to attain a just and comfortable society. Speaking from outside the commercial sphere, the leader of the world's Catholics explicitly recommended stable money, patient capital, and control of speculators. The Pope preached his gospel of economic integrity as follows:

> Economic activity, especially the activity of a market economy, cannot be conducted in an institutional, juridical or political vacuum. On the contrary, it presupposes sure guarantees of individual freedom and private property, as well as a stable currency and efficient public services. Hence the principle task of the state is to guarantee this security, so that those who work and produce can enjoy the fruits of their labours and thus feel encouraged to work efficiently and honestly. The absence of stability, together with the corruption of public officials and the spread of improper sources of growing rich and of easy profits deriving from illegal or purely speculative activities, constitutes one of the chief obstacles to development and to the economic order.[304]

Without using the expression, the Pope specifically warned about the dominance of ultra-capitalism:

> In this sense, it is right to speak of a struggle against an economic system, if the latter is understood as a method of upholding the absolute predominance of

---

[304] Pope John Paul II, *Centesimus Annus* (May 1, 1991) (Washington, D.C.: United States Catholic Conference, publication No. 436-8), pp. 72-93.

capital, the possession of the means of production and
of the land, in contrast to the free and personal nature
of human work. In the struggle against such a system,
what is being proposed as an alternative is not the
socialist system, which in fact turns out to be State
capitalism, but rather a society of free work, of
enterprise, and of participation. Such a society is not
directed against the market, but demands that the
market be appropriately controlled by the forces of
society and by the state, so as to guarantee that the
basic needs of the whole of society are satisfied.[305]

In so saying, the Pope pronounced a blessing on democratic
capitalism; every point he made parallels the theory and practice of
democratized capitalism.

The Famous Speculator: The old adage: "Ask the man who
owns one," pertains here to our understanding of the effects of ultra-
capitalism on social progress. George Soros's credentials as a
successful speculator lend credibility to his warnings about the
dangerous instabilities in finance capitalism, and his largesse as a
concerned philanthropist make him equally convincing in his
commitment to improving lives through an open society.[306]

The speculator side of Soros became famous in 1992, when he
bet on the German mark and shorted the British pound. The British
government used a good part of its national piggy-bank trying to
defend the pound, but the British were forced to give up. "Mr. Soros
closed out his bet, netting his funds $1 billion, plus another $1 billion
on related investments."[307]

The philanthropic side of Soros made him famous for
recycling billions to help Eastern European countries, including his
homeland, Hungary, become open societies. Time magazine also

---

[305] *Ibid.*, p. 68.

[306] George Soros, *The Crisis of Global Capitalism: Open Society Endangered* (New York: BBS- Public Affairs/Perseus Books Group, 1998).

[307] Mitchell Pacelle, "Breaking the Bank," *The Wall Street Journal*, December 13, 1999, p. C1.

reported on Soros's $1/2 billion megagift trying to help Russia: "Soros, who has amassed a $5 billion personal fortune trading currencies, and has given $1.5 billion to humanitarian projects worldwide, so far has only vague ideas about who gets the Russia money."[308]

Soros's warnings started with an article in the *Atlantic Monthly* in 1997, were repeated in another article[309] and a book in 1998. His record proves that he understands the system; we ought, therefore, to listen to his advice:

- An open government is the opposite of totalitarian government, but it can also be threatened by lack of government in selected areas and a lack of social cohesion.[310]

- Without supervision, the international financial system will not follow the supply/demand equation and return to equilibrium.[311]

- Global capitalism as now practiced results in uneven distribution of benefits.

- The burden of taxation has shifted from capital to citizens.[312] (In 1934, income taxes were .7% of GDP, in 1992 7.8%, and in 2000 close to 10%.)[313]

- Unemployment, and other social dislocations caused by global capitalism "increases the demands on the state to

---

[308] Douglas Waller, "Soros to the Rescue Again," *Time*, November 3, 1997, p. 74.

[309] George Soros, "Toward a Global Open Society," *Atlantic Monthly*, January 1998, p. 20.

[310] Soros, *Crisis, op. cit.*, p. x.

[311] *Ibid.*, pp. xvi-xvii, xx.

[312] *Ibid.*, p.112.

[313] Peter Brinelow, "Income Greed: Personal Incomes Are Rising, Washington's Take Is Rising Faster," *Forbes*, October 16, 2000, p. 126.

provide social insurance while reducing its ability to do so." [314]

- Every financial crisis is preceded by an enormous expansion of credit. [315]

- The conventional defense against better derivatives disclosure by bankers is faulty because the financial risk to banks from derivatives is not eliminated by cash transfers on any difference between cost and market, as was demonstrated in the Russian collapse: "Banks remained on the hook to their own clients. No way was found to offset the obligations of one bank against those of another. Many hedge funds and other speculative accounts sustained large enough losses that they had to be liquidated." [316]

- Society needs a common ideology to sustain itself. Global capitalism reduces everything to commodities, a buy/sell equation. The development of a global society has lagged behind the growth of a global economy. Unless the gap is closed, the global capitalist system will not survive. "After the collapse of the Soviet system in 1989, open society with its emphasis on freedom, democracy, and the rule of law, lost much of its appeal as an organizing principle and global capitalism emerged triumphant." [317]

- There is no international regulatory authority for financial markets, and there is not enough international cooperation for the taxation of capital. "The burden of taxation has shifted from capital to the citizens." [318]

---

[314] Soros, *Toward a Global Open Society, op. cit.*, p. 24.

[315] Soros, *Crisis, op. cit.*, p. 122.

[316] *Ibid.*, xiii.

[317] *Ibid.*, p. xxii.

[318] *Ibid.*, p. 112.

- Since 1971 when the dollar was floated, the single international currency in the form of convertible dollars backed by gold has been replaced with three major currencies, the dollar, the euro, and the yen. They are "rubbing against each other like tectonic plates, often creating earthquakes, crushing minor currencies in the process."[319]

- The belief in unsupervised financial markets or "market fundamentalism is today a greater threat to open society than any totalitarian ideology."[320]

- The United States has an identity crisis: Whether to be the only superpower or the moral and economic leader of the free world?[321]

- "The deficiencies of the political process have become much more acute since the economy has become truly global."[322]

- "The institutions of representative democracy have become endangered, and civil virtue, once lost, is difficult to recapture."[323]

- "In a transactional market, as distinct from a market built on relationships, morality can become an encumbrance."[324]

- Stability cannot be achieved by market participants alone; preserving stability must become an objective of public

---

[319] *Ibid.*, p. xxi.

[320] *Ibid.*, p. xxii.

[321] *Ibid.*, p. xxix.

[322] *Ibid.*, p. 199.

[323] *Ibid.*, p. 200.

[324] *Ibid.*, p. 199.

policy.[325]

Soros's solutions all depend on moral and economic leadership by the United States. No new world order is needed because the available international structures—the United Nations, the Bank for International Settlement, the International Monetary Fund, the World Bank, the World Trade Organization, the International Criminal Court, the International Labor Organization—are sufficient, if the United States will only lead. Economic policy at home and abroad, however, will continue to favor ultra-capitalism over the general welfare as long as no democratic lobbying power is organized to counteract the lobby power of ultra-capitalism, and as long as policy is determined by government officials whose priority is not to "upset the markets."

The Respected Investor: Warren Buffet is the world's best-known investor. Thousands of happy shareholders make the trip to Omaha, Nebraska, for his annual meetings that have more the good feeling of a family picnic than the stiff and frequently adversarial annual meetings. Buffet served on the SEC Advisory Board for Corporate Disclosure, and after that experience he "got serious," as he expressed it, about clear and unambiguous communication with his shareholders. In 1997, Buffet and Carol Loomis, his friend and Berkshire Hathaway shareholder, together wrote Buffet's letter in his annual report to the shareholders. Loomis, a senior *Fortune* writer, wrote the 1997 article on derivatives, titled "Alligators in the Swamp," quoted earlier in this chapter (see page 268).

In his 2002 report to his shareholders, Buffet began with his usual straight talk, saying that he and his partner, Charlie Munger, "are of one mind in how we feel about derivatives and the trading activities that go with them. We view them as time bombs, both for the parties that deal in them and the economic system."[326] Buffet explained to his shareholders why he and his partner were shutting down the derivatives business in their insurance company. He went on to warn of the systemic danger posed by derivatives.

---

[325] *Ibid.*, p. 58.

[326] Warren Buffet, "Avoiding a Mega-Catastrophe," *Fortune*, March 17, 2003, p. 82.

Buffet's letter was released on the website of Berkshire Hathaway on March 8, 2003, and published in the *Fortune* March 17 issue. On March 11, the feature editorialist in *The Wall Street Journal*[327] attacked Buffet's argument in a surprisingly *ad hominem* fashion. I mention the timing of these articles because the reaction by the defenders of ultra-capitalism was as quick as it was insulting.

The Wall Street Journal article describes Buffet as "grumpy" because his insurance company was not doing well. *The WSJ* featured in bold print: "Every great investor makes an occasional mistake." The article calls attention to a decline in the value of Buffet's stock to $60,000 that was "once worth more than $80,000"; it does not mention, however, that the stock had been at about $40,000 a little over a year earlier and as low as $11,450 ten years previously. The article concludes with the observation that Buffet "is not only shooting the messenger, he's also blaming the gun." Instead of grappling with the critical examination of the macroeconomic effects of derivatives proposed by Buffet, *The WSJ* article is patronizing and superficial. Calling derivatives "little miracles of financial engineering," *The WSJ* makes these points:

- Derivatives allow investors to shift and manage risk.

- Through this risk management, derivatives add to liquidity.

- By spreading risk, derivatives reduce the possibility of failure at one or more major institutions.

These are the standard microeconomic defenses of derivatives used by ultra-capitalists, including Fed Chairman Greenspan, to beat back efforts to get government regulation and oversight of derivatives even after disasters such as LTCM. In a puzzling way, however, *The WSJ* then proceeded to contradict themselves by stating agreement with some of Buffet's most important points:

---

[327] Editorial, "Derivative Thinking," *The Wall Street Journal*, March 11, 2003, p. A14.

- "Investors can't get a clear picture of potential dangers because disclosure remains inadequate."

- "Accounting for derivatives is a mug's game. Valuing derivatives on a mark-to-market basis can be an exercise in fantasy. The result is inflated earnings."

- "Limited and fanciful disclosure can also mask the possibility that risk, rather than being widely dispersed, has actually migrated to one or two sectors—insurance and pension funds come to mind—or even a few companies."

If one were to read these points while blocking out the earlier, cheap shots at Buffet, one would conclude that *The WSJ* editorialist agreed with Buffet that a marauding monster is out there and we'd better run, not walk, to get control of it. By the end of the article, however *The WSJ* describes these problems as merely needing "scrutiny." One must ask, however, "scrutiny" by whom and for what purpose? Is this, after all, a recommendation for government regulation and oversight of derivatives?

This difference of opinion between Buffet and *The WSJ*, which represents the view of Wall Street, is a special opportunity to examine the conflict in capitalism between democratic capitalism and ultra-capitalism. Ultra-capitalism demonstrates in this case the determination to deregulate financial services and oppose any regulation of new financial instruments such as derivatives. This is the fundamental error that shapes government policy but contradicts the capitalism of Adam Smith and classical economics. As George Soros and others emphasize, the financial markets will not find equilibrium without monetary and fiscal controls. Ultra-capitalism now has such power over our government, and reformers are so limited in their understanding of this subject, that the specific points made by both Buffet and Soros need to serve as a *study* agenda. Unless enough citizens are educated and aroused on these matters, Wall Street will continue to lobby self-serving policies, and the politicians will make them law. Warren Buffet's main points are as follows:

- "Reinsurance and derivatives both generate reported earnings that are often widely overstated because today's earnings are in a significant way based on estimates whose inaccuracy may not be exposed for many years."

- "Derivatives are usually paid on 'earnings' calculated by mark-to-market accounting. But there is often no real market and 'mark-to-model' is utilized. This substitution can bring on large-scale mischief." Profits should not be reported and bonuses paid on self-serving guesses.

- Enron demonstrated in the energy markets how to use derivatives and trading to hype earnings, "until the roof fell in when they actually tried to convert the derivative-related receivables on their balance sheet into cash. 'Mark-to-market' then turned out to be truly 'mark-to-myth.'"

- "Marking errors in the derivatives business have not been symmetrical. Almost invariably, they have favored either the trader who was eyeing a multimillion-dollar bonus or the CEO who wanted to report impressive earnings (or both). The bonuses were paid, and the CEO profited from his options. Only much later did shareholders learn that the reported earnings were a sham."

- "Derivatives exacerbate trouble that a corporation has run into for completely unrelated reasons. This pile-on effect occurs because many derivatives contracts require that a company suffering a credit downgrade immediately supply collateral to counter parties." By "counter party" Buffet means the person on the other side of the particular trade. (Think Enron).

- "Derivatives create a daisy-chain risk. A participant may believe his large credit exposures to be diversified and therefore not dangerous. Under certain circumstances, though, an exogenous event that causes the receivable from Company A to go bad will also affect those from

Companies B through Z." (Think LTCM and the Russian default on their bonds).

- "In banking, the 'linkage' problem was one of the reasons for the formation of the Federal Reserve System. Before the Fed was established, the failure of weak banks would sometimes put sudden and unanticipated liquidity demands on previously strong banks, causing them to fail in turn. But there is no central bank assigned the job of preventing the dominoes toppling in insurance or derivatives."

- "Large amounts of risk, particularly credit risk, have become concentrated in the hands of relatively few derivatives dealers." (Think CITI's lending money to Enron for their misadventures, then protecting themselves with credit insurance).

- LTCM used 100% leverage, that is, none of their own money, in total-return swaps, agreeing to accept the banks' future gain or loss on the stock or other instrument. "Total return swaps make a joke out of margin requirements."

- "Derivatives severely curtail the ability of regulators to curb leverage and generally get their arms around the risk profiles of banks, insurers, and other financial institutions."[328]

Buffet may have the luxury of abandoning derivatives, but the rest of the commercial world does not have such luck. Derivatives did not exist in any size before 1987, they grew to about $10 trillion in 1994, $20 trillion in '96, almost $40 trillion in '98,[329] and then, in 2002, according to a *Business Week* article: "The International Swaps & Derivatives Association estimated the worldwide market at $105 trillion. The Office of the Comptroller of the Currency says U.S.

---

[328] Buffet, *op. cit.*, p.82.

[329] Barboza and Gerth, *loc. cit.*

commercial banks held $56 trillion of derivatives at the end of 2002." These numbers can be compared to the total U.S. annual GDP of about $10 trillion. Peter Coy titled this article "Are Derivatives Dangerous?" and then answered his own question with the subtitle: "Without adequate collateral, one big default could set off a chain reaction imperiling the whole financial system." [330]

By considering the earlier warnings from economist Shelton and religious leader John Paul II, and coupling them with the warnings of Soros and Buffet, one must conclude that instabilities in financial markets do seriously threaten the world's economy. Throw in, as well, the negative examples of LTCM and Enron, and then I have to ask how much wisdom and how many clear examples do we need before the democratic will can be energized to combat the lobby power of the ultra-capitalists? If we continue to ignore these warnings, bad things will happen, and, as usual, those bad things will hurt the ordinary people who believed that their pensions and insurance money were being well protected by their government. The conclusion based on both logic and experience is that derivatives, more than any other financial instrument, urgently need government regulation.

Citizens' Choice: Peace and Plenty or Folly and Violence?

After World War II, the parts of the world that adopted economic freedom as the engine for progress improved the lives of hundreds of millions of people. In the 1990s, after the demise of Communism, more countries moved from tyranny to freedom, further validating the power of economic freedom to improve lives. During the 1990s, however, the corruptions of ultra-capitalism slowed the world's economic momentum and in many countries reversed it. Joseph Stiglitz, the 2001 Nobel Prize winner in Economic Science, summarized the record:

> A growing divide between the haves and have-nots has left increasing numbers in the Third World in dire poverty, living on less than a dollar a day. Despite repeated promises of

---

[330] Peter Coy, *Business Week*, March 31, 2003, p. 90.

poverty reduction made over the last decade of the twentieth century, the actual number of people living in poverty has actually increased by almost 100 million. This occurred at the same time that the total world income actually increased by an average of 2.5 percent annually.[331]

Our failure in economic leadership began in the 1960s: For half-a-century, each American President, whether Republican or Democrat, has made enormous mistakes in economic policy that have pushed the world toward the excesses of ultra-capitalism.

President Johnson's deficit spending in his "Guns and Butter" program initiated large inflation; President Nixon floated the dollar and initiated the excessive volatility that made the speculators more powerful than the central bankers; President Ford signed ERISA into law, causing the excessive liquidity that allowed Wall Street to dominate commerce; during Ford's presidency, Fed chairman, Paul Volcker fixed Johnson's mistake by taking interest rates up as high as 20%, with the unintended consequence of destroying the positive momentum in many emerging economies as well as undermining the domestic S&L industry; President Reagan added to the excessive volatility and liquidity caused by his predecessors, and he reinforced the "Great American Inversion" by deregulating finance capitalism at the same time that market disciplines were suspended; also during the Reagan Administration, taxes were moved from capital to wage earners; President Bush, the elder, trying to balance trade by changing the relationship of the dollar and yen, contributed to the Japanese bubble economy and the funding of overcapacity in Southeast Asia; President Clinton completed the damage by jawboning emerging economies into taking down their cross-border capital controls. This new mistake, combined with the excessive volatility, excessive liquidity, deregulation, and suspension of market disciplines caused by Clinton's predecessors, not only resulted in the reversal of economic momentum and social chaos in many emerging economies but also allowed Enron-style capitalism to flourish until the inevitable collapse at home. President George W. Bush has responded vigorously with military actions against people and nations espousing

---

[331] Stiglitz, *op.cit.*, p. 5.

violence, but the Bush Administration has not yet taken action to reform ultra-capitalism that was partly responsible for the violence.

America at the turn of the millennium, positioned to lead the world to peace and plenty through economic freedom, flunked the responsibility and led, instead, towards more folly and violence. Most of the world has become convinced that America is no longer the "light on the hill"; instead, the U.S.A. projects the image of arrogant American imperialism. Ultra-capitalism and its philosophical counterpart, militarism, have combined to condition many in the world to hate America. The depth and breadth of this antagonism surprises most Americans, but this environment encourages a few fanatics to do their terrible violence.

In this book, I offer an alternative: The agents of change—democratic capitalists, universities, institutional investors, religions, unions, new politicians, and citizens individually and in groups—have a responsibility more urgent than ever before to reform the economic system by purging the corruptions of ultra-capitalism and adopting democratic capitalism. Only a rising standard of living throughout the world accomplished through democratic capitalism can neutralize the fanatics and stop the reciprocal atrocities.

CHAPTER 8

Conflicts in Capitalism: An American Tragedy

This three-act play is my attempt to capture the human drama in the battle between ultra-capitalism and democratic capitalism. The scene is set at a strategy meeting of a mid-sized U. S. company whose stock is traded publicly on the stock market.

Dramatis personae
CEO (Chief Executive Officer) Alan
CFO (Chief Financial Officer) Dick
COO (Chief Operating Officer) Pete
VP Marketing Sheila
Bud, Sheila's brother, an Associate Instructor in Economics at the Community College

Act One

Scene: In the CEO's office; on stage: CEO Alan, CFO Dick, COO Pete, and VP Marketing Sheila

CEO Alan: We'll have our new CFO propose the mission for this discussion.

CFO Dick: Simply to study ways to enhance shareholder value. As you all know, we've done relatively well for years, and were sitting on a great deal of cash, but the analysts aren't very excited about next year.

COO Pete: I thought our preliminary budget showed another 7% profit improvement.

CFO Dick: It does, Pete, but all five of our major analysts have already figured that into their projected earnings-per-share of $2.15 to $2.18, and all it has produced is a yawn. Four of five analysts have pegged us as a "hold." One says we're "fully priced" and are not expected to exceed the whole stock market's movement next year. She's recommending sell because she's pushing a different industry as the hot stock pick.

VP Mktg. Sheila: We seem to discuss strategy in terms of what the analysts think or want. Shouldn't we give some attention to our own market opportunities?

CEO Alan: Obviously. Go ahead.

VP Mktg. Sheila: Our new telecommunications package is going great, as you know. The next three years are our opportunity to go for market share. We've got about an 18-month lead on competition, but we need to blanket the market with major additions to our sales coverage.

COO Pete: Sounds great, Sheila. We've got the plant capacity. Load us up. Just give us a week's notice before you double the volume!

[Laughter]

VP Mktg. Sheila: Don't get too excited, Pete. The budget guidelines from Dick's department allowed only a 5% increase in sales coverage; we need at least 20%.

CFO Dick: Do you want to blow our stock price? The Street isn't impressed with $2.15 a share for next year. How do you think they'd react to another $2.03? We've been on the road for three weeks with our dog-and-pony show, trying to convince the analysts that our steady growth should produce a better multiple. At 15 times earnings, we're way below the market's average. Add your sales coverage, Sheila, bring in faster growth, but the same $2.03, and we're dead. They'll punish us with a drop in the multiple of at least three points. How would you like to explain how the stock that has finally cracked $30 goes back under $25?

VP Mktg. Sheila: That's your job, but I'll be delighted to help you tell the story. If we make the big move on this market now, then the effect in a few years will be earnings improvements up in double digits. How does 10-12% grab you for long-term earnings growth?

CFO Dick: Sheila, you need a course in Wall Street 101! Short-term for them is a week from Tuesday, midterm is the next quarter, long-term is next year. Besides that, what are you going to do for an encore? You add sales people for more coverage for a few years, get the market penetration, but then what are you going to do—grow with the market?

CEO Alan: That's a good question, Sheila. Your market-growth plan is exciting, but it wouldn't be prudent to lay on additional salespeople for a few years to gain greater market penetration, only then to have to cut back.

VP Mktg. Sheila: Let me answer—now we're getting to the good part. For a couple of years, we've been developing a relationship with a skunk-works group out south of town. They are six design geniuses who opted out of the corporate world to concentrate on pure design. I think they've really hit it with a fully digital system that can be integrated into our telecommunications package beautifully. With this development, we can move out not months but years ahead of competition, including the Japanese.

COO Pete: I thought NAC just announced a new system with a lot of merchandising noise.

VP Mktg. Sheila: They did, but they opted for quick market entry, and their system is still partly analog. The skunk-works system, being fully digital, provides additional features and lower cost.

CEO Alan: How hard are your facts on that, Sheila? What's the development status? Give us some ball-park numbers on what we need to invest.

VP Mktg. Sheila: OK, Alan. They have completed a breadboard design and have confirmed function and theory. To move from breadboard to a fully producible design is going to be expensive.

This is going to be really high-volume in time, but that means big capital investment up front to get costs down. This group of designers recognizes that, along with the fact that they're not manufacturing people. That's why they're shopping for a partner. They have even less interest in messing with the marketing.

CFO Dick: Do they want a partner or a sugar daddy? What kind of a relationship are they interested in?

VP Mktg. Sheila: It's still being developed, but I think they'd like to sell 30% of their company for something like $25 million.

CFO Dick: $25 million for a gleam in the eye? Maybe they'd throw in the Brooklyn Bridge as part of the package!

VP Mktg. Sheila: Of course, they have no earnings; this is a start-up operation. But continuing, if we had rights to the product, including manufacturing rights, they'd want us to fund the remaining development, including capital equipment.

CEO Alan: Give us a ball-park, Sheila. Everything in—development costs, capital equipment, equity interest, market introduction, and working capital.

VP Mktg. Sheila: It would pretty much take care of that $125 million of cash that we're sitting on.

CFO Dick: It's not that simple. As you know, the costs that are chargeable to earnings will erode our e.p.s. further for the next few years. If $2.03 and a 12 multiple doesn't scare you, imagine what $1.90 and a 10 multiple would do to our total market capitalization! Get out your calculator and figure out how much we're talking about blowing.

CEO Alan: It's a loaded question, Dick. If your premises are correct, with 70 million shares, our present market capitalization is $2.1 billion. With your cataclysmic projections, we'd blow that to $1.3

billion and change, and I'd be on a railroad to nowhere, picking tar and feathers off my tired body.

COO Pete: I feel like Alice in Wonderland, listening to this conversation. I've been with this company for 25 years, and I've never been more excited about a development breakthrough than the one Sheila has outlined. With fast changing technology, this would really put us ahead of the curve. But I'm afraid I'm too unsophisticated to understand why a commitment to that program would blow 40% of our market value. I would think that this prospect would enhance it.

   I've put every nickel of my cash bonuses for 10 years into this company's stock, as well as subscribing to the limit on the stock-purchase program. I'd be prepared to bet what really is my net worth on such an opportunity. If the money-changers and the analysts are too short-term to see that, the hell with them! Take the punishment for a few years, and then when the earnings go over $3 a share, tell them to stick it in their ear!

   Besides that, your precious P/E ratio is another device that financial types use to fool people. I just saw a feature article in *The Wall Street Journal* that calls it "a moving target" and asks the question, "What is the P/E ratio?" Well, depends on what is meant by "earnings." I liked the next line best: "Earnings before bad stuff." I can remember Alan warning us about the non-repetitive annual events. Handling surprises was part of profit planning until you guys figured out how to x-out the bad stuff by changing definitions.

CFO Dick: I'm glad you prefaced your remarks with the confession of how unsophisticated you are, Pete. You've spent too much time on the factory floor. You've gotta pay attention to the big picture! If we sacrifice earnings momentum for a few years, then we'll be on the hit list. The institutions, pension-fund managers, insurance companies, and mutual funds own over 55% of this company. They get measured and ranked annually by outfits like the Becker Median. If they saw an earnings shortfall coming, they'd hammer this stock so badly, we'd all be on that track to nowhere with Alan.

   We've already been criticized for being too operations oriented. It's part of our low multiple and why our company is valued at only fifteen times our earnings. Worse, the takeover guys would be salivating at the prospects of grabbing us, and the analysts would be feeding them information and cheering them on.

COO Pete: Yeah, I read one of those analysts' reports. I never knew that "operations" was a dirty word until I read that. Alan brought you in, Dick, to provide some creative financial engineering—I guess that sounds a lot sexier than market growth and getting the cost-to-produce down. But just to show you how unsophisticated I really am, tell me how these institutions go around banging on companies for short-term earnings and, in many cases, pushing downsizing. They're investing the workers' money, aren't they? Don't they let the workers vote on whether they want to be downsized?

CFO Dick: Nothing is that simple, Pete. First, some of those institutions you're blaming for the short-term pressure are the managers of our company's pension fund. We had three of them in here last week for the quarterly review, and we dumped one of them because they missed the market last year. They invested in too many dull 15-multiple companies, like us, and missed the big move in hi-tech industries that now have an average multiple of over 40!

Some argue that the government blew it with ERISA back in 1974, when Congress forced full-cash funding of future pension obligations. I doubt that Congress knew what they were doing, but the law then sucked billions in growth capital out of companies and in effect gave it to Wall Street. A bull market is guaranteed when 100 billion dollars a year is added to the demand side.

VP Mktg. Sheila: It sounds like the government messed up the supply-and-demand equation.

CFO Dick: That's basically what happened; besides, ERISA also scared the hell out of Directors. The government wrote the law as if all Directors were responsible for Studebaker's going broke and stiffing the pensioners. Also, don't forget that most pensions at that time were defined benefits. A retiree got a fixed amount, say $500 a month or whatever, no matter what the pension money had earned. In an up-market, the companies and the states thought this was a good deal. They said that since they had the obligation to pay the fixed amount, then all the extra gains from the stock market were theirs. Some hollered that it was the workers' money, but they didn't get very far. But don't knock it; about four cents of our own earnings improvement last year was due to our reduction in pension expense. The market went up so much that we were able to drop our charge to earnings. It's a big impact. A study a few years ago showed that 44% of corporate earnings improvement that year came from reduction in pension cost.

CEO Alan: I'm afraid Dick's description is the reality, Pete. I happen to think that the government blew a beautiful opportunity—a plan that would have directed this cash to investments for job growth, not to the stock market, where most of it ended up pushing up stock prices. But that's the way it is. Certain punitive clauses in ERISA suggested that Board Directors would be personally liable if they screwed up the return on the pension funds. The Directors wanted maximum insulation. Spell that: having the pension committee, made up of company officers, not Directors, turning over poor performers judged on short-term performance. The government loaded the gun, but corporate America pulled the trigger!

COO Pete: This whole mess goes back to plans badly designed by Congress, that's what I get from what you're saying, Alan.

CFO Dick: Alan's right, Pete. Congress took ten years to design the plan and proved, one more time, that Congressional staffers and lobbyists are not good at designing anything that works.

VP Mktg. Sheila: It's worse than that. I read in *Fortune* that the biggest part of the hundreds of billions of dollars lost on the S&L debacle was Congressional delay—for years! Then they proved that no matter how bad the problem, Congress could fix it and make it worse. When they finally got off the dime, they passed a new law that went so far in the other direction that they put good thrifts out of business.

CEO Alan: All interesting, but let's wrap this up. We've got Sheila's proposal on the table. Now let's do our due diligence and see how we can pursue this opportunity without blowing the company. But we haven't heard Dick's proposal. In the interest of time, Dick, why don't you lay out all the moving parts, then we'll reconvene in two weeks for a fuller analysis.

CFO Dick: OK, Alan, I've got a tough package, but I think it makes sense in today's hard-ball world. I'm a little reluctant just to lay it out without all the background music, but it's your nickel, so here goes. First, the Georgia and California operations do not pass our hurdle rate for continued investment, even with a lot of depreciated equipment. Part of the benefit of the big-bang approach is that we can pull into one year all of the costs of shutting those operations down over the next three years but write them off this year.

VP Mktg. Sheila: Pardon the interruption, but you have to help me with this big-bang stuff. Give us a short course on this astrophysical phenomenon.

CFO Dick: Sheila, for years, companies have struggled to add a few cents a share to earnings, impress Wall Street, and build up the stock price. Then, when the takeover guys came in, they taught us all a lesson. After taking over a company, they would make an enormous charge against earnings for one-time "restructuring," a big bang. This would set them up to look good for a few years just on the accounting treatment. They would always test the outside auditors and the SEC to see how far they could push the accounting-rules envelope. Part of the benefit was, of course, big savings on taxes.

COO Pete: Us taxpayers subsidizing the speculators and deal-makers, again!

CEO Alan: Well, you're at least partly right, Pete. Of course these deal-makers were all one-trick ponies. They knew that the easiest thing to do was to dump people. All you have to do is to act real nasty and say, "We've got 10,000 people, take it down to 9,000!"

Capricious downsizing can help earnings only for a few years, but the damage it does can take five years to show up.

CFO Dick: That's one scenario, Alan, but don't you agree that there were plenty of situations where good companies had to make these moves in the face of tough world competition? Both downsizing and mergers were a matter of necessity.

CEO Alan: No question. As usual, the devil's in the details. Some restructuring moves were motivated in the best interest of the company; many others used world competition as an excuse to pursue greedy goals. In these deals, money in incredible amounts rains down on everyone involved. A good rule, I find, to understand a situation like this, is to check the personal motivation of those involved: Follow the money! But go ahead Dick, push on.

CFO Dick: Whatever the motivations, everyone began to see the benefits of downsizing and the big write-off, the big bang. Those who were really struggling, the ones with weak earnings, and had Wall Street down on them, found downsizing very seductive. Why not? Announce a big lay-off, and your stock goes up a few points. Company executives like it because it both buys them time and makes them wealthier. In many cases, they write off more than their annual earnings — in some cases, as much as half their net worth. Some executives took a while to comprehend that putting all these big negative numbers on the profit-and-loss statement didn't pull the house down; it was cheered by Wall Street.

VP Mktg. Sheila: It sounds like smoke and mirrors to me. Why is Wall Street so excited? Sounds to me as if they think that CEOs pass their manhood test by downsizing.

CEO Alan: As I said, with most of these questions comes the good, the bad, and the ugly. The availability of this accounting treatment for restructuring actually liberated some good companies to do necessary things. In many other cases, it is as you say, Sheila, clearly smoke and mirrors, and it allows management to fool the stockholders for a few more years. Can we continue, Dick?

CFO Dick: OK, Sheila's last two proposals have not quite made our hurdle rate, so they should be abandoned.

VP Sheila: Hey, wait a minute!

CEO Alan: Why don't we let Dick finish?

CFO Dick: Thirdly, we've now finished our five-year integrated data systems program. We're online with our dedicated satellite communications, and, most important, the whole company is on a single database. When this project was started, we had 13 different systems, from sales-prospecting to shipping. Now we're able to realize the benefits and lay off hundreds over the next few years. Their severance costs will be packaged in the big-bang. You can figure what this will do to improve profits in the next few years along with a windfall in cash from lower taxes.

COO Pete: That sounds like a blood bath! You weren't even here when that plan was laid out. It worked only because a lot of old dogs, starting with me, learned how to do new tricks. Most of our operating people went to training courses to learn how to assimilate this new technology along with doing their regular job. Fortunately, the hi-tech guys who came in knew from experience that if the new system weren't adopted by operations as their own, it wouldn't fly.

CFO Dick [Ignoring Pete]: Fourthly, the cost to produce in Ohio and Indiana has been going up for five years. Our major competitor has new plants in Mexico and Malaysia—they're eating our lunch. We'd better wake up and smell the coffee and shut these operations down. The shutdown will cost roughly $35 million and take three years, but it can all be written off now, this year.

COO Pete: That's all on top of the blood bath, right?

CFO Dick: Of course. Finally, the really big bang is when we take all of our savings on the layoffs, the tax savings, and the $125 million we're sitting on, and we buy back our own stock. Depending on how much our stock moves on the announcement of this package, we could purchase millions of shares. In the magic of Wall Street, our new earnings could be $2.19, and our new stock price almost $33— unless we're rewarded with a new multiple of 18, in which case our stock would be crowding $40! Even at $33, we've added over $200 million to our shareholder value.

COO Pete: This is obscene, Alan! Give us some time to respond to this tearing the company apart! You and I have spent our working lives building this company up. We've got great people, great spirit, and great opportunities. When this hot dog you insisted on hiring gets through with his razzle-dazzle, everything we've built will be gone. And me with it. Am I clear enough?

CEO Alan: Cool it, Pete! We all know it's a hard, cruel world. We now have two proposals on the table. Let's give them both a close look and reconvene in two weeks. OK?

COO Pete: I'd prefer to comment on this package while the flavor lasts. Leave this monster on the table, and it will start to grow.

CEO Alan: Meeting adjourned. You'll be advised of a meeting time in a couple of weeks. Pete, you can be the lead-off batter at that meeting. Thanks, gang! That's it for today.

Curtain

Act Two

Scene: At dinner in a restaurant; on stage: VP Marketing Sheila and her brother, Bud, Associate Instructor of Economics at the Community College

Sheila: Explain to me in simple terms, Bud, how building and selling things in a way that builds jobs is being dominated by those who make money on money.

Bud: I'll give you a formula: EL+LS−MD = 2C.

Sheila: You forgot the *simple!* What the hell does that mean?

Bud: The formula is EL (excessive liquidity) plus LS (leveraged speculation) minus MD (market disciplines) equals 2C (two catastrophes). EL or "excessive liquidity" means too much money chasing too few legitimate opportunities. The biggest example is the trillions of dollars of the wage earners' retirement money that the government gave to Wall Street to drive the bull market. It's a paradox! Alan Greenspan and the Fed inflation fighters watch for the slightest evidence that factory workers' wages are going up; at the same time, the government is passing laws that result in enormous asset inflation in stock values. This was the "excessive exuberance," as Greenspan later called it.

Sheila: Are there other examples of EL?

Bud: Many. Every economic crisis in emerging economies from South America to Mexico to Southeast Asia started with excessive liquidity that put economic growth into overdrive. They call it "hot money." It rushes into an economy in big quantities and funds risky projects and speculation, and then it rushes out so fast that severe damage is done to the economy and the people.

Sheila: Is there a solution?

Bud: Well, I'm not an expert on the international monetary system, but you would think that by now, bankers would know how to cooperate on judging the quality of loans. Isn't that what they get paid for? Another banking no-no that has been violated regularly in these loans to emerging economies is lending this hot money for longer-term investment. You cannot have an economy depending on investment capital that can flee the country at the slightest threat of speculative attack.

Sheila: How do you control hot money coming from so many directions?

Bud: For every problem there is an international agency somewhere. They just need the will and the way. The International Banking Settlement Commission, or something like that, is in Basel, Switzerland. It could write new protocols for international lending on the debt-to-equity ratio.

Sheila: The what?

Bud: Debt-to-equity is a measurement that's regularly applied to companies. If the percentage of impatient debt gets too high, compared to the percentage of patient capital or equity, then the rating companies downgrade the company. That makes it harder and more expensive for them to get more money, so the brakes get put on. A country's bonds are rated, but I don't think that there is any effort to keep tabs either on the amount of hot money pouring in or on its relationship to long-term, patient investment. A simple fix would be to require the banks to make long-term investments in these countries in some proportion to their short-term loans. I like built-in controls. This would make the bankers do their homework and direct the money to those activities that really build up the country.

Sheila: I started this, but now I know it's too deep for me. I'm getting a headache!

Bud: That's why I gave you the formula. It will make sense after we go through it a few times. Most people do not understand these arcane matters, and that's why the Wall Street foxes have been in charge of the chicken coop for too long.

Sheila: All right, Professor, continue with the lecture! I've got a fox in my own chicken coop, and what I need is a good fox trap.

Bud: Let's move on to LS for "leveraged speculation" or speculation with borrowed money. This borrowing privilege allowed by government regulation has been the cause of every economic problem in this country since the Panic of 1818. We have even more incredible stories now, though. Did you read about LTCM, the hedge fund, that took leverage to record levels? Would you believe they figured out how to make some bets when they did not use *any* of their own money? After they imploded, the Fed orchestrated a bailout on the usual pattern: Let finance capitalists screw up anyway they want, and then when the damage is too big to let them fail, bail them out!

Sheila: What's a hedge fund?

Bud: It's an investment pool for fat cats, throw in a million dollars and you can play. They use esoteric models designed by a bunch of Ph.D's to make money on money. And boy, do they make money! Would you believe a 40% return for several years and located in the Cayman Islands so the fat cats paid no taxes on these big wins!

Sheila: If they are so smart, how did they screw up?

Bud: They forgot to put Russia's defaulting on government bonds into their model. A guy wrote a book called *When Genius Failed.*[332] Read it — it'll make you cry!

Sheila: Incredible! But go ahead — you were giving me examples of LS.

Bud: The Crash of '29 is a good example. And so will the next one be. The leveraged speculation of the 1990s will be compared to the leveraged speculation of the 1920s. Think about when Alan Greenspan identified "excessive exuberance" in the stock market as the threat to the economy, and then think about what he did to respond to the threat.

Sheila: I can hardly wait. What did he do?

Bud: He raised the interest rate—it's the only thing he thinks he knows how to do! But that hurt people such as young couples trying to buy their first house. What he could—and should—have done,

---

[332] Roger Lowenstein, *When Genius Failed: The Rise and Fall of Long-Term Capital Management* (New York: Random House, 2000).

instead, was raise brokers' margins from 50% to say 75% of the speculators' bet. This would have reduced the percentage that speculators may borrow to gamble with. That would have placed the cure where even Greenspan said the sickness was.

Sheila: That seems to make so much sense. Why didn't Greenspan do that?

Bud: Greenspan? The water boy for ultra-capitalism? He would have lost his sainthood quickly if he had started cutting back on the ways to make money on money.

Sheila: So what's the long-term answer to leveraged speculation?

Bud: I told you, I am not a finance expert, but for starters how about a simple rule: Speculators can bet all they want as long as they do it with their own money? This is probably extreme, but split the difference between my rule and the crazy stuff that is going on now, and maybe you'll be making some sense.

Sheila: Great! That gets us back to *simple*. Now that I'm an expert on EL and LS, what is MD? Your formula is getting interesting.

Bud: MD is "market discipline," the forces of competition and the fear of failure that monitor the free economy. You know the old formula that every freedom needs a discipline. It's true in economic freedom, too. Wall Street has managed to lobby Washington to get the EL and LS, but their greatest merchandising job was to get rid of the disciplines that tended to get in the way of making money on money. The government invented the "too big to fail" rule for banks, took deposit insurance to new highs with the S & L debacle, and steadily found new ways to subsidize ultra-capitalists. One example was the "Greenspan spread," when the Fed nursed banks back to health after another series of dumb loans by lending money to the banks at less than 3% when the banks could turn around and make over 6% by investing in government bonds.

In this crazy world of unreality, they call this problem a "moral hazard." They borrowed the expression from the insurance industry as a more confusing way to say that they were trampling on the market disciplines upon which economic freedom depends.

Sheila: I can see the hazard, but where's the morality? Does the government have a credit card that I can get some of this 3% money with? I'm tired of paying from 9% to 18%!

Bud: Start a bank, make tons of bad loans, and maybe you can get a shot at 3% money, but let's get back to my formula. Follow the bouncing ball: First, the government allows EL, excessive liquidity, and then it stirs in a lot of LS, leveraged speculation. These in combination drive the economy up into the stratosphere. Then, after the inevitable climax and bust, the government says: "Gee, this is serious! We'd better get out the band-aids and patch it up." Then they forget to determine what caused this out-of-control problem in the first place and walk away, leaving it ready to repeat.

Sheila: I don't spend much time on these things, but I once saw a great picture of President Clinton and Secretary of Treasury Bob Rubin traveling the world preaching the gospel of free capital as the way to world prosperity. It sounded wonderful, are you sure about raining on this parade?

Bud: They were quite correct in describing the potential benefits of free trade, but it got me mad when they contradicted their own gospel by abandoning the market disciplines. Back in the '90s, these two great salesmen convinced the emerging economies to take down all of their cross-border controls to let this capital roam freely. But they forgot to warn these emerging economies that when no one was looking, they had torn down the disciplines that make the system work. Within a couple of years after removing the controls, EL and LS struck and devastated defenseless economies and innocent people. No wonder Malaysia thought that they had been set up for a fall by a new kind of Western imperialism.

Sheila: Talking about insurance, subsidies, and bailouts I suppose that the taxpayer pays for all of this, one way or the other. Listening to you, I thought of a bumper sticker for the money-changers — try this: "Privatize the profits, nationalize the losses!"

Bud: You catch on fast. It's good, but not original. Screwing the taxpayers in good ol' America is bad, but it's not so bad as the job done on the poor people, millions of them, in places like Mexico and Indonesia. The EL weakened their countries' economies, and then the currency speculators with their LS attacked like sharks, sensing blood in the water. They drove the currency value down 70% in Indonesia and devastated the country. The American media helped politicize the problem, so most people never understood what had really happened. Now, it looks like it will take a generation to get Indonesia back on track, unless the country devolves further in the meantime.

Sheila: This is getting too complicated — let's give it a rest! You're throwing in things like "devolve" like I knew what it meant.

Bud: Stay with me, Sheila! "Devolvement" means that the attack by lethal finance imperialism destabilizes a country that was fragile to begin with, so that it ends up breaking into small pieces, many of them fighting with each other. Ethnic and religious animosities contribute to the problems, but the root cause is economic.

Sheila: Ah, Mr. Economics Professor, there you go again, sounding like Karl Marx.

Bud: Karl got a few things right, and this is one of them. The form of commerce that underlies human culture makes the difference in whether that culture progresses or not. Human progress is not possible unless a form of commerce superior to whatever was in place before lifts the culture into its next stage of development. It's a Law of Nature!

Sheila: Or, at least, of Economics professors!

Bud: Touché! But listen, Sheila — you're a big champion of human rights. Frankly, most of your protests back in college were all "sound and fury signifying nothing." If you are really dedicated to human rights, think about how lethal finance capitalism deprived these millions of their basic rights for such luxuries as jobs, food, clothing, shelter, education, good health and hope for a better life for their kids. Then your protests will be getting real! But you have to do your homework first. Maybe we should require certification for protestors to make sure that they know enough about how the world works to protest. But we'll save that for another dinner, after which we can organize protest marches on Wall Street and Washington—two sides of the same street, Ultra-Capitalist Avenue!

Sheila: I'll be there! You have opened my eyes to a terrible human tragedy that, as you say, is not very well understood. OK, moving right along, what are the two C's in your formula?

Bud: I'm not a mathematician, either, but that's my way of calling attention to the two ways that EL+LS-MD adds up. It's the two different catastrophes that have resulted and will result from domination by ultra-capitalism. One is the ongoing danger that the whole international monetary system will blow up some day. Despite all of the warnings, there has been no correction of root causes. Too many people are making billions of dollars, pounds, euros, and yen on volatility for them to get serious about getting rid of the volatility.

The second dimension is slower, and for that reason it is more insidious. Financialization of the world's economy gradually puts the system into irreversible decline. You can follow this phenomenon throughout history. As an economy shifts from building and selling things to financial services, it slowly loses its economic vitality. Another way of putting it is that it abandons Adam Smith's dynamic. His progressive theory of commerce, according to which more volume drives the costs down, adding more volume, and so forth, doesn't happen in financial services. As a matter of fact, financialization ignores Smith's warning to beware of the "prodigals and projectors" who pull money away from growing the economy and put it into speculation.

Sheila: Sounds like there should be a lot of fire bells going off to warn people of this threat. How can all of this happen? I thought democracy was "of, for, and by the people," and that federal laws reflect their "will and wisdom." Whatever happened to the "general welfare?"

Bud: Sorry, Sheila, but bright people like you paid no attention to these matters. While you were protesting human rights abuses in China, you should have been spending your time learning how the system works in America, instead! It wouldn't have been as much fun, but it would have been more meaningful. The most basic human rights are for everyone to have adequate food, shelter, clothing, good health, education, and hope for the kids.

Sheila: Don't beat on me, Bud! The only thing I heard from my professors was how bad capitalism was. I never heard about the good capitalism. If you think that I should have gotten a functional knowledge of these financial matters from the educational process in a U.S. university, forget about it!

Bud: Right on! Nobody, not even my learned colleagues in the Economics Department, much less the Business School at the University, understand the connection between democracy and capitalism.

Sheila: Let's get back to the formula. I know from my company how amazingly interdependent the world is now. As I understand these monetary matters, it has to be a spirit of collaboration: "We're all in this together, gang, so let's play by good rules and make it work!" How do you get governments, with their history of fighting over what they thought to be finite resources, to shift gears and support "the superior form of commerce," as you call it, that can provide enough for everyone?

Bud: Good question. Right now, many governments are still playing politics with currency values and interest rates that should be harmonized for the world economy to work well.

Sheila: You keep slipping in these buzz words. "Harmony" — is this a music lesson?

Bud: In a sense, any activity to be governed works best in harmony; that's a Law of Nature, too. It is really no different from a great symphony orchestra. In the international monetary system, it means harmonizing the vital economic signs of various nations in order to provide monetary stability. The need is for a way to change currency values automatically as national circumstances fluctuate. This will not happen so long as finance capitalists lobby the rules, and xenophobic politicians start fighting whenever they hear anything about "world order." How-the-hell are we going to have a world economy that helps all people to live better lives without some order in the world? But we can't go there tonight, right?

Sheila: Right. If I had known how heavy a load you were going to dump on me tonight, I would have had *two* martinis. But seriously, these matters are hitting me where I live. I love my job, but in our company, we seem to be struggling over this very conflict in capitalism, and the bad guys are winning. What's the solution and where do we start?

Bud: I understand your frustration and I sympathize with you. Unfortunately, history shows that as long as ES and LS are not regulated, and MD has been suspended, the system will go up, up, and up until it bursts, and then it will go down, down, and down. In the up direction, the few make billions of dollars; in the down direction, many ordinary people get hurt. Did you ever hear of "the rich getting richer," Sheila? Maybe this time, the downer will be so bad that people like you and me will cooperate on an agenda to fix the system. How about a radical motto like this: "Control currency and credit for the general welfare?" Come on, I'll give you a ride home. You need your sleep; you've got a big meeting coming up, right?

Sheila: OK, let's go! I need to be at the top of my game, tomorrow morning. But you're right, so I'll accept your offer of a ride, but this time we'd better *walk the walk!*

Curtain

Act Three

Scene: CEO's office; on stage: CEO Alan, CFO Dick, COO Pete, VP Marketing Sheila

CEO Alan: OK, let's go! Pete, you're on.

COO Pete: I'll work off my notes on this one. I've been working pretty hard since the last meeting, and hope I have organized a convincing position. After all, we're only talking about the future of this great company.

CFO Dick: Don't start with undocumented premises!

COO Pete: That never seems to bother *you*!

CEO Alan: All right, guys, let's go!

COO Pete: Ten years ago, when Alan became CEO, and pulled me out of the plant to become COO, we had a decent company, but it had been around for a long time and our technology had tired blood. It worked, but in no way were we state-of-the-art. Our employees were also OK, but the majority were just putting in their time; they weren't very turned on. The unions were spending their time on grievances, and they were never included in company planning. The marketing group was likewise OK, but about as exciting as the product line.

Alan changed all that. We had a simple plan: Invest in the people for better productivity and participation, and remember that our mission is to serve the customer—not just sell them, but serve them. Alan's got some great buzz-words, but I think one of his best is "customer loyalty, not just satisfaction." I was never keen on consultants, but the ones we had at the time gave us a good emphasis: "Beware of internalizing; build your company from the customer perspective." The hardest ones to convince were the engineers. The new chip technology had gotten them so excited—what they could do with their chip—that they complicated the product with "freebies" that most customers didn't want.

At any rate, we had an old market and reasonably satisfied customers, and we had some standard products with huge profit margins. These oldies-but-goodies weren't going to be around too many more years, but they could sure spin off cash. We made reasonable earnings improvement—never worse than 5%, never better than 8%—because we were pumping so much money into product development and sales coverage. We got sales growth up to double digits, and we improved cash flow.

CFO Dick: You also got the analysts convinced that we didn't know how to leverage the business. When sales are growing 10%, the analysts are looking for profits to grow something like 12%, not 8%. How long can you go with a sales growth greater than earnings growth? You also spent a lot on your profit-sharing plan. Giving money to the workers may make you feel good, Pete, but it's a cost that most of our competitors don't have. The analysts aren't too keen on it, either.

COO Pete: I had planned to get to all those key areas, but you've interrupted. Perhaps just as well, as your business philosophy is so clearly contrary to mine. You have the benefit of advanced degrees, including a CPA and an MBA. I didn't have an opportunity to go to college, but I'll bet I've read more than anyone else in the room. It took me a lot of reading and thinking to realize just how special this democratic republic of ours is. We really blazed a trail for the rest of the world.

CFO Dick: Is there a point here?

COO Pete: An important point! This country was built on freedoms. They are all important, but anyone who works for a living knows that without economic opportunity, the others are pretty hollow. Several of the books I've read talk about a social contract, how we're all interdependent. The way I've always related this to my work and this company is to feel an obligation to *grow* the company by providing better opportunities for the workers and new jobs for new workers. This seems like such a fundamental obligation of a corporation that I don't know why we're deliberately destroying growth. All anyone talks about is e.p.s.! Why don't we measure company performance by sales growth and cash flow instead of stock price? The more I listen to you, the more I'm convinced not only that e.p.s. is something only accountants understand but also that e.p.s. doesn't even show an honest picture. You're always talking about world competition. We're bringing out great products, and with Sheila's plan will bring out more. Our products are great because our quality keeps going up while the prices go down every year. The market doesn't allow the big margins we used to get, but we're holding our own in this tougher market. Isn't that the way Adam Smith said it should work? Competition drives down prices for the benefit of the consumer, doesn't it?

CFO Dick: Listen, Pete, I don't see what all this flag-waving about the country and freedoms has to do with the problem at hand. And Adam Smith's dead, isn't he? Could you just get on with it?

COO Pete: Sure, Dick, I'll get on with it! Your comments on our profit-sharing and stock-purchase plans are stupid, too. To describe our plan as a giveaway shows particular ignorance of the facts. Profit-sharing and worker ownership is the best investment we ever made. It's the basis of everything else. Your own finance people confirm the productivity figures, Dick. More important than that, everyone in the company is involved, and that's why the products are so good. Our designers have learned that it's not enough to make it work—it has to be producible for the lowest cost and at the highest quality. Our shop people work with engineering, now, as though they themselves had written Dr. Deming's "Fourteen Points."

CFO Dick: All with a cost! Our training and education budget is ten times what it was when you started this program. When will your people be trained enough to get some profit leverage there? And, Peter, I hope you're not doing all this reading on company time! It's a joke, it's a joke! But who's this Dr. Deming — your dentist?

COO Pete: [Ignoring the barbs] I'll answer the training question first: We will never end our training program. With the product that Sheila has proposed, we will have to increase the budget. Incidentally, I thought Alan was nuts five years ago when he hired this little gal to run marketing, but it was a good move. She knows what she's doing.

VP Mktg. Sheila: The "little gal" thanks you, Pete; your heart's in the right place, so I've learned how to translate your language.

COO Pete: I'm not sure what that means, but we've got a great team. Dick, I can't believe that you're not familiar with Dr. Deming. What did you study to get that MBA? Maybe *that's* your problem. Take off your green eye-shade once in a while and see what's going on. W. Edwards Deming was a quality-control guru who couldn't get a hearing with the Big Three car companies, so he put the show on the road and taught the Japanese how to do it. After they stuck it to us with cars with both fewer defects and hours to produce, the U.S. car companies became very interested. There's nothing like a big loss of market share to get one's attention. Dr. Deming proposed 14 points that come down to a few simple concepts: Build it right the first time; build—don't try to *inspect*—quality into the product; get everyone involved and trained; and drive out the old-fashioned fear environment.

CEO Alan: Say a little bit more about the profit-sharing, stock-purchase plan, Pete.

COO Pete: With pleasure—it's my favorite subject. As I think you all know, 80% of our employees, or "associates" as we prefer to call them, are regularly buying the company's stock through a payroll-deduction plan. They have other options through their 401(k), but over half the money goes into our stock. It's probably a safer idea to encourage them to diversify with the rest. The company matches this payroll deduction with a minimum of 20 cents on the dollar, and up to a 100% match when we meet tough goals. All of the company's contributions are in stock. It's a great plan and has changed the company.

    Some people were a bit cynical about their involvement and cooperation, but when they saw people building serious net worth from this plan, they got interested and became converts. Some were amazed at how supportive the union officials were, but modern union statesmen recognize the connection between wages and job security on one hand, and quality and cost on the other. We have as high a participation in union plants as non-union. Grievances are almost a matter of history. The supervisors are trained to lead, not push, and problems are resolved on the spot and cooperatively.

One of the things that makes me most proud is that our associates now own over 10% of the company, and I hope that it will be 20% before I retire. Note carefully, Dick: They get nothing until they put up their own money. Most of them are raising families and are on tight budgets, but they dig down to enjoy that pride of ownership.

CFO Dick: Some people think that this company is in the Dark Ages. Instead of stock buy-backs, we dilute the stock with the profit-sharing plan; instead of stock options, we give stock grants that are both a charge against company profits and are taxable to those who receive them.

CEO Alan: All of those features were my decisions, Dick. We wanted a plan with discipline to it. A charge to earnings is just such a discipline; you don't reduce profits casually. Also stock grants, being considered a part of total compensation, are taxable. The profit-sharing plan is the same one for everybody, managers and secretaries. It offers different levels of participation depending on the individual associates' level of responsibility, but everyone understands the plan and that we're all in it together. We can and do explain this to anyone. There is no criticism of fat-cat plans here. It's part of the environment of trust. You can't buy trust, Dick; you have to earn it. Why do you have a problem with this, Dick?

CFO Dick: The plan has some benefit, Alan, but stock grants and the technique of funding from the company's stock drives me nuts. The earnings dilution, caused by steadily adding more shares and thereby lowering our earnings per share, is one of the reasons we have such a lousy multiple. Let me convince you that we should at least buy back the stock on the open market.

CEO Alan: Many associates elect to reinvest their dividends in more stock. This is low-cost, very patient capital to grow on, Dick. We just need to educate analysts better! The resulting productivity and innovation from the plan far exceed the dilution.

CFO Dick: Impossible! Anti-dilution is a matter of religious principle with them.

COO Pete: That's *their* problem. Most of them have never been in a factory; no wonder they don't understand it. Our plan has worked. We now have trained, motivated associates and the cash to make the big move that Sheila has outlined. Let me remind you that part of the profit-sharing spirit is a commitment to job security. It's a best-effort commitment to use attrition and retraining instead of lay-offs. We even absorb part of the cost if an associate moves to another plant. This is important: The whole program was put in place on the basis of trust, fairness, and cooperation. I guess you could simply use Alan's word and say it's based on integrity.

      The people now really believe that integrity also means meritocracy. You can go as far in this company as your brains and energy will take you. With this motivation and the training program, we've uncovered some incredible talent. Our top sales manager, Charlie, out in Chicago, was a materials handler in the Scranton plant. He had to leave school to support his mother and kid brothers and sisters, and now the guy's a winner for us as he was for his family. All we had to do was give him a shot at it.

      Maybe I'm going on too long about history, but this isn't merely history; it's about the spirit of our company; it's about potential, the potential of our associates and the potential of the company. This great spirit has also encouraged our associates to be more active in their communities. We take it for granted now, but we know how to really get things done by working together. Believe me, that's a rare talent in many community activities. One very successful program has been our adopt-a-school program. We're now experimenting with an adopt-a-church program. We've found that combining resources in the inner-city really does make a difference in people's lives. Besides, we get leads on some outstanding new employees that way.

CFO Dick: It's all very heart-warming, but …

COO Pete: And another thing, our suppliers tell us we're a different company. They know our commitment to integrity includes our relationship with them. Most of them have been keen on working with us, even at their own expense, on new-product development.

CEO Alan: It's a great history, Pete. You're describing the most satisfying experience of my working life. Nevertheless, we're caught in a dilemma: Either we run the company for the long-term benefit of associates and other stakeholders or we respond to the short-term threatening demands of Wall Street.

COO Pete: With all due respect, Alan, if the right move for the company is to invest in the future, then we're counting on you and Dick to merchandise the excitement of Sheila's product plan to the analysts and the money managers. Everyone has their own job to do, and that's yours, guys. We're close to the right product at the right time. The world is moving more and more towards free enterprise; more and more countries are moving into double-digit growth. Most of them badly need communications infrastructure. The bad news is that they have very little of it, the good news is that they can go immediately into wireless, fiber optics, satellites, and fully digital systems. The market's going to explode, and that means us!

VP Mktg. Sheila: Go, Pete!

COO Pete: Now, let me get to the shareholder question. The more I think about it, the more I think it's *B.S.*! Who is the shareholder anyway? Do you think our associate-shareholders would have any problem choosing the long-term plan? No way! They would say, "Build the company, do it right, and in time the stock value will be guaranteed."

And who are these money-manager Rock stars that intimidate Dick? The financial media love them because they are easier to write about than a long-term building plan. Besides, the media can make them out the good guys with us the bad guys, calling us the members of a club named "entrenched management."

And where did the analysts get perfect vision? Who taught them what a company should do or not do? More important, who gave them the authority to beat companies into short-term goals? These fund managers are investing the workers' money, but have they ever had a referendum with all those wage-earners who put their money into these funds? Have they ever asked the people they allegedly represent whether they prefer long-term or short-term?

CFO Dick: There you go again with voting on company policy, Pete! That ain't how it's done!

COO Pete: How it's done, Dick, is to do it right, whatever it takes! We're screwing around with the future of the country as well as our company, as you should know. This battle between capital and labor at least used to be between those with the capital and those who did the labor. Ultra-capitalists always knew how to screw the worker, but now they're doing it with the workers' own money. Danny DeVito did a movie on this: "OPM," Other Peoples' Money!

CEO Alan: You're giving me a headache, Pete, because even discounting your passions, some of what you say is probably true. But what are we going to do? We don't have a lobby that could convince Congress that they made a terrible mistake in pushing trillions of dollars of pension money onto Wall Street, and that it's time to redirect this "excessive liquidity," as the experts call it, away from Wall Street towards the general welfare. I have no question but that it's the government's industrial and fiscal policy, lobbied by Wall Street, that puts us in this box, but that won't change until we have educated citizens directing politicians with sufficient economic savvy to avoid mistakes like these. But Pete, I'm a businessman, not a politician. I have a company to run, whatever the circumstances!

CFO Dick: OK, now we're getting back to reality! All the feel-good stuff on company spirit is beautiful, but my job is to make this company more valuable. Since we don't have time to change the politics, as you say, Alan, then let's get to the bottom line.

CEO Alan: Have you finished, Pete?

COO Pete: I guess. I've given the background so that Sheila and Dick can have, I hope, a better sense of how long and hard you and I and the others have worked to build this spirit to realize the potential of our associates and the company. I'll comment as we go along on Dick's "bottom line."

CEO Alan: Sheila, do you have anything you'd like to add before Dick reviews his proposal?

VP Mktg. Sheila: No, Alan. Naturally, I'm as excited as Pete is about our new opportunity, and I know from my own marketing department that this spirit is real, and it can move mountains. I'm supposed to be the marketing expert, but I've learned a lot from Pete about the real meaning of potential. I've never before heard such emphasis on releasing the latent power of turned-on people as I've heard and seen in this company. I've seen it transform some of my steady performers into overachievers. I know it works!

I don't mean to gang up on you, Dick, but I also agree that we've got a wonderful story to tell Wall Street, and I'm sure you have the eloquence to do it. I don't know much about that part of the business; I'm just a simple-minded marketer, but if I can get our product message out to our customers, surely you can get our great company story out to the fund managers.

CEO Alan: Thanks for the comments, Sheila. Dick, you're on.

COO Pete: You must be in a good mood, Dick. The stock's behaving well, up a point and a half since our last meeting. Sheila's right! We've got a great story to tell, and you got out and told it.

COO Dick: That bump in our stock prices is not good news. You think it is, but I'll get to that later. At least you're consistent, Pete. You miss the mark on just about anything having to do with ultra-capitalism, including the idea that the wage earners are unhappy with how the money managers are investing their money. They're

347

delighted every time they look at their rising wealth on things like a 401(k) report. But let's get to Sheila's proposal. As Alan requested, my department did an EVA analysis, and, although the numbers are preliminary, they don't meet our hurdle rate.

VP Mktg. Sheila: I can't believe it! What growth-rate assumptions did you start with, and why wasn't I involved in the analysis?

CEO Alan: Easy Sheila! We didn't have the time for a full team effort. I asked Dick to do a talking paper for this meeting. We can debate his premises now, if you like.

VP Mktg. Sheila: We're only talking about the future of the company! Why didn't we take more time? Why the panic party?

CEO Alan: We'll get to the time pressure, but let's let Dick outline how EVA, the economic value added, analysis worked out.

CFO Dick: Here's the summary page, and it misses the hurdle rate by a full point.

VP Mktg. Sheila: You've cut the sales growth after year four from 14% to 8%. This is a breakaway plan. No, it's more of a vision. Even cutting it your 8%, sales growth still showed a pretty good profit return.

COO Dick: Unless Alan overrules me, I don't take visions to the Board. We've never had a program with better than a 10% growth; it's always better to be a bit conservative.

VP Mktg. Sheila: I hope you know what you're saying. This company and this country were built on vision and taking chances. It's the way to do it, we can make it happen! We can design and build a beautiful product and then make the 14% growth happen in the marketplace.

CFO Dick: Sorry, Sheila, I didn't see a place in the EVA analysis for cheerleading.

VP Mktg. Sheila: Alan, this can't work! The CFO cuts the growth rate and then concludes that the whole program doesn't meet the hurdle rate. I thought Dick would have his own agenda with his favorite ways to use our cash, and would try to shoot my program down, so I've been getting some help on his pet EVA theory. My brother teaches at the Community College—he's in Economics—and he thinks industry is shooting itself in the foot with this EVA hurdle rate, anyway.

CFO Dick: With due respect to the professor…

VP Mktg. Sheila: He's an Associate Instructor. They don't have "professors" at the Community College. But he knows his stuff!

CFO Dick: Whatever! I'm sure he's quite an authority. EVA became popular for the simple reason that any investment has first to earn the cost of money.

VP Mktg. Sheila: Exactly my brother's point! He says the real cost—I guess he means the prime rate, less inflation—is at a high level. Bud says that we need a growth rate of 3.5% to provide jobs and opportunity for everyone. As a country, we've done that and better, before. He says that the Federal Reserve works overtime worrying about inflation and slowing the economy, when all he hears from me is about prices going down. He also says that at the 3.5% level, the government will have sufficient revenues to help people, if they invest it wisely. What should the real cost of money be if we corrected it fully for the low inflation, Dick?

CFO Dick: About two points less, I guess. I must say, though, this is an interesting discussion. Between you and Pete, we go from gut feelings to arcane theory.

VP Mktg. Sheila: Dick, I stand on my high-growth projections. With them, even your constipated EVA goes right off the chart! It's Alan's call. Who has the better feel for market growth, the head of Marketing or the number-cruncher? I'm hedging my bets, however. I don't think

349

your other EVA assumptions hold up either. Tell us what the "cost of money" means.

CFO Dick: It means the prime lending rate plus one.

VP Mktg. Sheila: That's all that's in the equation?

CFO Dick: No, there's an assumed cost of equity. You can't tie up millions of dollars without recognizing that equity has a cost.

VP Mktg. Sheila: What's that number?

CFO Dick: It varies, but at the moment, it's 13%.

VP Mktg. Sheila: Wow! No wonder the country isn't growing its manufacturing. World competition is one thing, but with that number, no wonder good programs don't get started. Where does a number like that come from?

CFO Dick: It's an estimate of the rate of appreciation of the stock market.

COO Pete: Let me understand this: Because of ERISA, the workers' pension money was taken out of companies, and then it became such a monster wave of investable cash that it pushed the stock market up, and now we use the rising stock market values as a cost-of-equity to shoot down programs that would give jobs to the workers' kids. Have I got it right?

CEO Alan: A slightly biased description, but with some truth.

VP Mktg. Sheila: I'm missing something here, Dick. I just read somewhere that because of the bull market, the cost of equity is at a forty-year low; it's under 5%! Why are you using double digits?

CFO Dick: How did they measure that?

VP Mktg. Sheila: You know enough to lower my sales estimate, but you're asking me that question? Are you setting me up, or don't you know?

CFO Dick: Get off the soap box and define your terms!

VP Mktg. Sheila: OK, my brother helped me with this, but I think I've got it straight. It's pretty simple; it's the inverse of your beloved P/E ratio. Instead of price divided by earnings, it's earnings divided by price, how much capital we can raise on the stock market for every dollar of earnings. What I don't understand is why companies are not growing at supersonic speed with that under-5% cost of capital!

CFO Dick: There's a lot of initial-public-offering money being raised–didn't your brother tell you about IPOs? Besides, that's not the way companies look at cost of capital. Wall Street does not like the dilution of earnings that comes from selling more shares in the market. More shares reduces the earnings per share proportionately, and I suppose they don't like it adding to the total stock available in the market.

VP Mktg. Sheila: As a matter of fact, he did tell me about IPOs. Bud said that with this crazy market, IPOs are like Dutch tulips. They're a speculative commodity, and most of the money raised is paid off to the early investors and taken out of the company. Besides that, the ultra-capitalists learned how to low-ball the initial offering price, share the big first-day run-up in price with their selected fat cats, and then collect big fees. The entrepreneurs and the small investors get screwed, as usual.

CEO Alan: Dick, there was about three times as much new debt as new equity in last year's economy, despite the arithmetically low cost of equity. It's part of the well kept secret that the stock market has little to do with growth capital. Take away the IPOs and the conversion from debt to equity to clean up the balance sheet, and there's really very little new capital left to grow on.

COO Pete: I can't believe this! I thought that the reason why the media report the stock market with breathless, minute-by-minute coverage is because all that money pouring in was being recycled to help the economy grow.

CEO Alan: Afraid that's not the reality, Pete. Companies threw a lot more money into the stock market last year in stock buy-backs than they took out in growth capital. It's a lot like '29, when big companies were putting their surplus money into the stock market instead of investing in growth programs or putting it back into the economy in dividends.

COO Pete: Sounds like throwing all that money into a black hole.

VP Mktg. Sheila: Yeah! With all that EL pouring into the market from pension money, the demand went way up, but Wall Street figured out how to drive it even more by shrinking the supply of stock through buy-backs and mergers. The supply/demand equation was hit with a double whammy.

COO Pete: What's EL, Sheila?

VP Mktg. Sheila: Sorry, I thought everybody knew that, but I guess it's just Economics jargon. Bud says EL is "excessive liquidity," too much money chasing a diminishing amount of stock or too much money chasing a diminishing number of good business opportunities.

CFO Dick: Alan, we've got some urgent matters to consider. All of this theorizing is interesting, but if you are all pointing out that the stock market is a game of musical chairs dedicated to personal wealth, Keynes got there before you with that pitch in 1935. Can we accept reality and go from there?

CEO Alan: Unfortunately, we're trying to judge strategic moves for one good company in the middle of ultra-capitalism's takeover of the world. Short of writing your Congressman—and you know how much good that would do!—we'd better get back to the urgent. Unfortunately, the urgent always takes priority over the important.

VP Mktg. Sheila: May I finish my point on the capital requirements?

CEO Alan: Briefly, I hope.

VP Mktg. Sheila: We already have the capital to fund this program. Much of it came from the stock-purchase program and is zero-cost.

CFO Dick: Come again?

VP Mktg. Sheila: The associates put the money in, and because of motivation, from their feeling of ownership, they raised the productivity to pay for their profit-sharing. It was not a gift, as you, Dick, tend to describe it. They got it the old-fashioned way—they earned it! My brother is fascinated with our profit-sharing and stock-purchase plan. He says that it's the classic economics of Adam Smith: providing low-cost, very patient capital to grow on. But better than that, the capital itself comes from the workers themselves who raise their productivity enough to pay the cost of capital—it's their sweat equity. Voilà! Zero-cost capital. Besides that, Bud thinks that if there were enough of these plans, they would solve the distribution-of-wealth problem and put money in the hands of those whose spending would keep the growth going. He says that this was Adam Smith's vision, an economic perpetual-motion machine.

CEO Alan: It's an interesting argument, Sheila, but we can't change the world. Like most companies, we have to use commonly accepted ways of evaluating investment opportunities.

VP Mktg. Sheila: Alan, we don't have to change the *world* because we've already changed our own company. And when the current fads turn out to be financial machinations having little to do with building either companies or the country, the rest of the world can learn our little secret.

COO Pete: Sheila's comments are very interesting. I can almost see how as a country we're creating a self-fulfilling prophecy of slow manufacturing growth, and …

353

CEO Alan: [Interrupts] We'd better get the rest of the story from Dick. Tell them why our stock went up last week, Dick.

CFO Dick: We're "in play." Reports from two new analysts are coming out soon. Both of them trash our anemic earnings growth, and they describe our combination of cash and our unleveraged balance sheet as a huge bull's eye for some raider to take a shot at. They've concluded that we won't make the appropriate moves to find hidden asset value, and if *this* management won't go after those values, then there are dozens of corporate raiders who would like to move in and do it. Don't forget, that cash pile you've built up is like a flashing neon sign; it says: "Take me, I can pay for myself!"

COO Pete: This is crazy! We ran the company well to build up that cash. Why don't we pay it out in a special dividend?

VP Mktg. Sheila: Spend it on my new product plan!

COO Pete: In either event, that would stop the deal-makers from salivating.

CFO Dick: At least your naïveté is consistent, Pete. Wall Street hates special dividends. They want you either to keep the cash to stimulate a deal or else use it to buy stock back.

COO Pete: But they don't run our company, Dick, we do! How about announcing an increased dividend? We could double the dividend and still fund Sheila's project.

CFO Dick: A dud. Wall Street really doesn't like dividends. A few funds want a certain yield, a little income, but they still prefer deals or stock repurchase. They always use the ultimate argument: Dividends are not tax-efficient; they're taxed twice.

VP Mktg. Sheila: Yeah, wise people have been pointing out for years that a raider can take a tax deduction on the most extreme forms of junk bonds, but dividends, that help the economy, are doubly taxed, once to the company when the dividends are paid from after-tax earnings, and once to the stockholder when they are taxed as personal income.

CEO Alan: As Willie Sutton, the famous bank robber, said, you go where the money is. Look for the motivation! Deals and stock buy-backs have a wonderful benefit in immediate personal wealth for a few. Ultra-capitalists have an enormous lobby power in Washington. They don't like dividends, so the double taxation continues. Democratic capitalists, on the other hand, have little lobby power. It's that simple.

CFO Dick: Arbitrageurs are probably buying into our stock. That's why it's moved. They only buy on the assumption of a takeover.

CEO Alan: The word gets around so quickly! I've had three calls today from investment bankers who are eager to help us defend ourselves. But the arbitrageurs, if they make a killing in two months, will pay the same capital gains tax as our associates do, even if they hold on to their stock for twenty years. Can you imagine how quickly the situation would fix itself if the arbitrageurs had to pay 60% tax for trades done in less than six months, and our associates had no tax on their gains at retirement?

COO Pete: Unbelievable! Can you imagine how stock-purchase and profit-sharing plans would spread if the associates had more favorable tax treatment on dividends and capital gains? But what are you telling us, Dick? We're in play, so the game's over? Do it your way or else we're dead?

CFO Dick: Pretty much, Pete. Now that we're in play, there's a bunch of young hot-shots out there running their models till their computers smoke. They know the potential for lay-offs. In our annual report, we've been bragging about completing our integrated data system, with strong language about savings. That just convinces the raiders that the downsizing will be big, easy, and quick.

COO Pete: But the savings was to come from attrition over a five-year period. Many of those people could be retrained to build up Sheila's marketing force.

CFO Dick: You're going to retrain accountants and systems people to *sell*? Get real!

VP Mktg. Sheila: You'd be surprised, Dick! Some of my top producers have come from Accounting. We're selling big-ticket items to OEMs, original equipment manufacturers, and the ability to work out complicated program economics is as important as closing skills.

CEO Alan: All true, but Dick's telling us that it's all irrelevant. Either we go with the big-bang plan or someone else will.

COO Pete: I thought those expensive lawyers you had in here gave us some good defenses. Dick sounds like we're defenseless. You're a fighter, Alan, so let's fight.

CEO Alan: We've got the standard defenses, but we can't defend ourselves against an offer at maybe 40% over market, with financing clearly available. Our defenses provide us only bargaining time to try to get top buck.

COO Pete: What's the point of this meeting, then? Have you discussed this with the Board? Has a decision already been made?

CEO Alan: I've talked to them by phone. They're very supportive, and I'm sure they would stand with us in a fight, but they're sophisticated people. They know that if an offer for over $40 a share flies in, I'd be dog-meat if I didn't take it, after a certain amount of faking around.

COO Pete: Don't we have *any* alternatives? Can't we have a "little bang" and still push the new program? We'll get those savings in time through attrition.

CFO Dick: Listen, Pete, in a big bang, you accelerate the lay-offs, pull all those costs together, and write them off up front this year. Wall Street loves it. Your way, the costs drag on for years and hurt our earnings.

COO Pete: You mean the accounting rules favor a big bang?

CFO Dick: No question about it, but there are limits. Some big companies have gone to the well so many times that people began to raise serious questions about the quality of earnings. If companies get too cute, then the SEC gets involved, but that still leaves a lot of room to help future earnings.

VP Mktg. Sheila: It sounds like more smoke and mirrors, to me.

[Long silence]

COO Pete: Where do we take this, Alan?

CEO Alan: We'll have to lay out a plan with most of Dick's big bang in it. Then we'll announce a large stock buy-back. Perhaps we can spin off the Ohio operation. It's not core business, and the people out there could probably run it better on their own. Let's dodge this bullet Dick's way. We'll get the stock up, and then we'll have some breathing room to get serious about Sheila's big project.

CFO Dick: The layoffs are painful, but it is really a question of the greatest good for the greatest number.

COO Pete: Bullshit, Dick! You don't have a clue about company spirit. Our people aren't dopes. They'll know we sold our soul for stock price! Worse, they won't know how unfairly the deck was stacked.

CFO Dick: C'mon Pete! Most employees own stock. They'll be looking at a big win in their stock. And we haven't even discussed how well the people in this room will do.

COO Pete: If we stayed here a week, I couldn't convince you that a big short-term win is not very important to many of us.

VP Mktg. Sheila: We had a dream, but it's fading fast.

CEO Alan: Dick, do you have anything else?

CFO Dick: Yes. Our responsibility is to enhance shareholder value. If we go with the big-bang plan, we'll protect the company and probably see the stock settle at about $35. We're going to get some offers; we really are in play. If we move fast enough with the stock buy-back, we might duck a takeover. Our fiduciary responsibility, however, should make us look hard at this stockholder opportunity. We can probably get a 50% premium for change of control. That's a takeover expression for buying the whole thing for top bucks. Because several buyers will probably be interested, the game could turn into an auction, in which case the sky's the limit. We have a good shot at something in the mid-forties. It would take five to ten years to get to that value, even if your big project were to be a real winner.

CEO Alan: You're going too far with this, Dick. We're talking about how to keep this company alive, not how to shop it.

CFO Dick: I didn't put the company in play; it was you folks who didn't notice that someone had changed the rules. You kept thinking that you could do it your way. It's a new millennium. If we want to play with the big boys, we have to take a $45 possibility to the Board, and even more, if one of the high-multiple companies comes after us.

COO Pete: That did it! Alan, you've known me for a long time, and I hope you'll believe me when I tell you in sadness, not anger, that I am outa here! I feel for you, and maybe you have no choice, but neither a big bang nor an auction is how I had planned to finish up my career. I've spent a large part of the last ten years all over this company helping to build the spirit. Either of these options is contrary to my message. A company never gets the kind of productivity and support that we've generated without the people's believing that they have job security. They know that we're doing great and have a promising chance to expand. There's no way I can look our people in the eye and try to explain this razzle-dazzle. I don't believe in it, and I'm not going to lie about it. Good luck!

[Exit Pete]

VP Mktg. Sheila: Alan, I can only echo Pete's sentiments. You can't stop the world for either your big bang or your auction. Those geniuses at the skunk-works will make a deal with the Japanese. Some of my best people will start to drift out. Pete's 61—I'm 39. He can retire. I have to look for another dream.

[Exit Sheila]

CFO Dick: [Watching his colleagues leave] Downsizing is going to be easier than I thought, Alan.

CEO Alan: Enough with the stupid jokes, Dick! Two of the best people in the business just walked out, one of them a long-time friend.

CFO Dick: I'm sorry, but I can't help that, Alan. At least I think we can save your job, or at least make you a wealthy man.

CEO Alan: I don't think I would still want the job, and I'm not sure that I could enjoy the money.

Curtain

CHAPTER 9

Enron: Poster Boy for Ultra-Capitalism

The rich and powerful too often bend the acts of government to their selfish purposes, many of our rich men have not been content with equal protection and equal benefits, but have besought us to make them richer by acts of Congress.

Andrew Jackson, 1830[333]

Enron moved on many fronts in a wild ride of undisciplined capitalism to its record bankruptcy in 2001. Besides the original gas business formed in 1985 with the merger of several companies, Enron became the biggest trader in energy contracts, and it expanded into other commodities, including natural gas, paper, metals, crude oil, petroleum products, plastics, and strange areas like advertising, weather, and credit. This was the "asset lite" business that CEO Ken Lay hired Jeffrey Skilling to manage. At the same time, Lay entrusted Rebecca Mark with selling, building, and managing major projects around the world, including gas, water, steel, and power, a large percentage of which turned out to be big losers. After 1996, annual losses on many projects caused already thin profit margins almost to disappear. Chief Financial Officer Andrew Fastow was challenged to find ways to hide the losses, protect the high stock price and investment-grade rating, and keep the borrowed money flowing in. Enron's true financial condition became apparent in 2001, the same year that both the stock market and oil prices were going down, and the company imploded.

The internal reason for Enron's failure thus was Lay's incompetence, for he committed Enron management to an oversized task beyond their capacity to manage. The external reason for Enron's failure was that government-regulated banks kept pumping billions of

---

[333] Cited by Charles Sellers, *The Market Revolution: Jacksonian America 1815-1846* (New York: Oxford University Press, 1991), p. 62.

dollars of good money into bad loans and bad deals at Enron. Ultimately, Enron is a case study in how economic freedom can function well only when the government provides the proper fiscal, monetary, and regulatory disciplines.

Criticism can begin with a management that bet the shareholders' and employees' money on ventures of which the size of the risks and the size of the bets kept rising. At the very least, management was incompetent in balancing risk and reward, so they slipped into illegality, trying to hide the losses. The Board of Directors failed the shareholders by ignoring the decline in profit margins, the ballooning debt, and the erosion of business disciplines and corporate ethics. The Audit Committee of the Board failed in their more specific responsibility to assure integrity in the numbers and in the process. The outside auditors failed in their more comprehensive responsibilities to assure integrity in the numbers and procedures. Wall Street analysts failed to advise investors of deteriorating circumstances; instead, they continued to recommend Enron as a desirable investment until a few weeks before bankruptcy was declared. The bond-rating agencies failed to alert lenders or investors of the increasing risk and finally downgraded their investment-grade rating a few days before bankruptcy. Banks that lent billions of dollars to Enron failed to determine the quality of loans, used the artificial stock price as collateral for real money, and kept funding the game until it imploded. The institutional investors failed in their fiduciary responsibility to judge Enron as a bad investment. The lawyers failed in their public trust by structuring the partnership scams that allowed Enron to move debt off the balance sheet to add fictitious profits to earnings. The financial press failed to find the truth and inform the public.

A nation supports economic growth by controlling currency and credit for the benefit of the general welfare with money that is neutral, nonvolatile, and patient. This mission can be accomplished through free banking, national banking, or a combination of private and public banking. Free banking is monitored by market disciplines, and it worked well in Scotland at the time of Adam Smith when bad loans were punished locally, quickly, and visibly. Governments, however, do not trust private bankers with the opportunity to concentrate wealth for personal benefit, so they establish national banking through which the government has direct control of currency and credit. Private bankers, however, do not trust government to print and spend money at will, debase the currency, and cause inflation. The bankers exercise power over governments because they can withhold lending needed for war or defense. National banking was terminated by President Andrew Jackson in the 1830s (see chapter 7), after which private banking failed to prevent recurring capital crises. The American banking system was then made part public and part private in 1913 with the establishment of the Federal Reserve Board. By the end of the twentieth century, this compromise resulted in a banking system that was the worst of both worlds. On the one hand, the bankers enjoyed growing privileges to concentrate wealth in record amounts; on the other hand, the government assumed the obligation to bail out the bankers after the inevitable crises.

Financial crises are inevitable when two economic principles are violated: the neutrality of money and market disciplines. The neutral, nonvolatile, patient capital specified by Adam Smith as prerequisite to the proper functioning of economic freedom, has not been provided by the government's fiscal, monetary, and regulatory policies since the founding of the Republic. Easy credit, speculation, and lack of sensitivity to the quality of loans, however, became dramatically worse during the last quarter of the twentieth century when the banking system was deregulated, market disciplines were suspended, excessive volatility and liquidity were introduced by government mistakes, and electronic banking mushroomed in size, speed, and variety (see chapter 7). When money is dominant, not neutral, the market cannot find equilibrium, repetitive crises occur, and then, when the government violates the second economic principle by bailing out the private interests, greater disequilibrium and more crises are caused.

Economic disasters are caused by greedy people, and there will always be greedy people. In the republican spirit of the American Founders, we need to structure the system with the checks and balances that prevent greedy people from exploiting the economy and hurting the people. Every economic disaster thus far in American history has resulted from a structural failure of government to protect the people. The structure is one that must control currency and credit for the general welfare instead of allowing easy credit for the speculators and risk takers to do their damage. Freedom is functional only with discipline. Economic freedom depends on a structure in which money is a simple medium of exchange, not a marauding monster that dominates commerce.

The highly visible bankruptcy of Enron is an opportunity to examine the specific government policies that allowed ultra-capitalism to come to dominate our economy and cause its reversal. Enron also has a political dimension that should assure continued examination until the 2004 presidential election. Many in Congress, both Republicans and Democrats, posturing before the TV cameras, were the same politicians who had responded to corporate and Wall Street lobbying to pass the laws favoring ultra-capitalism during the quarter century that led up to the problem in the first place.

Citizens can learn about ultra-capitalism and how to apply democratic pressure to purge it from society by understanding the fundamental errors of those who support ultra-capitalism, and the collectivists who try to micromanage the economy. In the argument between the so-called "market fundamentalists" and the so-called "liberals," neither the terms nor the argument can survive careful examination, so unless citizens insure that the quality of the debate improves, ultra-capitalism will continue to dominate.

Let me tell you a story of greedy people managing assets with limited intrinsic value up to extraordinarily high artificial levels. The greedy people included the officers of the company, wealthy private investors, partners of the banks, and government officials. The company was run by people whose total concentration was the price of the stock. Every one of the participants benefited by the stock price going up and from the opportunity to leverage their investments with extremely easy credit. In time, short-sellers drove the share price down. Most of the wealthy got out with big gains while most of the ordinary investors were devastated. This is not only the story of Enron in 2001 but also the story of the South Sea Bubble in Great Britain in the 1720s.[334] Fiscal and monetary policies have been in the hands of the wrong people for a long time!

---

[334] Edward Chancellor, *Devil Take the Hindmost: A History of Financial Speculation* (New York: A Plume Book, 2000), pp. 68-72.

The Wall Street-Washington Roundtrip

Enron is a case study in how unregulated easy credit allowed this misadventure in corrupted capitalism to happen. Enron is also a case study in how "structured financing" has allowed both lenders and borrowers to move debt off of the balance sheet and hide it from the scrutiny of shareholders. Financial expert Martin Mayer regretted the loss of traditional bankers who were more fiscally reliable:

> [Traditional bankers were] trained to ask boring questions about how the investment of the money they lent would pay back the loan, and to follow up at regular intervals. An expanding business had to return repeatedly to its bank to finance its growth. The conditions of the loan forbade the entrepreneur from cashing in his stock while the bank stayed on the hook.[335]

Mayer went on to compare this basic banking to the age of ultra-capitalism ushered in by Congress:

> The guiding principle of the New Deal legislation was that sunshine is the best disinfectant, and that is still true. Chanting the mantra that big boys can take care of themselves, Congress in the 1980s and 1990s made it possible for consenting adults to do financially awful things behind closed doors.[336]

In the latter part of the twentieth century, the Chairman of the Fed and the Secretary of the Treasury contributed to the domination of the economy by ultra-capitalism. They believed that there could never be either too much deregulation or too much liquidity. Consequently, they supported the abrogation of market disciplines necessary to prevent bad loans, and they supported the lobbying by Wall Street that diverted the government from oversight of hedge

---

[335] Martin Mayer, "Banking's Future Lies in Its Past," *The New York Times*, August 25, 2002, p. 9.

[336] *Loc. cit.*

365

funds like Enron. These actions, in combination, caused repetitive economic problems, but instead of being red flags that attracted attention to the errors, they were used in support of additional abrogation of market disciplines in an effort to prevent systemic failure. Gradually the government's function changed from being a regulator of ultra-capitalism to being its protector.

In 2002, Paul Volcker was picked to head the damage-control committee at Enron's disgraced auditors, Arthur Andersen. The selection of Volcker was ironic because the root cause of the Enron scandal was not bad auditors, although they had added to the problem, but rather bad banking practices that were encouraged by Volcker's own having bailed out Continental Illinois in 1984, on the "too big to fail" principle (see chapter 7). The argument for bailouts is that the whole system is threatened, but the threat is not used as a reason to raise the bank reserves proportionate to the risk, and, to stop the bailouts, subsidies, and insurance. Until the system allows market disciplines to punish banks for bad loans, and until the leverage is taken out of speculation, Enrons will continue to happen.

The failure and bailout in 1998 of the unregulated hedge fund, Long Term Capital Management, was another unheeded warning of the damage to come from another unregulated hedge fund, Enron. The chairman of the Fed, despite persistent, demonstrable evidence that the banks were not fulfilling their responsibility, made this extraordinary statement: Greenspan advised Congress that hedge funds do not need regulation because they get their money from banks, and banks are regulated.[337]

Ultra-capitalism scored another impressive victory in 1999 when the Glass-Steagall Act was repealed. This law, signed by FDR in 1933, was passed to separate basic banking, especially the lending of money, from investment banking, especially the making of deals. It was passed because of evidence that mixing the two types of financial activities caused a conflict of interest and contributed to economic damage. This conflict was demonstrated again at Enron when beneficiaries of the repeal of Glass-Steagall, such as Citigroup, made multi-billion dollar loans at the same time they were obtaining the

---

[337] "Excerpts from Greenspan's Remarks to Congress," *The New York Times*, October 2, 1998, p. C3.

investment banking contracts for many of Enron's worldwide deals. Citigroup made bad loans to fund Enron's bad business in order to manage the bad deals that eventually brought Enron down.

Citigroup is special because they had been put together in anticipation of the repeal of Glass-Steagall. In 2001, CEO Weil's compensation was $26.7 million, excluding options. In approving this compensation, the Board commented, "Management had performed exceedingly well under these unusually difficult circumstances." Citigroup was reportedly "one of the biggest lenders to Enron Corp., and the bank has been forced to write down much of its exposure to the collapsed Houston energy company."[338] In other words, Citigroup was forced to reduce profits based on anticipated losses on the loans made to Enron. *The Economist* reviewed this history as follows:

> J.P. Morgan and Citigroup, two financial conglomerates exist in their current form and provide the range of financial services they did to Enron, only because of the abolition of the Glass-Steagall Act. This imposed statutory barriers between commercial banking, investment banking, and insurance, and was introduced in 1933 following public protests about conflicts of interest on Wall Street in the aftermath of the 1929 stock market crash. Rivals on Wall Street now whisper that conflicts of interest at these two banks may have played a role in Enron's collapse.[339]

Taken together, these details add up to a massive pattern of bad governance by leaders in government and banking. And yet American citizens so little grasp the implications that whispers in financial journalism never rise to the level of uproar of reformation. Only when voters, their elected representatives, and honorable people in government realize that the problem at Enron was not merely greedy executives but also the entire ultra-capitalist banking,

---

[338] Paul Beckett, "Citigroup's Weil Made $26.7 Million in 2001," *The Wall Street Journal*, March 13, 2002, p. A4.

[339] "Conflicts, Conflicts Everywhere. Was America Wrong to Scrap the Laws that Kept Commercial and Investment Banking Apart?" *The Economist*, January 26, 2002, p. 61.

investment, and governance system of the United States, will there be essential, structural change. In ultra-capitalism these monster financial services companies, courtesy of the U.S. government, mix money lending, deal making, and touting the stock of the same company. William Greider explored this triple play in the following words:

> J.P. Morgan and Citigroup provided billions to Enron while also stage-managing its huge investment deals around the world. The larger and more dangerous conflict of interest lies in the convergence of government-insured commercial banks and investment banks, because this marriage has the potential not only to burn investors, but to shake the financial system and entire economy.[340]

Greider went on to describe how these major houses of Wall Street play the game of doing deals and making loans to companies "while their stock analysts are out front whipping up enthusiasm for the same companies' stock."[341]

Citigroup was neither alone in funding Enron nor in finding ways on their own balance sheets to get around bank regulations, some of which backfired on them:

> They didn't want to do it, but they had no choice: J.P.Morgan, Citigroup, Bank of America and other banks shelled out unsecured loans of $3 billion to the doomed Enron Corp. in October, weeks before the firm collapsed into Chapter 11 amid accusations of fraud, self-dealing, and a cover-up.[342]

Just as Enron was moving debt off its balance sheet by shady deals, these loans were not shown on the banks' balance sheets: "Instead, the ill-advised promises were listed in the footnotes."[343]

---

[340] William Greider, "Crime in the Suites," *The Nation*, February 4, 2002, p. 13.

[341] *Loc. cit.*

[342] Robert Lenzer, "Time Bombs in the Vault: Like Enron, the Nation's Biggest Banks Have Risky Off-balance Sheet Liabilities that Are Barely Disclosed. Brace for the Next Disaster," *Forbes*, February 18, 2002, p. 58.

[343] *Loc. cit.*

These contingent loans were to be activated if Enron, and others, lost their financing from other sources. Something that was not supposed to have happened did happen. Apparently the capital division of corporations such as GE and Ford could sense troubled loans while the banks were ignoring it. The banks were forced to fulfill their promise to lend money to companies in the process of going broke.

Hundreds of billions of dollars of these bank obligations exist but cannot be seen by examining their balance sheets. Citigroup is distinguished by leading the list of these "off-balance-sheet commitments with a staggering total of $171.8 billion which is 15.7% of all of Citigroup's loans outstanding."[344]

The practice of bundling or securitizing loans to sell them to a third party was also an innovation of ultra-capitalism that began in the late 1980s in order to get more leverage than the balance sheet would normally allow. By 2001, use of this financial innovation in the U.S. had grown to over $1.3 trillion dollars per year! In earlier, simpler times, the quality of a company's balance sheet could be judged by such standard measurements as the relationship of debt to equity. If the debt percentage was too high, indicating an over-leveraged company, then new money would be harder to obtain and at higher cost. Special Purpose Entities (SPE) and securitization of debts make this examination irrelevant because the reported figures do not give any sense of this relationship between debt and equity.

The problem of securitization of assets was compounded not only by hiding the extent to which a company was over-leveraged but also to the extent that Wall Street and companies like Enron were successful in lobbying against better disclosure of these practices. Shareholders need transparency in order to ascertain an increase in risk. If one cannot examine debt and equity the old-fashioned way, at least one could check the footnotes of the financial reports to find out what the additional debt was and what implied guarantees had been given to get this debt off the balance sheet. In Enron's case, such a requirement would have exposed that the required 3% outside capital and the securitized assets were explicitly guaranteed and might as well have been pure debt. Some government officials did try to achieve better control in this matter:

---

[344] *Loc. cit.*

In late 1997, the Federal Reserve, the Office of the Comptroller of the Currency, the Office of Thrift Supervision, and the Federal Deposit Insurance Corp. proposed strengthening rules that required banks to set aside additional capital against possible losses on risky securitization deals. Such reserves, in addition to limiting a bank's freedom to make more loans, would have signaled investors that a lender was assuming greater risks.[345]

Because of political resistance, however, FASB's best effort was a watered-down version of higher reserves. By that time, at least five banks had failed from problems of improper accounting for securitization.[346] The FDIC paid out several billion dollars of taxpayers' money for these failures, but nowhere in the decade-long struggle was the ordinary taxpayer well represented. The lobby power of Wall Street and of corporations like Enron was too powerful, and in this case, the best efforts of government officials did not have enough democratic support. The reformers who claim to represent the peoples' interests did not feature this subject on their agenda.

Capitalism depends on a flow of nonvolatile, patient money to fund greater growth. One of the vital aspects of capitalism is the responsibility of the bankers to determine that the money they lend serves the economy well, rather than going to speculators who will waste it. Bailed-out, subsidized, insured bankers, who are motivated by stock price and options, did a disgraceful job in the last quarter of the twentieth century, thereby contributing to the dominance of the economy by ultra-capitalism. I have described the evidence of this dominance in chapter 7 in terms of the over-funding of South American countries in the 1980s, Mexico and South East Asian countries in the 1990s, LTCM in the late 1990s, and then Enron. In each case, the bankers failed in their judgment on the quality of loans because they were not clear about how much money was being

---

[345] Glenn B. Simpson, "Deals That Took Enron Under Had Many Supporters, Big Name Lobbying Stymied FASB Push to Disclose Off-Balance Sheet Entities," *The Wall Street Journal*, April 16, 2002, p 1.

[346] *Loc. cit.*

borrowed from other sources, what the money was to be used for, and what was the overall relationship between short-term money, "hot money," and long-term patient capital. The record indicates that they did not care.

For centuries, the empirical evidence has been convincing that excessive liquidity flows to speculation and high-risk projects. Demonstrably, the more volatile and impatient capital is, the greater are the opportunities to make more money on money. In the United States, the empirical evidence is that bank regulation does not provide the discipline requisite to direct money away from speculation into economic growth. Rather, the money is used for speculation and causes economic swings that slow economic growth and hurt people. The repeal of Glass-Steagall also illustrates the government's disinterest in both constraining easy credit and monitoring the growth of these financial empires. The new threat of "globalization" comes not from large companies that compete on product quality and price but, rather, from the huge financial services companies that have already caused great havoc in the world's economies and are nevertheless being allowed to acquire more companies and grow even larger. Both internationally and domestically, the fundamental error is the same: The use of free-market principles to spread ultra-capitalism, is upheld while the market disciplines and government control structure that the free market depends upon, are increasingly compromised.

Stock options are ultra-capitalism's coupling device between Wall Street and corporate executives because stock options motivate the corporate executive to short-term goals and deals. Senator Joseph Lieberman (D., Connecticut) was out in front getting great TV exposure on the Enron investigation as the chairman of Governmental Affairs Committee, but between 1991 and 1994, it was Lieberman who had been out in front leading the charge when Congress prevented FASB from issuing new standards on stock options that would have provided a needed discipline by incurring a charge against earnings. According to a *New York Times* editorial:

> In 1994, 88 members of the Senate voted for a "sense of the Senate" resolution in which they informed the FASB that its proposed standard would have grave economic consequences

for entrepreneurial ventures. At one point in the debate, Senator Lieberman introduced a bill that would have effectively destroyed the FASB's authority to set the standards for financial reporting.[347]

In the 1997-1998 session, Congress reviewed FASB's efforts to get control of derivatives. Hearings were held on the collapse of LTCM, but Congress backed away from "controlling currency and credit for the general welfare" and instead added to its record of encouraging ultra-capitalism. *The New York Times* editorial commented further:

> Congress paved the way for the current crisis. Congressional involvement in financial standard setting has been pure politics, fueled by a system of campaign financing that distorts the pursuit of the nation's legislative agenda. If members of Congress are sincere about identifying and correcting weaknesses in the standards used for financial reporting, then they should investigate the old-fashioned way: follow the money. They are likely to find a trail that leads to the nearest mirror.[348]

Enron has been described as a hedge fund sitting on top of a gas line. It was a specially privileged hedge fund, however, for its 28 lobbyists in Washington, a multi-million dollar budget for other lobbyists, and millions in campaign contributions to hundreds of politicians, allowed it to beat back efforts by the Commodities Futures Trading Commission to gain oversight of its trading activities. The hedge-fund oversight, proposed in 1998 after the failure of LTCM, would have been similar to bank oversight by the FED, and broker oversight by the SEC. The oversight proposal was defeated by Fed Chairman Alan Greenspan, Secretary of Treasury

---

[347] Michael H. Granof and Stephen A. Zeff, "Unaccountable in Washington: How Congress Set the Stage for Enron's Failure," *The New York Times*, January 23, 2002, p. 7.

[348] *Loc. cit.*

Robert Rubin, other government officials, and the lobbying efforts of Enron.

New legislation, instead, further freed Enron from government oversight and was passed in 2000 by the Senate Banking Committee, chaired by Senator Phil Gramm (R., Texas). Senator Gramm had received substantial political contributions from Enron, and he was the husband of Dr. Wendy Gramm, formerly head of the Commodities Futures Trading Commission, a Director of Enron, and a member of its Audit Committee.[349] As chair of the CFTC in 1992, Dr. Gramm "exempted energy swap derivatives from public scrutiny,"[350] another benefit for Enron. The special privileges nonetheless continued to flow from Congress when the Commodities Futures Act of 2000 was passed with additional opportunities for hedge funds to speculate with borrowed money.

The answer to the Enron blame-game question then is this: the United States government itself! After the fall of Enron, ten different Congressional committees were organized to determine blame and compete for TV exposure. There were so many candidates in the blame game that it will be easy for Congress to avoid blaming themselves and the bankers. Few recognize the Washington-Wall Street nexus as fundamentally responsible for the Enron failure. We Americans deplore "cronyism" in the commerce of other cultures, while at home we allow ultra-capitalists to dump huge amounts of money in various ways into the pockets of politicians, in return for which politicians dutifully pass laws and enact policies that result in more and more privileges for the few. Such is the mutual, interactive corruption of both capitalism and democracy.

Are not the citizens in a democratic republic responsible for their government? If democracy and capitalism are both being corrupted, is not the reform of both the responsibility of the citizens? "Of course!" anyone will answer, but that obvious answer is not enough to move the system out of its gridlock between the few who benefit from the special privileges; the political right that favors them; and the political left who, for lack of understanding, do not propose reforms that go to the root of the problems. This corruption of

---

[349] Bethany McLean, "Monster Mess," *Fortune*, February 4, 2002, p. 94.

[350] Greg Kaza, "Enron," *Chronicles*, March 2002, p. 7.

capitalism and democracy has gone on so long, and has now gained such power, that reform cannot come from within government itself. Reform and restructure can come, now, only from a collaboration of intellectuals, civic groups, universities, the media, and a new breed of politicians. Reform might more readily come from the institutional investors who are in charge of investing the collective wealth of America's working men and women, but the financial representatives of wage earners have not yet evidenced an understanding of their own democratic power and fiduciary obligation for reform. None of these groups has far to go in search of an appropriate reform agenda, for it is ready-made in a synthesis of the works of Adam Smith, Karl Marx, and John Stuart Mill that I detail in this book under the name of "democratic capitalism."

Enron: How Greedy People Hurt Employees and Shareholders Because of Faulty Government Structures

Ken Lay was an Economics professor before he became Deputy Undersecretary of Energy in the Interior Department. In both jobs, he was an evangelist for free markets and deregulation. Lay joined Humble Oil in Houston and became CEO of Houston Natural Gas in 1984. Later known as Enron, the original business was pumping natural gas through thousands of miles of pipelines across the United States. Natural gas became popular because it both filled the rising demand for energy and was an environmentally clean alternative to petroleum products.

Houston Natural Gas had come under attack by a famous takeover player, Irwin Jacobs, so Lay's first job was to keep the company away from Jacobs. Lay did this by acquiring Florida Gas, Transwestern Pipeline, and then he negotiated a merger with Nebraska-based Internorth. Although Internorth was the larger company, Lay became the CEO of the consolidated company within the year. Lay then got rid of Jacobs by paying "greenmail," that is, a premium over the market price of the stock. The money came from borrowing $230 million from the pension fund, and junk bonds organized by the famous Drexel Burnham junk-bond king—and later, convicted felon—Michael Milken.[351]

With the help of a New-York-based consulting firm, Lay changed the name of the newly consolidated company to "Enteron," in 1986, but this had to be changed to "Enron" when someone belatedly discovered that "Enteron" means "alimentary canal" or "digestive tract."[352]

Enron's first hedge fund was Enron Oil, located outside of New York City, and it was a disaster. After adding big profits to Enron's bottom line for a couple of years, Enron Oil was found to be cooking the books, went broke, and the top executive went to jail. Despite these early warnings about the self-destructive tendencies of ultra-capitalism, Lay pushed on and committed the same crimes that had caused the collapse of Enron Oil. In 2001, Enron became the largest bankruptcy in U.S. history, but, as ultra-capitalism had reached critical mass for self-destruction, Enron held its new record only a few months until WorldCom fell apart.

As Enron's $90 stock went into free fall down to 26 cents, Enron became a national scandal and a major media event because a few insiders took out hundreds of millions of dollars and left their employees and shareholders with virtually nothing. Many shareholders were also wage earners whose money had been invested in Enron through institutional investors.

Enron was symptomatic of a capitalism that subordinated everything, including integrity, to the price of the company's stock; a banking system that provided too much money for too many bad investments; and a government whose monetary, fiscal, and regulatory policies encouraged this short-term and greedy capitalism. Enron was a house of cards precariously balanced on a high-multiple stock price and an investment-grade rating. As losses developed in various misadventures, Enron had either to find ways to hide them or report weaker earnings and watch the house of cards collapse. Once companies have sold their soul to Wall Street, they must either deliver

---

[351] Peter C. Fusaro and Ross M. Miller, *What Went Wrong at Enron* (Hoboken, New Jersey: John Wiley & Sons, Inc., 2002), p. 5.

[352] Robert Bryce and Molly Ivins, *Pipe Dreams, Greed, Ego, and the Death of Enron* (New York: BBS Public Affairs, 2002), p. 32.

the earnings that Wall Street wants or be penalized by a drop in their stock market value by hundreds of millions, sometimes billions, of dollars. Enron played the game by fabricating e.p.s. (earnings per share) of 87 cents in 1997, then $1.01 in 1998, $1.18 in 1999, and $1.47 in 2000. In 2001, when the company was falling apart, they still managed to fabricate earnings for the first two quarters that annualized to a fictitious $1.87.

Free of government oversight, Jeffrey Skilling launched the world's largest energy trading activity by building up Enron North America, the trading company within the Enron company. Skilling, a Baker Scholar graduate of Harvard Business School and, later, a consultant with McKinsey, became president of his new company in 1997, and CEO in 2001. Skilling's career path mirrors the importance and apparent success of the trading operations, while also mirroring the growth of debt, erosion of profit margin, proliferation of bad deals, and increasing practice of fabricating profits.

Under Skilling's direction, the trading business in Enron North America grew from $20 billion in 1999, to an astounding $80 billion one year later, trading growth that catapulted Enron into the top ten of U.S. companies in terms of revenues. Those who questioned Enron's high-flying trading growth were described by Skilling as "assholes" who didn't "get it." [353] Chairman Lay talked about matching buyers and sellers in long-term energy contracts through innovation, flexibility, and Lay's word "optionality." Record trading activity was supported by a weak balance sheet but one, nevertheless, that had the crucial investment-grade rating from Standard & Poor's and Moody's.

Enron had a "laser focus," as Skilling called it, on e.p.s. growth. Along with an investment-grade rating, Enron's growth was based on a rising stock price that was used as collateral regularly to move debt off the balance sheet, and this enabled Enron to borrow more and more money from eager bankers. Although Enron's business had become 80% trading, its officials convinced a willing Wall Street that Enron deserved its price-earnings multiple that peaked in 2000 at 70, compared to a 17 P/E multiple for a top-quality trading company such as Goldman Sachs. Enron officials pointed to

---

[353] Wendy Zellner, "Jeff Skilling: Enron's Missing Man," *Business Week*, February 11, 2002, p. 39.

the reports of steady earnings improvement to demonstrate that they did not have the volatility associated with trading. Most Wall Street analysts ignored the evidence that the steady record was fabricated.

In the Alice-in-Wonderland world of ultra-capitalism, a high stock price and a high P/E ratio serve to do more than satisfy individual greed. They can be important tools in managing increased earnings. High P/E companies can acquire lower P/E companies and by that act alone improve profits; many are on acquisition binges for that reason. This is one of the many structural imperfections of the system. The bankers generally do not care whether they are getting collateral based on a 15 multiple stock price or a 70 multiple, although a prudent regulatory system would require significantly higher reserves for the obviously higher risk.

Enron had special ploys to fake profits. Along with the partnerships used as ways to manufacture profits, Skilling built a culture in which traders would change the assumptions and thereby seem to generate new profits. This was usually done at the end of a quarter when Enron was preparing to release their financial results and had to find the profits to meet Wall Street e.p.s. expectations. At that crucial time, traders were expected to "crank the dials," an expression used by a trader who said that his trading portfolio had been taken away from him because he did not manipulate the market values sufficiently to fake more profits.[354] Traders reportedly "cranked the dials" as follows:

> Reported profits were based on long-term trades that would not actually generate cash for many years. The value of those trades was largely based on the traders' own speculation in an environment where the traders' bosses were rewarded for higher reported profits. The trading desk used mark-to-market accounting. In a system where there was no established public market to set prices, a trader had to decide on a price curve.[355]

---

[354] James Horan, "Letters to the Editor," *Fortune*, April 15, 2002.

[355] Michael Brick, "What Was the Heart of Enron Keeps Shrinking," *The New York Times*, April 6, 2002, p. C1.

Under this pressure for profits, the traders learned how to "blend and extend," that is, to package and add years to the life of a deal and then take the profit increment into the report of current earnings (see Warren Buffet's attack on derivatives in chapter 7). When Enron went bankrupt, the trading-book value had fallen from $12 billion to $7 billion. According to a deposition by Enron's new president, that value had shrunk even more dramatically to $1.3 billion by January 2002.[356] How much of the enormous shrinkage was due to the earlier cooking of the books to produce needed profits is not clear; certainly the effects of the distress-sale environment substantially added to the shrinkage.

Deals, deals, deals—most of them bad!

Adam Smith conditioned the success of free markets on control of the prodigals and projectors, as he called them. Enron's Lay, Skilling, Mark, and Fastow were prodigals and projectors, and worse, they were not good at it. They deflected capital in the wrong direction, and then they messed up so many deals they had to resort to illegality to hide the damage.

Harvard Business School graduates Rebecca Mark and Jeffrey Skilling were competitors for the top job while in Lay's Office of the President. Skilling won the prize and did an amazing job building up the "asset lite" trading business. After Skilling was made President, Lay apparently gave the consolation prize of running around the world taking on complicated projects to Mark. Enron proceeded to overextend itself in foreign countries where its executives did not understand the people, the cultures, or the size and complexity of the projects. It should have been called the "asset heavy" business that demanded not trading brilliance, but, rather, old-fashioned experience, the ability to manage change, and the instincts properly to relate risk to reward. The combination of "asset lite" trading and "asset heavy" worldwide projects was Lay's terminal incompetence that placed an enormous management load of different types of business without the quantity or quality of talent to pull the load. Mark proceeded to deliver an annual crop of financial disasters to CFO Fastow whose job

---

[356] *Loc. cit.*

it was to hide the losses and protect the stock price and investment-grade rating. As the pile of losses grew higher, so did the criminality of the actions.

Typical of Enron's misadventures was the work of ECT Securities, launched in 1996 as Enron's in-house investment bank. ECT contributed to Enron's catalogue of bad deals by investing in a $650 million project to redevelop a steel mill in Chonburi, Thailand. ECT was involved in financing the company known as NSM, lent them $20 million, and then took a seat on the Board. "NSM went bankrupt without ever completing the project."[357]

ECT Securities registered with the SEC as a securities dealer to "conduct business as an investment-banking firm," structuring M&A deals, underwriting debt and equity offerings, and even doing financial advisory work. Revenues peaked at $30.4 million in 1998 and then dropped to $8.3 million in 2000. ECT's twenty traders in Houston and five in London who speculated in the shares of other companies were Skilling's top talent from his "intellectual capital," 150 MBAs recruited each year. ECT is an indicator of the incredible hubris of Enron management in their willingness to give financial advice to others.

Besides bad deals in the United States, other bad deals were made in England, Brazil, Bolivia, Panama, Ghana, Malaysia, Colombia, Thailand, Nigeria, Argentina, and India. Enron's power purchase agreement with India's Congress Party was particularly egregious. This was the first private power project that India had attempted, and under Enron management, partly insured by American taxpayers, it gave both America and capitalism a bad name in India. A year after the deal was signed, the power project had become so controversial that it was the only issue to be voted on in the Indian State of Maharashtra. After the opposition won the election, they scrapped the Enron agreement, having "accused the Congress party government of taking a $13 million bribe."[358]

---

[357] Bethany Mclean, "Is There Anything Enron Didn't Do?" *Fortune*, April 29, 2002, p. 23.

[358] Arundhate Roy, "Shall We Leave It to the Experts?" *The Nation*, February, 18, 2002, pp.17-18.

Chairman Lay and dealmaker Mark rushed to India and apparently spread around more millions for "education" of the new generation of politicians; they succeeded in getting the project reinstated at even better terms. Enron executives also involved the United States government back home to help pressure for re-ratification of the contract, and in this they were assisted in India by Ambassador Frank Wisner, himself later to become a director of an Enron operation. Reporter Arundhate Roy described the renegotiated deal as follows:

> In August 1996, the government of Maharashtra signed a fresh contract that would astound the most hard-boiled cynic. The "renegotiated" power purchase agreement makes Phase II of the project mandatory and legally binds the Maharashtra State Electricity Board to pay Enron the sum of $30 billion! It constitutes the largest contract ever signed in the history of India. The power that the Enron plant produces is twice as expensive as its nearest competitor and seven times as expensive as the cheapest electricity available in Maharashtra.[359]

The power plant, that had enough capacity to power two million U.S. type homes, required $1.5 billion from Indian banks. Two elements crucial to India's economic growth, electricity and capital, were wasted by Enron's combination of greed, incompetence, and connections in high places. Later, "the state disputed the amount it owed the plant, saying it was being overcharged for the power. The acrimony finally led to the plant's being shut down in the middle of 2001." In 2002, the multi-billion dollar power plant was described as "idle and rusting in the salty air of the Arabian sea."[360]

Enron's appetite for high-risk adventures included Mariner Energy, Inc., a 1996 investment in deepwater drilling. Mariner apparently had been profitable, but then as it was shuffled among

---

[359] *Ibid.*, p. 18.

[360] Saritha Rai, "Seeking Ways to Sell Enron's Plant in India," *The New York Times*, April 11, 2002, p. C1.

Enron entities, it gained a reputation as another "tool for earnings management."[361]

In 1997, Enron added to its catalogue of bad deals with a $400 million loss in a British natural gas transaction, and a $100 million loss involving a fuel additive.[362] An investor lawsuit claimed that 75 power plants and pipeline projects under Mark's management had failed to report expenditures. According to Enron's chief accountant, Jeff Skilling would not allow reporting these costs because "corporate did not have room to take a write-off, as doing so would bring Enron's earnings below expectations."[363]

A bad deal in Argentina managed by Rebecca Mark was arranged through Enron's Azurix division, which contracted to build a water and wastewater system in the province of Buenos Aires. "Azurix won the 30-year concession, in June of 1999, with a bid to pay the province $439 million, more than three times the offer from the second-place contender."[364] Argentina capped water rates allegedly at too low a level to make a profit. They also did not pay their bills, which is not surprising for a country that had defaulted on billions of dollars of foreign debt. The contract dispute over the water deal went into the courts between a bankrupt company and a bankrupt government.

In 2002, the slowly grinding legal process was identifying "Enron Alleged Corruption Abroad" with comments such as this: "Claims of corruption in Enron power or water projects have arisen over the years in many countries."[365] The article describes Federal prosecutors' investigation of Enron's alleged violation of the Foreign Corrupt Practices Act by bribing foreign government officials to win

---

[361] Mike France and Wendy Zellner, "Enron's Fish Story," *Business Week*, February 25, 2002, p. 38.

[362] Kurt Eichenwald, "Enron Investors Took Part in Fraud Scheme," *The New York Times*, April 8, 2002, p. A15.

[363] Kathryn Kranhold, "Enron Disputed Investors' Charge of Manipulated Cost Accounting," *The New York Times*, April 9, 2002, p. B7.

[364] Michelle Wallin, "Enron to Drop Utility Deal in Argentina," *The Wall Street Journal*, March 1, 2002, p. A7.

[365] John R. Wilke, "Enron Criminal Probe Focuses on Alleged Corruption Abroad," *The Wall Street Journal*, August 5, 2002, p. 11.

contracts. Along with the alleged bribes, Enron was favored in these foreign projects with more than $4 billion in U.S taxpayer loans and guarantees. "Among the lenders were the Overseas Private Investment Corp., Export-Import Bank, and the U.S. Maritime Administration. Enron got $3 billion more from other sources, including the World Bank, European Investment Bank, and U.K. export-credit agencies."[366]

Demonstrating that their affinity for bad deals was not limited to foreign adventures, Enron not only traded in fibre-optics but also invested $1.2 billion in a network just before others in the industry realized how overbuilt the networks were, and the whole market tanked.

Enron executives further enhanced their reputation with Braveheart. This deal with Blockbuster, the largest peddler of videos in the United States, was to deliver thousands of movies to consumers via pay-per-view TVs, purportedly on Enron's broadband network. The SPE (Special Purpose Entity) created for this project was the usual Enron razzle-dazzle with borrowed money and guarantees on the loans that violated the rules requiring 3% outside capital. Enron borrowed $115.2 million for Braveheart from CBIC World Markets, the investment-banking arm of Canadian Imperial Bank in Toronto, promising CIBC almost all of the earnings for ten years. The venture was barely getting off the ground in late 2000, when, in another audacious accounting move, Enron claimed profits from Braveheart of $53 million in the fourth quarter of 2000, and $57.9 million in the first quarter of 2001.[367] An Enron employee later commented: "I was just floored, I mean I couldn't believe it!"[368]

At analyst meetings in early 2001, Lay and Skilling predicted a $126 stock price, and they described the benefit to their broadband services from Braveheart. Blockbuster treated it as a pilot program and were amazed that Enron was anticipating revenues and profits in their financial results. A few months later, in March of 2001, Braveheart was on the rocks and Enron's end was near. The end must

---

[366] *Loc. cit.*

[367] Rebecca Smith, "Show Business, A Blockbuster Deal Shows How Enron Overplayed Its Hand," *The Wall Street Journal*, January 17, 2002, p. 1.

[368] *Loc. cit.*

have been nearer than Enron was letting anyone know, for they were faking a $57.9 million profit at the very time that the deal, the source of the alleged profit, was going belly-up.

The Wild Ride of Enron: 1996-2001

The following quick review covers the six-year period during which, despite the shrinkage of Enron's operating profit margin from 5.1% to 1.3%, its total market value increased from $12 billion to $70 billion! This disappearing operating margin happened despite Enron's best efforts to cook the books. One can hardly comprehend how all of the agencies responsible for protecting the shareholders and employees missed this dramatic profit erosion, for it was there for all to see.

1996: Operating margin was disappearing, but nobody was paying attention

Enron was valued by the stock market at $12 billion with a P/E ratio below the market average; Enron sales were about $13.3 billion; the operating profit margin dropped from 5.1% to 3.8% in the year; and reported long-term debt increased from $2.8 billion to $3.3 billion.[369]

Jeffrey Skilling became President and Chief Operating Officer, continuing as president of Enron Capital and Trade Resources. Rebecca Mark, CEO of Enron Operations Corp., made a power project deal in India.

1997: Big disappointment at Enron: The price of the stock was down.

Despite the determination of management, Enron's stock price went down for a time while the whole market was going up. Sales were up to over $20 billion, but the market value and the P/E multiple

---

[369] Figures for Enron for the five-year period are taken from *Value Line* #447, December 21, 2001, Sigourney B. Romaine, analyst. General Electric figures are from *Value Line* #1012, January 18, 2002, Edward Plank, analyst.

had improved little. For anyone who bothered to look, however, trouble signs were clear: The profit margin during the year fell from 3.8% to 2.6%, while the reported debt went up from $3.3 to $5.8 billion.

Besides shrinking profit margins and rising debt, Enron was faced every year with the problem of what to do with the latest losses on bad deals. In November, 1997, Enron's top executives found new ways to manage earnings. Lay, Skilling, and CFO Fastow attended "a meeting that would help put the energy-trading giant on a fateful and ultimately dangerous course."[370] A new partnership called LJM2 was put together in a hurry because if Enron had reported their real numbers, their stock price would have dropped. Enron got the money for LJM2 from their friendly bankers, J. P. Morgan, Citigroup, and Merrill Lynch; that is, the money came from both the institutions and from personal investments from the partners. The borrowed money, according to *The Economist*, was reported by Enron as fictitious profits:

> The Enron virus spreads still through Wall Street beyond J.P. Morgan, Chase, and Citigroup, whose roles as lenders and advisers to the firm have come under scrutiny. Nearly 100 executives at Merrill Lynch invested a combined $16 million in LJM2 an Enron off-balance-sheet partnership....Within seven days of the money coming in from the banks and the banking executives, Enron shifted a series of assets off its books in sales to LJM2. Those assets included a 75% interest in a Polish power plant and a 90% interest in an natural gas system in the Gulf of Mexico. [371]

SPEs (Special Purpose Entities) were not invented by Enron. Financial devices frequently have an honest beginning that are later turned into ways to fool the shareholders. In theory, an SPE matches companies that have more opportunities than money together with

---

[370] John R. Emshwiller and Rebecca Smith, "A Meeting that Would Put Enron on a Fateful and Dangerous Course," *The Wall Street Journal*, February 1, 2002, p. 1.

[371] "The Good Lay," *The Economist*, February 2, 2002, p. 70.

companies or individuals that have more money than opportunities. SPEs are covered by FASB Regulation 140 that specifies how to move assets off the balance sheet by giving up control.

That same year, Enron launched yet another new enterprise to bundle wholesale energy delivery and risk-management services, Enron Energy Services (EES), signing up contracts for $209 billion over two years.[372]

1998: Another tough year at Enron

Enron executives must have been disappointed in 1998 when, again, the stock price and P/E ratio improved only slightly. Enron's P/E multiple was up to 24.8, which is good compared to the market's sixty-year average of 15, but it was below market average in 1998 and compared poorly to GE's 30.3. GE, however, was gaining market value on performance, whereas Enron was trying to do it with smoke and mirrors. GE's 15.3% profit margin in 1995 improved to 16.8% in 1998, while Enron's 5.2% eroded in 1998 to 2.2%! GE slashed their long-term debt while Enron's continued to climb up to a reported $7.4 billion, despite Enron's sleight-of-hand in moving debt off the books. Enron's executives wanted GE's multiple without GE's performance; in time, Wall Street gave them that and more.

The use of outside partnerships built momentum in 1998: Chewco was presented to the Board, managed and partly owned by CFO Fastow. These vehicles were usually located in either the Cayman Islands or other tax friendly places where a portfolio of risky assets was dumped and accomplished the seemingly difficult task of getting rid of problems while making money at it. By 2000, partnerships were providing 40% of Enron's pre-tax income of $1.4 billion and more for Wall Street insiders.

Despite the rising debt, Enron continued to ignore other fundamental protocols of cash management. Although they were trying to be a high-growth, go-go company, they continued to pay out a large percentage of the alleged earnings in dividends. Back in the 1980s, when Enron had been a gas company, they paid out dividends with yields of 5-6%, typical for utilities. In the late 1990s, their high-

---

[372] Fusaro and Miller, *op. cit.*, p. 169.

growth time, they paid hundreds of millions of dollars in dividends with cash they did not have; consequently, they further escalated the debt.

1999: Enron finally on a roll

Now things started clicking for Enron. However they managed to do it, and Wall Street did not care, Enron produced steady earnings improvement and were rewarded with a P/E multiple of 31.8 and a stock price up 55%, doubling Enron's market value to $32 billion! GE's multiple, however, was still higher at 35.9.

During the year, Enron's Board waived Enron's Code of Ethics in January and again in June in order to expedite the addition of outside partnerships managed by Enron executives.[373] Enron's deal making included an electricity-producing barge to be anchored off the coast of Nigeria. When Enron needed to improve 1999 earnings, they got their friends at Merrill to "invest" $7 million in the deal. Enron got their money, managed their profits, and, in a few months, another Enron partnership bought the project from Merrill, who pocketed $775,000 for arranging the deal. LJM2 was then bought and sold several times with the "lazy Susan" technique of passing around assets that mysteriously gained in value each time they changed hands.[374] During the S&L scandal in the less sophisticated 1970s, this practice had been called "flipping assets."

2000: Enron in the promised land

In 2000, Lay, Skilling, and Fastow had accomplished what, with the right government structure and oversight, should have been impossible. Incredibly, Enron's stock was up 87%, and their market value had *doubled* again to $68 billion! Equally incredible, the reported debt had grown to over $10 billion, and the profit margin had almost disappeared at 1.3%—but, hey, who's looking! Enron was on

---

[373] Reed Abelson, "Enron's Board Quickly Ratified Far-Reaching Management Moves," *The New York Times*, February 22, 2002, p. C6.

[374] Anita Raghavan, "Enron's McMahon: Hero or Collaborator?" *The Wall Street Journal*, April, 9, 2002, p. C1.

a roll with an average P/E for the year of 50, which, for the first time, beat GE's 40.1. Enron's peak multiple for the year was an astronomical 70! Enron's sales were now over $100 billion. *Fortune* magazine reported it as America's sixth-biggest company.

Rebecca Mark was out. Poor results at Azurix and other sour deals gave Skilling the opportunity to push her out.[375] Mark took consolation from her generous severance contract and gross proceeds of over $82 million from sale of Enron stock.[376]

By the end of 2000, the difficulty of manufacturing earnings was stretching the creativity of the accountants and the auditors. The accountants were struggling to keep another SPE called Raptors afloat. The problem was $500 million of Raptors's losses that, unless a place were found to hide them, would have to be subtracted from Enron's profits, an event that would have dropped the stock price like a rock and destroyed the investment-grade rating that the trading depended upon. Raptors was financed indirectly with Enron's stock, and any drop in that value would have started an unraveling process like a margin call in a dropping market—the lower the price, the more money has to be found. Under pressure, the accountants became even more creative, and just before the end of the first quarter, they managed to refinance Raptors and hide the losses "by phony transactions that were still vulnerable to further decline in Enron's stock."

2001: Enron continued to present fabricated profits while the company was dying

In the strange world of ultra-capitalism, companies do not build a product and then try to make a profit; instead, they calculate what earnings Wall Street wants in order to support continued enthusiasm for the stock, and then they give it to them. In 2001, a few months before the company imploded, Enron reported a cosmetically attractive 20% plus improvement in profit, with 47 cents a share for the first quarter, followed by 45 cents a share in the second, compared to 40 cents and 34 cents in the same quarters a year earlier. Enron's

---

[375] Fusaro and Miller, *op. cit.*, p. 172.

[376] Bryce and Ivins, *op. cit.*, front cover.

reported debt was up to $13 billion—plus many unreported additional billions, were the stock price to have dropped. Despite this debt load, Enron paid the regular dividend. Most shareholders had no way of knowing that the dividend was the last value they would receive from Enron.

In early 2001, Lay, Skilling, and Fastow had to have known that the accountants were running out of tricks. As late as this, Enron management might have bitten the bullet and made a major restructuring effort, including a massive write-off to get all of the junk off their books. To face such a move takes courage and considerable expertise to execute. Enron's stock would have dropped, trading would have slowed, but the stock market is very forgiving of onetime corrections, considering them a bump in the road while anticipating good following-year results partly due to the extent of the write-offs. This would have been the only action possible to rescue some value for the general shareholders. Management did not choose that approach, however. Lay retreated, and a few months later, Skilling quit.

A few outsiders did take a hard look at Enron. Short-seller Jim Chanos took the look in early 2001. He had spotted the debt of $3.5 billion back in 1996 that had since ballooned to a reported $13.1 billion, as well as a lot more contingent debt taken off the books. By inspecting the partnerships, Chanos found that Enron was using the high stock price as credit support, according to which either a drop in the stock price or loss of the investment-grade rating would result in billions of dollars of debt crashing down on Enron's balance sheet, exactly what eventually did happen. After the bankruptcy, the off-balance-sheet debt was identified as $18.1 billion plus another $20 billion in other obligations and derivative trades. Chanos was shocked to find that Enron was not even covering their cost of capital, reporting less than a 7% return, despite the aggressive efforts to pump up profits and pull down capital. The Enron bubble had been kept aloft for years by Wall Street, but, as has to happen in time, it was punctured by a short-seller motivated to make money from a stock price decline.

At the time that Chanos was ready to attack, the whole stock market was in decline, gas prices were down, and the dot.com bubble had burst. The radio and TV analysts whipped up complicated explanations for the drop in the market as a whole, but the real cause was the typical speculative cycle: Assets had been bid up to artificial levels by greed, and now they were driven down by fear. Enron would have unraveled anyway, with the stock market decline, but attack by short-sellers such as Chanos accelerated and magnified the process.

Besides the short-sellers, others in 2001 suspected that things at Enron were bad. Sharon Watkins, V.P. Corporate Development, was the whistle-blower who wrote her now famous letter to Lay describing her nervousness that the company would implode from accounting scandals. Peddlers of credit protection were also onto Enron at that same time. The title of a *Forbes* article described them:

> Someone Knew, the Enron Belly Flop Stunned Almost Everyone, but a Select Group of Wall Street Pros Had an Early Warning System You Cannot Access.[377] It is an obscure electronic-trading market where banks and other big players buy and sell credit-protection contracts as an insurance policy against loans that might go bad. On August 15, the day after Enron Chief Jeffery Skilling abruptly resigned, Enron's stock barely budged, closing just above the $40 mark. But on the same day, the price of an Enron credit contract jumped 18%. By October 25, as the troubles sparked headlines, Enron stock had dropped more than 50%, while the credit contract had soared in price to $900,000 per $10 million annually. Even at the much higher price it was a great deal. Citigroup used the credit protection approach to insure $1.4 billion in loans to Enron.[378]

According to the crazy logic of ultra-capitalism, Citigroup was pumping excessive liquidity into Enron to speculate and engage in high-risk ventures at the same time that Citigroup could afford to pay for insurance on these loans. Why care about the quality of loans? Take out credit protection and relax!

Citigroup and the other big lenders are major targets for the contingency lawyers in the Enron scandal. These lawyers know how

---

[377] Robert Lenzer, *Forbes*, March 4, 2002, p. 78.

[378] *Loc. cit.*

to find the deep pockets, and they will inspect the corruptions of ultra-capitalism in great detail in numerous dispositions. Citigroup will be sued for their involvement in the questionable partnerships, sued for participation in the amazing number of bad deals around the world, just as Citigroup's Solomon Smith Barney operation was sued in 2002 for having misled unsophisticated investors. I find it bizarre that capitalism cannot be reformed by the democratic process, but rather has to be reformed, or at least punished, by short-sellers and contingency lawyers. Citigroup and the other bankers will settle out-of-court, take their slap on the wrist, and play again another day.

The collapse of Enron, directly and indirectly, financially and emotionally, devastated millions of people in various places around the world. The Enron employees were the ones most dramatically damaged because they lost hundreds of millions of dollars through the loss of their jobs, the value in their 401(k) accounts, and their pension money that was also tied to the value of Enron stock.

The few cashed out for hundreds of millions of dollars benefiting from their stock options, while the employees were locked in and could not sell. Lay, for example, made one of many sales on August 20, 2001, when the stock was still in the high 30s, netting another $2 million. On September 28, 2001, Lay exhorted the employees to take advantage of a great opportunity and buy stock! Shortly after that message, on October 16, 2001, Enron announced a $1.2 billion decrease in the company's value, and the stock went into free fall down to pennies.[379]

Besides the Enron employees, however, other millions were negatively affected by Enron. For example, the Florida State pension fund lost $328 million of their peoples' money because they had bought Enron aggressively during the autumn of 2001. The California taxpayers in 2002 were spending "the first $20 billion in State funds to stabilize a system torn asunder by power shortages and price pikes."[380] Part of this California waste of taxpayers' money was due to the games the Enron traders played in order to hype profits.

---

[379] Michael Duffy, "What Did They Know, and When Did They Know It?" *Time*, January 28, 2002, p. 19.

[380] Kathryn Kranhold, Bryan Lee, and Mitchel Benson, "Enron Rigged Power Market in California, Documents Say," *The Wall Street Journal*, May 7, 2002, p.1

All over America, wage earners incurred significant losses of their savings managed by professionals. All over the world, local economies were hurt by Enron misadventures, such as the useless power plant in India. But it is my belief that the greatest enduring damage from Enron will come from disgracing our economic system in the eyes of most citizens. Polls indicated that Enron was better known to the ordinary person than the Olympic Games.[381]

The incestuous relationship between the government and special interests was further exposed in Enron. Ken Lay allegedly gave $326 million of soft money to the George W. Bush campaign. Later, when Bush had become President, and "Lay complained to Bush that the head of the Federal Energy Regulatory Commission wasn't quite with the program, the man was replaced by a more docile successor."[382] These examples of the corruption of both democracy and capitalism included both Republicans and Democrats.

"Liberal" Democrats like Robert Kuttner, quoted above, used Enron to attack "free markets, *laissez-faire*, and market fundamentalism." Such attacks focus on what is profoundly wrong not with free markets but with the superficiality of the debate in American politics. Enron is an excellent example of the corruptions of free markets because of bad government policies but is rarely presented that way for the education of citizens. Instead, citizens are conditioned to believe that capitalism is an immoral monster badly needing more government control.

Enron was a tragedy for the many affected by the greed and incompetence of a few executives, and the greed and ineptitude of far too many elected representatives. The tragedy will be double if it goes into the memory bank as an indictment of the free market system instead of an opportunity for citizens to learn about the corruptions of democracy and capitalism so that they may reform the system.

---

[381] The Pew Center Poll, cited by Thomas Frank, "Shocked, Shocked! Enronian Myths Exposed," *The Nation*, April 8, 2002, p. 18.

[382] Robert Kuttner, "The Enron Economy," *The American Prospect*, January, 2002, p. 2.

A Reform Agenda

Perhaps a few Enrons will stimulate the study process, an examination leading to the reformation of ultra-capitalism. If Enron is a case study in what is wrong structurally and philosophically with the present political-economic system in the United States and in the world, what can be done to prevent another Enron? The answer to that question is the same as the answer to this question: What can be done to eliminate the corruptions of ultra-capitalism? Or this: What can be done to eliminate concentration of wealth due to special government privileges? Or this: What can be done to control currency and credit for the general welfare? Or this: What can be done to design monetary, fiscal, and regulatory rules through the democratic process, rather than by special interests?

The answer to all of these questions and the subsequent action to be taken by the voting public will determine whether the United States government can couple capitalism and democracy in a synergistic way in our own country, then to lead the world to peace and plenty through economic common purpose. If America fails in this ultimate test of its historic role to free people from want and oppression, it will have failed, to its great shame, in its essential Constitutional purpose.

Bright financial engineers could design a comprehensive, integrated fiscal, monetary, and regulatory policy to serve the general welfare. If an improved design were presented to American citizens, and compared to the present structure of privileged law, the pressure for reform would be overwhelming. The action for reform will have to come from a renewed democratic process, for the post-Enron "reforms" coming out of Washington are cosmetic and an additional insult to the American people.

I propose the following agenda for democratic examination and action. These structural corrections, I believe, address the root problems with nearly fail-safe solutions, that is, they will discipline the system, whether it be managed by people of integrity or greedy people. I begin with Adam Smith's concept of economic freedom that can eliminate material scarcity if money is kept neutral, and speculators are under control. I draw part of my agenda from Karl Marx who argued that social progress depends on movement to a superior economic system. Marx described a system as superior that would motivate each individual to maximum development, maximize surplus as the sum of this development, and distribute wealth broadly, a necessary outcome to sustain both individual motivation and the economic growth dynamic.

One would think that by now these attributes of a superior system would be upheld as a priori tenets of economic faith; instead, they are ignored by policy makers. These principles and practices have been validated through improvement in the lives of millions, but they continue to be ignored because the requisite structure has never been put in place for the system to function at full potential. Few debate the benefits of economic freedom, but many are confused about which disciplines are necessary for free markets to lead the world to full economic and social potential.

Reform #1: Democratization of capitalism through large dividends to low- and middle-income wage earners

A rededication by companies to paying large dividends to shareholders, encouraged by more favorable tax laws, would be the fastest and most effective way to move away from the corruptions of ultra-capitalism towards the worldwide benefits of democratic capitalism. Dividends return the surplus to the economy, thereby stimulating economic growth. A sound annual income from dividends encourages the spread of employee ownership plans and thereby improves productivity. Ownership plans with large dividend income on a global level would add more spendable income to workers in emerging markets and make free trade a universal benefit. The reform needed is a departure from exclusive focus on e.p.s., the short-term and greedy capitalism, to the capitalism that balances appreciation, income, and long-term security.

Enron, the dot-com bubble, and the drop in the whole market in 2001, demonstrated, as it did in the similar Wall Street catastrophe of 1929, the deficiencies of a market that has little security or income. Large regular dividends and stock appreciation, over a period of five years or more, provides more security and strikes the correct balance in capitalism.

393

Dividends have become an unfortunate victim of ultra-capitalism because the Wall Street emphasis on e.p.s. and stock price encouraged companies to reduce the portion of surplus paid out in dividends. Surplus should go into greater growth and dividends, but in ultra-capitalism it goes, instead, into stock buybacks and non-strategic acquisitions. This trend is an example of special privileges successfully lobbied by Wall Street because tax laws favor capital gains from stock and even favor stock buybacks. The pattern became so pervasive that many forgot the long-term importance of dividends in capitalism, but a study challenged the myths: "The return on stocks over the past two centuries has averaged 7% a year, a large part of it—close to 5%—came from dividends."[383]

During the bull market of the 1990s, Walls Street's dislike of dividends and preference for other uses of surplus cash became increasingly clear to companies. The institutional investors whose fiduciary responsibility should have prodded them into pressuring companies to pay large dividends, and should have prodded them into pressuring the government to eliminate tax penalties, did neither; in fact, they encouraged the dissipation of surplus in other directions. Huge stock options worsened the trend because dividends were of little interest to holders of options. Jeremy J. Siegel, an observer of the stock market, commented:

> The focus on earnings instead of dividends stood in sharp contrast to the entire history of stock returns. Until the last ten years, about three-quarters of stocks' real return has come from dividends. Federal tax law played a large role in creating the wrong incentives for both management and investors…. I do not wish to exonerate executives who looted their companies, auditors who committed fraud, and analysts who hyped stocks because of banking fees paid to their firms, but many of the problems that we have today have their roots in our Byzantine tax code that distorts incentives and invites fraud.[384]

---

[383] Daniel Fisher, "The Great Stock Illusion," *Forbes*, July 22, 2002, p. 194.

[384] Jeremy J. Siegel, "Stocks Are Still an Oasis," *The Wall Street Journal*, July 26, 2002, p. A10.

Where will all of the cash come from to pay large dividends? Much of it is produced internally, for many companies are cash rich from the efficiencies of the Information Age. Hundreds of billions of dollars will come from the money now wasted on stock buybacks, and hundreds of billions of dollars more will come from ending those acquisitions made primarily to keep the stock price going up. In 2002, companies like Microsoft, Ford, and Toyota had cash surpluses of $20 to $40 billion. IBM spent more than $40 billion on stock buybacks over two decades, much of it wasted, as a result of ultra-capitalism's exclusive devotion to the price of the stock. In 2001 for the first time, the Japanese government allowed stock buybacks, encouraging Toyota to waste their hoard of cash instead of returning it in dividends to an economy that had been starved for consumer demand for several decades. This action by the Japanese government also demonstrated that the infection of ultra-capitalism had spread around the world.

Reform #2: Measurement and Accountability

Integrity in financial reporting must start with recognition that quarterly and annual e.p.s. is a poor way to observe the complicated dynamics and normal time frame of corporate performance. Corporations ought to be made accountable by institutional investors, financial media, analysts, and shareholders not for a single year's performance but, rather, for a three-year moving average on sales growth, cash flow, and profits measured against management's predictions.

Measuring cash flow against plan makes tricky accounting more difficult to accomplish, and it exposes big mistakes earlier. Enron, under this proposed measurement, would have provided optimistic forecasts on profits and sales and then faked the results, but Enron would have been tripped up by the actual cash flow measured against estimates because it would have exposed the annual increments and cumulative debt, both on and off the balance sheet. The record suggests that Enron executives really did not know their cash needs because they did not know how many projects they were going to screw up that year. Enron executives were conditioned to the idea that the eager bankers would give them whatever they asked for.

395

At Enron, accountability for actual cash flow against executives' estimates would have exposed their growing problem earlier and forced the banks to examine the quality of the loans—an examination that the banks should have done within the existing system but didn't.

During the quarter century of ultra-capitalism, the quality of reported earnings steadily eroded. As the pressure for higher and higher short-term earnings built up, executives became willing to take riskier, trickier, and frequently illegal steps to feed Wall Street's voracious appetite, raise the stock price, and make themselves wealthy beyond their dreams. Wall Street encouraged the growing subterfuges that obscured true earnings: "pro forma," "EBITDA" (earnings before interest, taxes, depreciation, and amortization), "non-operational," and "restructuring reserves" were among the jargon to show a fictitious profit improvement while keeping the stock price going up. Enron was a textbook example of this pathology, but "cooking the books" became part of a general pattern so widespread and in such contradiction to public trust that respected investor Warren Buffet warned about the problem many times, including in his annual report: Buffet called them the "distortions *du jour*."[385]

Reform #3: Disclosure

Financial disclosure must be significantly improved. The large dividends and measurement and accountability reform described above would move the system from ultra-capitalism to democratic capitalism and at the same time significantly improve disclosure.

After ultra-capitalism reversed economic momentum in the Southeast Asian countries in 1998, U.S. officials self-righteously lectured the Asians about crony capitalism and inadequate disclosure. If the U.S. government had taken its own advice, perhaps the physician would have been healed and Enron would not have made us sick. Crony capitalism, American style, will stop when Congress promotes the general welfare, instead of drafting special-interest legislation in response to ultra-capitalist lobbyists. Clear disclosure is a fundamental requirement of economic freedom in order for the shareholders to be able to judge the health of the company, and it will

---

[385] "Buffet Blasts Accounting Tricks," *USA Today*, March 15, 1999, p. 1.

be mandated when the rules are written in support of democratic capitalism instead of ultra-capitalism. Enron officials were magicians at not disclosing the facts to the shareholders, analysts, rating agencies, auditors, and institutional investors. Banks are not included in this list because the disclosure problem at Enron could not have happened if the disclosure problems at the banks were not an even larger problem.

A few simple rules could have improved Enron's disclosure, the first of which is requiring a better definition of profits. Companies' statements to the public should in unambiguous language disclose profits consolidated into earnings through the movement of assets onto or off of the balance sheet. Similarly, companies should be required to present a worst-case scenario; for example, Enron should have been required to disclose all of the debt returning to its balance sheet, in the event that the credit support from stock price and investment-grade rating were to be lost. Others have suggested that profits should be defined and reported as those on which a company pays taxes. At least, the process of analyzing the differences between "profit" defined for tax purposes and "profit" as reported to the shareholder would improve disclosure.

The disclosure problem is not limited to Enron. Many companies play disclosure games with a "synthetic lease, an off-balance-sheet trick in which a corporation has all the practical effects of a heavily mortgaged piece of real estate but tells its share owners that it neither owns the property nor owes debt on it."[386] Many investors feel that return on invested capital is an adequate summary measurement of a company. With synthetic leases, however, that calculation is misleading. Banks are among the worst in disclosure because they regularly agree to take over a company's debt if the company is not able to keep borrowing from the commercial markets. This obligation becomes threatening in a down market, as bankers learned when Enron, K-Mart, and Tyco got into trouble, and they were forced to take over billions of dollars of debt based on obligations not shown on the bank's balance sheet.

---

[386] Seth Lubove and Elizabeth MacDonald, "Debt? Who Me?" *Forbes*, February 8, 2002, p. 56.

Why do the banks make these loans? "The best explanation is that banks make off-balance sheet pledges as a favor, hoping to win a client's business the next time it offers stock or buys a company."[387] In other words, banks do it for reasons that demonstrate why the Glass-Steagall Act should not have been repealed.

Government regulations must be tightened to eliminate the practice of moving debt off the balance sheet. The 3% outside ownership required for SPEs needs to be increased to 10%, with the stipulation that the 10% not be guaranteed or insured by the majority partner.

Reform #4: Control of currency and credit for the general welfare

The U.S. government's Constitutionally mandated responsibility to control currency and credit for the general welfare requires long-term, consistent fiscal, monetary, and regulatory policies and practices. The complex, fast-moving, worldwide economy requires consistent, universally applied rules. In the absence of such integrated, comprehensive policies, the rules are written by the lobbyists for ultra-capitalism, and the system is run for the benefit of the speculators. Most people, encouraged by the media, look to the Federal Reserve Board for control of the domestic economy, but they do not understand that the Fed regulates banks that now represent only about one-half of capital markets. The FDIC (Federal Deposit Insurance Corporation) insures the money in banks; the SEC (Securities Exchange Commission) regulates the stock markets; and the CFTC (Commodities Futures Trading Commission)) is supposed to regulate or provide oversight for the commodities futures market that grew to such great size during the last quarter of the twentieth century that it now dwarfs all commerce.[388] The Office of the Comptroller of the Currency "charters, regulates, and supervises national banks to ensure a safe, sound, and competitive banking

---

[387] Lenzer, *op. cit.*, p. 59.

[388] Michael Schroeder, "New Derivatives Regulation Is Opposed," *The Wall Street Journal*, November 10, 1999, p. C1.

system that supports the citizens, communities, and economy of the United States."[389] If only this official definition were the reality!

If this is the mission statement of the Comptroller of the Currency, one wonders who was watching the store when Enron came to do business. Instead of a coordinated program, the present arrangement encourages turf wars and makes each unconnected agency an easier target for lobbyists. If the office of the Comptroller has the mission to "control currency and credit for the general welfare," they will have to do it with a program that is protected from the *ad hoc* actions of politicians. The priority of this mission must be accepted by other agencies, and the Comptroller must have the staff and obligation both to act upon democratic principles and to resist and neutralize the lobby power of ultra-capitalists.

Part of the reason for the very threatening market crash of 1987 was proliferation of bureaucratic agencies. The Fed and SEC presumably watch the stock market while the CFTC watches the commodities futures market. When the market went into free fall, the volume was so great that the connection between the stock market and the commodities market was overwhelmed. This resulted in arbitrageurs trying to make money on small differences between stocks and their futures, getting misinformation that resulted in additional selling pressure. Other aspects of ultra-capitalism, such as hedge funds and program trading, contributed to the '87 crash, which points further to the need for either centralized or well coordinated control.

Chairman of the Fed Greenspan, a media favorite, was celebrated for his role in the crash of '87, for he pumped liquidity into the system. It was Gerald Corrigan, head of the New York Fed, however, who made sure that this liquidity did not stop at the banks. He jawboned the bankers into pushing the liquidity into the economy by extending new credit, instead of following the bankers' traditional instinct of tightening lending during a crisis. It is scary to realize that the stock market correction in 1987 threatened the whole economy and was prevented only by the intervention of one person using his

---

[389] http://www.occ.treas.gov/

personal clout to convince the heads of the largest banks to pass on the liquidity to their customers.[390]

When Brooksley Bonn, head of the CFTC, tried to get control of hedge funds in 1999, she was defeated by the "President's Working Group on Financial Markets." The group included the heads of the Fed, SEC, the Comptroller, and the Secretary of Treasury, and Ms Bonn's replacement at CFTC. This powerful group overwhelmed Bonn's best efforts to get control of hedge funds which could have either prevented or at least minimized the damage from Enron's collapse.[391] Enron's bankruptcy should at the very least provoke a review of the deliberations of this group, starting with the simple question: Why is oversight of hedge funds such a bad idea? (See chapter 7).

Part of the Enron examination should also be a review of the 1998 House Banking Committee hearings on the LTCM hedge-fund failure and bailout. Fed Chairman Alan Greenspan testified to Congress that the hedge funds did not need to be regulated because the banks that lent money to the hedge funds fulfilled that function—and he was not kidding![392] During that same time, Enron was successfully lobbying Congress for additional privileges.

The Constitutional mandate that the government control currency and credit for the good of the general welfare needs to be the responsibility of a single agency, one, however, that has never been established. The time has come for the American republic to extend the premises of democratic government more fully and substantially to the management of financial capitalism. In doing this, the government will be following the original specification of Adam Smith to make money neutral and control the speculators. If a Cabinet-level position of total oversight proves politically impossible, then a carefully negotiated consensus for a long-term plan, free of *ad hoc* political actions, should be legislated. The flow of capital to benefit the job-growth economy, instead of benefiting the speculators,

---

[390] Steven K. Beckner, *Back from the Brink: The Greenspan Years* (New York: John Wiley & Sons, 1996), p. 56.

[391] Schroeder, *op. cit.*, p. C1

[392] Roger Lowenstein, *When Genius Failed: The Rise and Fall of Long-Term Capital Management* (New York: Random House, 2000), p. 185.

needs oversight, and this includes particularly two tools of ultra-capitalism, hedge funds and derivatives. This kind of oversight is not possible so long as the responsibility is spread thinly among the SEC, FDIC, FED, CFTC, Departments of Treasury, Commerce and Labor, the U.S. Comptroller, and more than 10 Congressional committees, along with various private agencies such as FASB (Financial Accounting Standards Board).

Reform #5: Executive compensation congruent with the long-term interests of the shareholder

In the aftermath of Enron, stock options have become a popular subject whose defenders repeat the mantra that stock options make the interests of managers and stockholders congruent. This is a fiction because stock options are the coupling device between Wall Street and corporations that encourage executives to chase short-term earnings, and make them eager for mergers or acquisitions. Stock options are a tool of ultra-capitalism that has frequently encouraged top executives to cook the books to get the stock price up so that the CEO could quickly cash in for a few hundred million dollars.

Stock options are also defended as an important incentive for Information Age industries to attract top-quality people. This is a legitimate argument, but the same motivation can be accomplished by stock grants that incur a charge against earnings. The start-up companies are not making money anyway, so the cost of stock grants simply adds to cumulative losses with an eventual tax benefit. Besides this weak argument, the danger of proliferating stock options to too many people in an organization was demonstrated after the dot.com bubble burst. Even good companies, such as Microsoft, suffered many personal bankruptcies when the drop of the whole market hurt people who had borrowed money to exercise options that were then "underwater," that is, with a market price below the option price. Management of a solid company finds it difficult to explain to financially unsophisticated, trusting employees why the company is still profitable but the associates owe the bank thousands of dollars on pieces of paper that are worth nothing.

Until the last quarter of the twentieth century, investment bankers were paid an advisory fee for building up long-term relationships with companies; bankers were modestly paid executives responsible for prudent loans; and corporate executives were well paid but with total compensation rarely over $1 million. The feeding frenzy began on Wall Street when investment bankers began to "earn" 10 or 20 million dollars a year, or more, by pricing their services as a percentage of the deal. The money going to Wall Street executives went through the roof, and naturally so did the number of deals. In time, lawyers, too, learned how to make millions a year by abandoning their traditional per-hour charges. The accountants also decided that making millions of dollars a year looked like fun, so they raised their prices by several multiples. In the 1970s, few financial analysts made over $100,000 a year, and many made less than half that.

After ultra-capitalism became dominant, the analysts became the detectives of Wall Street, searching for companies with "hidden asset value," which usually means a potential for a takeover in which everyone shares in the plunder. As the analysts became more important to ultra-capitalism, searching the industrial landscape for hidden gold, their compensation moved up to millions of dollars per year. Henry Blodgett became famous as "Merrill Lynch's never-say-sell tout, for the same NASDAQ clients whose fees helped fuel Blodgett's $5-million-a-year income."[393] Jack Grubman of CITI's Solomon Smith Barney made Blodgett look underpaid with his average of $20 million a year. Grubman, however, provided additional services with an upgrade of AT&T at the request of his boss, Sandy Weil, a director of AT&T, and his famous buy support of WorldCom right up to the time of its bankruptcy. Grubman was implicated in a legal investigation into the activities of CITI; he resigned in August, 2002, with a $32 million severance.[394]

CEOs began eventually to realize that the percentage-of-the-deal philosophy could be stretched to measure astronomical individual compensation for them as a percentage of the increase in the company's market value, not hard to produce in a raging bull market. Most mergers happen because they rain so much money on

---

[393] Greider, *op. cit.*, p.13.

[394] Anthony Bianco and Heather Timmons, "Crisis at CITI," *Business Week*, September 9, 2002, p. 38.

investment bankers, commercial bankers, lawyers, accountants, acquiring executives, and acquired executives. Enormous stock options are freebies that have no cost at the time they are given to either the executive or the company. If a CEO receives a huge option, and a few years later is presented with a merger opportunity to cash out for tens of millions of dollars, he or she will usually do so. Similarly, most institutional investors are ready to support any deal that allows them to cash out and improve their position on the annual score-keeping of competing money managers.

Enron took this greed to new levels when newly recruited MBAs were told that they would make at least $100,000 in the first year and, with the benefit of options, be millionaires by the time they were 30. Enron was well aware of how the government had made the exercise of options an opportunity to avoid taxes. With this tax benefit and 692 subsidiaries in the Cayman Islands, and another 119 in the Turks and Caicos, Enron paid no taxes in four out of five years. When Enron executives exercised options, the company took the gain on the option as a deduction from taxes, but not a deduction from profits. Enron's reported profits benefited substantially: "Deductions for stock options alone turned what would have been a tax bill of $112 million in 2000 into a refund of $278 million."[395]

This tax treatment of options is an example of how ultra-capitalism lobbied government to shift taxes during the last quarter century from the wealthy and corporations to the wage earner. Claiming unwillingness to favor the wealthy, so-called reformers in Congress oppose ending double taxation of dividend income for worker-owners of the companies they work for, and yet they continue to uphold this kind of massive tax-dodging corporate welfare. This tax-dodging practice would not last long if wage earners ever found out the extent to which they are subsidizing wealthy individuals and wealthy corporations at the same time.

"Feeding frenzy" is the appropriate expression for an environment in which Enron's financial officers apparently saw nothing wrong with making millions of dollars in a few months from "investments" of a few thousand dollars in Enron partnerships. CFO

[395] Daniel Cay Johnston, "Enron Avoided Income Taxes in 4 out of 5 Years," *The New York Times*, January 17, 2002, p. 1.

Fastow's $30 million windfall received great publicity, but lesser lights, such as Treasurer Ben Glison, Jr., and Attorney Kristina Mordant, put up $5,800 for a quick return of $1 million.[396]

Harvard philosopher John Rawls proposed in his second principle of a just society that differences in wealth and power are appropriate only if they contribute to a system that benefits the least advantaged.[397] Compensation in ultra-capitalism, demonstrated in companies like Enron, is so far from this principle of a just society that the comparison is frivolous. Ultra-capitalists with compensation in the tens and hundreds of millions of dollars are blind to the effect of this on others. They do not recognize that they are presenting capitalism as an immoral, exploitive system to youthful protestors and the people of the world. The trust and cooperation required to maximize surplus in companies is destroyed by these compensation obscenities. At the international level, visibly greedy capitalism has become a target for extremists, and the excesses make it easier for terrorists to recruit adherents to their evil causes.

Corporations need to implement the following policies regarding the total compensation of executives. To reinforce the implementation of these reform policies, institutional investors should require that these policies of corporate governance be in place as a precondition for investing the collective wealth of employee-owners in any corporation:

- Executives and directors must not sell stock until six months after retirement or leaving the company.

- Stock options must be replaced by stock grants that incur a profit reduction to the company and a tax obligation for recipient at time of grant.

- Companies must not lend money to their executives.

---

[396] Kurt Eichenwald, "Deal at Enron Gave Insiders Fast Fortunes," *The New York Times*, February 5, 2002, p. 1.

[397] John Rawls, *Political Liberalism* (New York: Columbia University Press, 1993), p. 53.

- All bonuses must be paid in stock.

- Officers must have no financial interest in companies doing business with their company.

- The compensation of all employees, including the CEO, must be based on a professionally developed internal logic.

- All associates, from the CEO to the lowest paid, must participate in the same profit-sharing and stock purchase plan.

Reform #6: The mission of banks: Make good loans and do no harm

The capitalist system depends on a flow of money into the job-growth economy. Neutral money needed to support this flow requires three protections: Capital must not be too little to support the job-growth economy; it cannot be so excessive that it funds overly risky projects; it must not be deflected into speculation. Neutral money can be controlled by the cost of money, the size of the reserves that the banks are required to take out of profits, and—most importantly—by the bankers' motivation to make only prudent loans. The government is supposed to regulate banks for this purpose and through these tools. The time is gone, however, when appropriately paid bankers concentrated on the quality of their loans. They have been replaced by ultra-capitalist bankers who make deals, trade in futures, and enjoy multi-million dollar compensation. Bankers now use derivatives to make money and to hedge questionable loans. These techniques add to the excessive credit that allows ventures like Enron to be encouraged by the whole banking industry.

Banks are supposed to be regulated by the size of their reserves against the size of their loan risk. Based on the record of bad loans, protocols for these reserves need a major overhaul. Every case of rising artificial values should trigger proportionate increases in reserves; however, since increases in reserves come only from reduction in profits, and because bank executives are as influenced by stock price and stock options as are CEOs, the bankers' record of identifying artificial assets is notably poor. Based on the sad lending record of too-eager bankers, the government must improve regulation of banks, including monitoring how the banks fund high-risk hedge funds like LTCM and Enron.

When deposit insurance was proposed in 1933 to stop the runs on banks, FDR opposed it on the basis that it was an intrusion into market disciplines that would cause economic damage. He was talked into a policy of insuring deposit accounts of $5,000, but he proved to be prophetic in his concern.[398] To correct this situation, deposit insurance needs now to be limited to the small investor with less than a $50,000 deposit in a single banking location. Federal deposit insurance must be taken away from speculators; that can be done by rescinding $100,000 deposit insurance coverage in unlimited, multiple locations for a single investor. The extension of deposit insurance to large, multiple accounts, passed in 1982 by Congress, guaranteed federal bailout of insured funds that allowed the speculators to destroy the S&L banking industry. In 2003, government policy was still headed in the wrong direction: A bill before Congress would increase the amount of deposit insurance.

Enron demonstrated that the repeal of Glass-Steagall was a major government mistake. The inherent conflict among selling stocks, lending money, making deals, and selling insurance that had first provoked the law in the 1930s became even more apparent under ultra-capitalism. The amounts of money that now change hands, and the speed at which the transactions are now electronically traded, multiplies many times the threat to the world's economy. The Wall Street lobby has convinced the U.S. government that "free markets" means "free capital," not the neutral money and control of speculators specified by Adam Smith in the original version of capitalism.

It will not be easy to repeal the repeal of Glass-Steagall and to unravel J.P. Morgan and Citigroup, but specific reform is urgently needed. In addition to eliminating the conflicts of interest, the government also needs to control the enormous size of these institutions. Anti-trust actions that used to monitor the tendency to excessive growth has been virtually abandoned. The economic system needs to be protected from CEOs like Sandy Weil of CITI, serial

---

[398] Kathleen Day, *S & L Hell: The People and the Politics Behind the $1 Trillion Savings and Loan Scandal* (New York: W. W. Norton & Co. 1993), p. 43.

acquirers on ego trips, who acquire and fire up to a size beyond the capacity of any mortal to manage effectively.

Deregulation of banking, at the same time that market disciplines were suspended, resulted in easy credit and caused economic disasters. Bankers motivated by stock options and the short-term price of the stock contradicted the mission of making high-quality loans. Bankers ought to be compensated on long-term performance plans based on the quality of loans they made. The banking system in the United States has been compromised from the beginning: Whether as national banks, private banks, or a combination, the system has been dominated by finance capitalists with the mission of making money on money. For two centuries, this has resulted in a capitalism that has functioned at a fraction of its potential because of the concentration of wealth. Now that finance capitalism has grown into the monstrosity of ultra-capitalism, what was once only an impediment has escalated into a threat to the whole world's economic growth and consequently a threat to world peace.

Immediate reform of banking institutions may come not so much from an enlightened Congress as from court action. A *Consolidated Complaint,* a 500-page class-action suit, was filed early in 2002 against the "Enron Nine" (in William Greider's phrase). Citigroup and J.P. Morgan Chase led the list of financial institutions alleged to have "collaborated with the now bankrupt energy company in its financial sleight of hand in deals that enabled Enron to inflate its profits, conceal its burgeoning debts, and push its stock price higher and higher."[399]

Some of the country's toughest contingency lawyers are going after billions of dollars from those with the deepest pockets. Alas, since the ultra-capitalists knew that they could not survive a public trial, the bankers made new deals with the government, the case was settled out of court, and the lawyers got paid. Paid a lot! Estimates for the first-year legal bill is $300 million.[400] Although the courts are not the appropriate arenas, and litigation is not the best means, for the proper democratization of capitalism, the public class-action court

---

[399] William Greider, "Enron Nine," *The Nation,* May 13, 2002, p. 18.

[400] Mitchell Pacelle, "Enron Bankruptcy Is Fee Bonanza," *The Wall Street Journal,* December 11, 2002, p. C1.

fight might shed light on the corruptions. True reform must come, however, from an enlightened citizenry demanding legislation from a new breed of elected officials who take to heart their Constitutional mandate to "promote the general welfare." But time is running out! As long as America presents ultra-capitalism to the world as our economic system of choice, we will be snuffing out the "light on the hill" and giving the enemies of freedom undeserved support.

Reform #7: A simple rule for auditors

The governance of large, complex corporations requires clear measurement and accountability (see above, reform #2) and a fail-safe audit process. "Fail-safe" means that the system will work with either good people or bad people through a process that assures the integrity of all control systems. The core of audit reform is the requirement that the Audit Committee of a Board of Directors solicit bids and select a new auditor every five years, one who reports to the Board and has a no-cut contract for the five-year term. I have been in favor of this improvement in auditing for many years (see chapter 4). My experience includes over sixteen years as CEO and Chairman of ADT Inc., a NYSE public company, and my service on six Boards domestically and twelve in other countries. I was on the Board of Kroger, Inc., the country's largest food retailer, for about 20 years, including being chair of the Governance Committee, and I served on the audit committees of other companies. Because of this experience, I am able to judge the superficiality, even the hypocrisy, being proposed in Washington as part of the post-Enron reforms.

During 2002, support was growing for a change of auditors every five years. An article in *Harvard Business Review* put it in the perspective of high-quality auditing, not protection from criminality only:

> The deeper, more pernicious problem with corporate auditing, as it's currently practiced, is its vulnerability to unconscious bias. Because of the often subjective nature of accounting and the tight relationships between accounting firms and their clients, even the most honest and meticulous of auditors can unintentionally distort the numbers in ways that mask a

company's true financial status, thereby misleading investors, regulators, and sometimes management.[401]

Other events during 2002, however, demonstrated that the lobby power of the accounting industry was still capable of preventing clear and obvious reform. John Biggs, retired in early 2003 as CEO of the giant pension fund TIAA-CREF, had—according to all reports—the job of chair of the new Accounting Oversight Board, but then suddenly he did not get the job. Biggs was well qualified, and he would have been a tough chair, but the accounting industry knew that his interest in changing accountants every five to seven years was practice as well as theory at TIAA. Economist and pundit Paul Krugman hit the nail on the head: "The first big step in undermining reform came when Harvey Pitt, chairman of the SEC, backtracked on plans to appoint a strong and independent figure to head a new accounting oversight board."[402] Harvey Pitt himself was soon gone, but for other reasons. The accounting industry and their friends in Congress had closed ranks and beaten off real reform. The average citizen did not recognize the importance of what had happened.

Arthur Andersen had been the outside auditor of Enron since the merger of two gas companies in 1985. Andersen, in the 1990s, paid $100 million in fines for its auditing work at Sunbeam, and $7 million at Waste Management, two egregious cases of cooking the books. Enron's fees of $52 million, over half for consulting rather than for auditing, made them Andersen's second-largest customer. By the end of 2002, Andersen Accounting had almost disappeared, down from 28,000 employees to a skeletal 1,000. The destruction of one complicit audit firm, however, will not fix the system, but realization that that seventeen years with the same auditor is twelve years too long would be a good start.

The accounting industry fights the idea of separating auditing and consulting; they claim that consulting helps them recruit higher-quality people. Although the exaggerated claim has some truth to it,

---

[401] Max Bazerman, George Loewenstein, and Don A. Moore, "Why Good Accountants Do Bad Auditing," *Harvard Business Review*, November, 2002, p. 97.

[402] Paul Krugman, "Business as Usual," *The New York Times*, October 22, 2002, p. A31.

the accounting industry should welcome the proposal to change auditors every five years because this practice would allow them to stay in the consulting business except for their clients under a five-year audit contract.

The following are key points for audit reform:

- During the term of the audit contract, the auditors must not do consulting work, including tax work and internal auditing, with the client for whom they are the auditors.

- The Audit Committee of the Board must replace auditors every five years.

- The Audit Committee of the Board must have direct supervision of the outside auditors.

- The company must not hire any personnel from a contracted audit firm until six months after the contract is finished.

- The head of the internal audit department must report to the CEO (see chapter 4).

- The Internal Audit Department has a dual reporting responsibility to the CEO and to the Audit Committee of the Board (see chapter 4).

Reform #8: A simple rule for rating agencies

The agencies that qualify the risk level of a company's bonds have greater access to financial information than do stockholders and analysts. For that reason, rating agencies are an increasingly important source of early information about companies. Bonds are longer-term debt instruments, so any information suggesting that repayment is becoming more risky is vital information. In ultra-capitalism, bonds are far more volatile and are traded more frequently than they used to be. Bonds are now "stripped," that is, the principal and interest are separated into different tradable instruments. PO (Principal Only) bonds are broken into "tranches" based on different repayment schedules. "The final tranche, called Z-bonds because they were the last to repay the principal, were highly volatile and known as 'toxic waste' by the traders who handled them."[403] Ultra-capitalism has taken a simple instrument of known interest and term and has turned it into many different speculative instruments.

Because rating agencies are exempt from certain government regulations, companies can give them sensitive information that they are not supposed to reveal to stock analysts. Since most stock analysts' reputations under ultra-capitalism have changed from examiners to shills, "most Wall Street research has sold itself to the devil."[404] In this environment, the rating agencies must assume more responsibility; unfortunately, the rating agencies failed in the exercise of that responsibility when they did not alert the shareholders to growing trouble at Enron.

Ratings have been used since the Investment Company Act of 1940 created the "investment-grade rating" for bonds in which money-market funds could invest. Later, the SEC certified only three agencies that could make this judgment: Standard and Poor's, Moody's, and Fitch. After Enron, many criticized the rating agencies for having committed the same sins as the stock analysts: They sell so many different services that conflicts of interest inevitably arise. Some went so far as to recommend that free-market forces could do a better job: "Avoid heavy-handed central regulation. Instead, harness market forces in the shape of private-sector credit rating agencies."[405]

Enron's rapidly growing trading business and rapidly growing debt depended on an investment-grade rating by Moody's and Standard and Poor's. Derivatives in trillions of dollars are traded electronically every minute, and the trading parties use the investment-grade rating as evidence of the financial integrity of the other party involved in the trade. In Enron's case, despite the

---

[403] Chancellor, *op. cit.*, p. 246.

[404] Gretchen Morgenson, "Post-Enron, All Eyes on Rating Agencies," *The New York Times*, December 16, 2001, p. 61.

[405] "Let Go of Nanny: The Case for Taking Credit Ratings out of Financial Regulation," *The Economist*, February 8, 2003, p. 17.

disappearing profit margins, rapidly rising reported debt, an extremely high stock-price multiple, increasing evidence of large bad investments, aggressive accounting techniques in moving debt off the balance sheet, and moving profits onto the profit and loss statement, the rating agencies did not downgrade Enron until bankruptcy was but one week away. At that time, the agencies drastically downgraded Enron's bonds by six notches from investment-grade to almost a junk-bond rating. Before the rating agencies took this overdue action, the bond market had already priced the Enron bonds at 50 cents on the dollar.

The rating agencies' preposterous rationale for delaying action was that a downgrade in the sensitive trading business would have been a self-fulfilling prophecy that actually would have caused a bankruptcy. It is not the rating agencies' job to make that judgment. Rating agencies, like auditors and banks, bear an obligation to a broad constituency. Had they downgraded Enron one notch at a time, they might well have slowed the trading activity, but they could also have brought Enron in for a softer landing and avoided the enormous damage to stockholders and employees.

Rating agencies monitor the financial integrity of companies. To perform the work we need them to perform, they must indicate the direction and rate of change in a timely manner without consideration for the consequences of the rating change. The government ought to disqualify bond-rating agencies on evidence that they are compromising technical appraisal by concern over the effect of their appraisal. As obvious as this simple correction seems, the media headline, "Moody's and S&P, singed by Enron, may speed up credit downgrades,"[406] indicates that the essential purpose of rating agencies is not thoroughly understood. Of course they ought to speed up credit downgrades when they are deserved, and not on account of getting "singed!" The peddlers of credit protection raised the price of their credit contracts on Enron by 18% in August of 2001 for the benefit of the few, while the rating agencies sat on their hands for another three months and failed in their public trust.

---

[406] Gregory Zukerman and Christine Richard, "Moody's and S&P, Singed by Enron May Speed Up Credit Rating Downgrades," *The Wall Street Journal*, January 22, 2002, p. C1.

Reform #9: Protect pensions without slowing the spread of worker-ownership

American wage earners earn the hope of a certain income on retirement that a defined-benefit type of pension plan and Social Security can give them. This is American workers' money to live on in retirement. In addition to a secure basic pension, wage earners ought also to have the opportunity to participate in company-ownership programs, which includes taking some of the investment risk. Basic pensions enable wage earners to live in retirement; additional money from ownership plans enables them to live well. Even with profit-sharing and 401(k) plans, however, wage earners need to be encouraged to convert their stock holdings into guaranteed income instruments a few years before retirement.

Employees' profit-sharing and ownership plans, like *Care and Share,* which I designed and implemented at ADT (see chapter 2), must come in addition to the pension plan and never be used as a substitute. Many companies, like Enron, however, take the tax-favored 401(k) savings and repackage their whole pension obligation using company stock. Even though Enron provided a matching contribution, their mission was to reduce cost; at the same time, however, they increased the risk of devastating loss to company associates. With friendly treatment from the government, Enron combined aggressive efforts to find profits anywhere they could. "Enron, in an unusual move, offset the pension with the value of the ESOP accounts based on the price of the stock. In 1987, Congress banned ESOP-pension floor-offsets, but Enron had been excluded, 'grandfathered,' from the new rule."[407] One more time, Enron demonstrated its ability successfully to lobby Congress, use the artificial price of their stock, and ignore the added risk that was eventually destructive for the employees.

Politicians jump on the issue of the percentage of employees' pension and the 401(k) money invested in Enron stock, and they push for legislation to restrict the percentage of retirement money that may

---

[407] Ellen E. Schultz, "Pension Practices Used by Enron Come Under Fire," *The Wall Street Journal*, March 1, 2002, p. A4.

be invested in the employees' own company. This "too many eggs in one basket" concern is legitimate, popular, and easy to understand, but danger lies in moving too far in one direction. Ownership of stock by associates in the companies they work for is the way to maximize surplus and distribute it broadly, thereby solving the concentration-of-wealth problem that is now limiting world economic growth. The way to avoid the too-many-eggs problem is to separate ownership-investment money from retirement money, the latter being secured in various ways. Employees' pension money and investment money alike would benefit were the company to pay large dividends that would channel the rewards derived from capitalism into income and long-term appreciation (see reform #1). Instead of the wild swings and eventual economic dislocations caused by speculation in the short-term stock price, the peoples' money would become secure, and steady economic growth would be assured. Instead of capital being diverted into speculation in the stock market, it would, instead, be more productively invested in the job-growth economy.

Reform #10: Board of Directors

Most of the post-Enron reforms of the Board coming out of Washington are practices that have existed in most companies for decades, such as the percentage of outside directors, term limits, compensation, and annual performance reviews of both the CEO and the directors. Reforms #1 to #9, particularly large dividends and audit procedures would, however, significantly change the Board's responsibilities. Inherent in reform #1 is a new Board responsibility for the distribution of surplus. In this view, management is responsible for maximizing the long-term profit for the stakeholders, but the Board has oversight in determining the distribution of surplus. The question should be this: Is the surplus to be used for reinvestment in growth, large dividends, stock buy-backs, or acquisitions? In the case of an acquisition, the Board should question whether the acquisition is truly strategic or merely a way to hype short-term profits. During the heady days of the bubble economy, Boards allowed CEOs to waste around a trillion dollars on stock buy-backs and non-strategic acquisition to the detriment of both the company and the world's economy.

Another change in governance that has become a popular subject for reform is the separation of the jobs of Chairman and CEO. This is a bad idea because it will cause unnecessary politicizing, and in troubled companies, it can prevent the company from getting the best person for the job. The idea of outside directors meeting occasionally without the CEO and other insiders, however, is a useful one and not a regular practice on enough Boards. The simpler way to accomplish this goal is the appointment of a "lead director" whose function is to arrange and chair the meetings of outside directors at least twice a year. Appropriate times could include a meeting after the financials for the prior year are available, and another after the annual planning meeting.

The most important improvement in corporate governance will occur when Business Schools, institutional investors, universities, civic groups, unions, democratic capitalists, and religious groups join together to move the economy from ultra-capitalism to democratic capitalism.

Business as Usual

Enron and other corporate scandals provoked an outcry over corporate abuses and greedy CEOs. Even Wall Street executives lectured corporate America on the necessity for reform, while the financial media joined in with long lists of proposed reform actions. President Bush preached homilies on corporate integrity, and his Justice Department staged symbolic arrests of ultra-capitalists in handcuffs. Congress rapidly passed a reform bill that in no way goes to the root of the problems. Two common denominators of these events are the superficiality of analysis and the unlikelihood of real reform. As usual, the politicians and the media produced a great deal of noise and little substance. A *Business Week* article summarized this phenomenon:

> As Washington dithers, financial reform is going nowhere fast. Now the drive for post-Enron legislative reform is stalled, victim of Presidential indifference, Republican hostility, fierce

415

business lobbying, and disorganization among reform-minded Democrats.[408]

An example of the superficiality of half-reform recommendations is that audits be improved by changing the senior partner on the audit every five years. This move would change little, and beside that, it has been the practice in most companies for several decades! The much ballyhooed "reform" of having the CEO sign off on the company's financial statements is hardly new, but it is a reminder of the wrong attitude. Little improvement will be forthcoming if the attitude is adversarial, working on the "Gotcha!" principle. Most of these matters have little to do with solving the problems of an economic-political system in which finance capitalism is dominant, not subordinate, and writes the rules for our government.

Act Now to Democratize Capitalism!

The reforms proposed here as #1, balancing dividend income, appreciation, and security; and #2, measuring and making companies accountable on a three-year moving average of profits, sales growth, and cash flow, are the primary changes needed to move from the corruptions of ultra-capitalism towards democratic capitalism. The alignment of fiscal, monetary, and regulatory policies to these specific proposals would remove finance capitalism from its dominant position and make it subordinate to the commercial process, essential for the proper functioning of free markets.

Institutional investors are well positioned to press for reform both of government and of corporate policies. They can become effective agents of change after they accept their true fiduciary responsibilities, but to take that step forward, they need an epiphany that will sharpen their focus on these key points:

- Democratic capitalism's balance of dividends, appreciation, and security produces a superior long-term return for their constituents.

---

[408] Editorial, "What Clean Up?" *Business Week*, June 17, 2002, p. 26.

- Profit-sharing and ownership opportunities in democratic capitalism motivate all to maximize the surplus.

- The balance of dividend income, appreciation, and security, in combination with the inherently broad wealth distribution in democratic capitalism, will result in strong and sustained world economic growth.

The steady, sustained growth of companies and jobs from these reforms will help the world economy avoid the destructive, wild swings inherent in ultra-capitalism.

Institutional investors' opportunities to reform government and corporate policies are special to this unique group who function as representatives and managers of the collective wealth of American workers. Institutional investors have the responsibility, the democratic power, and more financial sophistication than most to accomplish this essential move towards the democratization of capitalism. Most other parts of the culture demonstrate an inability to foster reform consistent with their inability to comprehend. Institutional investors, if they are going to be faithful to the people whose money they invest, need to stand and deliver democratic capitalism as the superior economic system.

Banking reform is more complicated, and it will take more time because control of currency and credit for the sake of the general welfare has been done poorly for so long, in fact, from the beginning of this great democratic experiment. Capitalism has always functioned at only a fraction of its potential because the impediment of concentrated wealth has never been effectively addressed. Jefferson and Madison, the architects of the new republic, separated church and state, but they did not know how to separate finance capitalism and the government. That separation is now no longer a choice but an urgent need because bad capitalism is overwhelming good capitalism, and special interests are overwhelming democratic government. The traditional impediment of concentrated wealth has escalated to become a dominant force that has already slowed world economic growth and prevented economic common purpose from uniting the world.

True reform can begin when enough citizens recognize that free markets function and find equilibrium only after the government assures neutral money and control of leveraged speculation. CEO-bashing, post-Enron, became a popular sport because of the excesses that ultra-capitalists manifested. It is always fun to bash those who have more money and power, and many CEOs deserved the critical treatment. For some CEOs, ultra-capitalism has been an opportunity to become serial acquirers, stock-option pigs, and obscenely rich. For many CEOs, however, ultra-capitalism has been thrust upon them by the package of government mistakes that included excessive volatility, excessive liquidity, bad deregulation, and suspension of market disciplines. These CEOs were left with no alternative but to compromise their long-term building programs (see chapter 8).

To purge the American economy and the world's economy of these forces that have corrupted capitalism and are corrupting democracy, a coalition of stakeholders must be formed that comprises groups of people who hitherto have not found themselves on the same side of political, social, and economic issues: Ordinary people—wage earners, civic groups, educators at all levels, business organizations, unions, NGOs, and religious groups—must make common cause with such specialized forces as institutional investors and practicing democratic capitalist executives and Board members. Together they can save capitalism and advance democracy and find the way to a world of peace and plenty. Or, by doing nothing, they can let ultra-capitalism lead us into greater folly and violence.

In this new coalition, the practicing democratic capitalists play an especially important part because they have the practical experience that others lack in democratizing capitalism. Unfortunately, they also lack visibility in the same way that democratic capitalism, as an economic-political theory, lacks visibility. Reform action will emancipate these democratic capitalists to release the latent power of capitalism and demonstrate the enormous potential of people, companies, countries, and the world. As people are educated and inspired by this performance, more will recognize the attainability of the *ideal*, and understand the *process* to specify and support the *means*.

CHAPTER 10

The Way to a World of Peace and Plenty

*A program whose basic thesis is, not that the system of free
enterprise for profit has failed in this generation, but that it
has not yet been tried.*

Franklin D. Roosevelt, 1932[409]

The way to a world of peace and plenty is democratic
capitalism, the free enterprise system that can eliminate material
scarcity, elevate spirits, unify people, and stop the violence. Seventy
years after President Roosevelt's lament, the way was still blocked by
concentrated wealth and by violence in the relations among people
and nations.

Late in the twentieth century, the demise of Communism and
the demonstrable superiority of economic freedom gave the world an
unprecedented opportunity to move along the way towards a world of
economic common purpose. This opportunity was lost, however,
because the U.S. government was promoting ultra-capitalism instead
of the economic system that maximizes and distributes wealth
broadly.

From the beginning of the American republic, finance
capitalists successfully lobbied special privileges and impeded
economic and social progress through the concentration of wealth.
During the last quarter of the twentieth century, however, this nexus
of Wall Street and Washington combined government mistakes,
financial deregulation, and suspension of market disciplines to
escalate this traditional impediment into a dominant force. Ultra-
capitalism—defined as a combination of mercantilism that treats
workers as a cost commodity, together with finance capitalism that is
dominant over, rather than subordinate to, the commercial process—

---

[409] Cited by F. A. Hayek, *The Road to Serfdom* (Chicago: University of Chicago
Press, 1989; first published by Routledge and Kegan, 1944), p. 13.

has slowed the world's economy and provoked social tensions that range from populist protest to terrible violence.

Reformers with the democratic power to remove the impediments to economic and social progress have lost the way for over two centuries because they failed to understand fiscal, monetary, and regulatory policies well enough to counter the sophistication and lobby power of finance capitalists. At the end of the twentieth century, the size, speed, and complexity of the world's capital markets allowed ultra-capitalists to increase their domination and further confuse the reformers.

American citizens must come to understand the benefits of democratic capitalism in contrast to the corruptions of ultra-capitalism, and then refine capitalism and restructure government accordingly. With a democratic capitalist agenda, America will again be positioned to lead the world in the direction that improves all lives. The democratic capitalist way to a world of peace and plenty has been defined in this book and is summarized in this chapter.

My Experience

My experience at running companies (see chapter 2) gave me confidence that I understood the circumstances required to release the enormous latent power of people to produce and innovate. For many years, my job was to identify the full potential of companies, provide the circumstances conducive to realizing that potential, and neutralize the impediments. From experience, I learned that full potential is reached through *individual development in a harmonious whole* because total performance is the sum of individual performance enhanced by the cooperative environment. The governance template required to make this theory work includes the following four elements: *integrity*, a prerequisite to cooperation and trust; *maximum freedom* that motivates each individual to be involved and to contribute; *minimum structure* that provides the disciplines for freedom to function well; and *competence* accurately to relate task to resources and to execute effectively.

According to my understanding of these basics, I put this formula into practice. I had learned early from team sports that each is responsible for individual conditioning and skill development but also for contributing to that rewarding sense of team spirit. Later I recognized that this principle is consistent with the human duality of individual ambition and the instinct for social cooperation in which each lends his or her strengths to compensate for the weaknesses of others, and each borrows strengths wherein he or she may be weak. In this lending and borrowing process, I observed that each person both learns and teaches, and thus the whole becomes greater than the sum of its parts. Why, I wondered, was this way of individual development in a harmonious whole not also applicable to families, to education, to companies, to governments, and to the world as the universal way for each and all to reach their full potential?

This paradigm of democratic, progressive human behavior provided me with the *ideal*; my job was then to find the *means* to reach the *ideal*. I did not realize at the time that I was engaged in an interactive *process* of truth-seeking that would confirm the *ideal* by identifying, examining, and testing the *means*.

From experience, I learned that when individual ambition is properly coupled with social cooperation, the improvement of group performance is not slight but huge. Motivation and a positive attitude are the first priorities because people must want to be involved, to contribute, and to be trained. Motivated people with a positive attitude and a sense of common purpose make implementation easier, whereas people with a negative attitude make execution difficult.

If motivation and a positive attitude are the first priorities to individual development in a harmonious whole, where do they come from, how are they put in place? Further examination showed me that individual motivation and a positive attitude depend on individuals with a sense of freedom, dignity, self-respect, common purpose, and a fair share of the rewards. How can these circumstances be provided? Excellent education and training require a financial commitment and doing the job well; the sense of freedom, dignity, self-respect, fairness, and common purpose, however, are more complicated because they depend on the quality of leadership and the culture of the organization. Democratic capitalism offers the decentralized structure, but the requisite culture still depends on the right selection and training of leaders at all levels.

The final component to be integrated with high-quality leadership in the democratic capitalist culture is the sharing of financial rewards that have been generated by the improved performance. This opportunity for individuals to make their contributions and reap their rewards was the mission of the profit-sharing and ownership plan that I designed and put into place while CEO of ADT, Inc. The contest to name the plan was won by a lady who said that her understanding of the proposed plan was that "the more people care, the more they will have to share"; hence, *Care and Share*. The lady was correct: Whenever capitalism is properly democratized, individuals participate freely and think of themselves as owners, thus improving individual and group performance. In this environment, peer pressure and leadership replace top-down, command-and-control management; the fun and satisfaction that arise from involvement and cooperation displace fear and mistrust.

Among hundreds of branches, I found a shortcut to identify those ADT locations held back by the wrong culture and weak management. Because *Care and Share* was voluntary and required a financial sacrifice to participate, a low level of subscription in a particular branch was an early and accurate indicator of trouble. In effect, non-participation was a vote of no confidence in local management by the associates in that branch, which demonstrates that business, like politics, is local.

Ever since Karl Marx (1818-1883), "worker ownership" has had a threatening sound. Those with wealth thought it meant: "We have it, and the masses are trying to take it away." The worker ownership that I propose throughout this book is different from the Marxist revolutionary approach that spawned the fears of the wealthy. In democratic capitalism, no one takes anything away from anyone else; rather, the workers buy ownership with their own money, and they share in additional ownership accruing from the improved performance that they have helped to build. How can workers with tight budgets buy ownership? It is surprising how fast workers can build ownership from a modest weekly deduction from their pay, especially when the company adds more stock based on improved performance. From the beginning, workers feel and act like owners as long as the structure is decentralized and the culture is one of trust and cooperation. During ten years of *Care and Share,* the associates at ADT purchased and earned ownership of 13% of the company through their payroll deductions and the profit-sharing plan. Their ownership percentage would have continued to climb, had ADT remained an independent company.

My experience included an education in the corruptions of capitalism, for I was running ADT during the time when ultra-capitalism was growing to dominate the economy. I observed that Wall Street during the 1970s was making a profound change from providing long-term advisory services to transactional, basing the price of their services on a percentage of the deals they negotiated. Inevitably the number of deals exploded and rained money on all involved. This change on Wall Street initiated the compensation feeding frenzy that eventually infected the whole system.

During this time, the rush of hundreds of billions of dollars from ERISA pension funding (see chapter 7) gave the stock market new power to reward or punish CEOs, based on small changes in the quarterly earnings of their companies. Many CEOs learned how to parlay stock options into fortunes, many others were reluctantly forced to abandon long-range plans (see chapter 8). I was dismayed that the corporate mission to serve the broad constituency of stakeholders was ridiculed by many, including the financial press and Business Schools. The new mantra had become "shareholder value," a focus that ignored the growing excesses that, in time, destroyed shareholder value. The "American Model" that was flaunted to the world as the new, improved economic paradigm included the philosophy that "greed is good." This emergent ultra-capitalism was a contradiction of democratic capitalism, the management philosophy that I had learned and practiced from the time I was a young plant manager until I retired as a 62-year-old CEO.

In retrospect, I judge my management performance in terms of financial measurements to have been successful. ADT had a total market value of $97 million at the beginning of my term; by the end of my term, shareholders had received about $1 billion in dividends and cash for their stock. I judge the company's overall performance, however, to have been well below its potential. The reason for this, besides my own limitations, is that changing any corporate culture is a long process. Most of the managers were educated in an environment that gave tacit approval of the command-and-control style and no attention to democratic capitalism as a coherent system. Leaders have to be retrained away from the top-down management style, and away from the mercantilist philosophy that profits go up as wages and benefits go down, instead of profits going up as people are motivated to contribute. I found that managers are quick to agree philosophically with democratic capitalism, but, under stress, some will revert to the traditional style. Changing the organizational culture is a delicate process because months of slow progress can be wiped out quickly by the actions of a single supervisor who demeans people.

Many who have never had the experience of changing an environment to release the latent power of people, might think that the steps necessary are too obvious for comment, and the benefits exaggerated. More cynical observers would describe them as warm and fuzzy concepts with no place in the macho world of Social Darwinism, creative destruction, and downsizing. Only from experience, it seems, can one appreciate the magnitude of the human power that is released under the right circumstances. Rather than being anachronisms, these concepts have new currency in the Information Age because the release of the cognitive power upon which Information Age industries depend requires a democratic capitalist culture.

On retirement, I had a compelling curiosity to find out whether this system confirmed by my own experience and that of many others might well be the way to a world of peace and plenty. I wanted to find out whether wise people throughout history had arrived at a similar conclusion, but if they had, why the world was still full of misery and violence.

My Studies

I began my studies by reading through the 11 volumes of the *Story of Civilization* by Will and Ariel Durant.[410] I found their prodigious work invaluable because it provided a context of people, places, and times useful in truth-searching. The rest of my research was a matter of reading from my personal library and listening to educational cassettes and CDs. I regularly read over a dozen professional periodicals and a half-dozen newspapers from the far left

---

[410] Will and Ariel Durant, *The Story of Civilization* (New York: Simon & Schuster, 1954-1975).

of the political spectrum to the far right. Reading opinions from the far right and far left is an education in itself. Truth is not necessarily to be found by adding them together and dividing by two, but that is a good start.

Why is the world so full of misery and violence when an economic system is available that can eliminate both? If humans seek to be free of want, fear, and oppression, why do they not adopt the system that has demonstrated its capacity to satisfy these needs? Why do humans not use their unique rational abilities to understand this opportunity for freedoms, and then use their democratic power to put it in place? These hard questions led to the philosophers' query of whether history has a direction.

Pondering these questions led me to this overview of history: Ever since humans moved from being hunter-gatherers to being farmers and city-builders, we have demonstrated that trust and cooperation improve performance and generate the good feelings that foster social cohesion. Division of labor in a cooperative, trusting way, and present effort for future benefits, became civilized habits. Humans also found, however, that beyond the circle of rational social behavior, the violent have ever been ready to take away what human reason had produced.

Within the circle of trust and cooperation, people have knowledge of their neighbors and their circumstances; beyond the circle, relationships are dominated by a lack of knowledge that produces fear, suspicion, and frequently violence. Outside the circle of common purpose, people grab at and hold all they can get, and they build up political structures and armies to protect the wealth they have amassed and to gain more. From ancient empires, to the rise of the warrior state in the 16th century, to the world of weapons of mass destruction in which we live today, violence on a more massive scale, with more technologically sophisticated fire power, has continued to limit the growth of the circle of trust and cooperation among people trying to be free of want, fear, and oppression.

In the outside circle, the predatory bands were comfortable with the use of force, intimidation, and violence. They would regularly demonstrate quicker success, whether military or commercial, merely by taking what they wanted rather than by producing it. For this reason, defectors from the circle of trust and cooperation would occasionally join the predators in pursuit of short-term results. This defection continues because the distinction between visible short-term gain and longer-term expectation of gain requires a high-quality reasoning process as well as patience and discipline.

At the beginning of the 21st century, the revolutionary technology of the Information Age has moved us one giant step farther. Now, either the circle of economic common purpose can expand to encompass the whole world or the predators can use our new powers to commit unprecedented folly and violence. At this same time, various types of political societies—mature economies, emerging economies, democratic governments, and authoritarian regimes—have all demonstrated their ability to take advantage of the superior capacity of economic freedom to improve lives. Reason might well expect, then, that the circle of trust and cooperation would become worldwide, and that the competing circles of folly and violence would recede. It has not worked that way as yet, however; so my studies led me to dig deeper into history.

Society Advances; Predators Attack

Hammurabi (2123-2081 B.C.) was at first a successful warrior who brought order out of the incessant local warfare in lower Mesopotamia. He then drew up 285 laws and inscribed them in a public place for observance by all. When order had replaced violence, and society was based on justice under law, Hammurabi then addressed the general welfare by investing in the human and physical infrastructure. He dug canals, stored grain against famines, lent money at no interest to stimulate commerce, and prevented exploitation of the weak by the strong. Broad wealth distribution and better education improved the standard of living and stimulated momentum in all branches of knowledge, including astronomy, medicine, mathematics, physics, and philosophy.

This advanced society, in what is now mainly Iraq, lasted only a short time. Eight years after Hammurabi's death, Babylon was invaded and pillaged by the Kassites, a tribe of mountaineers from the northeast border. These predators, probably European immigrants, conquered and ruled in ethnic and political chaos for centuries.

Society had advanced quickly, but it was brought back to barbarism even more quickly.[411]

About four thousand years later, the world's largest Muslim nation, Indonesia, was attacked and left in economic and social chaos by foreign invaders. This time the weapons were hot money and currency speculation, the invaders were ideologues of the "liberalization of capital markets," but the destructive effect was the same.

In another part of the world fifteen hundred years after Hammurabi's civilization was destroyed, Confucius (552-479 B.C.), a Chinese humanist, manager, thinker, and teacher, spent his life analyzing the same question I was addressing: Why do so many live a life of misery and violence? I found Confucius's philosophy for the better organization of secular life to be consistent with the template of democratic capitalism. He included individual development in a harmonious whole, broad educational opportunities, moral discipline in the individual and within the family, civic order in the state, equal opportunity, meritocracy in the selection of leaders, broad wealth distribution, and an end to violence.

More than a century after Confucius, Aristotle (384-322 B.C.), the Greek philosopher of common sense, applied a scientific truth-seeking process to social organization. "Logic" was his term for this systemic method of seeking truth, and he used it to understand the nature of things, which he called "physics," and to understand the principles of social association, which he called "ethics." Aristotle likened the pursuit of individual virtue to learning how to play the flute because in both cases it takes practice, practice, practice.

The primary human elements that Aristotle emphasized are courage, temperance, justice, and wisdom. In each case, Aristotle urged the use of wisdom, close to the contemporary expression "street smarts," as the key to moderating the extremes and finding the workable "Golden Mean." Aristotle saw that all living things have certain common traits: nutrition, reproduction, and locomotion plus a distinguishing feature of each living being that he called its "essence." Aristotle believed that a living thing functions naturally because it

---

[411] Will Durant, *The Story of Civilization,* (vol.1) *Our Oriental Heritage* (New York: Simon & Schuster, 1954), pp. 218-222.

arises from its essence—or, as the pop song goes, "Fish gotta swim, birds gotta fly." The Aristotelian extension of that species essence is that "humans gotta reason." The record of human performance demonstrates that we humans need more practice in using our essential reason.

The Crusades opened the door to the Christian discovery of the Muslim culture, so that a larger collection of Aristotle's writings became available in Europe. Thomas Aquinas (1225-1274) undertook the daunting task of assimilating knowledge from Jewish, Greek, Muslim, and Christian philosophers whose literary works included science, medicine, humanities, philosophy, and religion. These were men of amazing intellectual range and practical accomplishment such as the Muslims, Avicenna (980-1037) and Averroës (1126-1198); and the Jewish philosopher, Maimonides (1135-1204). Avicenna (Abu ali al-Hussein ibn Sina), for example, wrote over 100 books, including medical texts that were used in Europe for the next 500 years.

For thousands of years, leaders and philosophers like Hammurabi, Confucius, Aristotle, Avicenna, Averroës, and Maimonides showed the way, but their social progress was reversed by predators who stole riches, and lands, and enslaved people. Despite these setbacks, from the human urge toward freedom came new philosophers who rediscovered the way and new leaders who rebuilt the circle of reason, trust, and cooperation. By the end of the 18th century, the acceleration of rational and technological progress was freeing the Western mind and facilitating improved industrial technology and more economic freedom, and this in turn was freeing more people from concern only with primitive needs. Was it possible that better educated, healthier people would use growing democratic power to widen the circle of reason and control the predators?

The 18th-Century Enlightenment: Freeing the Mind

The Enlightenment thinkers of Europe, the British Isles, and America were optimists who believed that history must have a rational direction, a direction that ought to move towards the human achievement of our full potential. The Enlightenment corollary to this rational hypothesis was that the means to attain the ideal could be found through a high-quality truth-seeking process.

Freedom to think, write, and act was a new and fragile thing: Galileo (1564-1642) had ended his days under house arrest; Descartes (1596-1626) was too fearful to allow publication of his best work until after his death; Bruno (1548-1600) paid the ultimate price for his insistence that the Copernican rearrangement of sun and earth was fact and not hypothesis. Even a century later, Montesquieu (1689-1755) Charles-Louis de Secondat, Baron de Montesquieu wrote cautiously of the French power structure only by putting his words of criticism in the mouths of Persian visitors. François Marie Arouet (1694-1778) came to be known as "Voltaire" during his first stay in the Bastille in 1718, when he was imprisoned for saying and writing what he thought. The struggle to free the mind in the search for truth had been a long and bloody battle over many centuries against the church-and-state power structure backed by legalized violence. In this environment, the truth-searching process and the quality of knowledge still improved, but slowly.

The Enlightenment drew on centuries of experience from many cultures all over the world. Their examination, however, was not random but of that human rationality so prized by Aristotle, now exerting its influence in a dynamic, collaborative, and cumulative truth-searching process described in the work of Francis Bacon (1561-1626), and coupled with the scientific methods of Isaac Newton (1642-1727). Adam Smith (1723-1790) interpreted the Enlightenment in terms of economics and presented his concept of a free market system that could eliminate material scarcity. Immanuel Kant (1724-1804) pointed the way forward for nations to substitute law for violence. The Marquis de Condorcet (1743-1794) summarized the direction for future human history based on the Enlightenment ideal and means (see chapter 3).

The Enlightenment also responded to John Locke's (1632-1704) challenge to find the best organization for human affairs: "God who hath given the world to men in common, hath also given them reason to make use of it to the best advantage of life and convenience."[412] Physician and philosopher, Locke was also a

---

[412] John Locke, *Concerning Civil Government: The English Philosophers from Bacon to Mill* (New York: Modern Library, 1967; first published, 1690), p. 413.

political thinker who specified that law should "have one rule for rich and poor, for the favorite at court, and the countryman at plough."[413]

Locke returned to England after the Glorious Revolution of 1688, encouraged by the promise of new constitutional freedoms, and continued his democratic advice by qualifying private property with sharing and limits: "What portion man carved to himself was easily seen, and it was useless, as well as dishonest, to carve himself too much, or to take more than he needed."[414] The father of inalienable rights for all, government by the consent of the governed, and the application of reason in the search for the better life, Locke did not leave out of his list of priorities either the broad distribution of wealth or a warning against speculators who were clipping coins and debasing the currency (see chapter 7).

Thomas Hobbes (1588-1679) had suffered through the chaos of civil wars and the Cromwellian regime. Hobbes concluded, contrary to Locke's later optimism, that humans are inherently murderous animals, and that only an all-powerful state, a *Leviathan*, could keep them in control.[415] Like Niccolò di Bernado Machiavelli (1469-1527) before him, Hobbes's bleak view of people allowed little expectation that the world might become a better place. Machiavelli, writing to impress the powerful Medici family in Florence, had proposed that "whoever organizes a state and establishes its laws must assume that all men are wicked and will act wickedly whenever they have the chance to do so."[416] Machiavelli, Hobbes, and others who believed evil to be inherent in human beings, offered a rationale for suppressing individual freedoms. Unfortunately, the Machiavellis and Hobbeses, men of little accomplishment in their own time, have been elevated in the eyes of posterity to undeserved celebratory status by those in power seeking philosophical support for exploitation of the many by the few and the continued use of violence as a means to this goal.

---

[413] *Ibid.*, p. 461.

[414] *Ibid.*, p. 423.

[415] Thomas Hobbes, *The Leviathan: The English Philosophers from Bacon to Mill* (New York: The Modern Library, 1967; first published, 1651), p. 162.

[416] Niccolò Machiavelli, *The Prince with Selections from The Discourses* (New York: Bantam Books, 2003; first published, 1513), p. 106.

Voltaire was one of the first in the West to study Confucius, and he developed great respect for the advanced Chinese culture. From his stay in England, Voltaire brought back an appreciation of English constitutional freedoms, Newton's scientific method in the examination of order in the universe, and Locke's challenge to apply reason to the organization of human affairs. As Locke had done before him, Voltaire advocated tolerance as the rational minimum on which basis social progress could be made.

The Enlightenment job of absorbing the wisdom of many cultures and ages was an impressive accomplishment, distilled from the thought of Arab, Jewish, Greek, and Chinese philosophers, as well as of European and American Christians, humanists, atheists, and deists. The Enlightenment philosophers had come to the same conclusion that I had found in the factory. Performance can be maximized when one builds up from worth and great potential of each individual functioning in harmony with the group. Individual ambition is natural to humans, but concepts of the harmonious whole seem common in the thoughts of secular humanists such as Confucius's "Reciprocity," Kant's "Categorical Imperative," or what religion calls the "Golden Rule."

By the end of the 18th century, the struggle was continuing, but humans were winning their freedoms, and the way to a world of peace and plenty was well defined.

The 18th Century Enlightenment: Freeing Society from Material Scarcity

The technology of the Industrial Revolution had raised the wealth-producing capacity of the economic system such that a properly organized society could produce more than enough for everyone. Adam Smith in *The Wealth of Nations* [417] described an economic system that could free humans of material scarcity. Smith also wisely articulated the circumstances required and the impediments to be avoided. For the first time in human history, a system was available that could eliminate material scarcity, unify

---

[417] Adam Smith, *An Inquiry into the Nature and Causes of the Wealth of Nations* (New York: Modern Library, 1937; first published, 1776).

people in economic common purpose, and purge the violence that had been associated with the battle over scarce resources. The economic system that Smith envisioned was based on the theory that a free-market economy would self-correct and reach equilibrium with minimum governmental involvement. Smith published his seminal work in 1776, the same year that Thomas Jefferson (1751-1826) and others in America wrote their *Declaration of Independence*, presenting a political philosophy and structure that complemented Smith's vision of economic freedom.

The American Founders expressed their idealism in the phrase "life, liberty, and the pursuit of happiness" for all. Jefferson, who had spent years in France, was acquainted with Smith and the Marquis de Condorcet, and he knew that these men of the Enlightenment were counting on the new American republic to lead the world to reach the ideal. Condorcet expressed this view of America:

> One nation alone escapes the two-fold influence of tyranny and superstition. From that happy land where freedom had only recently kindled the torch of genius, the mind of man released from the leading strings of its infancy, advances with firm steps toward the truth.[418]

The Enlightenment thinkers had undertaken their extraordinary examination in a Europe that had been dominated by violence and was heading for even more violence. They could see, nonetheless, that the American democratic experiment could demonstrate to the world that the ideal was attainable and that economic freedom was the means. The United States had then, as it still does now, a special opportunity with its people, resources, freedoms, and until recently, geographical isolation. With that opportunity came a continuing responsibility to confirm the ideal and refine the means for all of society.

Near the end of the eighteenth century, Condorcet summarized the work of the Enlightenment (see chapter 3) and penned a liberal manifesto that challenged society to free the mind, body, and spirit.

---

[418] Cited by Edward Goodell, *The Noble Philosopher, Condorcet and the Enlightenment* (Buffalo, New York: Prometheus Books, 1994), p. 214.

Condorcet's manifesto of *liberalism* advanced what Confucius had taught, and it included the new principles of Smith and Jefferson. Condorcet's manifesto remains as fresh in the 21st century as it was revolutionary in the 18th:

> Free trade, freedom of speech, freedom of press, the end of censorship, the end of slavery, the enfranchisement of women, universal free education, equality before the law, the separation of state and church, religious toleration, the adoption of a written constitution to insure the recognition of those rights, the establishment of a representative or parliamentary form of national government, and local self-government to encourage the independence and the participation of the peasants in government.[419]

Condorcet was a remarkable man in his range of knowledge and his experience in science and government. I marveled more, however, at his optimism for a better life for future generations which he expressed while he was in hiding and then in prison waiting to die during the Reign of Terror.

The theoretical conclusions of the Enlightenment about the human response to better circumstances received practical confirmation early in the nineteenth century through the management of a spinning mill in Scotland by Robert Owen (1771-1858). Owen invested in the quality of life of his workers and their families, and his results experimentally verified that the form of capitalism that elevates people is more profitable than mercantilist capitalism that suppresses workers' wages, benefits, and spirits to maximize owners' profits. Owen felt that he had confirmed the system that was the way to a world of peace and plenty, so he took his discovery to the Church of England, to Parliament, and to European and American leaders assembled for a conference following the Napoleonic Wars. Few leaders listened and learned; consequently, the direction of history continued to be a struggle between the rational and the predatory.

The work of the Enlightenment answered the philosophical question about human violence and misery with a potentially positive

---

[419] *Ibid.*, p. 152.

reply: Nothing *reasonable* accounts for human want, fear, or oppression; human reason argues for a natural human right to plenty, and for a right to many kinds of freedom, including freedom from fear and freedom from oppression. The American experience inspired much of the world, but the coupling of democracy and capitalism proved too difficult for many nations, such as those in South America, to accomplish in face of the opposition from their traditional establishments. The freeing of the mind before and during the 18th century had led to the economic-political system that freed some from the lack of necessities but left many still living unnecessarily in want, and most living in fear and oppression.

The question for me then changed: Why has society not followed the Enlightenment way to peace and plenty during the two centuries following? The short answer is that too few people received the quality of knowledge from their education to be applied with growing democratic power to break the cycle of violence and exploitation. The long answer took me back to the study of the 19th century.

The 19th Century: Freeing the Spirit

German Idealist G. W. F. Hegel (1770-1831) saw history's direction as one of struggle and contradiction. Progress is energized by the human urge towards freedom, and reason is employed to reach this end, but reason can be contradicted and progress opposed by countervailing predatory forces; consequently, human history is a three-steps-forward-and-two-steps-backward process.

History was stumbling along this confused direction in the middle of the 19th century when another German Idealist, Karl Marx, focused on Smith's economic system with a capacity to eliminate material scarcity. Marx identified the reason that Smith's system was functioning at only a fraction of potential: concentrated wealth. Marx then identified the solution: Change the mode of production, that is, the relationship between capital and labor in order to release the enormous productivity from involved workers. Genius lay in Marx's tying progress in the human condition to the mode of production and the associated wealth-producing capabilities. Marx therefore proposed that history's direction had been, and would be, based not on changes in culture or political structure but, rather, in movement towards a superior economic system.

Marx's historical retrospection began with the limited wealth production that existed at the time of Aristotle when the mode of production was slavery. Wealth had grown in limited ways, Marx realized, because the mode of production had changed slowly over many centuries from slavery to serfdom to the wage-slaves of his time. Marx predicted that the productive evolutionary history of the human species was positioned for a great leap forward through individual development within a harmonious whole, though he worded it differently: "The free development of each is the condition for the free development of all."[420] Marx's equivalent to "the harmonious whole" was the "elimination of alienation." Marx was convinced that his evolutionary theory of workers who thought as owners, instead of as wage-slaves, would result in greater productivity and innovation and would supercede all prior theories about how to improve the human condition. Marx's way included "plenty" from the greater wealth production, and "peace" because the spreading wealth would unite people in economic common purpose and eventually reduce the power of the warrior state and eliminate violence.

Marx's idealism was similar to John Stuart Mill's (1806-1873), for each foresaw an explosion of additional wealth coming through freeing the spirits of the workers. Mill connected the dots among profits, spirits, and a moral environment in this way:

> It is scarcely possible to rate too highly this material
> benefit, which yet is nothing compared to the moral
> revolution in society that would accompany it; a new
> sense of security and independence in the laboring
> class; and the conversion of each human being's daily
> occupation into a school of the social sympathies and
> the practical intelligence.[421]

---

[420] Karl Marx and Friedrich Engels, *The Communist Manifesto* (New York: Penguin Books, 1967; first published in London, 1848), p. 105.

[421] John Stuart Mill, *Principles of Political Economy with Some of Their Applications to Social Philosophy* (Fairfield, New Jersey: Augustus M. Kelley, 1987; first published in London, 1848), p. 789.

Mill endorsed the benefits of worker ownership (see chapter 5), proposing that profits, quality of life, and a moral environment can be synergistically combined (see chapter 3). In the middle of the 19th century, Mill's proposal was radical because the economic system had not been reformed to provide neutral money, control of the speculators, broad distribution of wealth, and emancipation of the wage-slaves, all of which Smith had specified as prerequisites for the success of free markets. In the early-21st century, Mill's proposal still seems radical because ultra-capitalism concentrates wealth in record amounts, and ultra-capitalists would continue to treat workers as wage-slaves.

Marx's discovery coupled with Smith's system refined by Mill's insights might well have ended the conflict over resources because there was potentially more than enough for everybody. The end of exploitation and violence, however, required acknowledgement by those with power and authority of this better and broader way to wealth. With the backing of government, religion, and learning, society could have followed the Enlightenment roadmap towards a new understanding of history's rational direction. Smith provided the vehicle, Marx and Mill showed how to increase the power and speed. It did not happen that way, however.

The 20th Century: The Lost Way

At the end of the 19th century, optimism prevailed for further social progress during the twentieth century. America had demonstrated the benefits of economic freedom, and the Europeans had managed to limit the number of wars and even make wars more civilized by limiting the number of civilians included in the carnage. The twentieth century, however, instead of building on this positive momentum, became the most violent century in human history. In economic maneuvers equivalent to this political and military devastation, finance capitalists managed to concentrate more wealth than ever before, while collectivists did not use growing democratic power to reform capitalism but rather used it to concentrate political power. Instead of a world uniting in economic common purpose, the nations reverted to barbarism and atrocity, including two world wars, ethnic cleansing of many peoples, the holocaust, the fire-bombing of cities, and the atomic bombs over Hiroshima and Nagasaki.

This human failure to move toward a world of peace and plenty during the twentieth century discouraged philosophers and forced many to conclude that humans were incapable of using reason to improve lives and eliminate the violence. Along with the millions of people killed by governments during the century, the ideal of a world free from want, fear, and oppression was itself a causality. In this vacuum of idealism, the world became dominated by those whose mission was to amass greater wealth, and by those comfortable with the use of violence for religious, ethnic, and nationalistic purposes.

Among the casualties in the death of idealism, for example, were two celebrity philosophers: Isaiah Berlin (1904-1998) and John Rawls (1921-2002). Both reacted to the century of record violence by declaring idealism an illusion and the Enlightenment search for truth useless. Berlin used the failure of the "single solutions" of Hitler, Stalin, and Pol Pot as evidence that no solutions of any complexity are available. Rawls, who had contributed much to the examination of a just society, gave up on the effort to apply reason to find a better organization of human affairs:

> Whether there is or ever was such an Enlightenment project (finding a philosophical secular doctrine, one founded on reason and yet comprehensive), we need not consider it, for in any case, political liberalism, as I think of it, and justice and fairness as a form thereof, has no such ambitions.[422]

Who killed idealism? Why did the great promise for society during the twentieth century turn so violent and bloody? Were Berlin and Rawls correct in abandoning idealism and the Enlightenment challenge? Let us rather, I suggest, lay the blame where it belongs: Reformers failed to realize the ideals of the Enlightenment because they failed to synthesize the means presented by Smith, Marx, and Mill, and consequently failed to modify the political structures in

---

[422] John Rawls, *Political Liberalism* (New York: Columbia University Press, 1993), p. xviii.

support of the superior economic system. Capricious leaders were still allowed to fumble their way into WWI followed by more failure of leadership that made WWII inevitable. Subsequently, other untrained leaders continued to make mistakes in power politics resulting in violence. The process was imperfect, the quality of knowledge poor, and the tragic mistakes inevitable from this failure.

The circle of people united in trust and working in cooperation continued to build wealth and good feelings, demonstrated in the improvement in the lives of hundreds of millions in America and other countries that moved away from tyranny towards economic freedom.

Economic and social progress was constrained, however, as it always had been, by those motivated by greed and comfortable with exploitation and the use of violence.

The 21ˢᵗ Century: Another Chance to Find the Way

Another new and promising opportunity for society seemed to arise in the 1990s when all could see that collectivism with its central planning and state control had failed to deliver on its social contract. With the fall of the Berlin Wall and the collapse of the international Communist movement, the contrast between collectivism and economic freedom demonstrated again that freedom, not collectivism, is the way to improve the peoples' lives. Besides this empirical evidence of what works and what does not work, other developments also put in a new light the understanding of Marx's proposed changes in the relationship of capital and labor. The Information Age added enormous productivity to the economic system that could be attained only in the democratic capitalistic culture that eliminates the alienation between labor and capital. Equally dramatic, workers in the United States became a major source of new investment capital. Class struggle between capital and labor must be at an end when the wage earners and the capitalists are one!

Reflecting these profound developments, new idealists were again proclaiming a world of economic common purpose that would lead to a world of peace and plenty for all. Francis Fukuyama, for example, gained recognition by affirming that the world was moving in the direction of liberal democracy and free markets, for, he reasoned, with the demise of Communism and the failure of collectivism, no other ideologies remained to compete.[423] Fukuyama's *End of History* thesis was contrasted, however, with Samuel Huntington's *Clash of Civilizations,* a proposal that a half-dozen major cultures would not converge but would remain fracture lines for global conflict.[424] After the events of 9-11, Fukuyma's critics reported that "history has returned from vacation."[425] Fukuyama defended his thesis, placing 9-11 in the context of fanatics in a shrinking world who had reacted to the inevitability of their young people's demand for the freedoms and comforts that they could now view on television and visit on the internet. Fukuyama expressed it this way:

> The struggle we face is not the clash of several distinct and equal cultures like the great powers of nineteenth-century Europe. The clash consists of a series of rearguard actions from societies whose traditional existence is indeed threatened by modernization. The strength of the backlash reflects the severity of this threat.[426]

Fukuyama and Huntington thus brought the historic dichotomy up-to-date: Will society adopt the rational economic system that can eliminate material scarcity, elevate spirits, and unite people in economic common purpose, or will society continue to struggle in the grip of destructive emotion and violence? Fukuyama's argument had economic and social logic on its side; Huntington's had the human history of folly and violence.

Despite favorable circumstances at the turn of the millennium, the idealists were dashed again! The impediment of concentrated wealth had grown because ultra-capitalism dominated the world's

---

[423] Francis Fukuyama, *The End of History and the Last Man* (New York: The Free Press, 1992).

[424] Samuel Huntington, *Clash of Civilizations and the Remaking of the World Order* (New York: Simon & Schuster, 1996).

[425] Francis Fukuyama, "History Is Still Going Our Way," *The Wall Street Journal,* October 5, 2001, op-ed p. 1.

[426] *Loc. cit.*

economy. The reformers still did not know how to synthesize Smith, Marx, and Mill in order to learn how to democratize capitalism. A large part of investment capital, most of it the workers' money, went into speculation rather than being directed towards the job-growth economy. Corporate surplus was not being distributed in dividends to the wage earners but was being diverted to Wall Street priorities. The bubble economy of the 1990s rewarded the few in the up direction and hurt the many in the down, as it had done before in similar economic swings many times since the beginning of the American republic.

The same corruptions of ultra-capitalism that were damaging the domestic American economy were doing even worse damage on the international scene to emerging economies. Few recognized the connection between the reversal of strong economic growth in Indonesia and the attacks of terrorists on 9-11. The connection was indirect, but after U.S.-led ultra-capitalism had destroyed the Indonesian economy (see chapter 7), social tensions and violence in this largest of Muslim nations displaced the sense of economic common purpose associated with a rising standard of living. Terrorists then found a fertile environment for the recruiting and training of more terrorists.

Optimism at the end of the nineteenth century was destroyed by WWI. Optimism at the end of the twentieth century was destroyed even more quickly on a single day, September 11, 2001. Before this atrocity, America was regarded by many as an arrogant unilateralist with a cop-of-the-world attitude. After the tragedy, some American officials ignored the history of all empires, apparently convinced that the U.S. could run the world. Others recognized that terrorism is guerrilla warfare and particularly requires multilateral U.N. action, and, further, that the only thing that can break the cycle of reciprocal atrocities is a rising standard of living worldwide.

The Crossroads in Human History

By the middle of the 19th century, the way to a world of peace and plenty had been made clear in theory, was available in principle, and was being validated in practice. Why, then was society still debating the attainability of the ideal at the beginning of a new millennium? Why, then, had the impediments to that superior form of commerce that is the basis for social progress not been removed? Why, then, were the folly and violence escalating? I have written my answer to these questions in this book, now I summarize in these few lines:

- Before the Industrial Revolution: Concentrated wealth among the elite, and violence among nations and people, dominated society because resources were in fact limited. The miserable majority found idealism primarily in the spiritual realm.

- Late-18th century: The Enlightenment in Europe, the British Isles, and America proposed the secular ideal, the means to attain it, and the process to identify both.

- Mid-19th century: Marx and Mill confirmed that Adam Smith was correct: Material scarcity could be eliminated. They proposed ways to increase wealth further and spread it broadly to eliminate the impediment of concentrated wealth.

- 20th century: Reformers chose collectivism instead of the free-market principles of Smith and the worker-ownership proposed by Marx and Mill. This choice caused the bloodiest century in human history.

- Beginning of the 21st century: A world of peace and plenty through economic freedom and economic common purpose has its best opportunity to succeed for these reasons: The Information Age requires the democratic capitalist culture; the Information Age has added multiples of productivity; the Information Age is itself a unifying influence; wage earners in America have become a major source of new capital; and the evidence of the benefits of economic freedom have been demonstrated not only in democratic but also authoritarian countries.

- Beginning of the 21st century: America should be leading the world to peace and plenty through economic freedom but is, instead, supporting ultra-capitalism that has slowed the world's economy and reversed economic momentum in many countries. The world's wealthiest nation is supporting a system that further concentrates wealth; the world's most militarily powerful nation is being trapped in reciprocal atrocities by a relatively few fanatics.

This crossroads in human history sets before us the choice whether to follow the way to peace and plenty or to take the well-troden way to more terrible folly and violence. At this intersection, I want to erect some guideposts, and so I propose the following hypotheses. They are arranged according to a sequential logic: The validation of one hypothesis is necessary before moving on to the next. Assuming that the validation has successfully proceeded from #1 through #7, then hypotheses #8 and #9 suggest movement to required action.

I find myself again in agreement with Karl Marx that only after the world is improving lives through a superior economic system will it be possible to stop the violence. Thus the ultimate success of the United Nations in substituting law for violence among nations, proposed in hypothesis #10, is predicated on the visible success of economic freedom worldwide, success that I believe will be attainable if we act according to these hypotheses.

I propose that Enlightenment II, an undertaking by teams of multi-disciplinary, multi-cultural truth-searchers in the universities, examine these hypotheses and develop a curriculum for the education of citizens and the training of leaders (see below, hypothesis #8). Institutional investors and other groups could from their own examination and by cooperation with the universities more quickly derive an action agenda to refine capitalism and restructure government (see below, hypothesis #9). A hopeful solution in these troubled times is emergence of leaders with the intellect of Jefferson, the relentless determination of Washington, and the capacity of Franklin to get things done, people of statecraft who will draw on the will, wisdom, and votes of the majority to reform America and lead the world to peace and plenty. I invite examination, challenge, debate, rejection, refinement, or validation of these hypotheses.

Hypothesis #1—The Ideal: A world of plenty is attainable on the basis of a superior economic system supported by the culture and the political structure.

Economic freedom has demonstrated the capacity to eliminate material scarcity, elevate spirits, and unite people. The satisfaction of the basic needs for food, clothing, and shelter through economic freedom is naturally coupled with improvement in health and education; this, in turn, stimulates hope for further improvement in future generations. Changes in the culture and political structure, unless directed to improve the economic system, do not improve the lives of people and frequently make them worse.

A world dominated by violence among nations and concentrated wealth does not improve lives; instead, it leaves a large part of the world living in misery, not free of want; a good part of the world living under tyranny, not free of oppression; and most of the people of the world fearful for the future. During the twentieth century, 160 million people were killed by governments, and wealth was concentrated in record amounts. This empirical evidence demonstrates that the direction of the world is under the control of those whose mission is to build and use nationalistic power, no matter how many innocent people are killed, and to concentrate wealth, no matter how badly they damage the world's economy. The most fundamental of all principles in human affairs, the worth of each individual, was obscenely violated throughout the century by the killing of so many innocent people. The obscenity was so pervasive and repetitive that many citizens were conditioned to accept it as the norm as they watched its repetition early in the 21st century.

In prioritizing the support of the economic system by the culture and political structure, we begin with affirmation of the most basic tenet that all people can reach their potential only after satisfaction of their needs for adequate food, shelter, clothing, health, and education, and that only the economic system can satisfy these needs. A superior economic system provides jobs, income, products, and services to fulfill these needs of society, and it also generates the tax revenues through which we can assist those not included in the benefits of the economic system. The economic system, further, underwrites good education and health that elevate peoples' spirits and foster an expanding sense of shared community. On the first premise, that a superior economic system ought to be sustained by the culture and the political structures, the ideal of individual development for all in a harmonious whole is attainable.

As obvious as this may seem, the world has been managed another way because leaders have repetitively given priority not to the economic system but to the culture and political structure. If the terms of this hypothesis are both obvious and ignored, then we must acknowledge the economic and social tragedies caused by failing to act according to them, and we must acknowledge that similar or worse tragedies are liable if we do not validate hypothesis #1 and act accordingly. For example, Woodrow Wilson tried to substitute fuzzy idealism for economic principles at the post-WWI conference with tragic consequences for the direction of history during the rest of the 20th century. Wilson's biographer wrote the following:

> Wilson had little time to ponder deeply on the economic causes of war, from the beginning of the peace process he had relegated economic matters to subordinate places. Wilson's first love was politics, not economics.[427]

The most powerful man at the post-WWI peace talks ignored the principles and implications of hypothesis #1 that social progress depends on movement to a superior economic system. Others at the peace talks were appalled at Wilson's ignorance. John Maynard Keynes (1883-1946) left the British team to go home and write a book on the subject.[428]

I propose that Marx's priority for the superior economic solution can be applied in retrospect as the way to have avoided

---

[427] Arthur Walworth, *Woodrow Wilson: American Prophet* (New York: W. W. Norton Company, 1979), vol. II, p. 335.

[428] John Maynard Keynes, *The Economic Consequences of the Peace Process* (New York: Harper & Row, 1971).

violent events in history. At the time of the American Revolution, as another example, British Parliamentarian Edmund Burke warned King George III that British economic interests were being sacrificed in the effort to maintain political control of the Colonies. George III did not listen.

The American Civil War killed 620,000 young Americans and added enormous economic cost to the national tragedy. Most Americans, including many Southerners, had realized that slavery was an ideological contradiction to everything that America stood for, but slavery was also an economic problem that in the course of a generation could have had an economic solution.

The Russian Bolsheviks stole the 1917 Revolution and made radical changes in the political structure that deflected attention from Marx's intended rearrangement in the relationship between labor and capital. This priority for changes in the political structure, instead of economic reform, led to decades of violence and misery!

The Social Democrats in Germany in the 1920s were poorly trained in economics and could not overcome the problems left over from the faulty peace talks of 1919, Wilson's legacy. The resulting desperate economic circumstances in Germany destroyed social cohesion and set the stage for Hitler and his reign of evil.

The argument that the bloody 20th century was the result of avoidable errors can be demonstrated both by analyzing the failures and by evidence of other leaders who gave the necessary priority to economic freedom. After WWII, the United States used its power and money to repair the ravages of war and set the world on the way to economic growth and better lives for many. The Marshall Plan was one of America's proudest moments because President Harry Truman and General George Marshall understood history and economics well enough to make the right moves. Any criticism that it was self-serving, and in time helped the U.S. economy, misses the point, for mutually beneficial results are the essence of economic common purpose.

The United States provided the money and encouragement, but free market-experts such as Ludwig Erhard, German Finance Minister and later Chancellor, made it work with an amazing 8% sustained national growth rate. The economic recovery in both Germany and Japan demonstrates what can be accomplished when the national mission is improving the lives of the people through economic freedom, not through war and geopolitics.

Each of these cases, I argue, supports hypothesis #1: When the priority is movement to the superior economic system, not changes in the culture or political structure, then the lives of the people can be improved. The ideal of plenty through economic freedom, as proposed by the Enlightenment, has never been reached because neither have conducive circumstances been put in place nor have the impediments been removed. At the head of this chapter, I cite FDR's observation: The problem is not that free enterprise has failed; the problem is that free enterprise has never yet been tried on a sustained basis.

Validation of hypothesis #1 will serve as the first building block for the improved organization in human affairs. The examination can then proceed to a definition of the superior economic system, hypothesis #2.

Hypothesis #2—The Means: The superior economic system is democratic capitalism based on economic freedom, private property, competition, neutral money, and protection from speculators. Democratic capitalism maximizes wealth because workers are motivated to produce and innovate in a trusting, cooperative environment in which they share in the surplus of improved performance. Worldwide economic growth becomes stronger because of the workers' motivation, and steadier as a result of the broader distribution of wealth.

By the latter part of the nineteenth century, economic freedom had been experimentally verified through improvement in the lives of millions of people, particularly in America. The great wealth that was produced by this system was then distributed to those whose purchases kept the economy growing and spreading through free trade. This was the free market system summarized by Adam Smith in these words:

> Little else is required to carry a state to the highest
> degree of opulence from the lowest barbarism, but
> peace, easy taxes, and a tolerable administration of

justice; all the rest being brought about by the natural course of things.[429]

The dynamic that Adam Smith proposed is an economic perpetual-motion machine. Leave it free and it will steadily reduce costs, add volume, and spread wealth around the world through free trade (see chapter 6). Economic freedom will not only eliminate material scarcity, the source of the traditional struggle, but also it will foster the harmony and trust that has been thwarted throughout human history.

Adam Smith was not an apologist for greed, as he has been frequently translated to be; he was, rather, a champion of the workers. He was an enemy of mercantilism and the concentration of wealth, and he qualified the success of his system in terms of the availability of non-volatile, patient money, and the control of speculators. Smith warned that the "prodigals and projectors," as he called them, would deflect money from the job-growth economy and waste it on speculation. In Smith's vision, strong and steady economic growth would spread wealth broadly if the wild and destructive swings in the economy were purged by directing currency and credit to the job-growth economy.

Karl Marx and John Stuart Mill were inspired by Adam Smith's description of a system that could actually eliminate material scarcity. The message that Marx and Mill got from Smith was of economic freedom that combines the productivity and innovation of involved workers, the technology of the Industrial Revolution, the motivation of private property, the monitoring influence of competition, and a government that secures ample, low-cost, non-volatile, patient money. Mill integrated all of these vital components, but Marx failed to assimilate the importance of private property and competition.

Mill studied socialism carefully and concluded that the Socialists had taken a wrong turn when they took competition and private property out of the economic equation. Subsequent history proved Mill correct, for central planning not only is inefficient but also it destroys motivation at all levels. The prospect of honest

---

[429] Smith, *op. cit.*, p. xiii.

competition is the fuel that energizes Smith's economic perpetual-motion machine, for competitors constantly raised the levels of productivity and excellence in product design, reduced the cost to produce, and improve their marketing skills.

This economic system that offers to improve the quality of life in a moral environment can be rationalized in several ways. Mechanical engineers could explain the superiority of democratic capitalism on the principle of friction and force: More friction results in less force; less friction results in more force. The parallel in human relations is this: More alienation results in poorer performance; less alienation results in better performance.

Social scientists could explain the superiority of democratic capitalism because it appeals to both sides of the human duality: individual ambition and the instinct for social cooperation. Democratic capitalism rejects the motivation of "greed is good" morality and the theory of Social Darwinism as one-dimensional and overly individualistic. The self-centered approach ignores, and in fact contradicts, the more powerful benefits resulting from combining individual ambitions with cooperative efforts.

Statisticians could verify the superiority of democratic capitalism by referring to the large database of democratic capitalist companies that have demonstrated superior long-term performance in competition with those who treat workers as a cost commodity (see chapter 4). This comparative record would be even more impressive if Business Schools presented democratic capitalism for student examination, thereby adding substantially to the pool of young managers inspired by the philosophy and trained in the protocols. Instead, democratic capitalism has had to be reinvented through trial and error by successive generations of democratic managers.

Democratic capitalism is superior to other economic systems because it is freedom based and enhances the natural characteristics of humans. The human urge is to bond together in order to be free of want, fear, and oppression. Nevertheless, humans throughout history have been forced to settle only for freedom from want in a commercial world that was run on the basis of fear and oppression. Democratic capitalism, by contrast, is based on the natural human state in that it allows everyone to be free of want, but it accomplishes this in a working culture that frees people from both fear and oppression.

The superiority of democratic capitalism can be tested and verified in many ways, but how universal can it become? Is it a "Western" phenomenon only? What political structures are required for its success? In hypothesis #3, I propose that it can be a universal system.

Hypothesis #3—The Universal Economic Solution: Democratic capitalism can be universal because it has demonstrated the capacity to raise the standard of living and improve the quality of lives under both democratic and authoritarian governments.

Economic freedom works best within a democratic structure because freedoms are complementary: Economic freedom contributes to and enhances political and social freedoms; social and political freedoms contribute to and enhance economic freedom. Economic freedom has been demonstrated to work, nonetheless, under authoritarian governments so long as the government's true mission is the welfare of the people. Economic freedom cannot work in a totalitarian structure, but in our increasingly interdependent world, people recognize the failure of totalitarian governments to improve lives; therefore, younger generations in most societies are applying long-term political pressure to move their governance towards economic freedom.

Both Adam Smith and the Marquis de Condorcet recognized that the new American republic would have the best chance for economic freedom to work because democracy and capitalism are inherently synergistic. Despite the impediments of concentrated wealth and collectivism, economic freedom in America did improve the lives of many millions, thus confirming Smith's theory and Condorcet's optimism.

In the late-twentieth century, Lee Kuan Yew demonstrated in Singapore that economic freedom can also improve lives under an authoritarian government. Singapore's transition from being a third-world to a first-world economy was used as the title of Lee's book.[430]

---

[430] Lee Kuan Yew, *From Third World to First: The Singapore Story: 1965-2000* (New York: Harper Collins, 2000).

Even more impressive was the improvement in the standard of living and quality of life in authoritarian Indonesia, the world's largest Muslim country, with a total population of over 220 million people (see chapter 7).

Authoritarian China is a work-in-progress, but it has already improved the lives of more people through the introduction of economic freedom than any other country in history has done. All of these efforts under authoritarian governments have included serious imperfections, as also do efforts at economic freedom in democratic cultures, but if the criterion of success is the improvement in the quality of millions of lives, then they succeeded.

Many believe that economic freedom should be paralleled by political liberties, such as the freedoms of the press, assembly, religion, civil rights, due process, and democratic elections. This perception that economic freedom and democratic rights go hand-in-hand is correct in the long term. Short-term, however, economic freedom is so powerful that it can work under conditions of limited political freedom; indeed, it becomes a compelling force towards greater political freedoms. This assumption is based on the belief that once the freedom genie is out of the bottle, once people are more economically comfortable and better educated, then political freedoms will follow. Some political activists give priority to political freedoms over economic freedom, but it has been demonstrated that this sequence does not work well. Many American politicians seek political gain by criticizing other country's human-rights violations, but they fail to place the complex management of change from tyranny to economic freedom in the context of a long process that must begin with economic improvement.

Jean-François Revel, a former editor of *L'Express* and winner of many European honors, proposed that "economic freedom sooner or later leads to political liberty." Revel then made this distinction:

> What is needed is less state and more government. The democratic renewal stems from nothing so much as the practical necessity of diminishing statist omnipotence and impunity while enhancing governmental

competence and responsibility—for humanity cannot persist in self-destruction.[431]

This sensitive relationship between liberty and democracy, including the dangers in rushing to democratic elections before economic momentum has been gained, has been well examined by reporter Fareed Zakaria in *The Future of Freedom*.[432] Zakaria points out that a rush toward democracy can be counterproductive unless a structure of law is in place.

The proposal that economic freedom will eventually lead to political freedoms is particularly convincing in the Information Age because the profile of the educated, independent-thinking employee is the same as the profile of the citizen who will demand political freedoms.

In the latter part of the twentieth century, the universal system of economic freedom was improving lives throughout the world. The American government, however, reversed this momentum by making mistakes that escalated the traditional impediment of concentrated wealth into destructive ultra-capitalism. Hypothesis #4 describes this impediment.

Hypothesis #4—The Impediment of Ultra-Capitalism: At the beginning of the twenty-first century, the worldwide economic system is functioning at only a fraction of its potential because of U.S.-led ultra-capitalism which combines mercantilism, that treats the worker as a cost commodity, and finance capitalism, that dominates the economy instead of supporting it.

During the last quarter of the twentieth century, the combined effect of the demise of Communism and of the demonstrated ability of economic freedom to improve lives, presented the world with an unprecedented opportunity to unite in economic common purpose. Tragically, the United States government responded to Wall Street

---

[431] Jean-François Revel, *Democracy against Itself: The Future of the Democratic Impulse* (New York: The Free Press, 1993), p. 156.

[432] Fareed Zakaria, *The Future of Freedom: Illiberal Democracy at Home and Abroad* (New York: W. W. Norton & Company, 2003).

lobbying with mistakes and bad policies that wasted this wonderful opportunity. The U.S. led the world consequently into ultra-capitalism that slowed the world's total economy, reversed the economy of many countries trying to move toward economic freedom, and provoked populist protest and new forms of violence.

These mistakes and bad policies included Nixon's floating of the dollar in the early1970s without an alternative stabilizing mechanism in the international monetary system, thus causing volatility that made the speculators more powerful than central bankers. This volatility mistake was followed by ERISA, the liquidity mistake, that took active capital used in growing companies and gave most of it to the stock market where it caused the bubble economy, little of that capital going back to the job-growth economy. During this period, finance capitalism was deregulated at the same time that market disciplines were abrogated. The suspension of market disciplines began in the late-1970s with the dramatic expansion of bank deposit insurance in multiple locations that contributed to the S&L scandal, followed in 1984 by the bailout of the Continental Illinois Bank. Short-term "hot" money, easy credit, and speculation with extraordinary leverage then combined with the pressure on the emerging economies by U.S. officials to take down cross-border capital controls. Easy credit was further expanded by "structured finance," a euphemism for new ways to avoid disclosure, fool the people, avoid regulation, and make more money on money (see chapter 9). The total effect resulted in severe economic and social damage in a number of developing nations and another boom/bust cycle in the mature economies.

The human tragedy lies in that those who control wealth have yet to recognize the system that does provide more for everybody, and could provide still more for the whole world. The financial elite still lobby policies that concentrate wealth because they presume that wealth is finite and must be battled over. Human tragedy lies also in the failure of those whose mission it is to improve the human condition but who have yet to reform the prevalent system in a way that would improve the human condition. For these reasons, Adam Smith's vision of eliminating material scarcity has not been realized. For these reasons, Marx's and Mill's visions of improving the world by releasing the latent power of motivated workers has not been realized. For these reasons, the broad wealth distribution anticipated by Smith, Marx, and Mill, upon which free trade depends, has not been realized.

I find it paradoxical and tragic that the country with the greatest record of improving lives through economic freedom was, at the turn of the millennium, leading in the wrong direction and becoming known as an economic imperialist with a cop-of-the-world attitude. The traditional weakness of capitalism, concentrated wealth, was escalating to new record levels under ultra-capitalism. The worldwide benefits of free trade could not be realized in emerging economies because that same concentration of wealth was limiting the spendable income that free trade depends upon. Sadly, the reality of "globalization"—with its potential to bring material comforts, education, and improved health to the world's people—was corrupted to such an extent that the word "globalization" became, instead, a rallying cry for populist protest.

The superficial success of the U. S. economy in the latter part of the twentieth century resulted in many bragging about the "American Model." Others saw more clearly that unchecked individual greed was taking America down a dangerous path. In 1993, Michel Albert, a French executive, captured this threat in *Capitalism vs. Capitalism* and warned in his subtitle: *How America's Obsession with Individual Achievement and Short-Team Profits, Has Led It to the Brink of Collapse.*[433] Albert was prescient in his examination, but it took another eight years for the damage to become public and blatant.

During this time, I watched with concern the exploitation of South American countries and Mexico by U.S.-sponsored ultra-capitalists who put forward the theory of "free capital roaming the world seeking its most efficient investment." The reality was short-term and speculative capital, protected by the U.S. government, searching the world for quick profits. For centuries, strong countries had exploited weaker countries, but this time it seemed to be different.

---

[433] Michel Albert, *Capitalism vs. Capitalism: How America's Obsession with Individual Achievement and Short-term Profits Has Led to the Brink of Collapse* (New York: Four Walls Eight Windows, 1993).

People in these emerging economies were beginning to earn a better life, when, suddenly, it was snatched away.

My concern changed to shock when Southeast Asian countries were devastated in 1998. The ideal of economic common purpose gradually improving lives and purging the violence, went right down the drain in several countries, most notably Indonesia, a showcase of the benefits of economic freedom. Suddenly, their economy was destroyed by a lack of control of hot money and by speculators driving the Indonesian currency down by as much as 70% of its earlier value. No country, and few businesses in the country, could absorb an economic shock of this magnitude. The fragile political structure went down with the currency, jobs, and wages. Inevitably, ethnic and religious tensions surfaced and provoked violence. The IMF, dominated by the United States, then made matters worse with bankers' policies that slowed growth even further. The myopia of U. S. Treasury officials and the IMF was so great that they found ways to blame the victims, even while opening up new markets for Wall Street firms (see chapter 7).

I almost cried! The world was so close in the early 1990s to building irreversible momentum towards peace and plenty, then to have the momentum reversed in a way that was quick, ugly, and unnecessary. Economic exploitation is not admirable, but it is at least understandable. The 1998 reversal of economic and social momentum, however, was not old-fashioned imperialist exploitation but, rather, mistakes in government policies in response to Wall Street lobbying.

The events in Southeast Asia were too remote and complicated to arouse popular concern in America, particularly since most of the popular press did not grasp the meaning of these events as opportunities to inform citizens about the corruptions of ultra-capitalism. Instead, they turned the economic disaster in Indonesia into a political event, much easier to describe than are complicated economic realities. Suharto, president for 32 years at that time, was an easier target than were the speculators and hot money bankers. Suharto's positive record in having reduced the percentage of his people under the poverty line from 40% to 10% was rarely mentioned.

The economic collapse was accompanied by a moral collapse in commerce: In 2003, an executive doing business in Indonesia reported that whereas "he never had to bribe local officials during the Suharto days, [he] now pays off scores of them."[434] Suharto had greedy kids and allowed "crony capitalism," but his civic order controlled broad-scale bribery along with everything else.

In my studies, I learned that society has been warned throughout history about the harm to economic growth and social cohesion from concentrated wealth. Confucius understood the necessity for diffused economic power two and one-half millennia ago:

> The centralization of wealth is the way to scatter the people, and letting it be scattered among them is the way to collect the people. They produce wealth, but do not keep it for their own gratification. Disliking idleness, they labor but not alone with a view to their own advantage. In this way, selfish schemes are repressed and find no way to arise; robbers, filchers, and rebellious traitors do not exist.[435]

The 18th-century European Enlightenment added their wisdom to that of Confucius. Claude Adrien Helvétius (1715-1771), a wealthy man, wrote with special authority on the persistent impediment of concentrated wealth and its negative effect on social cohesion:

> The almost universal unhappiness of men and nations arises from the imperfections of their laws, and the too unequal partition of their riches. There are in most kingdoms only two classes of citizens, one of which wants necessaries, while the other riots in superfluities. If the corruption of the people in power is never more manifest than in the ages of the greatest

---

[434] Richard Borsuk, "In Indonesia, a New Twist of Spreading the Wealth," *The Wall Street Journal*, January 29, 2003, p. A16.

[435] Cited in Durant, *op. cit.*, vol. I, p. 673-4.

luxury, it is because in those ages the riches of a nation are collected into the smallest number of hands.[436]

Benjamin Franklin (1706-1790), that Enlightenment man of America, actually proposed legal limits to concentrated wealth:

> That an enormous Proportion of Property vested in a few Individuals is dangerous to the Rights, and destructive of the Common Happiness, of Mankind; and therefore every free State hath a Right by its Laws to discourage the Possession of such Property.[437]

Condorcet denounced special privileges from the government to the few as the root cause of the concentration of wealth:

> Wealth has a natural tendency to equality if the administration of the country did not afford some men ways of making their fortune that were closed to other citizens.[438] We shall reveal other methods of ensuring equality, either by seeing that credit is no longer the exclusive privilege of great wealth or by making industrial progress and commercial activity more independent of the existence of great capitalists.[439]

Condorcet correctly identified non-democratic privileges lobbied by, and given to, the few as the source of concentrated wealth, but his vision of broad wealth distribution was only a utopian ideal in the eighteenth At the beginning of the twenty-first century, however, the U.S. economy had begun to fulfill Condorcet's prophecy: Wage earners had supplanted the "great capitalists" as a source of investment money. Unfortunately, this watershed event has yet to

---

[436] Cited in Durant, *op. cit.*, vol. IX, *The Age of Voltaire*, 1965, pp. 688, 689.

[437] Edmund S. Morgan, *Benjamin Franklin* (New Haven, Connecticut: Yale University Press, 2002), pp. 307-308.

[438] Cited by Goodell, *op. cit.*, p. 231.

[439] *Ibid.*, p. 233.

change the pattern of government privileges for the few to make more money on money. While the source of capital has been democratized, the rewards from capitalism have not yet been democratized.

By 2001, ultra-capitalism began to unravel in America in a spectacular fashion as big company after big company failed when their corruption was exposed. This public failure of ultra-capitalism, the drop in the stock market, and the sight of corrupt CEOs being led away in handcuffs, all became media and political events. Many of the politicians in Congress who rushed to reform capitalism had been the same politicians who earlier had been responsible for passing the laws that gave ultra-capitalists the privileges that caused these problems in the first place (see chapter 9). CEOs had become easy targets, but it was the government structure itself that provided Wall Street such power to reward and punish CEOs based on how thoroughly they adopted ultra-capitalism or not. For every corrupt CEO, hundreds more were forced victims of ultra-capitalism (see chapter 8).

The fundamental conflict between finance capitalism and democratic capitalism in America goes back to the beginning of the republic when non-democratic privileges to make money on money flowed from many government officials who could be influenced or bribed. Since then, the neutral money needed for free markets to work well has been displaced by easy credit for speculators, and wild swings in the economy have been the result. Removal of this impediment is the intent of hypothesis #5.

Hypothesis #5—The Bad Banking Impediment: From the beginning, the banking system in the United States has limited the capacity of economic freedom to spread wealth and improve lives. Under ultra-capitalism, this impediment has escalated to a force that threatens the world's economy.

Commercial banks have a simple mission: make high-quality loans in support of the job-growth economy. Government policies, instead, now allow banks at various times and in various ways to provide easy credit to fund excessively speculative and high-risk ventures, to trade in futures, to slow growth during a credit crunch, and to hide total debt through structured finance and securitization.

Government policies then insure, subsidize, and bail out the banks, assuring a continuation of bad loans. In a down market, bank policies then deprive credit-worthy businesses of critical funds because the bankers are trying to fix their loan reserve ratios that they screwed up with their bad loans.

Adam Smith predicted that free markets would spread wealth and improve lives through "the natural course of events" and the "invisible hand," if money were low-cost, ample, non-volatile, and patient. Smith warned particularly that the system could be compromised by the "prodigals and projectors" who would deflect money from the job-growth economy, waste it, and destroy free-market benefits.

In this hypothesis, I affirm that the U.S. government has failed to protect the system from the "prodigals and projectors"; it has, rather, encouraged, funded, insured, subsidized, and bailed them out. Extreme examples of this corruption of free-market principles include LTCM (see chapter 7) and Enron (see chapter 9), but many other cases could be cited. This contradiction of Smith's free-market philosophy has slowed economic and social progress for two centuries, and the privileges and corruptions have now escalated to a level that deprives the world's economy of its best opportunity. The global economy cannot function if the speculators on borrowed money have more power than do central bankers, a power that the speculators demonstrated many times during the last quarter of the twentieth century. Leveraged speculation would be purged from the system in a heartbeat *if citizens understood the corruption.* The way to a world of peace and plenty lies before us, but we cannot follow it until the economic system implements a 21st-century version of the free-market principles proclaimed by Adam Smith and refined by Marx and Mill so long ago.

While Adam Smith and the classical economists believed that the free markets could do most of the job without assistance, that belief was qualified by the expectation that government exercise its responsibility to assure that money remain a neutral medium of exchange, and that capital for investment be patient. The government can fulfill this responsibility either through free banking that is monitored by market disciplines or through government regulation.

The banking system in the United States is the worst of both possible worlds because it has deregulated at the same time that it was suspending the disciplines that free markets depend upon. The result is a banking system that privatizes the profits for the few and nationalizes the losses to the taxpayer. Instead of allowing the market to seek equilibrium, the U.S. government's policies cause large swings in the economy that are economically and socially damaging.

Since the beginning of the American government, the politicians have experimented with national banks, State banks, private banks, and the present system of half-public/half-private banking. None of these efforts has succeeded in serving the general welfare.

The present banking system in the United States has limited the power of economic freedom to improve lives because it has been cobbled together in pieces, and designed under the influence of Wall Street lobbyists whose mission is to make money on money. No integrated banking policy; no long-term government plan for currency and credit control; and no thoroughly articulated responsibility for fiscal, monetary, and regulatory practice is in place. What does exist is spread among so many governmental agencies that the overlap, confusion, and turf squabbles cause a policy vacuum that is filled by Wall Street lobbying. This approach has limited growth, concentrated wealth for the privileged, slowed the world's economy, and prevented improvement in the lives of billions of people.

The more recent policies lobbied by the special interests of ultra-capitalism generated the excessive liquidity that funded the bubble economy, lately popped. From one extreme to the other, the policies then switch to a credit crunch just when the economy needs stimulation to regain momentum. Similar policies have been applied around the world by the U.S. dominated IMF with the same boom/bust economic damage, over-funding in the up direction, under-funding in the down.

Adam Smith's qualification that free markets function only when capital is not deflected to the speculators, has not only been ignored by the American government but has been denied at the highest level. When Chairman Greenspan famously described the "excessive exuberance" in the stock market in the mid-1990s, he not only did not reduce the percentage of money that could be borrowed

for speculative purposes but also he advised Congress that no
relationship exists between the money available for speculation and
the rise in the stock market (see chapter7). In a later speech,
Greenspan reviewed the 1990s bubble economy and concluded that if
high interest could not prick the bubble, then the Fed had no other
tools to do the job. In other words, Greenspan was acknowledging the
government's powerlessness to prevent the boom-and-bust pattern
that has caused such enormous social damage over the past two
centuries. Greenspan commented:

> If low-cost, incremental policy tightening appears
> incapable of deflating bubbles, do other options exist
> that can at least effectively limit the size of bubbles
> without doing substantial damage in the process? To
> date, we have not been able to identify such policies.[440]

This view is not only unacceptable and dangerous but also
incorrect. Many options are available to a government willing to
follow its Constitutional mandate to control currency and credit for
the general welfare, and these options await only an aroused citizenry
that will demand their implementation. This, however, is the same
chairman that helped repeal the Glass-Steagall Act and helped prevent
regulation of derivatives, and, oversight of hedge funds like LTCM
and Enron. This type of powerful support from top government
officials has led to a fundamental error in government economic
policy, namely the deregulation of finance capitalism, with a claim
that unregulated finance capitalism constitutes the "free market." This
wrong turn was taken at the same time that the market disciplines that
could have kept the market free were being suspended.

Many tools are available to prevent the boom/bust cycle. For
example, if bank examiners can come in after the bubble has burst and
make matters worse by tightening credit, then why can they not come
in earlier and raise reserves, limit the availability, and raise the cost of
money for speculation that causes asset inflation in the stock market

---

[440] Alan Greenspan, speech, August 30, 2002, Jackson Hole, Wyoming, quoted by
David Malpass, "The Fed's Moment of Weakness," *The Wall Street Journal*,
September 25, 2002, p. A14.

and real estate in the first place? Reserves must be increased when the stock market rises beyond improvement in corporate earnings, and reserves must be increased when real-estate values grow at a rate faster than inflation. Following this protocol will require determined democratic support because reserves are increased only by a reduction of profits, which affects the price of the bank's stock and the value of bankers' stock options.

Whether the problem is the over-funding of Enron or Southeast Asian countries, another control tool is the reintroduction of the debt-to-equity ratio discipline. The relationship of short-term hot money and other debt to long–term patient capital, whether in a company or a country, must be subject to regulation. When hot money becomes disproportionate to long-term equity, the risk goes up; therefore, the availability of money should go down, and the cost of money should go up. An accurate debt/equity comparison, however, depends on full disclosure of all off-balance-sheet debt, but disclosure has been so corrupted under ultra-capitalism that both the lenders' and borrowers' balance sheets are works of fiction. International bankers chasing profits through hot money need to be disciplined simply by requiring that a portion of their money invested in emerging economies be in the form of long-term debt or equity, or, in a crisis, a requirement that hot money be cooled by automatic conversion to long-term debt or equity.

The mission of commercial bankers ought to be to make good loans to help the economy grow. Ultra-capitalist bankers, however, are motivated and rewarded based on deal-making, short-term earnings, and stock options that are incongruent with the mission of making good loans. Bankers' compensation over a period of years should be penalized by write-offs for bad debts. The all-important sensitivity to making good loans will come back only after the insurance, subsidies, and bailouts are eliminated. Deposit insurance, for example, must be returned to the original intention of protecting the small depositor in a single banking location.

William Isaac, former chair of the FDIC (Federal Deposit Insurance Corporation), warned about the potential damage to the economy from the "too big to fail" policy (see chapter 7). He pointed out that bankers would be convinced by a bailout that they could make stupid loans for short-term gain and be protected from punishment. Fed Chairman Volcker ignored Isaac's warning in 1984 and bailed out the Continental Illinois Bank. In 1991, the Bank of New England, the third largest bank-holding company in the Northeast, failed. The FDIC, under new leadership, then demonstrated how far it had gone in protecting bad loans by paying off not only the insured deposits, the limit of which had been raised from $40,000 to $100,000 in the 1982 S&L bailout law, but also *all depositors*. As the abrogation of market disciplines became steadily worse, so also did the quality of bankers' loans.

How could this Constitutional contradiction persist while democratic power was growing in a country "of the people, by the people, and for the people?" The answer to this question is that the people's elected representatives have not been reflecting the will and wisdom of the people; instead, the politicians have been influenced by the lobby power of Wall Street and the banking interests. Liberal Democrats have also ignored the will and wisdom of the majority, and instead of reforming ultra-capitalism, they have concentrated political power to micromanage commerce and redistribute wealth. Hypothesis #6 is about the resulting political gridlock that impedes appropriate reforms.

Hypothesis #6—Gridlock: America is in an intellectual and political gridlock between those who support ultra-capitalism and those who are trying to use government to redistribute wealth. This gridlock prevents urgently needed reform of monetary, fiscal, and regulatory policies.

Since the beginning of the American republic, the financial oligarchy has held both economic and political power. During the twentieth century, the Liberal Democrats (collectivists) challenged this concentration of wealth and influence with growing democratic power promoting a poorly designed agenda to help people through a more equitable distribution of wealth. In this process, the American collectivists raised the percentage of the nation's annual production (GDP) taken in all taxes during the century from 3% to over 30%. They did not, however, reform the economic system, they did not prevent ultra-capitalism from dominating, and they wasted much of the money.

In addition to the impediments from ultra-capitalism described in hypotheses #4 and #5, the free market has been impeded, then, both by "liberal" collectivists and by "conservative" ultra-capitalists. Ultra-capitalism impedes the building of wealth by concentrating it; collectivism impedes the building of wealth in these three ways: Central planning is inefficient; neither the workers nor the recipients of government assistance are motivated; and taxes take wealth from investment in economic growth and waste it in poorly designed government programs. Finance capitalists and the new breed of ultra-capitalists are good at lobbying privileges to make more money on money, whereas the collectivists, pursuing noble goals but limited in their grasp of economics, have not been effective at achieving what they hoped to achieve.

The Liberal Democrats failed to examine and validate hypothesis #1, that social progress depends on movement to a superior economic system; as a consequence, they failed to reform capitalism; instead, they moved towards a collectivist imitation of Socialism and state solutions. The failure of Communism and Socialism, in contrast to the evident success of free markets, has left the collectivists without an agenda, whereas the financial capitalists have the feeling that they have won both more political influence as well as the intellectual argument. The polarized extremes sustain support of their followers by attacking the errors of their opposite, meanwhile leaving true reform unaccomplished in the resulting vacuum.

The present gridlock is a philosophical and political impasse between those who believe, on the one hand, in Social Darwinism and the prerogatives of the rich and powerful to govern the confused masses, and, on the other hand, well-meaning collectivists whose mission is to pass laws to help people and muzzle what they consider to be the animal instincts of generic capitalists. The middle class and the general welfare are ignored in this gridlock between the well-focused supporters of ultra-capitalism, mainly Republicans, and the poorly focused collectivists, mainly Democrats.

This gridlock goes back to the beginning of the Republic when Alexander Hamilton (1757-1804), the first Secretary of the Treasury, won the battle with Thomas Jefferson, the first Secretary of State, over the type of government that the nation was to have. Believing that the elite would know how to govern the masses better than the people could govern themselves, Hamilton favored a strong central government with privileges for the financial establishment.

Jefferson, James Madison (1751-1836), and other Founders had crafted a structure of governance that would give democratic power to many, protect minorities from the tyranny of the majority, and diffuse political power among the legislative, executive, and judicial branches of government. Jefferson's governmental structure was intended to diffuse both political and economic power, whereas Hamilton's structure was intended to concentrate both. Although Jefferson's design for government was a huge leap forward in the human quest for freedom, his political structure, nevertheless, did not prevent the accumulation of non-democratic special privileges for finance capitalists, and his skill as an economic theorist fell behind his capacities as a political thinker. Because Jefferson was weak where Hamilton was strong, Hamilton carried the day on the financial front with President George Washington (1732-1799), whose extraordinary abilities and leadership, like Jefferson's, did not include depth in economics and finance.

The core of the debate between Jefferson and Hamilton is their respective perceptions of ordinary people: Hamilton did not trust them to govern themselves, whereas Jefferson did. That is not to say that Jefferson was unaware of the dangers of mob rule, and that is why the government was structured with protection for minorities. Neither did Jefferson believe that the people would necessarily get it right the first time, but he did believe that with universal education, and with leadership by those he called the "aristocracy of talent and virtue," the people would get it right in the long run. This belief in the extraordinary potential of people, given the proper circumstances, is one that I share with a passion. It is also the humanistic core of the democratic capitalist philosophy.

Despite Jefferson's and Madison's intentions, the Hamiltonian financial establishment ever since has dominated the U.S. government's fiscal and monetary policies, with the result that wealth has been, and continues to be, concentrated. Presidents Jefferson, Madison, Jackson, Lincoln, Johnson, Theodore Roosevelt, Wilson, and Franklin D. Roosevelt all made proclamations about getting control of the "money changers," and they all failed (see chapter 7).

They failed sometimes because their need to finance a war deflected their reforms, often because they and their advisors lacked financial sophistication adequate to reform the large inventory of special privileges lobbied by finance capitalists, and almost always because the peoples'elected representatives in Congress were well treated by Wall Street. Special privileges were the result of "crony capitalism," American style, according to which some finance capitalists lobbied public figures outright and others served their time in senior government positions before, during, and after which they could directly determine legislation and policies that resulted in a constant flow of special privileges. It has been that way for over 200 years, and it is still that way. Congress, the Executive Branch, the Supreme Court, State legislatures, and the federal and state court systems have all promoted, passed, and interpreted laws that concentrate wealth. In the early 19th century, laws upheld by local judges included jail time for labor organizers and strikers.

Aristotle long ago warned of governments controlled by the extremes of the rich and the poor. He proposed, instead, that the middle class was best qualified to structure government for the general welfare. Aristotle's theory has been confirmed many times, but the middle class in the United States is now underrepresented, over-taxed, and overwhelmed by the lobby power of special interests. The paradox is that the group with the greatest voting power has the least political influence; the shame is that they are neither doing sufficient homework on these critical problems nor using their democratic power for reform.

Friedrich Hayek, who shared the 1974 Nobel Prize in Economics and was the recipient of the 1991 American Medal of Freedom, was both a market fundamentalist and a liberal in the original sense of the word. A twentieth-century idealist in the tradition of the Enlightenment, Hayek had a clear view of this double impediment to social progress: concentrated wealth of the conservatives and concentrated political power of the collectivists. His book, *The Road to Serfdom* (1946), had shocked many in the intellectual community who were, at that time, convinced that the wave of the future, the inevitable replacement for capitalism, was collectivism. Hayek, to the contrary, advocated the benefits of free

markets and pointed out that collectivism led to totalitarian
government and loss of freedoms.

He described the collectivist and conservative extremes that
polarized and gridlocked the political process—then as now—as
follows:

> *Socialists* increasingly recognized the incurable economic
> inefficiency of central planning; *collectivists* then simply
> discovered that redistribution through taxation and aimed
> financial benefits was an easier and quicker method of
> achieving their aims.[441]

> *Conservatism,* though a necessary element in any stable
> society, is not a social program; in its paternalistic,
> nationalistic, and power-adoring tendencies, it is often closer
> to socialism than true liberalism, and with its traditionalistic,
> anti-intellectual, and often mystical propensities it will never,
> except in short periods of disillusionment, appeal to the young
> and all those others who believe that some changes are
> desirable if this world is to become a better place.[442]

Although Hayek is often celebrated as a conservative
economist, he understood the pathologies of both *collectivism* and
conservatism, and he pointed the way to the system that combines the
freedoms of the original liberal philosophy with the economic
capabilities of free markets, conditioned by a finance capitalism that
is subordinate to the commercial process, and money that is neutral.
Hayek added:

> A conservative movement, by its very nature, is bound
> to be a defender of established privilege and to lean on
> the power of government for the protection of
> privilege. The essence of the liberal position, however,
> is the denial of all privilege, if privilege is understood

---

[441] F. A. Hayek, *New Studies in Philosophy, Politics, Economics, and the History of
Ideas* (Chicago: University of Chicago Press, 1974), p. 300.

[442] Hayek, *The Road to Serfdom, op. cit.*, preface to the 1956 edition, p. xxxvi.

in its proper and original meaning of the state granting
and protecting rights to some which are not available
on equal terms to others.[443]

Guru of conservative economics to both the American
President, Ronald Reagan, and to Great Britain's Prime Minister,
Margaret Thatcher, Hayek nevertheless qualified the effective
coupling of the free-market economic system with the liberal mission
of improving lives. Hayek repeated Adam Smith's advice that money
must be neutral, that is, without influence on the process.
Unfortunately, as the triumph of ultra-capitalism demonstrates, both
the conservatives and collectivists ignored that part of the economic
principles of both Hayek and Smith.

Seeking the system that combines the best of the political left
and the right is confused even by the terms: *Collectivists* have stolen
the good word *liberal* for their purposes, even though most of their
programs are not based on individual freedom. *Conservatives* and
market fundamentalists have stolen the good phrase *free markets*, for
they pretend to free the world's capital markets while they, at the
same time, contradict economic freedom through their reliance on
federal insurance, subsidies, and bailouts. The suspension of market
disciplines is also confused by being termed a *moral hazard,* a
deliberately vague expression.

Resolution of this gridlock between ultra-capitalists, the so-
called "market fundamentalists," and the collectivists, the so-called
"liberals," will determine the direction of history in the twenty-first
century. Shall Americans take further strides in history's greatest
democratic experiment and learn how to democratize capitalism, or
shall we drift towards economic collapse and more violence? If we
are going to be able to take the path to progress, then our venturing
forth awaits an epiphany by *collectivists* in which they discover that
their mission of improving the human condition is best accomplished
through the material and spiritual benefits of democratic capitalism.
The conservatives and market fundamentalists also await an epiphany
to discover that the best way to maximize profits is through
democratic capitalism, holding finance capitalism subordinate.

---

[443] *Loc. cit.*

A bridge between the collectivists and conservatives will not be built on political theory; it will be built by collaborators who examine and validate hypothesis #1, that is, by people who accept Marx's axiom that social progress depends on movement to a superior economic system. Once this intellectual hurdle is passed, the examination can proceed to hypothesis #2, identification of the superior economic system in our time, and agreement that this system can eliminate material scarcity. The collaboration must continue with examination of the original social ethic of *liberalism*, in which progress is made toward full human potential by encouraging individual development in an environment of trust and cooperation. This liberalism was the philosophy of the eighteenth-century Enlightenment that informed both Adam Smith's economic system and the political wisdom of the American Founders. Although impeded, this economic-political-social-philosophical system has demonstrated in practice over two centuries that it is the means to improve lives around the world.

If the truth-seeking process is of high quality, then the collaboration between the political left and political right that leads to social progress should not be difficult because most components of *liberalism* are common to both sides, and they include the following elements:

- Integrity
- Economic freedom
- Political freedom
- Religious freedom
- Freedom of expression
- Freedom of assembly
- Individual responsibility
- Rule of law
- Tolerance
- Representative government
- Cost efficiency in government
- Equal opportunity
- No non-democratic privileges
- Diffusion of economic power

- Diffusion of political power
- Universal education
- Due process

This examination of the political gridlock raises yet more troubling questions: Why have reformers failed who had the democratic power to restructure government for the general welfare? Why has this failure gone on for so long? Why is this failure so profound that many have lost hope in the democratic process? The answer is that whereas the Enlightenment grounded the ideal and the means on the proper truth-seeking process, successive generations of thinkers and managers have failed because they abandoned the *process* that is the focus of hypothesis #7.

Hypothesis #7—The Process: The ideal of a world of peace and plenty achieved through the means of democratic capitalism has not been reached because of failure in the truth-seeking process.

The inability of reformers to connect social progress with the superior economic system led me to an analysis of truth-seeking. If the economic system that could eliminate material scarcity, elevate spirits, and unify people had been so well defined by Smith, Jefferson, Condorcet, and others, and if the key impediment of concentrated wealth had further been identified and resolved in theory by Marx and Mill, why does the bottom one-third of the people of the world still live in misery. Why is so much of the world still so violent? Why have so many brilliant philosophers abandoned idealism when the opportunities seem so great? I have concluded that the reason is an egregious, persistent failure in the truth-seeking process. This failure itself seemed inexplicable because the process had been tested by the Enlightenment and has been available for use for 200 years. The culture, particularly the universities, I concluded either have not done their job or did it poorly.

Thousands of idealists for thousands of years have grappled with the question of how to seek knowledge to improve the human condition. In my studies, I found that coupling the philosophy and protocols of Aristotle and Francis Bacon provides the best process for that mission. Aristotle used his training as a biologist to determine the

469

growth potential of all living things, and then he addressed the conducive circumstances required and the impediments to be removed. This seems to me to be a straightforward way to find what the fullest growth potential of the human species might be. Aristotle's process seems familiar because it is how most managers seek excellence: "What's the best we can do if we do everything right? Which tools do we need to do it? What obstructions do we need to get out of the way?"

Most of the Enlightenment thinkers were inspired by the work of Francis Bacon who was Lord Chancellor of England before being driven out of office by his political enemies. He then dedicated his life to examining the correct process to ascertain truth. One of the stars of the French Enlightenment, Jean Le Rone d'Alembert (1717-1783), praised Bacon in these words: "At the head of these illustrious personages should be placed the immortal Chancellor of England, Francis Bacon, whose works, so justly esteemed, deserve our study even more than our praise."[444]

Bacon was convinced that the curriculum in the universities neither equipped students for leadership in business or government nor did it teach them to think clearly. Bacon attacked the resulting superficiality in the thought process:

> The primary notions of things, which the mind readily and passively imbibes, stores up and accumulates, are false, confused, and over-hastily abstracted from the facts. Whence it follows that the entire fabric of human reason, which we employ in the inquisition of nature, is badly put together and built up like some magnificent structure without any foundation.[445]

Bacon had to attack the Aristotelian curriculum of his time as it was being interpreted by 17th century Scholastics, and he did this in part by calling for a return to a more authentically Aristotelian investigation of things in the search for their essences, study of their

---

[444] Cited by Durant, *op. cit.*, vol. IX, p. 637.

[445] Francis Bacon, *The Great Instauration: The English Philosophers from Bacon to Mill* (New York: Modern Library, Random House, 1939) p. 5.

growth potential, discovery of the favorable circumstances required, and identification of impediments to be removed.

Bacon espoused learning from experience, testing the resulting generalizations, and then moving onto higher levels of generalization in a process that is *dynamic, collaborative, and cumulative:*

- The process is *dynamic* because it is a reiterative process that is modified by improved knowledge and experimental verification assimilated through a feed-back system.

- The process is *collaborative* because multicultural and multi-disciplinary participation neutralizes narrow cultural conditioning.

- The process is *cumulative* because it is based on adding verified blocks of knowledge to the structure of understanding upon which to lay new, further blocks of knowledge.

Drawing upon Aristotelian examination and Baconian process, the 18th-century Enlightenment made available to successive generations as their legacy an attainable *ideal*, a workable *means*, and the *process* to identify both.

In the latter part of the 19th century, despite availability and clarity, the culture and the political community failed to follow the path because they failed to follow the process. Instead of reforming the economic system as the way forward, ideologues and politicos took a wrong turn: Contradicting hypothesis #1, they tried to reform society by changing the political structure. This process failure resulted in the misdirection of reform energies into political structure rather than into greater wealth creation and broader wealth distribution. The terrible result of this process failure was a twentieth century in which millions of innocents were killed and hundreds of millions lived in misery. By the end of that century, the leaders of culture and the elected politicians, instead of viewing the damage and correcting the errors, were continuing to make the same mistakes with the same threatening economic and social consequences.

Mistakes by American leaders during the 20th century violated Bacon's process because the truth-seeking was inadequately dynamic, collaborative, and cumulative. Among the examples of these process errors that contributed to the folly and violence, one may include President Wilson's fuzzy idealism and disinterest in economics that contributed to the flawed peace talks in 1919, and the failure to get American participation in the League of Nations; President Hoover's three egregious errors that exported the stock market correction into the Great Depression (see chapter 7); and the misreading of the nationalistic motives of Ho Chi Minh and Vietnamese leaders that caused the war in that country. In the last quarter of the 20th century, successive Presidents made mistakes in economic principles that caused excessive volatility and liquidity; these, combined with deregulation and the suspension of market disciplines, launched ultra-capitalism on an unsuspecting world. Both the ideologues of the "liberalization of capital markets" and the proponents of a worldwide manifest destiny for America in which we unilaterally determine which governments should survive, violate Bacon's process in every respect. They are not sufficiently reiterative; they fail badly on the diversity of disciplines and cultures and they are not cumulative in their assimilation of historical evidence.

The *process* failure in all of these examples manifested the usual errors of imperial-minded formalists applying old answers to old questions, for the process has been secretive and static instead of dynamic and reiterative. The process has been authoritarian and punitive rather than collegial and collaborative, for it lacked representation by various disciplines and the multiple perspectives of different cultures. The process perpetuated ideological concerns even after the evidence of error became obvious. Finally, no unifying intelligence collected and codified their knowledge which would have added validated building blocks to the edifice for the organization of human affairs.

At the turn of the millennium, the world was making the same mistakes it had made a century before. Not only were our leaders failing to seize the opportunity to unite in economic common purpose but also they were going backwards economically and backwards to new forms of violence. The sad record of the 20th century validates hypothesis #7, that global social progress has been retarded by persistent and egregious mistakes that should have been avoided by the correct truth-seeking process. The common denominators in all of these errors were ignorance and arrogance in the otherwise bright minds of sincere people who nevertheless lacked understanding of economics, the management of change, and the structure needed before freedoms can become functional. Among the first agents of change to employ the correct truth-seeking process in order to reconfirm the ideal and specify the means ought to be the universities; this is hypothesis #8.

Hypothesis #8—Agents of Change: American culture, led by the universities, must train leaders and educate citizens in the functional requirements of economic freedom. Citizens with this knowledge can develop an agenda for structural reform of both industry and government.

The world is whirling in a vicious cycle: The failure to follow an efficacious truth-seeking process to harness knowledge for human betterment has resulted in grievous mistakes by nations' leaders, causing enormous economic and social damage and bloodshed, in turn causing many intellectuals to abandon idealism, which, in turn, saps the energy that might be directed to true reform. To break this cycle, the universities and the intellectual community must initiate a determined effort at Enlightenment II by assimilating the wisdom of the first Enlightenment, and then by following the process that will reaffirm the ideal and specify the contemporary means.

Enlightenment II is an opportunity for the universities to regain the lost mission of unifying and elevating society. Citizens of Enlightenment II, engaging in an improved, cooperative truth-seeking process among many disciplines and many cultures, will examine the hypothesis that democratic capitalism is the way to peace and plenty and an end to violence. In this process, the humanists will sensitize the economists, the economists will educate the humanists in the superior economic system, and the whole will be greater than the sum of the parts. Most will eventually recognize that Marx was right: Social progress does depend on movement towards a superior economic system.

Enlightenment II will have a difficult responsibility in analyzing the lessons of the twentieth century. Will the demonstrable capacity of economic freedom to improve lives be copied and spread worldwide, or will the violence of governments and terrorists be repeated? Many twentieth-century philosophers viewed the horrors of their time and abandoned idealism; others, such as Peter Drucker, saw the dawning Information Age as a new opportunity, if only a new synthesis could be developed. This synthesis could finally bridge the "thinkers" and the "managers," along with scientists, humanists, economists, and the religious, that is, combining cultures and disciplines into teams cooperatively engaged in Enlightenment II. Drucker believed that "to transcend this dichotomy in a new synthesis will be a central philosophical and educational challenge for the post-capitalist society."[446]

Case studies are available, such as Enron (see chapter 9), for a provocative curriculum that will contrast the fundamentals of democratic capitalism with the corruptions of ultra-capitalism. When this curriculum becomes available for courses in Adult Education, it will educate and stimulate business groups, civic groups, religious groups, unions, and others, availing the voting public with the economic literacy they require to elect leaders who will structure government in support of free-market principles.

All parts of universities and colleges have the obligation to educate citizens in order for economic freedom to work, but Business Schools and Law Schools have a more particular responsibility to train leaders. Many Business Schools, infected by ultra-capitalism, have joined in celebrating the "American Model," that is, the economic system that is individualistic, greedy, and devoid of any social contract. In hypothesis #2, I propose that democratic capitalism, not ultra-capitalism, is the system that can maximize long-term wealth, the result that is presumably the mission of business and, therefore, the mission of those who teach Business Administration. As the economic and social damage from ultra-capitalism increases, the obligation of Business Schools becomes more urgent to present their students with the theory and practice of democratic capitalism.

---

[446] Peter Drucker, *Post-Capitalist Society* (New York: Harper Business, 1993), p. 9.

Young people coming into Business Schools are roughly divided into those determined to become millionaires by the time they are thirty, and those with a still vague desire for a contributory career, the wish to "make a difference." As long as the Business Schools fail to present democratic capitalism, those potential moral leaders default to ultra-capitalism. Conversely, when the Business Schools do present democratic capitalism as a coherent and integral system for student examination, those with a conscious moral instinct will grab democratic capitalism and run with it. Those on the margin, partly conditioned to the idea that morality and the profit motive are mutually exclusive, will recognize instead the synergy, and become enthusiasts for democratic capitalism.

Law Schools are the breeding ground for many politicians; therefore, they have a responsibility analogous to the Business Schools to train leaders in those matters that will generate social progress. Law students with a tilt to the political left will gain from Enlightenment II by an understanding of the pathologies of collectivism, and the enormous opportunities for the state to do more for people at a fraction of the cost simply by applying to governance the philosophy and protocols of democratic capitalism. Those with a tilt to the political right will recognize the opportunity to reduce the role of government by supporting the economic system that produces strong and steady growth, thus allowing many families now needing government assistance to become part of the positive economic momentum. New leaders, thus educated and inspired, will, in time, break the gridlock.

Another college at the university that needs to become fully engaged in the exploration of democratic capitalism by way of Enlightenment II is the School of Education. One outcome of Enlightenment II will be a curriculum for citizen education, pre-K through graduate school, including Adult Education. A curriculum in democratic capitalism will inevitably stimulate a new democratic political agenda.

Citizens will examine the proposition that democratic capitalism solves the persistent problem of the maldistribution of wealth. Citizens should examine the proposition that as the standard of living in the world rises through economic common purpose, so the violence will go down. Citizens will learn to structure fiscal and monetary policies to support economic freedom, assist those inadequately prepared to participate in the economy, and engage in cooperative U.N. actions to stop the violence.

Long before any of these good things can happen, school children, starting in pre-K, must be educated for their dual participation in individual development and social cooperation. National educational standards are useful points of reference, but they remind us of massive failure without addressing root causes. Top-down application of remote standards do little to educate the kids, and they burden teachers and principals with another time-consuming distraction. Only integration of the philosophy and protocols of democratic governance can free education from the bottom up, and release the latent power of principals, teachers, and students. Only then, and in time, will there be a chance for all schools to meet national standards.

Multi-disciplinary truth-seeking for the improved curriculum for citizen education and training of leaders is neither a precise science nor need it be, as Aristotle cautioned:

> It is the mark of an educated man to look for precision in each class of things just so far as the nature of the subject admits; it is evidently equally foolish to accept probable reasoning from a mathematician and to demand from a rhetorician scientific proofs.[447]

Human history is not about small misses; it is about large, persistent mistakes and violence. No great precision is required for humans to determine what is required to stop killing hundreds of millions of our own species. Similarly, no great precision is required to adopt the commercial system that has demonstrated its capacity to eliminate material scarcity, and elevate and unite people.

Disciplined by the correct process, the model produced by many minds assimilating knowledge from different cultures would have a tremendous benefit for the education of citizens. The model could serve as a template for all international agencies, most

---

[447] Aristotle, *The Basic Works of Aristotle: Nicomachean Ethics* 1:3 (New York: Random House, 1941), # 1094, p. 936.

importantly the United Nations, to provide consistent advice to nations trying to improve the lives of their people. The new model could show the conservatives how actually to attain the reality contained in the slogan "compassionate conservative," and it could give the collectivists a new identity not as bureaucrats and micromanagers but as true liberals. Further, it could give true liberals on both sides of the ideological aisle an effectual political agenda to improve the human condition. The potential political power of this agenda is vast because it provides focus for the feelings of most citizens.

What is the benefit of an excellent Liberal Arts education if it sensitizes many wonderful young people to the desire to improve the human condition, but it also sensitizes them to a contempt for capitalism, and provides them no education in the fiscal and monetary matters upon which improvement in the human condition depends. I do not suggest that everyone needs to major in Economics and minor in Accounting; rather, I am suggesting that the college curriculum include a basic understanding of socio-economic principles and issues, and raise broad questions of policy and social implications. For example, ought not every citizen know about "easy credit," "leveraged speculation," and in general the history of the government's failure to control currency and credit for the general welfare? Ought not a future citizen know that Adam Smith warned about the "prodigals and projectors" who, uncontrolled, would deflect capital from the job-growth economy to speculation? Ought not every citizen know how free markets depend on "neutral money," and understand the government's responsibility to assure that money be not "volatile and impatient?" Ought not future tax-payers legitimately expect their college professors to teach them why bank subsidies, bailouts, and deposit insurance are abrogations of the disciplines needed for the free market to work properly?

A democratic republic depends for success on educated citizens; the universities in an open society are responsible for the education of those citizens. The job is not now being done, and that is the root cause for a society that is blundering along the well-worn path of folly and violence.

Enlightenment II is the long-term movement to peace and plenty that will gain positive momentum with each generation of students and citizens. Other agents of change, people who can press for reform more rapidly, are to be found among institutional investors, the concern of hypothesis #9.

Hypothesis #9—Agents of Change: Institutional investors have the fiduciary responsibility and the democratic power to democratize capitalism by reforming company practices and government policies.

Institutional investors could move the American economy towards democratic capitalism in a surprisingly short time by using means that already exist, namely by influencing the policies of companies that are largely owned by working people, and by bringing to bear both on companies and the government the democratic voting power that this ownership of shares represents.

During the last quarter of the twentieth century, a new wage-earner capitalism emerged, called either "pension fund socialism" or "employee capitalism" by Peter Drucker,[448] but I prefer to call it "democratic capitalism." This new capitalism is a realization of Marx's and Mill's visions of a synergistic relationship between labor and capital, a development that has come about not through radical restructure or political revolution but through evolutionary means.

This new relationship between capital and labor was expedited by ERISA, a new federal law passed in 1974, that mandated the funding of future pension benefits out of current corporate earnings. The flow of funds started by this law increased with the 401(k) law that encouraged savings from pre-tax dollars. As a result of these new laws, the ownership of American public companies has shifted towards wage earners. Pension funds, mutual funds, insurance companies, banks, foundations, and university endowments increased the amount of money to be managed from under a half-billion in 1970, to $8.5 trillion by 2001. Ownership of public companies by wage earners grew from under 15% to over 50%.[449]

The explosive growth of wage-earner capitalism should have diffused economic and political power. Instead of diffusion, however,

---

[448] Peter Drucker, *op. cit.*, p. 82

[449] Jeff Gates, *The Ownership Solution: Toward a Shared Capitalism for the 21st Century* (Reading, Massachusetts: Addison Wesley Longmans, 1998), pp. 2-3.

wealth and political influence became more concentrated. Instead of becoming more accountable for the long-term financial and social benefits of their majority owners, most of the wage earners' money managers supported ultra-capitalism, attracted by its presumed better short-term results. Ultra-capitalism came to dominate the economy because the enormous flow of new cash into the stock market gave new power to reward or punish CEOs based on how closely they follow Wall Street dictates (see chapter 8). If this observation sounds like a lament by an ex-CEO, consider the words of an ex-banker, David A. Hartman:

> Corporate CEOs got the message. Forecast 20% growth and 20% return—or fake it. Does this provide any clue as to why the fictitious earnings of Enron, WorldCom and the like have become so widespread? Either CEOs and auditors play ball, or Wall Street has them replaced with more "performance oriented" players.[450]

Wall Street's new power came from an extraordinary contradiction in which more democratic ownership resulted in more concentration of wealth and a less socially sensitive capitalism. This contradiction can be traced to the egregious government mistakes that caused the excessive volatility and liquidity that launched ultra-capitalism (see chapter 7 and hypothesis #4). Instead of using the growing democratic power to counteract the lobby power of ultra-capitalism, institutional investors in most cases supported ultra-capitalism.

The Congressional designers of ERISA failed to analyze alternative uses of this new flow of democratic capital. In the early 1970s, when ERISA was being designed, Senator Russell Long (D., Louisiana) and his committee proposed, and Congress passed, new tax laws that encouraged employee ownership through ESOPs (Employee Stock Ownership Plans). A magic opportunity was missed to design new financial instruments to invest tax-favored ERISA funds in the job-growth economy, which would have resulted in large

---

[450] David A. Hartman, "Wall Street's Turn," *Chronicles*, December, 2002, p. 43.

dividends, long-term appreciation, and security. The government, instead of responding to the needs of the people and recycling the capital into economic growth, responded to the Wall Street lobbyists and sent the money to the stock market where it pushed stock prices to artificially high levels in the bubble economy. A new chapter in the book of making money from special government privileges was being written: Since the beginning of the Industrial Revolution, finance capitalism had exploited the workers' labor; now, in the early stages of the Information Age revolution, ultra-capitalism was learning how to exploit the workers' capital!

We need to listen to, and act upon, the insight of Peter F. Drucker, who skewered ultra-capitalism in these words:

> What emerged from this frantic decade [hostile takeovers, leveraged buy-outs, downsizing, *et al.*] was a redefinition of the purpose and rationale of big business and the function of management. Instead of being managed in the best balanced interests of stakeholders, corporations were now to be managed exclusively to "maximize shareholder value." This will not work, either. It forces the corporation to be managed for the shortest term, but that means damaging, if not destroying, the wealth-producing capacity of the business. It means decline and finally swift decline. Long-term results cannot be achieved by piling short-term results on short-term results. They should be achieved by balancing short-term and long-term needs and objectives. Furthermore, managing a business exclusively for the shareholders alienates the very people on whose motivation and dedication the modern business depends: The knowledge workers. An engineer will not be motivated to work to make a speculator rich.[451]

The alienation that Marx identified as the impediment to greater and more widely distributed wealth, should have disappeared

---

[451] Drucker, *op. cit.*, p. 80.

with the advent of the Information Age and wage-earner capitalism. An industrial environment that releases the cognitive power of people is mutually exclusive with alienation because the working class ("labor") is now also the owner class ("capitalists"), as well as the bosses ("management"). As Drucker pointed out, however, the alienation will persist as long as ultra-capitalism prevails.

I argue, therefore, that institutional investors ought to examine and accept the hypothesis that democratic capitalism maximizes long-term shareholder value because the system that maximizes the innovation and productivity of each will add up to the maximum profits to be shared by all. Exclusive concentration on short-term profits is eventually self-defeating because it destroys the motivation upon which the long-term success of any enterprise depends. Drucker made this point many years before the 2002 crash of ultra-capitalism, and so did I!

The first priority of the institutional investors should be to put pressure on companies to invest capital surplus in more growth and to pay the stockholders large dividends, rather than wasting surplus on non-strategic acquisitions and stock buy-backs. At the same time, institutional investors can become the antidote to Wall Street lobby power by lobbying changes in the tax laws for tax-free dividends and tax-free capital gains for low- and middle-income shareholders. This simple change will have the benefit of recycling surplus into stronger economic growth, and it will also build momentum towards greater worker-ownership plans and the full benefits of democratic capitalism. Most wage earners will be pleased to put their money into a plan that provides not only secure long-term appreciation but also large annual dividends that can be spent or reinvested in more equity, both stimulants to still greater economic growth.

Another change that institutional investors could implement is to measure corporations by making them accountable for management's predictions for sales growth, cash flow, and profits over a three-year period. Adoption of this measurement and accountability—combined with large, tax-free dividends, with no capital-gains tax for the wage earner; control of the feeding frenzy in executive compensation; and a change of auditors every five years (see chapter 9)—would move the economy towards the stronger, steadier growth of democratic capitalism, and away from the boom/bust cycle of ultra-capitalism that has done such unnecessary economic and social damage.

After ultra-capitalism is purged from the system in part by the voting power of institutional investors, and after democratic capitalism receives support from the American culture and political structure, it will spread wealth throughout the world and unite people in economic common purpose. The visible improvement in the lives of hundreds of millions of people will then set the stage for a steady reduction and eventual elimination of violence among people and nations. The United States is positioned to lead towards this economic common purpose and its promise of global social progress. That ideal prospect, including cooperation with the United Nations in its mission to substitute law for violence, is the focus of hypothesis #10.

Hypothesis #10—The Ideal of World Peace: Democratic capitalism will result in a rising standard of living and a growing sense of economic common purpose worldwide, which will provide the environment for the United Nations, backed by the United States of America in a cooperative role, to displace violence with law in the relations among nations.

The *ideal* of a world of *plenty* through the *means* of economic common purpose is placed as hypothesis #1 because democratic capitalism must be demonstrably spreading wealth worldwide before the *ideal* of a world of *peace*, hypothesis #10, can become attainable and perceived as attainable. The repositioning of American foreign policy to be a strong team player within the United Nations must be supported by a clear demonstration that America is leading the world towards the benefits of economic freedom.

The full capacity of capitalism to provide basic comforts to the people of the world has never been realized. The opportunity for nations to substitute law for violence has never been accomplished. Underlying these two persistent failures is the perception of inherent tension between capitalism and democracy. Democratic capitalism that draws its strength from an inherent synergy between capitalism and democracy has been obscured because most have believed that commerce is inherently immoral, or amoral at best. Lacking a unifying ideal, many have concluded that idealism is dead and violence inevitable.

One might argue that stopping the violence could have a quicker effect on improving the condition of the world, but the cycle of violence is so institutionalized in human affairs that the cycle will be broken and the reciprocal atrocities will cease only when the standard of living is steadily going up throughout the world.

In my studies, I found a correlation among many of the great thinkers regarding the enormous potential of people in a world free of want and violence. Many of these great thinkers over many centuries emphasized the same virtues that I had learned from experience, the direct correlation between improved performance and trust and cooperation. These great thinkers also observed the interconnected impediments to social progress: the concentration of wealth and violence among nations and people.

Confucius, for example, knew that a world of law, not violence, begins with trained and virtuous leaders, though he was realistic in his awareness that the elimination of violence would be a long process:

> When the great principle prevails, when the world
> becomes a republic, they elect men of talents, virtue,
> and ability; they talk of sincere agreement and
> cultivate universal peace. After a state has been ruled
> for a hundred years by good men, it is possible to get
> the better of cruelty and do away with the killing.[452]

Mencius (371-289 B.C.), one of Confucius's interpreters and a teacher of universal love, denounced war as a crime against humanity: "There are men who say 'I am skillful at marshalling troops, I am skillful at completing a battle.' They are great criminals, there never has been a good war." Mencius marveled that a thief who steals a pig is condemned and punished, whereas an emperor who invades and appropriates a kingdom and enslaves its citizens is called a hero and is held up as a model for posterity.[453]

---

[452] Durant, *op. cit.*, vol. I, p. 673.

[453] *Ibid.*, p. 685.

Young Edmund Burke (1729-1797), before he became a famous British Parliamentarian, pondered the human failure to stop the violence. He asked these questions: Why has every human effort to structure society for peace and plenty been a failure? Why does the only animal capable of reason kill more of its own species than does any other animal? Burke included in his litany of civil society's failures the exploitation of the poor by the rich, and then, after viewing them in their demeaned condition, the conclusion by the rich and powerful that ordinary people are incapable of participating in their own governance.[454]

German philosopher Immanuel Kant, later in the eighteenth century, searched for the perfect constitution that would allow humans to reach their full potential. Kant's "Eighth Thesis" was his elaboration upon "a perfectly constituted state as the only condition in which the capacities of mankind can be fully developed, and also bring forth that external relation among states which is perfectly adequate to this end."[455] Kant, in his seventies, took a dim view of the quality of truth-seeking then being practiced in international relations:

> [Kant expressed] …a certain indignation when one sees men's actions on the great world stage and finds, besides the wisdom that appears here and there among individuals, everything in the large woven together from folly, childish vanity, even from childish malice, and destructiveness.[456]

Condorcet in his summary of the work of the Enlightenment did not miss this vital subject. Buoyed by his optimism about improving the condition of humankind through universal education and rising affluence, he foresaw the establishment of organizations like the United Nations, "more intelligently conceived than those

---

[454] Edmund Burke, *A Vindication of Natural Society, or a View of the Miseries and Evils Arising to Mankind from Every Species of Artificial Society* (Indianapolis, Indiana: Liberty Classics 1982; first published in 1756), pp. 39-40.

[455] Immanuel Kant, *Selections. Idea for a Universal History from a Cosmopolitan Point of View* (New York: Scribner/Macmillan, 1998; first published in 1784), p. 422.

[456] *Ibid.*, p. 415.

projects of eternal peace which have filled and consoled the hearts of certain philosophers," and he believed that these would "hasten the progress of the brotherhood of nations." Condorcet expressed his hope that when war departed and peace arrived, "Wars between countries will rank with assassinations as freakish atrocities, humiliating and vile in the eyes of nature and staining with indelible opprobrium the country or the age whose annals record them." Condorcet saw a moral society founded on economic principle:

> When at last the nations come to agree on the
> principles of politics and morality, when in their own
> better interests they invite foreigners to share equally
> in all the benefits people enjoy either through the
> bounty of nature or by their own industry, then all the
> causes that produce and perpetuate national
> animosities and poison nations' relations will
> disappear one by one, and nothing will remain to
> encourage or even to arouse the fury of war.[457]

Condorcet thus placed economic common purpose as the prerequisite to stopping the violence. A little over a half-century later, Marx arrived at the same conclusion. Marx first emphasized that social progress depends on movement to a superior economic system, and then he concluded that, with the elimination of material scarcity through this superior economic system, the warrior state would lose power.

Early in the twenty-first century, the United States was confused about the kind of capitalism to support and the nation's proper role in the world. Was America an example of democratic principles in action, one person, one vote? Or was it a new imperial nation with the responsibility to run the world, one nation, all of the votes? Enormous military might and economic strength was affording the United States all the hard power it needed to be imperialistic, and it so chose in the invasion of Iraq.

At the same time, America also had great soft power through its traditions of American freedoms, comfort for most, work ethic,

---

[457] Goodell, *op. cit.*, p. 244.

inventiveness, and rule of law. Early in the new century, both types of hard power, both economic and military, were securely in place, but America was losing its soft power at the same time that soft power was gaining in importance in our more interconnected world.

Joseph S. Nye, Jr., Dean of the Kennedy School of Government and former Assistant Secretary of Defense, reasoned in his examination of hard and soft power that while America is likely to continue to be number one in hard power, in a world where soft power is more important, America cannot go it alone:

> In this global information age, number one ain't gonna be what it used to be. To succeed in such a world, America must not only maintain its hard power but also must understand its soft power and how to combine the two in the pursuit of national and global interests.[458]

The United States has the hard economic power to lead the world towards democratic capitalism, but it has, unfortunately, used that power to push the world toward ultra-capitalism. The economic and social damage done by ultra-capitalism has fed anti-American sentiments to such an extent that the U.S. has had to use its military hard power both to fight terrorists and to threaten other countries.

The more the United States tries to "go it alone," the more other governments such as China, India, Russia, France, and Germany feel pressured to build a hard-power coalition to challenge what most of the world views as America's arrogance of power. China can surpass the United States in economic power during the 21st century. Their high economic growth rate can benefit the American people in a world united by economic common purpose, but if China is forced to divert growing economic power to build up military hard power, not only will China have squandered its national wealth but also the sense of global economic common purpose will devolve into mutual suspicion. Nye commented on this choice:

---

[458] Joseph S. Nye, Jr., *The Paradox of American Power: Why the World's Only Superpower Can't Go It Alone* (New York: Oxford University Press, 2002), p. 171.

Global governance requires a large state to take the lead. But how much and what kind of inequality of power is necessary—or tolerable—and for how long? If the leading country possesses soft power and behaves in a manner that benefits others, effective counter-coalitions may be slow to arise. If on the other hand, the leading country defines its interests narrowly and uses its weight arrogantly, it increases the incentives for others to coordinate to escape its hegemony.[459]

Nye offered this wisdom a year before the Iraq War.

Senator Robert Byrd (D., West Virginia) warned the Senate on February 12, 2003, that they were standing by, passively mute, while the nation was lurching toward war, "the most horrible of human experience." Senator Byrd placed the impending attack on Iraq in this context:

This coming battle, if it materializes, represents a turning point in U.S. foreign policy and possibly a turning point in the recent history of the world. This nation is about to embark upon the first test of a revolutionary doctrine applied in an extraordinary way at an unfortunate time. The doctrine is preemption— the idea that the United States, or any other nation, can legitimately attack a nation that is not immediately threatening but may be threatening in the future—a radical new twist on the traditional idea of self-defense.[460]

Senator Byrd went on to describe the destabilizing effect that this new policy and action would have as nations would now have to judge whether to attack or whether they were about to be attacked.

---

[459] *Ibid.*, p. 15.

[460] Robert Byrd, "We Stand Passively Mute," speech to the U.S. Senate (February 12, 2003), *Congressional Record*, February 12, 2003.

Byrd regretted that these destabilizing actions were under consideration in a world "where globalism has tied the vital economic and security interests of many nations so closely together." Byrd understood that 9-11 had changed the world, but he commented:

> Calling heads of state "pygmies," labeling whole
> countries as "evil," denigrating powerful European
> allies as irrelevant—these types of crude insensitivities
> can do our great nation no good. We may have massive
> military might, but we cannot fight a global war on
> terrorism alone.[461]

Shortly after the Senator's speech, America and a few allies invaded and conquered Iraq contrary to the wishes of most of the world.

The theory that any nation has the preemptive right to invade another country entails extraordinary implications, for it leads the world in a direction in which each nation would feel responsible for adding to its military capability either to be an attacker or a defender against another's attack. At the same time that the U.S. chooses to arm selected nations, including tyrannical ones, America also decides which other nations are not allowed to be similarly armed, and which ones are to be attacked because they think that they have the same prerogatives for military preparation as the U.S. and its allies.

The demilitarization of all nations, not just the ones targeted by American patriots, is an urgent and overdue event that should be managed by the United Nations and led by the United States. Demilitarization of selected parts of the world while adding to one's own and one's allies military strength, however, is not only hypocritical but also impossible. All citizens should be concerned with American hypocrisy in the elimination of weapons of mass destruction. For example, thousands of nuclear-armed missiles in America and Russia are still in the ready position, aimed at each other. With a desperately poor Russia trying to be friends with the United States, why are those weapons still there?

---

[461] *Loc. cit.*

Those weapons would not be there if Soviet leader Gorbachev and American President Reagan, when they met in Reykjavik, Iceland, had concluded their agreement for a sweeping nuclear weapons ban. According to *The Nation*:

> That was the 1986 summit where only the panicked intervention of several presidential aides—some of whom advise the current U.S. administration (George W. Bush)—pulled Ronald Reagan back from the brink of agreement.[462]

> In 1988, Gorbachev tried again in his December U.N. address, a vision of deep, unilateral arms cuts; rejection of ideology in international relations; and a call for a new world order of cooperation in solving such global problems as poverty, pollution, crime, and *terrorism*.[463] (Emphasis added)

President Bush, the senior, was well known for his disinterest in "the vision thing," and the Cold War warriors in his Administration had not assimilated the opportunities for a world relieved of that bipolar confrontation. The leaders of Russia, the country destroyed by that confrontation, had the vision; the leaders of America, the country with the power to put the vision into practice, continued, instead, on its path to more folly and violence.

In a world of reason and vision, preemption might have a place in a long-term U.N. plan to demilitarize the world. Force would be occasionally necessary, but the need would diminish rapidly as the world witnessed a coordinated, determined plan to convert the trillions of dollars wasted on military expenses to education, good health, and economic development. Those few madmen who opposed this movement would provoke the moral and military might of the rest of the world.

Where did this extraordinary new policy of preemption come from? With its enormous ramifications for the direction of history in

---

[462] Robert D. English, "The Revolution Within," *The Nation*, May 26, 2003, p. 36.

[463] *Ibid.*, p. 35.

the 21st century, it must have been the product of high-quality truth-seeking by people of different disciplines and cultures. Not at all! Preemption came out of the minds of a few Conservative ideologues. Their new mission began in 1998 when a new, small Washington think tank, the "Project for the New American Century," wrote President Clinton to urge the elimination of Saddam Hussein's weapons of mass destruction and, in time, the elimination of Hussein himself. Eighteen concerned people signed that letter, one-half of whom ended up in senior positions in the George W. Bush Administration.[464]

In September 2002, these ideologues now with political power, produced *The National Security Strategy of the United States* in which foreign policy emanated from the existence of great military power that was left over from the bipolar confrontation between the U.S. and the U.S.S.R., now improved with hi-tech developments. The policy conclusion is that America has the power and is obliged to use it to run the world.

Robert Kagan's essay on this subject caused a stir that encouraged him to restate it in a small book in which he concluded as follows:

> The United States remains mired in history, exercising power in an anarchic Hobbesian world where international laws and rules are unreliable, and where true security and the defense and promotion of a liberal order still depend on the possession and use of military might.[465]

Kagan did not reference the success of the European Union in substituting cooperation and law for centuries of killing a large percentage of their people in wars. That example would have supplied experimental verification that such a transition could be made at the world level, if America would put its power behind the U.N. Kagan called the U.N. "a pale approximation of a genuine multilateral

---

[464] Robert S. Greenberger and Karby Leggett, "President's Dream: Changing Not Just Regime but a Region," *The Wall Street Journal*, March 21, 2003, p. 1.

[465] Robert Kagan, *Of Paradise and Power: America and Europe in the New World Order* (New York: Alfred A. Knopf, 2003), p. 3.

order,"[466] but he did not address how thoroughly the U.N. had been undermined by the U.S. or how badly it needed structural reforms that would come about only with American support. Instead, Kagan presumed to interpret the level of American idealism this way:

> One of the things that most clearly divides Europeans and Americans today is a philosophical, even metaphysical disagreement over where exactly mankind stands on the continuum between the laws of the jungle and the laws of reason. Americans do not believe we are as close to the realization of the Kantian dream as do Europeans.[467]

A few hawkish, power-adoring ideologues are trying to preempt traditional American idealism. If their view prevails, America will turn even worse folly and violence in the 21st century into a self-fulfilling prophecy. The United Nations will continue to be emasculated by the United States, and the world powers will be forced to build a coalition to challenge America in the worst arms race in human history, and that will include nuclear capability, chemical, biological, and all other weapons of mass destruction.

The policy of these ideologues of military power expressed in the *National Security Strategy* must become a matter of exhaustive public debate. This madness must be fully examined by the American people. Give the citizens a clear choice, and they will vote their idealism!

The hawks in the United States need perceived enemies to sustain their enormous military budget. China had become the designated enemy for them since the demise of the U.S.S.R. until Iraq or North Korea—or whoever is next—would become a more inviting target. Military preparation can become a self-fulfilling prophecy, too. Thucydides (471-399 B.C.), the Greek historian, warned at the time of the Peloponnesian War between Sparta and Athens that a belief in the inevitability of war can be a major cause of war's taking place.[468]

---

[466] *Ibid.*, p. 40.

[467] *Ibid.*, p. 91.

[468] Will Durant, *op. cit.*, vol. II, *The Life of Greece* (1939), p. 440.

The group that determined the Iraq agenda violated the same part of Bacon's truth-seeking process that former Secretary of Defense Robert McNamara identified as the fatal flaw in the team deliberations over American involvement in Vietnam. McNamara, a pivotal figure in the Vietnam decisions, described what he had learned from that searing experience: "We are not practicing in an international context what we preach, and what we practice domestically—which is *democratic* decision making. We are not omniscient."[469]

In both the Vietnam and Iraq wars, the teams responsible for American policy were not sufficiently *collaborative,* that is they did not have the multi-disciplinary and multicultural participation necessary to neutralize mistakes by those joined by the same narrow cultural conditioning. The Iraq war was another government policy founded on a desirable mission in the abstract but with threatening and unintended consequences for the rest of the century. Massive military expenditures around the world; balance-of-power geopolitics that target one group of nations differently from how other nations are treated; increasing violence, this time to include wide-spread and suicidal terrorism that will bring the battle to North America; and a further denigration of the power and prestige of the United Nations, the only available forum of international dialogue—all of these last-gasp behaviors of a warrior state are now out-moded by the inherent morality and effective promise of democratic capitalism. The new policy of preemption re-ignites the Cold War competition for weapons of mass destruction in a world where eight nations already have 32,000 nuclear weapons. These nuclear-armed nations include India and Pakistan, contiguous countries consumed by religious and nationalistic passions engaged in war more often than not. Preemption practiced by either of those densely populated nations would result in a human catastrophe beyond measure.

The Iraq War can have positive effects: American troops can be taken out of Saudi Arabia, oil profits can be directed to the Iraqi people, Israel can get security, and the Palestinians a state. Even if all

---

[469] Robert S. McNamara and James Blight, *Wilson's Ghost: Reducing the Risk of Conflict, Killing, and Catastrophe in the 21st Century* (New York: BBS Public Affairs, 2001) p. 53.

of these good things happen, these ends did not justify that means, and the residual effects will still be catastrophic.

The Alternative

What will it take for the United States to reassume its historic role as a leader nation to bring about a rising standard of living, a growing sense of economic common purpose, and peace to the world? The 21st century presents an extraordinary opportunity for the United States to exercise its soft power and spread the benefits of democratic capitalism, to teach by word and example the only economic system that combines elimination of material scarcity and broad wealth distribution with the enduring values of freedom, trust, and cooperation.

During the transition to peace, the U.S. must be an enthusiastic supporter of the United Nations as the only agency available to displace violence with the rule of law in the relations among nations. This does not mean abrogation of the national sovereignty of any country, but it does mean that all nations—including the U.S.—must be held accountable to the high standards for international behavior set by the charter and other declarations of the U.N. The U.N. must be the starting place for the occasional use of force against nations that refuse to abide by the rule of law. Military coalitions and even unilateral actions will continue to be necessary, and they can be acceptable, but only with U.N. approval. The delicate problem of supporting a multilateral approach to the use of military force without compromising sovereignty, broadly defined, will be solved for the simple reason that the world cannot afford the alternatives.

For example, the war on terrorism ought not to be fought unilaterally by the United States but be coordinated by the U.N. Immediately after 9-11, the U.N. Security Council passed a resolution in support of the U.S., pointing out that the U.N. had the infrastructure in place to conduct the long fight throughout the world against terrorism. President Bush, however, never mentioned the U.N. in his address to Congress following 9-11.

The U.N. is an imperfect organization needing both reform and further development. But why would one expect the United Nations to be anything other than imperfect when one considers how

493

many officials in the world's most powerful nation have treated it with contempt? For years, the U.S. refused to pay our U.N. dues, and in January 2000, Senator Jesse Helms (R., North Carolina) even appeared before the Security Council and told them that they had to do it "our way" or America would quit![470]

The necessary reforms depend on steady support by the United States for a strong U.N. and renewed American leadership of the world in economic common purpose. The standard of living will then go up, and the violence will go down, when global corporations work with governments to help the poor countries. As costly as this undertaking shall be, global corporations will do this work for two reasons: A moral obligation and good business. Each country that joins the world's free markets adds to total growth, and as long as the wealth is broadly distributed, all countries will benefit from free trade.

Many of the politicians who undermine American support of the U.N. are the same people who keep America's contribution to foreign aid at one of the lowest percentages of GDP of any mature economy. Foreign aid has often been poorly managed, but similar to attitudes about the United Nation, the American focus needs to be on fixing what is amiss, not using the failures as an excuse to abandon its obligations. Weak U.S. foreign aid, the contradiction of free trade implicit in agricultural subsidies, and other unilateralist policies, as well as the corruptions of ultra-capitalism, now combine to portray to the world the image of an arrogant, greedy, self-centered America, nothing like the "light on the hill" that inspired the world two centuries ago. The spirit of ordinary Americans has not changed, I believe, but the quality of the leadership has; the quality of leadership, however, is ultimately the responsibility of the people.

Those Muslim nations suffering from the tyranny that results when religion and state are coupled, will either have to move towards economic freedom or explain to their people why they are being systematically deprived of the good things in life that can be viewed on television or read about over the internet. Once America espouses the system that not only can eliminate material scarcity but does so in a moral way, then the enemies of freedom and their repressive

---

[470] Jesse Helms, speech before the United Nations (January 20, 2000), *The New York Times*, International Edition, January 21, 2000, p. A1.

ideologies will lose credibility as morally superior among their followers.

After the ultra-capitalist dragon has been slain, and wealth is more broadly distributed in each country and around the world, then people can unite in economic common purpose. Better education and a rising standard of living go together, and once the building momentum becomes visible, the violence will recede and the U.N. can begin to foster positive competition that will come to mean a contest of nations vying with one another to improve the lives of their people.

Instead of geopolitical power struggles and wars, the international community will, for the first time, concentrate on measurement and accountability in improving lives. This new positive focus can be based on the existing U.N. Human Development Index that is a composite assessment of a nation's GDP that measures productive growth, life expectancy that measures efforts to improve health, and literacy that measures how well countries are educating their people.

People naturally like to compete and keep score. After the U.N. Human Development Index comes into broader use, people will become interested in which countries are in the top positions, and which are toward the bottom. The U.N can then add to the Development Index predictions made by countries' leaders based on three-year average improvement targets. Competition can then expand from absolute standings to how well countries are doing in comparison to their own plans.

Some may think that such measurement and accountability is game-playing, simplistic, or naïve in a violent world, but perhaps they have not had the experience in how quickly and powerfully people respond to a positive message. The positive message is that we can do better, and that we can do better in competition with those countries just ahead of us in the standings.

When rich nations and powerful global corporations join together with emerging economies, performance will improve as it always does with trust and cooperation, except the improved performance will now benefit all of the world's citizens. Great benefit will accrue when rich countries are measured not only in terms of their own performance but also in terms of their sponsorship of emerging economies. When global corporations are added to this roster of international commercial coaches, the competition will become even greater and more productive of progress. Instead of begrudged foreign aid, conceived as international welfare and dominated by bankers with limited experience in the management of change, competitive managers, experienced in training, motivation, and resource application, will compete to parlay funds from the mature economies into profitable long-term programs among the emerging economies. These experienced team managers will not predetermine failure by under-funding and inadequate training.

In this scenario, dramatic improvement in the lives of people in various countries will put economic freedom on display as the universal solution, and best practices will spread under the monitoring influence of competition. Those countries stuck at the bottom of the list in absolute terms, or in terms of meeting their improvement targets, will be subject to pressure from their own citizens to restructure governmentally for better support of economic freedom. Over time, the benefits of economic freedom will lead to political and social freedoms. Democracy will grow naturally throughout the world, not from a political campaign for human rights but, rather, because of recognition that political freedoms enhance the capacity of economic freedom to get the job of improving lives done better.

Aristotle, the philosopher of common sense, laid out the plan almost two and one-half millennia ago, but the system of production at that time did not have the capacity to feed, clothe, shelter, educate, and provide good health and hope for all the people. Now that the productive system has demonstrated its capacity to do all of these things, Aristotle's *eudaimonia*, life lived to its full potential, is no longer limited to the fortunate few but has become available for all. This is the same promise of the American Founders: "life, liberty, and the pursuit of happiness" for all; it is the vision of the French Enlightenment: "liberty, equality, and fraternity;" and it is the challenge of Marx's manifesto: "The full development of all is the sum of the full development of each."

When the impediments are removed, and the conducive circumstances are in place, momentum towards a world of peace and plenty will be enormous and irreversible. The momentum will be irreversible because rising affluence and better education will equip more and more people to accelerate the progress and passionately oppose its reversal. The progress will be irreversible because the U.N.'s Human Development Index will shine a bright light on any nation that is not improving lives, and an even brighter light of stardom on every nation that is leading the way. Future generations will benefit from this self-perpetuating momentum toward the realization of full human potential, but they will wonder why it took so long because it will all seem so essentially human, so *reasonable*!

Democratic Capitalism

BIBLIOGRAPHY

Abelson, Reed, "Enron's Board Quickly Ratified Far-Reaching Management Moves," *The New York Times*, February 22, 2002, p. C6.

Aguayo, Rafael, *Dr. Deming*. New York: Lyle Stuart, 1990.

Albert, Michel, *Capitalism vs. Capitalism: How America's Obsession with Individual Achievement and Short-Term Profits Has Led to the Brink of Collapse*, with an introduction by Felix Rohatyn. New York: Four Walls Eight Windows Publishers, 1993.

Andres, Edmund L., "Study Shows How World Banks Panicked over Asian Troubles," *The New York Times*, January 30, 1998, p. 1.

Aquinas, Thomas, *Treatise on Man*. Westport, Connecticut: Greenwood Press, 1981.

Aristotle, *The Nicomachean Ethics*, in *A New Aristotle Reader*. Princeton: Princeton University Press, 1987.

Ibid., The Politics of Aristotle, edited and translated by Ernest Barker. New York: Oxford University Press, 1958.

Ibid., The Basic Works of Aristotle. New York: Random House, 1941.

Bacon, Francis, *The Great Instauration: The English Philosophers from Bacon to Mill*. New York: Modern Library, Random House, 1939.

Ibid., New Organon and Related Writings. Indianapolis: Bobbs-Merrill, 1960.

Banning, Lance, *The Sacred Fire of Liberty*. Ithaca, New York: Cornell University Press, 1995.

Barboza, David, and Jeff Gerth, "On Regulating Derivatives: Long-Term Capital Bailout Prompts Calls for Action," *The New York Times,* December 15, 1998, p. C1.

Bazerman, Max, George Lowenstein, and Don A. Moore, "Why Good Accountants Do Bad Auditing," *Harvard Business Review,* November 2002, p. 97.

Beckett, Paul, "Bankers Trust's Newman to Be Paid at Least $55 Million Over Five Years," *The Wall Street Journal,* February 1, 1999, p. B5.

Ibid., "Citigroup's Weil Made $26.7 Million in 2001," *The Wall Street Journal,* March 13, 2002, p. A4.

Beckner, Steven K., *Back from the Brink: The Greenspan Years.* New York: John Wiley & Sons, 1996.

Bell, Daniel, *The Coming of Post-Industrial Society.* New York: Basic Books, 1973.

Berger, Peter L., *The Capitalist Revolution: Fifty Propositions about Prosperity, Equality, and Liberty.* New York: Basic Books, 1986.

Berle, Adolf A., Jr., and Gardiner C. Means, *The Modern Corporation and Private Property.* New York: The Macmillan Company, 1932.

Berlin, Isaiah, *The Proper Study of Mankind.* New York: Farrar, Straus and Giroux, 1997.

Bianco, Anthony, and Heather Timmons, "Crisis at CITI," *Business Week,* September 9, 2002, p. 38.

Blackburn, Robin, "The Great Pension Crunch: How the Crisis Is Destroying Jobs— and What Can Be Done About It," *The Nation,* February 17, 2003.

Blasi, Joseph R., *Employee Ownership: Revolution or Rip-off?* Cambridge, Massachusetts: Ballinger Publishing, 1988.

Blasi, Joseph R., and Douglas L. Kruse, *The New Owners: The Mass Emergence of Employee Ownership in Public Companies and What It Means to American Business.* New York: Harper Business, 1991.

Blasi, Joseph R., Douglas Kruse, and Aaron Bernstein, *In the Company of Owners: The Truth about Stock Options (And Why Every Employee Should Have Them).* New York: Basic Books, 2003.

Blinder, Alan, "The Speed Limit: Fact and Fancy in the Growth Debate," *The American Prospect,* September-October, 1997, p. 57.

Bloom, Allan, *The Closing of the American Mind: How Higher Education Has Failed Democracy and Impoverished the Souls of Today's Students.* New York: Simon and Schuster, 1987.

Bluestone, Barry, and Irving Bluestone, *Negotiating the Future.* New York: Basic Books, 1992.

Blustein, Paul, *The Chastening: Inside the Crisis that Rocked the Global Financial System and Humbled the IMF.* New York: Public Affairs, 2001.

Bok, Sissela, *A Strategy for Peace: Human Values and the Threat of War.* New York: Vintage Books, Random House, Inc., 1990.

Boorstin, Daniel J., *The Creators: A History of Heroes of the Imagination.* New York: Random House, 1992.

Borosage, Robert L., "The Global Turning," *The Nation,* July 18, 1999, p. 20.

Borsuk, Richard, "In Indonesia a New Twist of Spreading Wealth," *The Wall Street Journal,* January 29, 2003, p. A16.

Branch, Shelly, "The 100 Best Companies to Work For," *Fortune,* January, 11, 1999, p. 134.

Brick, Michael, "What Was the Heart of Enron Keeps Shrinking," *The New York Times,* April 6, 2002, p. C1.

Brinelow, Peter, "Income Greed," *Forbes,* October 16, 2000, p. 126.

Bruck, Connie, *The Predators' Ball: The Junk Bond Raiders and the Men Who Staked Them.* New York: Simon & Schuster, 1988.

Bryce, Robert, and Molly Ivins, *Pipe Dreams: Greed, Ego, and the Death of Enron.* New York: BBS Public Affairs, 2002.

Buffet, Warren, "Avoiding a Mega-Catastrophe," *Fortune,* March 17, 2003, p. 82.

Burke, Edmund, *A Vindication of a Natural Society, or a View of the Miseries and Evils Arising to Mankind from Every Species of Artificial Society.* Indianapolis: Liberty Classics, 1982.

Ibid., Reflections on the Revolution in France. London: Penguin Books, 1986.

Byrd, Robert, "We Stand Passively Mute," speech in the United States Senate, *Congressional Record,* February 12, 2003.

Cassidy, John, *Dot.con, the Greatest Story Ever Sold.* New York: Harper Collins, 2002.

Catechism of the Catholic Church. New York: Catholic Book Publishing, 1994.

Cato, *Cato's Letters: Essays on Liberty, Civil and Religious.* New York: DaCapo Press, 1971.

Chancellor, Edward, *Devil Take the Hindmost: A History of Financial Speculation.* New York: A Plume Book, 2000.

Chardin, Teilhard de, *The Divine Milieu.* New York: Perennial Library, Harper and Row, 1959.

Ibid., The Phenomenon of Man. New York: Perennial Library, 1959.

Cohen, Stephen F., *Failed Crusade: America and the Tragedy of Post-Communist Russia.* New York: W. W. Norton & Co., 2000.

Collins, James C., and Jerry I. Porras, *Built to Last: Successful Habits of Visionary Companies.* New York: Harper Business, 1994.

Colvin, Geoffrey, "GE Succession," *Fortune,* January 8, 2001, pp. 85-89.

Condorcet, *Sketch for a Historical Picture of the Progress of the Human Mind*, with an introduction by Stuart Hampshire. Westport, Connecticut: Hyperion Press, 1979.

Confucius, *Analects.* London: Penguin Classics, 1979.

Coy, Peter, "Are Derivatives Dangerous? Without adequate collateral, one big default could set off a chain reaction imperiling the whole financial system," *Business Week,* March 31, 2003, p. 90.

Crankshaw, Edward, *Bismarck.* Middlesex, England: Penguin Books, 1981.

Crystal, Graef S., *In Search of Excess: The Overcompensation of American Executives.* New York: W. W. Norton, 1991.

Dante, Alighieri, *The Inferno.* New York: Mentor Press, 1954.

Darwin, Charles, *The Descent of Man.* Princeton: Princeton University Press, 1981.

Day, Kathleen, *S&L Hell: The People and the Politics Behind the $1 Trillion Savings and Loan Scandal.* New York: W. W. Norton & Co., 1993.

Deming, W. Edwardss, *Out of the Crisis.* Cambridge, Massachusetts: MIT, Center for Advanced Engineering, 1982.

Descartes, René, *Discourse on the Method* and *Meditations on First Philosophy.* New Haven, Connecticut: Yale University Press, 1996.

Drucker, Peter F., *Post-Capitalist Society.* New York: Harper Business, 1993.

Ibid., "Beyond the Information Age Revolution," *Atlantic Monthly,* October, 1999, p. 57.

Ibid., "They're Not Employees, They're People," *Harvard Business Review,* February, 2002, p. 73.

D'Souza, Dinesh, *Illiberal Education: The Politics of Race and Sex on Campus.* New York: The Free Press, 1991.

Duffy, Michael, "What Did They Know, and When Did They Know It?" *Time,* January 28, 2002, p. 19.

Dumaine, Brian, "Creating a New Company Culture," *Fortune,* January 15, 1990, p. 127.

Dumaine, Brian, Brian O'Reilly, Faye Rice, Patricia Sellers, Stratford P. Sherman, Sarah Smith, "Leaders of the Most Admired," *Fortune,* January 29, 1990, pp. 40-43, 46, 50, 54.

Durant, Will, and Ariel Durant, *The Story of Civilization.* New York: Simon & Schuster.

Vol. I	1935	*Our Oriental Heritage*
Vol. II	1939	*The Life of Greece*
Vol. III	1944	*Caesar and Christ*
Vol. IV	1950	*The Age of Faith*
Vol. V	1953	*The Renaissance*
Vol. VI	1957	*The Reformation*
Vol. VII	1961	*The Age of Reason*
Vol. VIII	1963	*The Age of Louis XIV*
Vol. IX	1965	*The Age of Voltaire*
Vol. X	1967	*Rousseau and Revolution*
Part II	1975	*The Age of Napoleon*

Economist, The, "Safety First: How to Handle Bank Regulation," May 3, 2003, p. 20.

Ibid., "Unleashing the Trade Winds," December 7, 2002, p. 27.

Ibid., "Conflicts, Conflicts Everywhere. Was America Wrong to Scrap the Laws That Kept Commercial and Investment Banking Apart?" January 26, 2002, p. 61.

Ibid., "Let Go of Nanny: The Case for Taking Credit Ratings Out of Financial Regulation," February 8, 2003, p. 17.

Editorial, "Derivative Thinking," *The Wall Street Journal,* March 11, 2003, p. A14.

Editorial, "The Hypocrisy of Farm Subsidies," *The New York Times,* December 1, 2002, p. 8.

Editorial by ten correspondents in eight countries, "In an Entwined World Market, No Man (or Nation) Is An Island," *The New York Times,* February 17-18, 1999, p. A8.

Editorial, "The Good Lay," *The Economist,* February 2, 2002, p. 70.

Editorial, "What Clean Up?" *Business Week,* June 17, 2002, p. 26.

Ehrbar, Al, "The Great Bond Market Massacre: A Perilous Rise in Leverage," *Fortune*, October 17, 1994, p. 77.

Eichenwald, Kurt, "Deal at Enron Gave Insiders Fast Fortunes," *The New York Times,* February 5, 2002, p. 1.

Ibid., "Enron's Investors Took Part in Fraud Scheme," *The New York Times,* April 8, 2002, p. A15.

Emshwiller, John R., and Rebecca Smith, "A Meeting That Would Put Enron on a Fateful and Dangerous Course," *The Wall Street Journal,* February 1, 2002, p. 1.

Engels, Friedrich, *The Condition of the Working Class in England.* Stanford, California: Stanford University Press, 1958.

English, Robert D., "The Revolution Within," *The Nation,* May 26, 2003, p. 1.

Erdal, David, "Employee Ownership Models in Europe," paper presented at "Ownership for All" conference, Capital Ownership Group (COG), Kent State University, May, 2001.

Ferrara, Peter J., and Michael D. Tanner, *Common Cents, Common Dreams.* Washington, D.C.: Cato Institute, 1998.

Field, William C., "Banks Heap Windfall from Falling Rates," *Asbury Park Press,* February 17, 2002, p. 1.

Fingleton, Eamonn, *In Praise of Hard Industries: Why Manufacturing, Not the Information Economy, Is the Key to Future Prosperity.* New York: Houghton Mifflin Company, 1999.

Fisher, Anne B., "Employees Holding the Bag," *Fortune,* May 20, 1991, p. 83.

Fisher, Daniel, *Payback: The Conspiracy to Destroy Michael Milken and His Financial Revolution.* New York: Harper Business, 1995.

Ibid., "The Great Stock Illusion," *Forbes,* July 22, 2002, p. 194.

France, Mike, and Wendy Zellner, "Enron's Fish Story," *Business Week,* February 25, 2002, p. 38.

Friedman, Milton, *Money Mischief: Episodes in Monetary History.* New York: Harcourt Brace & Company, 1994.

Friedman, Milton, and Rose Friedman, *Free to Choose: A Personal Statement.* New York: Harvest/HBJ, 1990.

Fukuyama, Francis, *The End of History and the Last Man.* New York: The Free Press, 1992.

Ibid., Trust, The Social Virtues & the Creation Prosperity. New York: The Free Press, 1995.

Ibid., "History Is Still Going Our Way," *The Wall Street Journal,* October 5, 2001, op-ed p.1.

Fusaro, Peter C., and Ross M. Miller, *What Went Wrong at Enron?* Hoboken, New Jersey: John Wiley & Sons, 2002.

Gabor, Andrea, *The Man Who Discovered Quality: How W. Edwards Deming Brought the Quality Revolution to America.* New York: Random House, 1990.

Galbraith, John Kenneth, *Economics in Perspective: A Critical History*, Boston: Houghton Mifflin, 1987.

Ibid., The Great Crash, 1929. Boston: Houghton Mifflin, 1997.

Gates, Jeff, *The Ownership Solution: Toward a Shared Capitalism for the Twenty-First Century.* Reading, Massachusetts: Addison Wesley Longmans, 1998.

Ibid., Democracy at Risk: Rescuing Main Street from Wall Street, Cambridge, Massachusetts: Perseus Publishing, 2000.

Gilder, George, *Wealth and Poverty.* New York: Bantam Books, 1981.

Godwin, William, *Enquiry concerning Political Justice.* New York: Penguin Books, 1985.

Goodell, Edward, *The Noble Philosopher: Condorcet and the Enlightenment.* Buffalo, New York: Prometheus Books, 1994.

Goodwyn, Lawrence, *Democratic Promise: The Populist Movement in America.* New York: Oxford University Press, 1976.

Gorbachev, Mikhail, *Perestroika*, New York: Harper & Row, 1987.

Granof, Michael H., and Stephen A. Zeff, "Unaccountable in Washington," *The New York Times,* January 23, 2002, p. 7.

Greenberger, Robert S., and Kathy Leggett, "President's Dream: Changing Not Just Regime but a Region," *The Wall Street Journal,* March 21, 2003, p.1.

Greenspan, Alan, "Excerpts from Greenspan's Remarks before Congress," *The New York Times*, October 2, 1989, p. C3.

Ibid., speech, Jackson Hole, Wyoming, August 30, 2002, quoted in *The Wall Street Journal,* September 25, 2002, p. A4.

Greider, William, *Secrets of the Temple: How the Federal Reserve Board Runs the Country.* New York: Simon & Schuster, 1987.

Ibid., Who Will Tell the People?: The Betrayal of American Democracy. New York: Simon and Schuster, 1992.

Ibid., One World, Ready or Not: The Manic Logic of Global Capitalism. New York: Simon & Schuster, 1997.

Ibid., Fortress America: The American Military and the Consequence of Peace. New York: Public Affairs, 1998.

Ibid., "Crime in the Suites," *The Nation,* February 4, 2002, p. 13.

Ibid., "Enron Nine," *The Nation,* May 13, 2002, p. 18.

Griswold, Daniel T., *"Free Trade, Free Markets: Rating the 105th Congress,"* Washington, D.C.: Cato Institute, February 3, 1999, #6.

Halberstam, David, *The Reckoning.* New York: William Morrow and Company, Inc., 1986.

Ibid., War in a Time of Peace: Bush, Clinton, and the Generals. New York: Scribner, 2001.

Hamilton, Alexander, James Madison, and John Jay, *The Federalist Papers.* New York: New American Library, 1961.

Hammer, Michael, *Beyond Reengineering: How the Process-Centered Organization Is Changing Our Work and Our Lives.* New York: Harper Business, 1996.

Harrison, J. F. C. , *Robert Owen and the Owenites in Britain and America: The Quest for the New Moral World.* London: Routledge and Kegan Paul, Ltd., 1994.

Harry, Mikel, and Richard Schroeder, *Six Sigma: The Breakthrough Management Strategy Revolutionizing the World's Top Corporations.* New York: Currency, 2000.

Hartman, David A., "Wall Street's Turn," *Chronicles,* December 2002, p. 43.

Hayek, Friedrich August, *The Constitution of Liberty.* Chicago: University of Chicago Press, 1960.

Ibid., The Fatal Conceit: The Errors of Socialism. Chicago: University of Chicago Press, 1988.

Ibid., The Road to Serfdom. London: Routledge and Kegan, 1944. University of Chicago Press, 1989.

Ibid., New Studies in Philosophy, Politics, Economics, and the History of Ideas. Chicago: University of Chicago Press, 1974.

Hegel, G. W. F., *Introduction to the Philosophy of History,* from *Lectures on the Philosophy of History.* New York: Modern Library, 1960.

Heilbronner, Robert L., *The Worldly Philosophers.* New York: Clarion Books, Simon and Schuster, 1967.

Helms, Jesse, speech before the United Nations, January 20, 2000, *The New York Times, International Edition*, January 21, 2000, p. A1.

Himmelfarb, Gertrude, *One Nation: Two Cultures, A Searching Examination of American Society in the Aftermath of Our Cultural Revolution*. New York: Alfred A. Knopf, 1999.

Hobbes, Thomas, *The Leviathan: The English Philosophers from Bacon to Mill.* New York: W. W. Norton, 1997.

Hof, Robert D., "Stock Options Aren't the Only Option," *Business Week*, April 14, 2003, p. 60.

Holbach, Baron Paul Henri Dietrich d', *The System of Nature*, New York: Burt Franklin, 1970.

Horan, James, "Letters to the Editor," *Fortune,* April, 15, 2002.

Hovanesian, Mara der, "The Mutual Fund Mess," *Business Week,* December 17, 2001, p. 102.

Hume, David, *A Treatise on Human Nature*, New York: Penguin Classics, 1984.

Huntington, Samuel P., *The Clash of Civilizations and the Remaking of the World Order.* New York: Simon & Schuster Touchstone, 1996.

InteliQuest, *Historical Biography Series: The World's 100 Greatest People* (vol. 1 and 2). Danville, California: InteliQuest Learning Systems, 1995.

John XXIII, *Pacem in Terris* (April 11, 1963). Washington, D.C.: United States Catholic Conference Publication no. 342-6, 1963.

John Paul II, *Centesimus Annus* (May 1, 1991). Washington, D.C.: United States Catholic Conference, Publication No. 436-8, 1991.

Ibid., Crossing the Threshold of Hope. New York: Alfred A. Knopf, 1995.

Johnson, Paul, *A History of the American People*, New York: Harper Collins, 1997.

Ibid., A History of the Jews. New York: Harper & Row, 1987.

Ibid., Intellectuals. New York: Harper & Row, 1988.

Johnson, Chalmers, *MITI and the Japanese Miracle*, Stanford, California: Stanford University Press, 1992.

Ibid., Blowback: The Costs and Consequences of American Empire, New York: Metropolitan Books, Henry Holt and Company, 2000.

Johnston, Daniel Cay, "Enron Avoided Taxes in 4 out of 5 Years," *The New York Times,* January 17, 2002, p. 1.

Josey, Alex, *Lee Kuan Yew: The Struggle for Singapore.* London: Angus E. Robertson, 1980.

Kagan, Robert, *Of Paradise and Power: America and Europe in the New World Order.* New York: Alfred A. Knopf, 2003.

Kagan, Donald, *On the Origins of War, and the Preservation of Peace.* New York: Anchor Books, Random House, 1995.

Kant, Immanuel, *Critique of Pure Reason.* New York: Modern Library, 1960.

Ibid., Critique of Judgment. New York: Harper Press, 1951.

Ibid., Selections: Idea for a Universal History from a Cosmopolitan Point of View and Perpetual Peace. New York: Scribner/MacMillan, 1998.

Kaplan, Lawrence F., and William Kristol, *The War over Iraq: Saddam's Tyranny and America's Mission.* San Francisco: Encounter Books, 2003.

Kaplan, Robert D., *The Coming Anarchy: Shattering the Dreams of the Post Cold War.* New York: Vintage Books, 2000.

Kaza, Greg, "Enron," *Chronicles,* March 2002, p. 7.

Keegan, John, *A History of Warfare.* New York: Alfred A. Knopf, 1993.

Kelly, P. H., *Locke on Money.* New York: Oxford University Press, 1991.

Kelso, Louis O., and Mortimer Adler, *The Capitalist Manifesto.* Westport, Connecticut: Greenwood Press, 1958.

Kelso, Louis O., and Patricia Hetter Kelso, *Democracy and Economic Power: Extending the ESOP Revolution.* Cambridge, Massachusetts: Ballinger Publishing, 1986.

Kennedy, Paul M., *The Rise and Fall of the Great Powers: Economic Change and Military Conflict from 1500 to 2000*. New York: Random House, 1987.

Ibid., Preparing for the 21st Century. New York: Random House, 1994.

Keynes, John Maynard, *The Economic Consequences of the Peace Process*. New York: Harper & Row, 1971.

Ibid., The General Theory of Employment, Interest, and Money. New York: Harvest/HBJ, 1964.

Kissinger, Henry, *Does America Need a Foreign Policy? Toward a Diplomacy for the 21st Century*. New York: Simon & Schuster, 2001.

Knowledge Products, The Audio Classic Series: *The World of Philosophy: The Giants of Philosophy; Science and Discovery; The World's Political Hot Spots; Great Economic Thinkers; Religion, Scriptures & Spirituality*. Nashville, Tennessee: Carmichael & Carmichael, 1990s.

Kranhold, Kathryn, "Enron Disputed Investors' Charge of Manipulated Cost Accounting," *The New York Times,* April 9, 2002, p. B7.

Kranhold, Kathryn, Bryan Lee, and Mitchell Benson, "Enron Rigged Power Markets in California, Documents Say," *The Wall Street Journal,* May 7, 2002, p. 1.

Kristol, Irving, *Two Cheers for Capitalism*. New York Basic Books, 1978.

Krugman, Paul, *The Age of Diminished Expectations: U.S. Economic Policy in the 1990s*. Cambridge, Massachusetts: MIT Press, 1990.

Ibid., "Business As Usual," *The New York Times,* October 22, 2002, p. A31.

Kurtzman, Joel, *The Death of Money: How the Electronic Economy Has Destabilized the World's Markets and Created Financial Chaos*. New York: Simon & Schuster, 1993.

Kuspit, Donald, "Midwife of the Future!" *Critical Review* vol. II, no. 2, spring 1997.

Kuttner, Robert, *The End of Laissez-Faire: National Purpose and the Global Economy after the Cold War*. New York: Alfred A. Knopf, 1991.

Ibid., Everything for Sale. New York: Alfred A. Knopf, 1997.

Ibid., "The Enron Economy," *The American Prospect,* January 2002, p. 2.

Lancaster, Hal, "A New Social Contract to Benefit Employer and Employees," *The Wall Street Journal,* November 29, 1994, p. B1.

Lazare, Daniel, *The Frozen Republic: How the Constitution Is Paralyzing Democracy.* New York: Harcourt Brace, 1996.

Lee Kuan Yew, *From Third World to First: The Singapore Story: 1965-2000.* New York: Harper Collins, 2000.

LeGoff, Jacques, *Your Money or Your Life: Economy and Religion in the Middle Ages.* New York: Zone Books, 1988.

Lenzer, Robert, "Archimedes on Wall Street," *Forbes,* October 19, 1998, p. 53.

Ibid., "Time Bombs in the Vault," *Forbes,* February 18, 2002, p. 38.

Ibid., "Someone Knew, the Enron Belly Flop Stunned Almost Everyone, But a Select Group of Wall Street Pros Had an Early Warning System You Cannot Access," *Forbes,* March, 4, 2002, p. 78.

Leo XIII, *Rerum Novarum: Contemporary Catholic Social Teaching.* Washington, D.C.: National Conference of Catholic Bishops, 1991.

Levering, Robert, Milton Moskowitz, and Michael Katz, *The 100 Best Companies to Work for in America.* Reading, Massachusetts: Addison-Wesley, 1984.

Levitt, Arthur, *Take On the Street: What Wall Street and Corporate America Don't Want You To Know, What You Can Do To Fight Back.* New York: Pantheon Books, 2002.

Lindquist, Sven, *A History of Bombing.* New York: A New Press, 2001.

Litwin, Shirley Robin, *The Pursuit of Certainty: David Hume, Jeremy Bentham, John Stuart Mill, Beatrice Webb.* Indianapolis: Liberty Funding Inc., 1988.

Lipton, Martin, "Corporate Governance in the Age of Finance Corporatism," *University of Pennsylvania Law Review*, vol. 136, num. 1, November, 1987, pp. 1-72.

Locke, John, *An Essay Concerning the True Original Extent and End of Civil Government: The English Philosophers from Bacon to Mill.* New York: Modern Library, 1939.

Ibid., On Money. New York: Clarendon Press Oxford 1991.

Logue, John, "Thinking Globally, Acting Locally," paper presented at *Ownership for All* conference, Capital Ownership Group (COG), Kent State University, May 2001.

Lohr, Steve, "In a Surprise, Microsoft Says It Will Pay a Dividend," *The Wall Street Journal,* January 17, 2003, p. C1.

Loomis, Carol, "The Risk That Won't Go Away: Like Alligators in a Swamp, Derivatives Lurk in the Global Economy," *Fortune*, March 7, 1994, p. 40.

Lowenstein, Louis, *What's Wrong with Wall Street: Short-Term Gain and the Absentee Shareholder.* New York: Addison-Wesley, 1988.

Lowenstein, Roger, *When Genius Failed: The Rise and Fall of Long-Term Capital Management.* New York: Random House, 2000.

Lubove, Seth, and Elizabeth Macdonald, "Debt? Who Me?" *Forbes,* February 8, 2002, p. 56.

Machiavelli, Niccolò, *The Prince* with selections from *The Discourses.* New York: Bantam Books, 2003.

Malpass, David, "The Fed's Moment of Weakness," *The Wall Street Journal,* September 25, 2002, p. A14.

Mandel, Michael J., "How Most Economists Missed the Boat," *Business Week,* November 15, 1999, p. 102.

Manuel, Frank, *A Requiem for Karl Marx.* Cambridge, Massachusetts: Harvard University Press, 1995.

Mapp, Alf J., *Thomas Jefferson.* New York: Madison Books, 1987.

Marx, Karl, *Capital.* New York: Penguin Classics, 1990.

Ibid., A Contribution to the Critique of Political Economy. New York: Penguin Classics, 1994.

Marx, Karl, and Friedrich Engels, *The Communist Manifesto.* New York: Penguin Books, 1967.

Matthews, George, "China: Struggle for Basic Democracy," *The Times of India,* November, 2002, p. 1.

Mayer, Martin, *Nightmare on Wall Street.* New York: Simon and Schuster, 1993.

Ibid., The Fed: The Inside Story of How the World's Most Powerful Financial Institution Drives the Markets. New York: The Free Press, 2001.

Ibid., "Banking's Future Lies in its Past," *The New York Times,* August 25, 2002, p. 9.

McGeehan, Patrick, "Wall Street Deal," *The Wall Street Journal,* December 21, 2002, p. C1.

McKeon, Richard, *The Basic Works of Aristotle.* New York: Random House, 1941.

McLean, Bethany, "Monster Mess," *Fortune,* February 4, 2002, p. 94.

Ibid., "Is There Anything Enron Didn't Do?" *Fortune,* April 29, 2002, p. 23.

McNamara, Robert S., *In Retrospect: The Tragedy and Lessons of Vietnam.* New York: Times Books, 1995.

McNamara, Robert S., and James G. Blight, *Wilson's Ghost: Reducing the Risk of Conflict, Killing, and Catastrophe in the 21st Century.* New York: BBS Public Affairs, 2001.

Micklethwait, John, and Adrian Woodridge, "It Could Happen Again," *Forbes ASAP,* August 21, 2000, p. 186.

Mill, John Stuart, *Considerations on Representative Government.* New York: Prometheus Books, 1991.

Ibid., On Liberty. New York: Penguin Classics, 1986.

Ibid., Principles of Political Economy with Some of Their Applications to Social Philosophy. Fairfield, New Jersey: Augustus M. Kelley, 1987.

Miller, Rich, "The Future of the Fed," *Business Week,* December 16, 2002, pp. 95-104.

Mises, Ludwig von, *The Theory of Money and Credit.* Indianapolis: Liberty Classics, 1980.

Democratic Capitalism

Ibid., Planning for Freedom. South Holland, Illinois: Libertarian Press, 1952.

Ibid., Human Action. Chicago: Contemporary Books, 1966.

Montesquieu, Charles-Louis de Secondat, *The Spirit of the Laws.* Berkeley: University of California Press, 1977.

Morgan, Edmund S., *Benjamin Franklin.* New Haven, Connecticut: Yale University Press, 2002.

Morgenson, Gretchen, "Some Suffer Tax Hangovers from Microsoft Option Spree," *The New York Times,* April 18, 2001, p. 1.

Ibid., "Post-Enron, All Eyes on Rating Agencies," *New York Times,* December 16, 2001, p. 61.

Moynihan, Daniel Patrick, *On the Law of Nations.* Cambridge, Massachusetts: Harvard University Press, 1990.

Mudge, Eugene T., *The Social Philosophy of John Taylor of Carolina.* New York: AMS Press, 1968.

Myrdal, Gunnar, *An American Dilemma: The Negro Problem and Modern Democracy.* New York: Harper and Brothers, 1944.

Narvaez, Alfonso A., "Louis O. Kelso who advocated worker-capitalism, is dead at 77," *The New York Times,* February 23, 1991, p. B10.

Niebuhr, Reinhold, *Moral Man and Immoral Society.* New York: Charles Scribner & Sons, 1932.

Niskaner, William A., *Reaganomics.* New York: Oxford University Press, 1988.

Novak, Michael, "A Phrase with a Ring," *Forbes,* August 7, 1989, p. 56.

Ibid., The Spirit of Democratic Capitalism. New York: Touchstone Book, 1982.

Noyes, John Humphrey, *Strange Cults & Utopias of 19th Century America.* New York: Dover, 1966.

Nye, Joseph S., Jr., *The Paradox of American Power: Why the World's Only Superpower Can't Go It Alone.* New York: Oxford University Press, 2002.

O'Reilly, Charles A., III, and Jeffrey Pfeffer, *Hidden Value: How Great Companies Achieve Extraordinary Results with Ordinary People*. Boston, Massachusetts: Harvard Business School Press, 2000.

Owen, Robert, *A New View of Society*. New York: AMS Press, 1972.

Owen, Robert Dale, *Threading My Way*, New York: Augustus M. Kelley, 1967.

Pacelle, Mitchell, "Breaking the Bank," *The Wall Street Journal,* December 13, 1999, p. C1.

Ibid., "Enron Bankruptcy Is Fee Bonanza," *The Nation,* May 13, 2002, p. 18.

Paine, Thomas, *Age of Reason.* Secaucus, New Jersey: Citadel Press, 1974.

Ibid., Rights of Man. New York: Penguin Books, 1984.

Perlez, Jane, "At Trade Forum, Clinton Pleads for the Poor," *The New York Times,* January 31, 2000, p. 8.

Peters, Tom, *Liberation Management.* New York: Alfred A. Knopf, 1992.

Phillips, Kevin, *Arrogant Capital: Washington, Wall Street, and the Frustration of American Politics.* New York: Little Brown, 1994.

Ibid., Boiling Point: Republicans, Democrats, and the Decline of Middle-Class Prosperity. New York: Random House, 1993.

Ibid., Wealth and Democracy: A Political History of the American Rich. New York: Broadway Books, 2002.

Piñera, José, and Aaron Lukas, "Chile Takes a Bold Step toward Trade," *The Wall Street Journal,* January 15, 1999, p. A11.

Pizzo, Stephen, Mary Fricker, and Paul Muolo, *Inside Job: The Looting of America's Savings and Loans*. New York: McGraw-Hill, 1989.

Plato, *Gorgias.* New York: Penguin Books, 1988.

Ibid., The Laws. London: Penguin Classics, 1970.

Ibid., The Last Days of Socrates. New York: Penguin Books, 1988.

Ibid., Protagoras and Meno. New York: Penguin Books, 1956.

Ibid., The Republic. New York: Penguin Books, 1982.

Raghavan, Anita, "Enron's McMahon: Hero or Collaborator?" *The Wall Street Journal,* April 9, 2002, p. C1.

Rai, Saritha, "Seeking Ways to Sell Enron's Plant in India," *The New York Times,* April 11, 2002, p. C1.

Rauch, Jonathan, "The New Old Economy," *The Atlantic Monthly,* January 2001, p. 39.

Rawls, John, *A Theory of Justice.* Cambridge, Massachusetts: Belnap Press of Harvard University Press, 1971, revised edition 1990.

Ibid., Political Liberalism. New York: Columbia University Press, 1993.

Rebello, Joseph, "Greenspan Denies the Fed Is Acting to Deflate Markets," *The Wall Street Journal,* March 31, 2000, p. A6.

Reich, Robert B., *The Resurgent Liberal (And Other Unfashionable Prophecies).* New York: Times Books, 1981.

Ibid., The Future of Success: Working and Living in the New Economy. New York: Alfred A. Knopf, 2001.

Reichheld, Frederick F. with Thomas Teal, *The Loyalty Effect: The Hidden Force Behind Growth, Profits, and Lasting Value.* Boston: Harvard Business School Publishing, 1996.

Revel, Jean-François, *The Flight from Truth: The Reign of Deceit in the Age of Information.* New York: Random House, 1991.

Ibid., Democracy against Itself: The Future of the Democratic Impulse. New York: The Free Press, 1993.

Ricardo, David, *Principles of Political Economy and Taxation.* New York: Dutton, 1973.

Rifkin, Jeremy, *The Hydrogen Economy: The Creation of the Worldwide Energy Web and the Redistribution of Power on Earth.* New York: Tarcher/Putnam Books, 2002.

Roberts, Cokie, *Sunday Morning News,* ABC, October 7, 2001.

Rohrabacher, Dana, *Human Events,* February 2, 1991, p. 11.

Romero, Simon, "The Rise and Fall of Richard Scrushy, Entrepreneur," *The Wall Street Journal,* March 21, 2003, p. C4.

Ropke, Wilhelm, *A Humane Economy: The Social Framework of the Free Market.* Lanham, Maryland: University Press of America, 1960.

Rothschild, Emma, *Economic Sentiments: Adam Smith, Condorcet, and the Enlightenment.* Cambridge, Massachusetts: Harvard University Press, 2001.

Rousseau, Jean-Jacques, *The Social Contract or Principles of Political Right* (abridged), in *The European Philosophers from Descartes to Nietzsche*, edited by Monroe S. Beardsley. New York: Modern Library, 1960.

Roy, Arundhate, "Shall We Leave It to the Experts?" *The Nation,* February 18, 2002, pp. 17-18.

Rummel, R. J., *Death by Government.* New Brunswick, New Jersey: Transaction Publishers, 1994.

Rutland, Robert A., *James Madison, The Founding Father.* New York: Macmillan Publishing Company, 1987.

Samuelson, Paul A., and William D. Nordhaus, *Economics.* New York: McGraw Hill Book Company, 13th edition, 1989.

Say, Jean-Baptiste, *Treatise on Political Economy.* New York: A. M. Kelley, 1967.

Schlesinger, Arthur M., Jr., *The Age of Jackson.* Boston: Little, Brown, 1953.

Schlesinger, Jacob, "Fed Signals Comfort with Faster Growth," *The Wall Street Journal ,* August 28, 2000, p. C1.

Schroeder, Michael, "New Derivatives Regulation Is Opposed," *The Wall Street Journal,* November 10, 1999, p. C1.

Schultz, Ellen E., "Pension Practices Used by Enron Come Under Fire," *The Wall Street Journal,* March 1, 2002, p. A4.

Sellers, Charles, *The Market Revolution: Jacksonian America, 1815-1846.* New York: Oxford University Press, 1991.

Sen, Amartya, *Development as Freedom.* New York: Alfred A. Knopf, 1999.

Shelton, Judy, *Money Meltdown: Restoring Order to the Global Currency System.* New York: The Free Press, 1994.

Shiller, Robert J., *Irrational Exuberance.* New York: Broadway Books, 2000.

Shilling, A. Gary, "Dividends Back in Style," *Forbes,* May 27, 2002, p. 170.

Sidelsky, Robert, *John Maynard Keynes.* New York: Penguin Press, 1994.

Siegel, Jeremy J., "Stocks Are Still an Oasis," *The Wall Street Journal*, July 26, 2002, p. A10.

Simpson, Glenn B., "Deals that Took Enron Under Had Many Supporters," *The Wall Street Journal,* April 16, 2002, p.1.

Smith, Adam, *An Inquiry into the Nature and Causes of the Wealth of Nations.* New York: Modern Library, 1937.

Ibid., The Theory of Moral Sentiments. Indianapolis: Liberty Classics, 1959.

Smith, Randall, and Susan Pullman, "Two More Wall Street Firms Are Targeted in Trading Practices," *The Wall Street Journal,* April 25, 2002, p. 1.

Smith, Rebecca, "Show Business: A Blockbuster Deal Shows How Enron Overplayed Its Hand," *The Wall Street Journal,* January 17, 2002, p. 1.

Smith, Roy, *The Global Bankers.* New York: Truman Talley, 1989.

Ibid., The Money Wars. New York: Dutton, 1990.

Smith, Vera C., *The Rationale of Central Banking and the Free Banking Alternative.* Indianapolis: Liberty Press, 1990.

Soden, Roger, ed., *Democracy, Education, and the Schools.* San Francisco: Jossey-Bass Publishers, 1996.

Solomon, Jay, "Indonesia's Poor Will Suffer Most as Nation Tightens Its Belt," *The Wall Street Journal*, October 15, 1997.

Solomon, Steven, *The Confidence Game: How Unelected Central Bankers Are Governing the Changed Global Economy.* New York: Simon & Schuster, 1995.

Soros, George, "Toward a Global Open Society," *Atlantic Monthly*, January, 1998.

Ibid., The Crisis of Global Capitalism: Open Society Endangered. New York: Public Affairs, Perseus Books Group, 1998.

Ibid., Open Society. New York: BBS, Public Affairs, 2000.

Soros, George, with Byron Wien and Krisztina Koenen, *Soros on Soros: Staying Ahead of the Curve.* New York: J. Wiley, 1995.

Sosnoff, Martin, "Don't Get Greenspanned," *Forbes,* September 6, 1999, p. 27.

Speiser, Stuart M., *Ethical Economics & the Faith Community: How We Can Have Work and Ownership for All.* Bloomington, Indiana: Meyer-Stone Books, 1989.

Spencer, Herbert, *On Social Evolution.* Chicago: The University of Chicago Press, 1972.

Stack, Jack, *The Great Game of Business.* New York: Currency Doubleday, 1992.

Stewart, James B., *Den of Thieves.* New York: Simon & Schuster, 1991.

Stewart, Thomas A., "See Jack Run," *Fortune,* September 27, 1999, p. 136.

Stiglitz, Joseph E., *Globalization and Its Discontents.* New York: W. W. Norton, 2002.

Sweeney, John, with David Kusnet, *America Needs a Raise: Fighting for Economic Security and Social Justice.* Boston: Houghton Mifflin, 1996.

Taylor, A. J. P., *The Origins of the Second World War.* New York: Touchstone Books, Simon & Schuster, 1961.

Ibid., From the Boer War to the Cold War. London: Penguin Press, 1995.

The Great Courses, *The Great Ideas of Philosophy; Great Presidents: Power Over People: Classical and Modern Political Theory; Great Minds of the Western Intellectual Tradition.* Audiocassette and CD collection. Chantilly, Virginia: The Teaching Company, 1995-1997.

Thorow, Lester, *Head to Head: The Coming Economic Battle among Japan, Europe, and America.* New York: William Morrow, 1992.

Ibid., The Future of Capitalism: How Today's Economic Forces Shape Tomorrow's World. New York: William Morrow and Company, 1996.

Tocqueville, Alexis de, *Democracy in America*. New York: Random House, 1990.

Toffler, Alvin, *Power Shift: Knowledge, Wealth, and Violence at the Edge of the 21ˢᵗ Century*. New York: Bantam Books, 1990.

Tuchman, Barbara, *The March of Folly: From Troy to Vietnam.* Boston: G.K. Hall, 1984.

Tyson, Laura D'Andrea, "The Farm Bill Is a $200 Billion Disaster," *Business Week,* June 3, 2002, p. 26.

Vandetter, Jim, and David Rogers, "Bush Seeks $5 Billion Foreign Aid Boost Over Three Years to Quell Charges of Stinginess," *The Wall Street Journal,* March 15, 2002, p. A12.

Volcker, Paul, and Toyoo Gyohten, *Changing Fortunes: The World's Money and the Threat to American Leadership.* New York: Times Books, 1992.

Voltaire, *Candide.* New York: Signet Books, 1961.

Waller, Douglas, "Soros to the Rescue Again," *Time,* November 3, 1997, p. 74.

Wallin, Michelle, "Enron to Drop Utility Deal in Argentina," *The Wall Street Journal,* March 1, 2002, p. A7.

Walsh, Mary Williams, "Many Companies Fight Shortfalls in Pension Funds," *The New York Times,* January 13, 2003, p. 1.

Walworth, Arthur, *Woodrow Wilson: American Prophet* (2 vols.). New York: W. W. Norton & Company, 1978.

Wanninski, Jude, *The Way the World Works.* New York: Basic Books, 1978.

Weber, Max, *The Protestant Ethic and the Spirit of Capitalism,* Talcott Parsons, trans.; introduction by Anthony Giddens. Glouster, Massachusetts: Peter Smith, 1988.

Weil, Jonathan, "Moving Target," *The Wall Street Journal,* August 21, 2001, p. 1.

Welch, Jack, with John A. Byrne, *Jack: Straight from the Gut.* New York: Warner Business Books, 2001.

White, Lawrence, *Competition and Currency: Essays on Free Banking and Money.* New York: New York University Press, 1989.

Wilke, John R., "Enron Criminal Probe Focuses on Alleged Corruption Abroad," *The Wall Street Journal,* August 5, 2002, p. 11.

Wilson, Edward, *Consilience: The Unity of Knowledge.* New York: Alfred A. Knopf, 1998.

Winans, R. Foster, *Trading Secrets: Seduction and Scandal at the Wall Street Journal.* New York: St. Martin's Press, 1984.

Wollstonecraft, Mary, *Vindication of the Rights of Women.* New York: Penguin Books, 1975.

Woodward, Bob, *Maestro: Greenspan's Fed and the American Boom.* New York: Simon & Schuster, 2000.

Ibid., Bush at War. New York: Simon & Schuster, 2002.

Zagorin, Perez, *Francis Bacon.* Princeton, New Jersey: Princeton University Press, 1998.

Zakaria, Fareed, "Lousy Advice Has a Price," *Newsweek,* September 27, 1989, p. 40.

Ibid., The Future of Freedom: Illiberal Democracy at Home and Abroad. New York: W. W. Norton & Company, 2003.

Zedillo, Ernesto, "Will the Doha Round Implode in 2003?" *Forbes,* February 3, 2003, p. 29.

Zellner, Wendy, "Jeff Skilling, Enron's Missing Man," *Business Week,* February 11, 2002, p. 39.

Zukerman, Gregory, and Christine Richard, "Moody's and S&P Singed by Enron May Speed Up Credit Rating Downgrades," *The Wall Street Journal,* January 22, 2002, p. C1.

Zukerman, Gregory, and Joanne Craig, "High Rollers: In a Risky Period, Goldman Sachs Depends More on Riskier Bets Using Firm's Own Cash," *The Wall Street Journal,* December 17, 2002, p. 1.

Democratic Capitalism

INDEX

398, 400, 401

Chancellor, Edward, 364, 411, 445, 470, 502

Chanos, Jim, 388, 389

Chardin, Teilhard de, 502

Charlemagne, 245

Chase Manhattan, 290

Chewco, 385

Chile, 155, 515

China, 82, 159, 200, 287, 337, 431, 450, 486, 491, 513

chip technology, 103, 339

Choi, Jay, 160

CITI, Citigroup, 298, 299, 300, 315, 366, 367, 368, 369, 384, 389, 390, 402, 406, 407, 500

Citibank, 260, 290

Citicorp, 261, 269, 270

citizens' choice, xi, 1, 8, 10, 316

civic groups, v, 12, 14, 225, 374, 415, 418, 474

Civil War, 58, 249, 445

class conflict, 50, 54, 81, 89, 166

classical economics, 202, 204, 209, 210, 212, 216, 301, 313

classical liberalism, 73

Clinton, Bill, 192, 197, 199, 227, 280, 295, 296, 297, 299, 317, 334, 490, 507, 515

COG, Capital Ownership Group, 158, 159, 160, 504, 512

Cohen, Stephen F., 7, 286, 502

Cold War, 30, 33, 232, 489, 492, 509, 510, 519

Collectivists, 10, 90, 212, 222, 224, 225, 227, 364, 436, 462, 463, 465, 466, 467, 468, 477

Collins, James C., 99, 100, 101, 502

command-and-control, 75, 89, 422, 423

Commerce Department, 192

commercial banks, 249, 260, 316, 368

Commodities Futures Act of 2000, 300, 373

common ideology, 4, 5, 17, 240, 241,

309

Communism, 73, 92, 209, 211, 229, 237, 240, 278, 316, 419, 439, 451, 463

compensation, xiii, 4, 118, 119, 120, 121, 122, 141, 157, 176, 189, 256, 294, 343, 367, 401, 402, 404, 405, 414, 423, 461

Compensation Committee, 118, 119, 121, 156

competition, ix, 2, 4, 50, 54, 74, 82, 86, 87, 89, 95, 96, 97, 108, 112, 119, 122, 143, 144, 160, 168, 171, 172, 193, 195, 205, 209, 236, 261, 320, 321, 327, 333, 341, 350, 446, 447, 448, 492, 495, 496

Comptroller of the Currency, 265, 315, 370, 398, 399, 400, 401

concentration of wealth, xi, 205, 243, 392, 407, 419, 447, 453, 456, 462, 479, 483

Condorcet, xii, 62, 63, 64, 65, 66, 67, 68, 69, 70, 71, 72, 73, 78, 82, 429, 432, 433, 449, 456, 469, 484, 485, 502, 506, 517

conflicts in capitalism, xv, 102, 319

Confucius, 60, 427, 428, 431, 433, 455, 483, 502

Congress, U.S., 29, 58, 147, 149, 154, 161, 187, 194, 218, 222, 239, 248, 257, 261, 262, 264, 267, 270, 291, 298, 299, 300, 324, 325, 346, 361, 364, 365, 366, 371, 372, 373, 396, 400, 403, 406, 407, 409, 413, 415, 457, 460, 465, 479, 493, 506, 507

Conservatism, 466

Conservatives, 463, 467

Constitution, U.S., 8, 44, 58, 247, 511

Constitutional Convention, 57, 58

consumer choice, 195

contempt for commerce, xiii, 90, 91

Continental Illinois Bank, 264, 265, 366, 452, 462

continuous process, 113, 127

liquidity, 212, 250, 270, 271, 272, 280, 281, 284, 285, 301, 302, 303, 312, 315, 317, 330, 363, 365, 399, 452, 472, 479
liquidity crisis, 280, 281, 284, 285
LJM2, 384, 386
Locke, John, 57, 82, 246, 429, 430, 431, 509, 511
Logue, John, 158, 512
Lohr, Steve, 512
Long, Russell, 147, 149, 150, 153, 479
Loomis, Carol, 268, 311, 512
Louis XVI, 63
Louisiana Purchase, 174
low-cost, non-volatile, patient capital, 9, 55, 56, 127, 128, 139, 173, 174, 195, 209, 228, 447, 458
Lowe's, 139
Lowenstein, Roger, 250, 269, 270, 271, 287, 289, 290, 291, 332, 400, 512
LTCM, Long-term Capital Management, 206, 208, 213, 218, 242, 287, 288, 289, 290, 291, 298, 303, 312, 315, 316, 331, 366, 370, 372, 400, 406, 458, 460, 512
Lubove, Seth, 397, 512
M&A, (mergers and acquisitions), 102, 120, 121, 187, 212, 256, 265, 266, 327, 352, 361, 374, 401, 402, 403, 409
Machiavelli, 61, 430, 512
macroeconomics, 171, 223
Madison, James, 50, 57, 58, 78, 248, 249, 417, 464, 507, 517
Maharashtra, India, power plant, 379, 380
Maimonides, 428
Malaysia, 6, 240, 278, 328, 334, 379
Malpass, David, 512
managed trade, 196, 197
management, 7, 13, 31, 34, 39, 43, 44, 45, 48, 52, 75, 96, 98, 100, 102, 104, 105, 108, 109, 112, 113, 114, 115, 116, 117, 119, 121, 122,

124, 125, 129, 130, 138, 143, 145, 149, 151, 161, 204, 223, 230, 236, 237, 257, 265, 284, 312, 327, 346, 354, 361, 362, 378, 379, 381, 383, 385, 388, 394, 395, 400, 409, 414, 422, 423, 433, 450, 473, 480, 481, 496
Mandel, Michael J., 85, 192, 512
Manuel, Frank, 81, 512
Maoist China, 92
margin calls, 251, 275, 276, 387
Mariner Energy, Inc., 380
Maritime Administration, 382
Mark, Rebecca, 361, 378, 380, 381, 383, 387
market discipline, 9, 136, 139, 170, 173, 197, 209, 213, 222, 230, 234, 241, 252, 255, 261, 271, 277, 287, 296, 317, 330, 333, 334, 362, 363, 365, 366, 371, 406, 407, 452, 458, 460, 462
market fundamentalism, 167, 202, 205, 209, 227, 310, 391
market neutral, 288
market share, 39, 104, 113, 320, 342
mark-to-market, 301, 302, 313, 314, 377
Marshall Plan, 231, 445
Marshall, George, 445
Marx, Karl, xi, xii, xiii, xvi, 2, 3, 6, 7, 8, 15, 22, 31, 49, 50, 51, 55, 73, 81, 82, 83, 84, 85, 86, 87, 88, 89, 91, 92, 108, 133, 137, 142, 143, 144, 146, 148, 166, 168, 178, 179, 211, 226, 235, 236, 237, 242, 249, 280, 284, 335, 374, 392, 393, 422, 434, 435, 436, 437, 438, 440, 441, 442, 444, 445, 447, 452, 453, 458, 468, 469, 473, 478, 480, 485, 496, 512
Marxism, 133, 166, 237, 284
maximum freedom, 22, 100, 125, 130, 136, 420
maximum surplus value, 21, 55
Mayer, Martin, 365, 513
MBA, Masters in Business

About the Author

Ray Carey learned through managing companies for 33 years how to change the work culture to provide employees with their best opportunities to develop and contribute. This experience began as a 28-year old plant manager and later president of an electric motor company, and concluded with eighteen years as president, chairman, and CEO of ADT, Inc.

At ADT, Carey implemented a profit-sharing and stock-purchase plan for all associates as part of the work culture change needed to move the relationship between management and wage earners from alienation to cooperation.

Carey demonstrates how economic freedom in a culture of trust and cooperation is the way to a world of peace and plenty, and why passing on this world to our grandchildren is our opportunity and obligation.

See Carey's autobiography of his work career in chapter two. For more information about Ray Carey and his advocacy of democratic capitalism, visit the website of the Carey Center for Democratic Capitalism: *www*.democratic-capitalism.com

264232BV00002B/97/A

9 781418 428099